Henry Moore: **Writings and Conversations**

Notes on Sculpture

It is a mistake for a sculptor or a painter to speak or write very often about his job. It releases ~~tension~~ tension needed for his work. By trying to express his aims with rounded-off logical exactness, he can easily become a theorist whose actual work is only a caged-in exposition of conceptions evolved in terms of logic + words.

But though the non-logical instinctive, subconscious part of the mind must play its part in his work, he also has a conscious mind which is not inactive. The artist works with a concentration of his whole personality, + the conscious part of it resolves conflicts, organises memories, + prevents him from trying to walk in two directions at the same time.

It is likely, then, that a sculptor can give, from his own conscious experience, clues which will help others in their approach to sculpture, and this article tries to do this, and no more. It is not a general survey of sculpture, or of my own development, but a few notes on some of the problems which have concerned me from time to time.

Three Dimensions

Appreciation of sculpture depends upon the ability to respond to form in three dimensions. That is perhaps why sculpture has been described as the most difficult of all arts; certainly it is more difficult than the arts which involve appreciation of flat forms, shape in only two dimensions. Many more people are "form-blind" than colour-blind. The child learning to see first distinguishes only two-dimensional shape; it cannot judge distances, depths. Later, for its personal safety + practical needs, it has to develope (partly by means of touch) the ability to judge roughly three-dimensional distances. But having satisfied the requirements of practical necessity, most people go no further. Though they may attain considerable accuracy in the perception of flat form, they do not make the further intellectual + emotional effort needed to comprehend ~~form~~ in its full spatial existence.

This is what the sculptor ~~must~~ do. He must strive continually to think of, + use form in its full spatial completeness. He gets the solid shape, as it were inside his head;—he thinks of it, whatever its size, as if he were holding it completely enclosed in the hollow of his hand; he mentally

Henry Moore: **Writings and Conversations**

Edited and with an introduction by Alan Wilkinson

Lund Humphries

In memory of Betty Tinsley
Secretary to Henry Moore 1957–1986

First published in 2002 by

Lund Humphries
Gower House
Croft Road
Aldershot
Hants GU11 3HR

www.lundhumphries.com

Lund Humphries is part
of Ashgate Publishing

ISBN: 0 85331 847 6

British Library Cataloguing in
Publication Data
A catalogue record for this book is
available from the British Library

Designed by Ray Carpenter
Typeset in Garamond by Tom Knott
Printed in China by Midas Printing

Frontispiece: 'Notes on Sculpture' 1937, HMF
archive; published as 'The Sculptor Speaks',
see p.193

EDITOR'S NOTE

Both published and unpublished texts have been respected as far as
possible, although it was considered desirable to adopt some overall
consistency of style. To this end, the spelling of proper names has been
corrected, as have some words consistently misspelt by Moore, such as
'symmetry'. English rather than American spelling has been used.

Henry Moore's handwritten notes and letters have been transcribed as
written, except where lack of punctuation was thought to obscure the
meaning. The use of 'sic' has been avoided. Simple factual errors such
as dates are corrected in the text in square brackets; other inaccuracies
are dealt with in the footnotes. All extracts whose sources are given
as 'Unpublished notes' are handwritten. Extracts described as 'In
conversation with …' are taken from tapes, films and transcripts in the
Henry Moore archive. Subheadings ranged to the left of the page are part
of the original text. Ellipses in original material are given as …; words or
passages deliberately omitted as […].

Moore's works are referred to by their archive reference numbers: LH
(Lund Humphries) for sculptures; HMF (Henry Moore Foundation) for
drawings; CGM (Cramer, Grant, Mitchinson) for graphics. All titles of
works are by Moore unless otherwise stated. In accordance with HMF
house style, measurements of sculptures are given in centimetres, those
of works on paper in millimetres (height first).

Sources frequently quoted appear in abbreviated form (e.g. Berthoud
1987); details of these may be found in the list of bibliographical sources
on p.311. Other references are given in full. All periodicals and newspapers
were published in the United Kingdom unless stated otherwise.

A.W.

This book would not have been possible without the generous support
of the Henry Moore Foundation.

CONTENTS

ACKNOWLEDGEMENTS

I wish to thank Sir Alan Bowness, Prof. Andrew Causey, Margaret McLeod, the late David Sylvester, Trustees of the Henry Moore Foundation, and Prof. Bernard Meadows for their support. I am most grateful to Tim Llewellyn, Director of the Henry Moore Foundation, for his encouragement, and to members of his staff who assisted me in various ways during my research in the library and archive at the Foundation: Alice Beckley; Tracy Charge; James Copper; Colin Corden; Martin Davis; John Farnham; Johnny Hayes; Janet Iliffe; Charles Joint; David Mitchinson; Helen Piper; Margaret Reid; Geoffrey Robinson; Sheila Savill; Emma Stower; Anne Unthank; Rosemary Walker. My thanks to Catherine Ames, Lucy Clark and Lucy Myers of Lund Humphries, and to John Taylor, publisher, and Ray Carpenter, designer. My excellent editor Angela Dyer, with her broad knowledge of Moore's life and work, provided indispensable assistance and support.

I would like to thank a host of friends and colleagues who assisted me in many different ways: Jane Aitken; Helen Ashton; Wendy Baldwin and Ian Parker; the late Dr A.M. Beattie; Roger Berthoud; Barbara Boutin; Dr Sophie Bowness; Julia Brown and Robert O'Rorke; Paddy-Ann and Latham Burns; Sarah Burrell; Georgiana Butler; Sir Anthony Caro; Janet Charlton; Harriet Cochrane; Mary and Malcolm Cochrane; Desmond L. Corcoran; Deborah Cowley; Caroline and Martin Davis; Edmund Davis; Sharon and James Edwards; Gila Falkus; Lady Antonia Fraser and Harold Pinter; Ann Garrould; Debby and George Gibbons; Dr John Golding; Dr Christopher Green; Patricia Jackson and Ramsay Derry; Nicola and John Jennings; Nancy Lockhart and Dr Murray Frum; Anna and Francesco Macchi; Fiona MacDonald and Bob McElwain; Miriam Macgregor; Donald Matthews; John Matthews; Renwick and Bob Matthews; Jane and John Lorn McDougall; Jane and Michael Meredith; Sandy and Peter Merry; Iain Miller; Michael O'Connor; David Pinchin; John Randle; Dr Ben Read; Judith Robertson; Leila and Tim Rose Price; Diana and Graham Rowley; Janet and Bill Rowley; Jonathan Sale; Susan Sharratt; Hugo Stringer; Jenny and Jack Stringer; Joy Tinsley; Alan Toff; Katie and Fred Valentine; Jenny and Denzil Wadds; Maggie Walker; S.C.B. Walker; Judy and Graham Weeks; Nina and Graham Williams.

Alan Wilkinson

FOREWORD

The first reaction is likely to be astonishment. How could Henry Moore have written some three hundred pages of such entertaining and interesting commentary about art? He is after all famous for the hundreds of sculptures and thousands of drawings and prints that he made during his long career. And yet he still found time to write (and talk) so much. What better example of the sheer energy and drive that those of genius often possess?

Moore loved using words and doing something creative with them. Had he not, as a young student teacher, written a play, *Narayana and Bhataryan*? At one time he was a passionate novel reader. He kept his love of theatre, and in the 1970s and later he regularly attended the opening nights at Olivier's National Theatre.

He was fortunate too in spending the early part of his career, up to 1939, among a close and intellectually stimulating group of friends. Both Barbara Hepworth and Ben Nicholson spoke and wrote eloquently, and one can imagine the arguments and private conversations of Britain's most advanced artists of the period (particularly about abstract or surrealist art), living as they did on top of one another in Parkhill Road, Hampstead. Their great friend and champion was Herbert Read, who was, more than anyone, inventing the language to write about contemporary modernist art in such books as *Art Now* (1933) and of course the first Moore monograph in 1934. A new language was needed to describe a new art, and the making of it is an exhilarating experience. Though Herbert Read once told me that he had helped Moore with the text of the *Unit One* statement in 1933-34, the fascinating unpublished material unearthed by Alan Wilkinson shows very clearly how hard Moore himself had worked at it.

The *Unit One* piece, and its successor, 'The Sculptor Speaks' of 1937, constitute Moore's attempt at a personal credo. They make a serious artistic statement, but much of what Moore wrote after the mid-1930s is more occasional, and perhaps in later life he lacked a challenging environment. (The Venice speech of 1952, 'The Sculptor in Modern Society', is more self-revealing than profound, and he attempted nothing similar later.) But Moore was a born teacher, and he loved to talk, and could do so with great intelligence and frequent insight. He was never difficult to interview, as I found when we arranged the 1970 Hayward Gallery Rodin exhibition together. Many artists are suspicious of words, but Moore always wanted to share his ideas about sculpture with others, and talking was his natural way of doing so. As he grew older, he became loquacious and sometimes a little repetitive, but conversation with Henry was always stimulating and a privilege, and much of this comes over in the pages that follow.

Alan Wilkinson has trawled the rich material with exemplary thoroughness, greatly aided by Alex Davis's meticulous five-volume Bibliography – surely the most exhaustive bibliography ever devoted to an artist. Wilkinson has also searched the extensive archive held by the Henry Moore Foundation, and from unpublished notes and early letters has been able to throw new light on the artist's formative years. The nature and purpose of Moore's writing are illuminated. The introduction reflects Alan Wilkinson's long friendship with Moore, and the commentary and notes testify to a remarkable knowledge of his work, his circle and his ideas – ideas that are so important to anyone seeking a richer understanding of Henry Moore's work and of sculpture in general.

Alan Bowness

INTRODUCTION

'PERFECT SYMMETRY IS DEATH'[1]

Yorkshire men are imaginative, like all northmen, but a matter-of-factness, a strong sense of objectivity, a faculty for vivid visualisation, keep them from being profoundly mystical. The same qualities make them wary in their actions, and canny in their reckonings. But their most extraordinary characteristic – a characteristic with which in the process of time they have leavened almost the entire English race – is their capacity for masking their emotions. [...] Passion, of course, does blaze from many a poem of Wordsworth's; but not the direct passion of profane love, not even the direct passion of sacred love, but passion transmuted into impersonal things – rocks, and stones, and trees.[2]

It would be difficult to find a more apposite and succinct description of the imaginative, verbal world of Henry Moore, with its powerful imagery and vivid similes and metaphors, than these observations of Herbert Read on the Yorkshire imagination and the poetry of Wordsworth. Indeed, as Moore's sculpture may be said to represent the continuation and perhaps the culmination of the English romantic tradition, Read's remarks also provide a fortuitous comment on his work, in which passion for the human figure was often transmuted into the forms of hills, cliffs and mountains, stones, pebbles, bones and shells. Moore's voracious curiosity about the three-dimensional world around him was reflected in the language and imagery of his writings and conversations. For example on 12 March 1917 writing to Alice Gostick, the art mistress at Castleford Secondary School, from the army camp at Hazeley Down, near Winchester: 'You ought to see me with my equipment on, I dont know what I really look like but I feel like a walking saddler's shop, all belts buckles & straps.' Or, talking to me in the early 1970s, a single sentence that encapsulated his long-standing admiration for the pre-Columbian Chacmool carving, ending with a powerful architectural simile: 'Its stillness and alertness, a sense of readiness – and the whole presence of it, and the legs coming down like columns.' He described Michelangelo's sculpture as having 'a kind of lazy heavy

---

[1] From unpublished notes for 'A View of Sculpture' 1930, HMF archive; see p.17.
[2] Herbert Read, *Wordsworth*, Cape, London 1930; Faber and Faber, London 1965, pp.37, 38.

ponderous slowness as though slowly turning in thick treacle –.' Giacometti wanted to make sculpture 'like a spring onion'. In a tribute to his friend T.S. Eliot: 'He was not effusive not outwardly full blooded not wetly warmhearted – rather he was dry like a hard grain of human wheat – but a grain you knew could germinate – & did, in his poetry.' To return to Wordsworth's poetry and the 'rocks, and stones, and trees', Moore could hardly have expressed more vividly or directly his romantic yearning for the English countryside than when he wrote from Italy on 12 March 1925 to William Rothenstein, Principal of the Royal College of Art: 'I do not wonder that the Italians have no landscape school – I have a great desire – almost an ache for the sight of a tree that can be called a tree – for a tree with a trunk.'

Thirty-six years have passed since the publication in 1966 of *Henry Moore on Sculpture*, a collection of the sculptor's writings and spoken words edited and with an introduction by Philip James.[3] The Trustees of the Henry Moore Foundation felt that a new book on Moore's writings and conversations was almost certainly needed, not only to cover the last two decades of the sculptor's life, but also to publish earlier material not included by James. Any initial concerns which the trustees and the editor may have had that there would not be enough interesting material, both pre- and post-1966, to justify the publication of another volume, proved to be unfounded. With Alexander Davis's extraordinarily comprehensive five-volume *Henry Moore Bibliography* (1992-94) – a staggering achievement of bibliographical research – as my guide, and the excellent research facilities of the Henry Moore Foundation archive and library at my disposal, I was swamped with pre-1966 unpublished manuscripts, together with numerous articles, interviews and casual conversations, none of which appeared in *Henry Moore on Sculpture*, as well as the considerable quantity of material from the last twenty years of the artist's life.

From his play *Narayana and Bhataryan* of *c*.1916 and the letters to Alice Gostick of 1917-18, to his comment at the age of eighty-seven on the need to go out for a drive each afternoon in the Hertfordshire countryside to refresh his vision, Moore's writings and recorded conversations span some seventy years; so extensive are they that a comprehensive exhibition catalogue could readily be compiled from that material alone. Some sixty monographs and the 435 one-man exhibition catalogues mentioned in the introduction to Volume 1 of Davis's Bibliography make it abundantly clear how often and extensively the authors have relied on Moore to tell his own story and to comment on his work. He must surely be one of the most frequently quoted artists in the history of Western art. As the table of contents in this volume indicates, the scope of his writings and conversations encompasses a remarkably wide variety of other subjects: affectionate tributes to friends and

---

[3] Philip James was appointed keeper of the library of the Victoria and Albert Museum in 1935. From 1942 to 1958 he was Director of Art at the Arts Council of Great Britain.

colleagues; notes and articles on pre-Columbian and African sculpture, on primitive art and on Mesopotamian art; statements condemning the attitude of the Royal Academy of Arts towards contemporary art; general statements on art, and on art and society; lively comments on critics and art criticism; notes, interviews and tributes to painters and sculptors whom he admired, from Giovanni Pisano and the little known Heinrich Brabender to Picasso, Hepworth, Nicholson and Rothko; and finally, extensive notes, articles and discussions about the art of sculpture: on carving and modelling; on truth to material; on space and form; on size and scale; on subjects and sources of inspiration; on materials; on bronze and lead casting; on drawing and sculpture; on sculpture and architecture; and on sculpture in landscape.

Moore's declaration in 1937 that 'It is a mistake for a sculptor or painter to speak or write very often about his job. It releases tension needed for his work'[4] seems curious, in that he must have discussed and written about his work more prolifically than any other twentieth-century artist. The index in Volume 5 (1994) of the *Henry Moore Bibliography* lists 598 entries under MOORE Henry dating from 1920 to 1991 in which, in whole or in part, his writings and conversations are to be found.[5] These include books, exhibition catalogues, letters, articles in newspapers and periodicals, transcripts of interviews, sound recordings, films and video cassettes, print albums and miscellaneous publications. Despite his concern, the 'tension needed for his work' was never threatened or in short supply: during the sixty-five years of his working life, Moore produced some 1,200 individual sculptures, at least 5,500 drawings and some 700 editions of original graphic works.

Among the 598 bibliographical entries are some sixty films solely on Moore, all of which feature the artist in interview. Why was Moore so extraordinarily accessible? How many films were made on Picasso, and of these how many featured Picasso in interview? How many eager students, architects, museum curators and directors, collectors, journalists, film-makers and art dealers would have even considered telephoning Picasso's secretary in the hope of arranging a meeting or interview, as one did when one rang Mrs Tinsley, Moore's secretary, on Much Hadham 2566? Access to Picasso was virtually impossible; access to Moore, his studios and sculpture garden was rather like planning a visit to Regent's Park and telephoning ahead to arrange an interview with the head gardener. Moore was as willing to meet and discuss his work with an unknown MA student (as he did with me in 1969 and continued to do for the next five years) as he was to welcome to Hoglands W.H. Auden, Lauren Bacall, Joan Miró, François Mitterrand and I.M. Pei. Anthony Caro, who was an assistant to Moore from 1951 to 1953, told me the quintessential story of his accessibility. Without an appointment, he knocked on

---

[4] 'The Sculptor Speaks', *The Listener* 18 August 1937, p.338 (see p.193).

[5] Many of the entries do, however, refer to items that were reprinted from earlier published articles.

the door of Hoglands and when Moore appeared, announced that he would like to work for him. 'You might have telephoned,' Henry said, 'but come in and have a cup of tea.'

Moore was by nature the most open, friendly and gregarious of men, who never seemed to lose his enthusiasm for discussing his life and work, even though he had been asked the same questions and had given more or less the same answers hundreds of times before. He was an engaging conversationalist – conversation came to him 'as naturally as leaves to a tree', as Keats thought poetry should come – and a brilliant communicator who throughout his life both enjoyed and, I believe, felt compelled to explain and promote his own work in particular, and the art of sculpture in general.

Moore was a dedicated teacher. One must not forget that he taught at Temple Street Elementary School, Castleford, in 1915-16 and 1919, was sculpture instructor at the Royal College of Art from 1924 to 1931, and was appointed the first head of sculpture at Chelsea School of Art, where he taught from 1932 to 1939. Caro has paid tribute to the dedication of his mentor: 'When I think back I'm amazed by how much time and trouble Henry took over me. I wanted to learn, I really wanted to learn from him. I learned more in the two years I was there than in the five years I spent at the Royal Academy Schools. […] Here was somebody who talked about things in sculpture, in art, in life in a way that struck a chord, rang a bell.' Caro also commented: 'He was very intelligent – intelligent in a way that a sculptor or an artist is intelligent. By that I mean he was visually aware and listened to what his gut instinct told him and he used his brain to develop that. But he could also talk well to people and explain things. He knew how the world worked. He had a real gift for explaining things, he enjoyed explaining things – he did to me, anyway.'[6]

Forging a Reputation: 1920-49

And so I think it is likely that a sculptor can in talking about some of the problems which occupy him, drop clues which will be of help to others in their approach to sculpture.[7]

Between 1920 and 1949, from the 'History of Sculpture: Notes' signed 'H.S. Moore 1920', entry 00001 in the *Henry Moore Bibliography*, to the German translation of his statement in *Unit One* 1934, which was published in the periodical *Thema*, Munich 1949 (01179), there are forty-one entries on Moore as an author in the index in Volume 5 of the Bibliography. In only fourteen of these is he the sole author.

---

[6] *Celebrating Moore: Works in the Collection of the Henry Moore Foundation*, selected by David Mitchinson, Lund Humphries, London 1998, pp.119, 237.
[7] Unpublished notes for 'The Sculptor Speaks' 1937, HMF archive.

Thirteen entries are letters and documents signed by Moore and others, usually artists, which were published in newspapers and periodicals. The letters address a variety of issues and concerns, from uniting artists opposed to war and Fascism and calling for arms for the people of Spain, to deploring the fact that, under new customs regulations, sculptures by Brancusi and others had in 1938 been refused admission to Great Britain as works of art. Twelve of the forty-one entries record material that was reprinted from items listed earlier in the Bibliography. In addition, there is the material that was not cited. Moore's personal letters, with a number of notable exceptions, were not included. The most interesting and historically important of the unpublished writings are manuscripts in the Henry Moore Foundation archive, which include: from the 1920s, notes on Mexican and Negro sculpture (pp.97, 98); from the 1930s, notes for 'A View of Sculpture' 1930, and for the recently identified, unsigned foreword to the catalogue of the 1933 *Primitive African Sculpture* exhibition at the Lefevre Galleries, London (p.99), drafts for his contributions to *Unit One* 1934 and *Circle* 1937, and drafts for 'Mesopotamian Art' 1935 and 'The Sculptor Speaks' 1937; and from the 1940s, notes for 'Primitive Art' 1941.

A chronological list of Moore's published and unpublished writings and conversations from these years provides a perspective on their evolution that is not apparent from the thematic arrangement of this book:[8]

1920 'History of Sculpture: Notes', manuscript, Leeds City Art Gallery

1930 'Contemporary English Sculptors: Henry Moore', *Architectural Association Journal* May 1930 (later republished as 'A View of Sculpture')

1931 Answers to a questionnaire on the Royal Academy of Arts, *Architectural Review* June 1931

1932 'On Carving' (A Conversation: Henry Moore and Arnold L. Haskell), *New English Weekly* 5 May 1932

1933 Unsigned foreword, *Primitive African Sculpture*, The Lefevre Galleries, London May 1933 (not in Bibliography)

1934 *Unit One: The Modern Movement in English Architecture, Painting and Sculpture*, ed. Herbert Read, Cassell, London 1934

1935 'Mesopotamian Art', *The Listener* 5 June 1935

1937 *Circle: International Survey of Constructive Art*, ed. J.L. Martin, Ben Nicholson, N. Gabo, Faber and Faber, London 1937

[8] Apart from the two entries marked 'not in Bibliography', all are listed in the *Henry Moore Bibliography*; the majority appear in the index in Volume 5 under MOORE Henry, but the film *Out of Chaos* may be found only under 1944 VIDEO, AUDIO & MICROFORM PUBLICATIONS and the last two articles only under 1947 PERIODICALS.

1937 'The Sculptor Speaks', *The Listener* 18 August 1937

1938 'Collective Security', *The Yorkshire Post* 31 March 1938

1939 On modern English buildings, *Architects' Journal* 4 May 1939

1941 'Primitive Art', *The Listener* 24 April 1941

1941 'Art and Life', *The Listener* 13 November 1941

1942 Letter to Wolfgang Paalen, 11 April 1942, *Dyn*, Mexico July-August 1942

1942 'Answering You', BBC 15 and 16 November 1942 (not in Bibliography)

1943 Discussion of *Madonna and Child* 1943-44 LH 226, *Church of S. Matthew, Northampton, 1893-1943*

1944 *Out of Chaos*, film directed by Jill Craigie, G.F.D. Two Cities, London *c*.1944

1947 John D. Morse, 'Henry Moore Comes to America', *Magazine of Art*, New York March 1947

1947 James Johnson Sweeney, 'Henry Moore', *Partisan Review*, New York March-April 1947

1947 *Henry Moore*, film narrated by J.J. Sweeney, Falcon Films, New York 1947

This survey includes Moore's first published article (1930), interview (1932) and book review (1935); first published letter, as sole author, to a newspaper (1938); first radio discussion, with Clark, Pritchett and Sutherland (1941); first published statement on one of his own sculptures (1943); and the first film in which Moore and his work appear, with a brief commentary by the artist (*c*.1944).

The 1920s

After the entry for 1920, there is a gap of nine years in which no entries for writings or conversations are recorded in the Bibliography. However, further written sources provide some fascinating nuggets of information from this otherwise more or less silent decade.

The earliest of these are Moore's letters. The first surviving letters are thought to be those of 1917-18 to Alice Gostick, which give an invaluable, if fragmentary, account of army life and war (p.40). Extracts from two letters to his friend Jocelyn Horner have been included. In the one dated 29 October 1921 Moore discussed his second visit to the British Museum and his discovery, after he tore himself away from the rooms of Egyptian and Assyrian sculpture, of 'the ecstatically fine negro sculptures' in the Ethnographic Gallery (p.45). This letter not only documents and dates Moore's second visit to the British Museum (he later recalled that he went weekly, sometimes twice weekly), it also provides an invaluable account of his discovery of primitive art, and of its immediate impact on him. Although he had already seen a few examples of African sculpture in Sir Michael Sadler's collection in Leeds, and had read Roger Fry's essays 'Negro Sculpture' and 'Ancient American Art' in *Vision and Design* (1920), the real shock of recognition was experienced during those early visits to the British Museum in October 1921.[9] Moore's letter from Paris to his friend Raymond Coxon, written on 7 February 1925, includes his impression of the French capital – 'it's a dull hole' – and a discussion of paintings and sculpture which he found of particular interest in the Musée Guimet (p.51). A letter to William Rothenstein, written from Florence on 12 March 1925, provides details of his itinerary while on a travelling scholarship, and gives his reactions to the work of Giotto, Masaccio, Michelangelo, Donatello and others (p.52). Whatever difficulties Moore was to experience later when writing about sculpture, it is obvious that he enjoyed writing to his friends. The letters have much of the warmth, boyish charm and playfulness that were so apparent in his conversation.

The second meagre but significant batch of unpublished material from the 1920s comprises four pages of undated manuscript notes on 'Mexican Sculpture' (see p.97) and four pages on 'Negro Sculpture' (see p.98), almost certainly written in tandem. That the former was on Royal College of Art headed paper suggests they were composed while Moore was sculptor instructor at the R.C.A. between 1924 and 1931, probably *c.*1925-26. These two short pieces were Moore's earliest writings on primitive art. At the end of the notes on 'Negro Sculpture', he identifies the three works in Walter Lehmann's *Altmexikanische Kunstgeschichte* (1922) 'which I think are the best sculptures', the third of which, plate 45, is the pre-Columbian Chacmool carving (fig.33) in the Museo Nacional de Antropología, Mexico: 'The last is about as good a piece of sculpture as I know.' This remark, the first reference to what Moore told me was the single most important influence on his early work, could just as well have been made at the end of his career as at the beginning.

The 1930s

In his first, short, published article of 1930, later called 'A View of Sculpture' (p.187), Moore propounds seven principles on the nature of modern sculpture in general, and his own work in particular – 'sculptural beliefs and aims', as he later called them, which were to remain, with one considerable modification (to truth to material in 1951), the bedrock of his philosophy of art. These were: seeking

[9] Eighty years on, in 2001, the new Sainsbury African Galleries in the British Museum were dedicated to 'Henry Moore OM, CH'.

inspiration outside what Roger Fry called 'the tyranny of the Graeco-Roman tradition';[10] truth to material; the importance of the intrinsic emotional significance of shapes; looking to nature for inspiration; the fully three-dimensional realisation of form; asymmetry; and the analogy of the human figure and landscape.[11] Moore has acknowledged his debt to Fry in making him aware of 'three-dimensional realisation' and 'truth to material' (p.44). The influence of the writings of the French sculptor Gaudier-Brzeska is even more pronounced, with clear echoes of his ideas and even his language. (For Moore's brief account of his excitement in reading Ezra Pound's *Gaudier-Brzeska: A Memoir* 1916, see p.151.) In the third paragraph of 'A View of Sculpture', 'This removal of the Greek spectacles from the eyes of the modern sculptor' must surely have been lifted from Gaudier-Brzeska's 'The Indians felt the hamatic [African] influence through Greek spectacles.'[12] In the last paragraph, 'its component forms are completely realised and work as masses in opposition' appears to be a paraphrase of Gaudier-Brzeska's 'Sculptural feeling is the appreciation of masses in relation.'[13] Finally, one of Moore's best-known statements, that the sculpture which moves him most 'is not perfectly symmetrical, it is static and it is strong and vital, giving out something of the energy and power of great mountains', could hardly be closer to one of the French sculptor's most famous pronouncements, 'Sculptural energy is the mountain.'[14]

Fortunately, Moore kept the notes and drafts for all his articles of the 1930s and early 1940s: 'A View of Sculpture' 1930; the foreword to *Primitive African Sculpture* 1933; his contributions to *Unit One* 1934 and *Circle* 1937; 'Mesopotamian Art' 1935; 'The Sculptor Speaks' 1937; and 'Primitive Art' 1941. The five pages of notes for 'A View of Sculpture' reveal just how seriously he took his writing, and the effort that went into polishing a phrase or sentence. For example, in three of the four drafts for the last paragraph on the qualities of sculpture which move him most, he wrestles with the concept of symmetry and with the mountain metaphor, quoted above as it appeared in the article:

'~~it is strong & vital giving out the same kind of energy & power possessed by a mountain, static as a mountain is, not perfectly symmetrical (symmetry is death nothing living is perfectly symmetrical~~)'

'~~it is strong & vital giving out the same kind~~ it is not perfectly symmetrical – it is static as a mountain is, it is strong & vital, (giving out the same kind of power & energy ~~as mountains~~ possessed by mountains.) giving out something of the energy & power of great mountains.

[10] *Vision and Design*, Chatto and Windus, London 1920; Pelican Books, Harmondsworth 1961, p.92.
[11] The 1930 green Hornton stone *Reclining Woman* LH 84 was originally called 'Mountains'.
[12] Ezra Pound, *Gaudier-Brzeska: A Memoir*, John Lane/Bodley Head, London 1916, p.10.
[13] Ibid., p.9.
[14] Ibid. Moore quotes this statement in 'Some definitions of sculpture', *c.*1953-54, p.204.

'It is static in the sense that a tree or a mountain are static (though it will have growth & rhythm as a tree has, energy & power as a mountain has) it will not be symmetrical, symmetry is death, nothing living is perfectly symmetrical.'

In some of the drafts, ideas are often expressed more vividly and forcefully than they are in the published article. For example, in the notes for 'A View of Sculpture' Moore's remark on symmetry exudes a revolutionary fervour reminiscent of some of Gaudier-Brzeska's statements. 'Symmetry is death', which appears twice in the drafts, has in the article been watered down to the bland statement that the sculpture he most admires 'is not perfectly symmetrical'. The drafts also contain much interesting material which was later left out. To take one example, also from the notes for 'A View of Sculpture', Moore ingeniously finds an analogy for the difference between stone carving and modelling: 'the kettle gives a sense of power emitting steam through the spout, in contrast with [an] open pan of water boiling –' (p.231). The article ends: 'It has a life of its own, independent of the object it represents.' A much more lively draft reads: 'A great work of sculpture has a life of its own independent of the object it represents, it can create its own atmosphere, it is a personality in the world, a living presence.'

Three other items from the early 1930s are indicative of the disparate subject-matter of Moore's first published pieces. His outspoken attack on the standards and usefulness of the Royal Academy of Arts, published in the *Architectural Review* in June 1931 (p.111), is of interest both for the views expressed and for the fact that at this relatively early stage in Moore's career his opinions were valued and sought after. (For the comments he made in 1973 on the R.A., see p.112.) Moore's first and very important published interview, 'On Carving' (*New English Weekly* 5 May 1932, see p.188), has been largely forgotten because it was not included in the selection of early writings reprinted in *Henry Moore: Sculpture and Drawings* 1944. Herbert Read wrote the introduction to this first edition of Volume 1 of the six-volume catalogue raisonné of the sculpture, published by Lund Humphries. (Nor was 'A View of Sculpture' included, although it was republished in 1957 in the fourth edition of Volume 1, edited by David Sylvester.) The third item, Moore's foreword to the catalogue of the 1933 exhibition *Primitive African Sculpture* at the Lefevre Galleries, London (p.99), was his first published piece on primitive art; one wonders why it was not signed.

Moore's statement in *Unit One* 1934 (p.191), his first contribution to a collection of writings by a group of painters, sculptors and architects, was the most expansive airing to date of his views on sculpture. He enlarged on three of the key issues he had touched on briefly in 'A View of Sculpture': truth to material; full three-dimensional realisation; and the observation of nature, by which he meant the human figure, and natural objects such as pebbles, rocks, bones and trees. At the end of his first, detailed description of the structural qualities of natural forms, which may have been influenced by D'Arcy Wentworth Thompson's *On Growth and Form* (1917),[15] Moore introduces two new topics with the headings 'Vision and expression', and 'Vitality and Power of expression'. Here for the first time he offers his views on abstraction, beauty and vitality in his sculpture.

Herbert Read, the editor of *Unit One*, drew up a questionnaire which he sent to the eleven members of the group. It consisted of nineteen questions on theory, education, technique and policy.[16] Among Moore's extensive drafts for his *Unit One* article are two sets of answers to the nineteen questions, but apart from the notes in reply to question 7, 'Do you study natural objects or embody observation of the natural object in your sculpture?', very little of this interesting material was used. I have included several of Moore's brief written replies to some of the questions, including number 16: 'Have you any political convictions of a party kind (conservative, fascist, communist)?' This produced a rare and revealing statement on his political beliefs in the mid-1930s (see p.131). He obviously abandoned the idea of submitting his answers to the questionnaire, and decided instead to write his article under the following headings:

Points of Article
Truth to material
Full three dimensional realisation
Asymmetry
Sculptural principles from observation of natural objects (pebbles bones etc)
Qualities of vision & expression
Vitality & Power of expression
Beauty v. Power
Pure Abstraction – & Abstract qualities plus the Human element
Difference between Architecture & Sculpture [not discussed in *Unit One*]
Art not an escape from Life.

Among the notes is an isolated sentence which reads: 'I have no conceit as a writer, in fact I find it very difficult to start writing about sculpture generally & my aims in particular.' The copious notes and drafts for the articles of the 1930s suggest that in fact the ideas flowed fairly easily, even though, as we have seen, he wrestled with the choice and order of words. It is curious that a man who always radiated such confidence about his life and work did not think more highly of his obvious abilities as a writer.

[15] For the influence of Thompson on Moore's ideas on the structure of natural forms, see Christa Lichtenstern, 'Henry Moore and Surrealism', *Burlington Magazine* November 1981, pp.651-2.
[16] The questionnaire that appears on pp.14 and 15 of *Unit One* is the one sent to the painters. Some of the questions were modified to suit the subject-matter of architecture and sculpture.

'Mesopotamian Art', Moore's first book review, published in *The Listener* on 5 June 1935 (p.100), was also his first substantial article on a period of art history, and the forerunner of extensive writings and conversations on art and artists, many of which are included in Chapter Three. Among the most interesting of the later pieces are 'Primitive Art' 1941 (p.102), 'Tribal Sculpture' 1951 (p.106), Epstein 1959 (p.149), Michelangelo 1964 (p.156), Nicholson 1969 (p.161), Pisano 1969 (p.169), Rodin 1970 (p.176), Hepworth 1975 (p.153) and Brabender 1984 (p.142). Moore seemed almost as willing to write about and discuss the work of other artists and periods of art as he was his own life and sculpture.

Moore's minimal contribution to *Circle: International Survey of Constructive Art* 1937 (p.193) would seem to indicate that he did not fully embrace the ideals of Constructivism and abstract art (see p.113). The first statement, except for the opening sentence, was lifted almost verbatim from the last paragraph of the *Unit One* article; the second was based on notes already made for 'The Sculptor Speaks' (see p.193, notes 7 and 8). There are no notes or drafts marked 'Circle article' in the HMF archive.

'The Sculptor Speaks', published in *The Listener* on 18 August 1937 (p.193), Moore's longest piece of writing to that date on any subject, is in my opinion his most crucial treatise on sculpture, the one to save for posterity if a single article had to be chosen. As with the *Unit One* material, there are extensive notes and drafts which reveal interesting variations on the published text. For example, the previously quoted opening, 'It is a mistake for a sculptor or a painter to speak or write very often about his job. It releases tension needed for his work' is a distillation of the more tentative but fulsome 'For a sculptor or a painter or any artist (though probably least for the writer) to speak or write, in public, about his job, very often is a mistake. It (perhaps) releases (some of the) urge & tension needed to do his work with intensity –'.

The manuscript that Moore sent to *The Listener* was headed 'Notes on Sculpture', though this was changed to 'The Sculptor Speaks' – a title that may have been borrowed from the book *The Sculptor Speaks: Jacob Epstein to Arnold L. Haskell, A Series of Conversations on Art* (1931). The brief introduction is followed by seven sections: Three Dimensions; Brancusi; Shells and pebbles – being conditioned to respond to shapes; Holes in Sculpture; Size and Scale; Drawing and Sculpture; Abstraction and Surrealism. These headings, which appear in the manuscript and in *The Listener*, were unfortunately omitted when the article was reprinted in *Henry Moore: Sculpture and Drawings* 1944, and in *Henry Moore on Sculpture* 1966.

Moore opens the otherwise perceptive section on Brancusi with: 'Since the Gothic, European sculpture had become overgrown with moss, weeds – all sorts of surface excrescences which completely concealed shape. It has been Brancusi's special mission to get rid of this overgrowth, and to make us once more shape-conscious.' These comments have understandably raised a few eyebrows, the earliest being those of Douglas Lord (Douglas Cooper), whose letter in *The Listener* (8 September 1937) appeared three weeks after 'The Sculptor Speaks', and referred to this 'extraordinary statement' (see p.194, note 10). Did Moore *really* mean to dismiss the sculpture of Donatello, Michelangelo, Bernini and Rodin? It seems more likely that he was echoing the views of his friend Herbert Read, whose writings on art had a considerable impact on him in the 1930s.[17] In the opening two sentences of his review of Moore's exhibition in London at the Leicester Galleries (*The Listener* 22 April 1931), Read makes the equally sweeping claim: 'Since the fifteenth century sculpture has been a lost art in England. Perhaps it has been a lost art in Europe generally, for it is possible to argue that the whole Renaissance conception of sculpture was a false one.' I suspect that Moore, who would certainly have read Lord's attack in *The Listener*, wished that he had expressed less forcefully his belief in the need to simplify form. For one who wrote and spoke so much, there were bound to be some flats among the elevations, to borrow a phrase from Dryden.

The sculptural beliefs and aims which Moore formulated in his published articles and conversations of the 1930s were to remain the cornerstones of his future statements on the nature of sculpture and on what he was trying to achieve in his own work. In much of the subsequent written and spoken material (of which there was a staggering amount) he was simply elaborating on and reinforcing those concepts which had first emerged in embryonic form in 'A View of Sculpture' 1930, and which were added to and reached their full and mature expression in *Unit One* 1934, and above all in 'The Sculptor Speaks' 1937. Sometimes an idea or image first expressed during the 1930s would lie dormant and resurface many years later. For example, his simile of 1930 about the difference between carving and modelling being like that between the steam emerging forcefully through the spout of a kettle and that rising randomly from the surface of an open pan of boiling water (see p.231) reappeared in an interview in 1973 (p.201).

Moore never wavered in his commitment to explaining and promoting his views on such fundamental issues as the full, three-dimensional realisation of form, the intrinsic emotional significance of shapes, asymmetry, and the study of nature – the human figure and natural forms – as the necessary foundation for a sculptor. There was only one fundamental tenet from the 1920s and 1930s that was later considerably modified and redefined, and that was his almost fanatical belief in the doctrine of truth to material (p.200). According to his view at that time, a sculpture carved in stone or wood was quite simply superior to one modelled in clay, wax or plaster and later cast in bronze. He always maintained that one shouldn't try to make stone behave and look like flesh and blood, dimples and drapery, as Bernini

[17] David Sylvester told me, however, that he thought Read was reflecting Moore's ideas.

did. Nor would Moore have even contemplated the supreme challenge to the stone carver, posed by Leontes in the last scene of *The Winter's Tale* as he witnesses the miraculous transformation of the statue of Hermione[18] into a woman:

> 'Still, me thinks,
> There is an air comes from her: what fine chisel
> Could ever yet cut breath?'

Moore's writings of the 1930s – to which I would add the article 'Primitive Art' 1941 – and the copious notes from which they were distilled, are imbued with a richness of ideas and imagery, and a sense of passionate conviction, which set them apart from much of the subsequent voluminous material on similar or related subjects. In later articles and conversations, although he never seemed to lose his enthusiasm for communicating, something of the freshness of concepts shaped and formulated for the first time, and the sense of urgency in the crusade to explain his aims and beliefs, were lost in the telling and retelling. In discussing the art of sculpture, Moore never again quite recaptured the intensity, nor improved on the insights and observations of those 1930s articles. They remain the most lucid, original and ultimately the most important statements that he made on the art of sculpture.

The 1940s

If Moore's writings of the 1930s were mainly concerned with the formulation of his aims and beliefs, the material from the 1940s, though comparatively sparse, appeared in more varied media, as can be seen in the list on p.15; it includes two group radio discussions (1941 and 1942), the first published statement on one of his own sculptures (1943), his first two appearances on film (*c.*1944 and 1947), and two interviews (1947). In his article 'Primitive Art' of 1941 Moore continued to promote non-European sculptural traditions, as he had done in the 1930s with his pieces on African sculpture and Mesopotamian art. Although he wrote less than he had done in the previous decade, much more was written about him and his work. The 1940s brought the dissemination of his writings to a wider public; of the nineteen entries for the 1940s listed in the *Henry Moore Bibliography* with Moore as an author, nine refer to items that were reprinted from earlier published articles. Of these, the one publication that should be mentioned again is the first edition of *Henry Moore: Sculpture and Drawings* 1944, in which for the first time a group of his writings was published together: 'The Sculptor's Aims' (the title was new) from *Unit One* 1934;

---

[18] A little earlier, in Act V.ii of *The Winter's Tale*, the statue is described as being 'by that rare Italian master, Julio Romano'. The Renaissance painter and architect Giulio Romano (1492-1546) – he was not a sculptor – is the only artist named in Shakespeare's works.

'Notes on Sculpture', originally published as 'The Sculptor Speaks' in *The Listener* 18 August 1937; and 'Primitive Art', *The Listener* 24 April 1941.

Although 'The Sculptor Speaks' had been reprinted in whole or in part in three books published between 1937 and 1941, Moore's articles of the 1930s and early 1940s were not readily accessible, and did not reach a larger public until three of them were included in *Henry Moore: Sculpture and Drawings* 1944. What better way of helping the reader to understand and appreciate Moore's sculpture and drawings than by letting the artist speak for himself about the art of sculpture in general, about his own work in particular, and, in his article on 'Primitive Art', about his deep admiration for prehistoric European, Egyptian, Assyrian, Sumerian, archaic Greek, African, Oceanic, and above all pre-Columbian sculpture, all of which in the 1920s and 1930s had played such a vital role in the formation and consolidation of his vision of three-dimensional form. Little wonder that since the publication in 1944 of *Henry Moore: Sculpture and Drawings*, authors of articles, catalogues and monographs on the artist have relied on and quoted so frequently and extensively from the writings: it is impossible to compete with Moore on Moore.

'Primitive Art' 1941 (p.102), Moore's only article from the 1940s, is by far his most perceptive treatise on the subject. It had been preceded by the two short unpublished essays from the mid-1920s on pre-Columbian and African sculpture (pp.97, 98), and by the introduction to the catalogue of the 1933 Lefevre Galleries exhibition *Primitive African Sculpture* (p.99); it was followed by the interview with William Fagg in 1951 in the form of a review of the exhibition *Traditional Art from the Colonies* at the Imperial Institute, London (p.106), and, towards the end of his life, by his comments on Aztec, Oceanic, African, American and Caribbean sculpture in *Henry Moore at the British Museum* 1981.

In the letter to Jocelyn Horner of 29 October 1921, Moore had described the excitement of his discoveries in the Ethnographical Gallery of the British Museum (p.45). Twenty years later, in his article 'Primitive Art', he takes us on a tour of the British Museum, and recalls the impact that the sculpture collections had made on him during those first visits. The descriptions of the formal characteristics of the works are typical of Moore's prose at its most vivid and assured: it is punchy, packed with concrete images, similes, metaphors and associations. In a rare musical simile, he describes the life-size female figures in the archaic Greek room as 'seated in easy, still naturalness, grand and full like Handel's music'. He admired the 'contained bull-like grandeur and held-in energy' of some of the Sumerian sculpture (fig.34). Of the Palaeolithic 'tender carving of a girl's head', he gives us a sense of its size not by vaguely describing it as 'small', or giving an impersonal measurement, but with the words 'no bigger than one's thumbnail'. The works in the display cases in the Ethnographical room are not simply crowded but 'overcrowded and jumbled together like junk in a marine stores'. Oceanic, as compared to African, sculpture 'has a livelier, thin flicker', and the carvings from New Ireland 'have, besides their vicious kind of vitality, a unique spatial sense, a bird-in-a-cage form' (fig.36).

Whereas in the most interesting and informative section of 'Primitive Art' Moore looks back and relives his discovery in the early 1920s of African, pre-Columbian and Oceanic art, the contents of the other discussions, statements and interviews of the 1940s are very much rooted in the present. In 'Art and Life' 1941 (p.124), his first published radio broadcast, Moore, V.S. Pritchett, Graham Sutherland and Sir Kenneth Clark discuss such current topics as Picasso's *Guernica*, and the fact that Moore's work looks to the average man fairly remote from human experience. In the first published text on one of his own sculptures, included in the 1943 booklet *Church of S. Matthew, Northampton, 1893-1943* (p.267), Moore recounts his initial misgivings about accepting the commission to carve a Madonna and Child, and goes on to describe the qualities of austerity, nobility and grandeur which he felt were demanded. Although in articles of the 1930s he had discussed his aims, beliefs and sculpture in general terms, not once, as far as I know, did he refer to a specific work by name. It was not until the 1950s that Moore began in earnest to comment on individual carvings and bronzes, sometimes while a work was in progress and often not long after it had been completed.

Moore's reputation, both at home and abroad, grew steadily throughout the 1940s. His first museum exhibition in England, shared with John Piper and Graham Sutherland, was held in 1941 at Temple Newsam, Leeds. In 1941, 1942 and 1944 his wartime drawings were shown in three exhibitions under the title *War Pictures at the National Gallery*. In 1946 the retrospective exhibition of his work at The Museum of Modern Art, New York, firmly established his reputation in the United States. During his visit to New York in 1946 Moore was interviewed by James Johnson Sweeney, the organiser of the exhibition, and by John D. Morse, and material from those interviews, the first since 'On Carving' in 1932, was published the following year (see list on pp.14-15). On that same visit, Moore was the subject of a film made at the exhibition, narrated by Sweeney and released in 1947. In it he comments on his discovery of Londoners sheltering during the Blitz on the station platforms of the London Underground, and discusses his Shelter Sketchbook. Finally, in 1948 Moore was awarded the International Prize for Sculpture at the XXIV Venice Biennale.

If the writings and conversations from the first three decades of Moore's career were so few in number that they are as readily discernible as Orion and Ursa Major in the winter sky, the 557 entries in the Bibliography with Moore as an author for the years 1950 to 1986 are as overwhelming as the myriad fainter stars contrasting with the vivid constellations.

In the Public Eye: the 1950s

Because some of the notes & writings on sculpture which I have made in the past have been quoted without their dates, or go on being quoted as though I said them yesterday – it has been necessary to make a few refutations.[19]

This statement appears in a notebook of *c*.1951 – unusually, full of handwritten notes, not of drawings – the single most extensive source of unpublished writings since the drafts for the articles of the 1930s. It is the first of six possible opening sentences of the introduction to a piece which, as the inscription 'Tate Article' on another page seems to suggest, Moore was writing for David Sylvester's catalogue of the Tate Gallery's 1951 exhibition, but which, Sylvester has told me, had not been commissioned. What did appear in the catalogue were 'Notes by Henry Moore', which consisted of ten brief passages: five extracted from articles of the 1930s, one taken from 'Primitive Art' 1941, and four based on material in this *c*.1951 notebook. The subjects of these four notes were truth to material; the human figure; humanist trends in contemporary painting and sculpture; and sculpture in landscape.

The first topic, truth to material, was really the only one of his earlier principles that Moore needed to amend; as he wrote in the second draft for the opening sentence, he did not intend to refute his previous statements so much as 'to qualify some of the beliefs & aims they expressed, for not all of them are what I now completely believe.' It must be remembered that since the late 1930s, as well as carving as he had always done, Moore had also been modelling in clay, wax and plaster so that his work could be cast in lead or bronze. He obviously felt the need to explain his present position and to justify his radical change in attitude towards the once sacred doctrine of truth to material (see p.202).

It is interesting to compare the subjects listed for discussion in the *c*.1951 notebook – truth to material, opening out of form, drawing, humanist qualities, sculpture and nature, the human figure, conflict, and 'separate sentences' – with those addressed in *Unit One* and 'The Sculptor Speaks' in the 1930s. In the intervening years, the principal preoccupations remain the same, are amplified and considered with fresh insights. One addition to the long-standing topics of interest is conflict, previously discussed in J.J. Sweeney's 1947 published interview (p.54). In one of the unpublished notes on the subject, Moore wrote: 'Conflict, or rather Tension is necessary to the artist as to everybody else in life – otherwise he stagnates – One welcomes "Tension" as the "growing" periods & "Harmony" as the "achieving" periods.' Conflict was a subject to which he returned (p.116). Another was the useful idea of 'separate sentences', brief, self-contained statements on a variety of subjects, as for example the one in the 1951 Tate Gallery catalogue,

---

[19] Unpublished notes *c*.1951, HMF archive.

beginning 'In my opinion, long and intense study of the human figure is the necessary foundation for a sculptor' (see p.218). Some of Moore's best known and most frequently cited statements are separate sentences, such as another from 1951 which starts: 'Sculpture is an art of the open air. Daylight, *sunlight* is necessary to it, and for me its best setting and complement is nature' (see p.245). As Roger Berthoud perceptively observed, Moore 'liked to deal in homespun, quotable verities.' Of the 'sculpture is an art of the open air' remark, Berthoud continued: 'That is an archetypal Moore statement. It looks good, it sounds good. It makes you feel: Isn't he wise, simple and down-to-earth, unlike all those pretentious old critics! Yet the harder you scrutinize each sentence, the less convincing it seems.'[20] Moore's 1939 wood and string *Bird Basket* LH 205 (see p.257) should no more be displayed in the open air, exposed to the elements, than should a delicate medieval ivory, a wooden Gothic altarpiece, a terracotta by Clodion, or a wax sculpture by Degas. Many of the best of Moore's 'separate sentences' were those not written for public consumption but spontaneous pensées, often one-liners, such as: 'I mean even when he makes the women, they've got skin like rhinoceros, really, I mean in certain ways I dislike Michelangelo's women.' Or, 'Renoir has a sinuous flowing snakelike rhythm whereas Cézanne has a short staccato, stratified rocklike rhythm as though his forms were chopped into their shape by an axe –' The palpable imagery of Moore's descriptions is nowhere more in evidence than in these concise, pithy sentences.

The 1950s was for Moore a very public decade. In 1951 there was the retrospective exhibition at the Tate Gallery, and the commission for a sculpture for the Festival of Britain (p.275). In 1952-53 he created the stone screen and the bronze reclining figure for the Time–Life Building, London (p.278), and in 1957-58 he carved the huge marble reclining figure for the Unesco headquarters in Paris (p.286). In 1951 John Read wrote and produced his first film on Moore, in which the sculptor discussed primitive art and the qualities of natural forms. The following year, on one of the few occasions when he agreed to speak in public, Moore gave a long and considered speech, 'The Sculptor in Modern Society', at the International Conference of Artists in Venice (p.136). *Henry Moore, Volume Two: Sculpture and Drawings Since 1948* was published in 1955, with an introduction by Herbert Read and texts by Moore. These were 'Notes on Sculpture', reprinted from the 1951 Tate Gallery catalogue; 'Some Notes on Space and Form in Sculpture' and 'Notes on the Sculptures made for the Time–Life Building, London', both reprinted from Felix H. Man's *Eight European Artists* 1954; and 'Notes on the Draped Reclining Figure', reprinted from the exhibition catalogue *Sculpture in the Open Air*, Holland Park, London 1954. The following year the nine-page typescript *Sculpture in the Open Air: A Talk by Henry Moore on his Sculpture and its Placing in Open-Air Sites*, edited by Robert

[20] *The Life of Henry Moore*, Faber and Faber, London 1987, p.134.

Melville, provided invaluable comments, on the early works in particular, from the 1928 relief *West Wind* LH 58 (p.252) to the 1952-53 bronze *Draped Reclining Figure* LH 336 (p.280). Whereas during the period 1920 to the late 1940s Moore wrote very little about his individual sculptures and drawings, by the mid-1950s he was beginning to discuss his current as well as his earlier work on a regular basis. For example, the year after the large elmwood *Upright Internal/External Form* 1953-54 LH 297 was completed, Moore wrote to Gordon Smith at the Albright-Knox Art Gallery, Buffalo, and explained how the sculpture evolved, as well as suggesting how it should be lit (p.277).

In both his written and spoken words and in his work, the year 1958 marked the end of Moore's social role as public sculptor. The *Unesco Reclining Figure* 1957-58 LH 416 (p.286) was his last public commission in the sense that the sculpture was created for a specific site; it was not enlarged from a maquette that already existed, as in the case of *Three Way Piece No.2: (The) Archer* 1964-65 LH 535 (p.294) and almost all future 'commissions'. As a spokesman on the international stage for the art of sculpture, his speech in Venice in 1952, expounding the need for the interaction of the artist and society and discussing the role of patronage, was to be his first and last major public address. Moore's role as an adjudicator, which had included being a member of the organising committee for The Unknown Political Prisoner sculpture competition in 1952, came to an end in 1958 when, as President of the Jury, he reported on the progress in selecting a sculpture to be erected on the site of Auschwitz–Birkenau concentration camp (p.134).

Alan Bowness was the first to identify the year 1958 as a watershed, marking 'the beginning of a new, more personal, late period. From this date forward Moore has seemed more inclined to please himself, exploiting all the possibilities of working on a grand scale that were now open to him as a successful sculptor, indifferent to fashion and caring little about what other people might think.'[21] As far as his writings, conversations and interviews were concerned, however, he seemed more and more inclined to please and accommodate everybody. Including the items with Moore as an author, there are 2,411 entries for the years 1920 to 1958 in the *Henry Moore Bibliography*, and an astounding 8,300 for the years 1959 to 1986. The more books, catalogues, exhibitions, articles, radio, newspaper and television interviews and films were produced, the greater the demand became, the more generous his response, so that it could be said of him:

> 'For his bounty,
> There was no winter in't; an autumn 'twas
> That grew the more by reaping.'[22]

---

[21] *Henry Moore: Complete Sculpture, Volume 4 1964-73*, ed. Alan Bowness, Lund Humphries, London 1977, p.8.
[22] William Shakespeare, *Antony and Cleopatra* V.ii. 86-88.

Despite the marked increase during the 1950s in publications with Moore as an author, those that are significant – which include his first tributes to friends, Curt Valentin in 1954 (p.92), Peter Gregory and Jacob Epstein in 1959 (pp.86 and 149) – are still readily discernible. From 1960 onwards, however, there are no such focal points and it would be monotonous and futile to attempt anything more than a brief outline of the material and the patterns that emerged during the last twenty-seven years of Moore's life. The most frequently quoted sources from which the writings and conversations have been extracted are listed at the back of this book.

The Great Communicator: 1960-86

When I've finished a sculpture and through it expressed my ideas, emotions and feelings, then I can look and philosophise about the reason for doing a particular piece. But it would never be exact. Who can tell if an experience which occurred yesterday, or ten years ago, or a lifetime ago was an influence or not? I can't.[23]

His own life and sculpture were the subjects most often discussed in the countless interviews which Moore gave during the 1960s to 1980s. In the first chapter of this book, 'Life and Influences', almost all the material was written or recorded between 1960 and 1986. In Chapter Five, 'Works by Henry Moore', the comments on the sculptures and drawings up to the end of the 1940s were written or recorded later, mostly after 1960, with the exception of Moore's letter of 15 March 1939 to Kenneth Clark about transporting the 1938 *Recumbent Figure* LH 191 to New York, his 1943 text on the Northampton *Madonna and Child* LH 226, and an extract from Sweeney's 1947 article, discussing the Shelter and Coalmine drawings and their influence on his later work.

Moore's tributes to friends and colleagues appear in Chapter Two. (Those to his closest artist friends – Epstein, Hepworth, Nicholson, Piper, Richards and Sutherland – appear in Chapter Three, 'Art and Artists'.) These portraits, most of which date from the 1960s and 1970s, were expressed in letters, obituaries, radio broadcasts, and in the case of the birthday tributes to J.D. Bernal and Anton Zwemmer, in short published texts. The admiration and affection that Moore felt for his friends and colleagues radiate from these reminiscences, nowhere more so than in the Herbert Read obituary in *The Sunday Times* 16 June 1968 (p.91); they gave rise to some of his most perceptive observations on character, such as the simile already quoted that describes T.S. Eliot as 'dry like a hard grain of human wheat'. Such tributes represent the more private and personal side of Moore's writings, and

[23] *Henry Moore: My Ideas, Inspiration and Life as an Artist*, photographs by John Hedgecoe, Ebury Press, London 1986, p.181.

were composed with a great deal of care and effort. Alfred Barr appreciated this when he wrote to Moore on 9 March 1973 (see p.81): 'Dear Henry: I am most grateful to you for your letter of February 19th and really touched that you should have troubled to write it in longhand.'

Most of Moore's statements on ancient and non-Western art, on art in general, on art and society, which appear in Chapter Three, date from the 1920s to the early 1950s. However, during the last twenty-five or so years of his life Moore turned his attention to discussing the work of painters, sculptors and draughtsmen whom he admired, from Giovanni Pisano to Picasso. The earliest tribute had been to Brancusi in 'The Sculptor Speaks' 1937 (p.194); one of the last was to Donatello in 1978 (p.148). Moore had changed his tune since he wrote in 1925 that 'in the influence of Donatello I think I see the beginning of the end – Donatello was a modeller, and it seems to me that it is modelling that has sapped the manhood out of Western sculpture,' (see p.52); his 1978 *Three Bathers – After Cézanne* LH 741 was modelled in plasticine and later cast in bronze (p.307). Moore wrote obituaries for *The Sunday Times* on Epstein in 1959, and Hepworth in 1975 (pp.149 and 153); and on the death of Picasso in 1973 he was interviewed for a tribute programme on BBC radio (p.167). It was at Moore's suggestion that Michael Ayrton's *Giovanni Pisano: Sculptor* (1969) and Paul Pieper's book on Heinrich Brabender (1984) were produced, and to both he contributed a carefully considered introduction (see pp.169 and 142).

Moore's extensive comments on the nature, techniques and materials of sculpture, which are the subject of Chapter Four, consist of those seminal articles of the 1930s, later frequently elaborated upon in considerable detail, and added to as new working methods were introduced and new styles evolved. Bringing together in this chapter these later observations from so many sources, and adding them to the 1930s articles, has created a comprehensive treatise on sculpture by a great sculptor.

In the early 1950s, in one of those isolated sentences that are scattered throughout the notebooks and manuscript pages, Moore mused rather wistfully, 'Will sculpture ever be generally appreciated?' Perhaps he had in mind Herbert Read's opening remark in the 1934 monograph *Henry Moore*: 'Sculpture is certainly the most difficult of all the arts – the most difficult of all arts to master, the most difficult to appreciate.' From the mid-1920s, when he proclaimed that pre-Columbian artists 'were true sculptors in sympathy with their material & their sculpture has some of the character of mountains, of boulders, rocks & sea worn pebbles', to the delightful aside in 1985, in one of the last interviews, that female backs 'are beautiful – although they don't have a lot of incident on them, like the front of a figure', I do not believe that any artist has done as much as Henry Moore to explain and promote the art of sculpture.

Alan Wilkinson

1 Adel Rock, Alwoodley Crags, about five miles north of Leeds

CHAPTER ONE

LIFE AND INFLUENCES

Yorkshire 1898-1921

Family Life

I was the seventh in the family. By the time I came along, one brother and two sisters had already become teachers, and this was the sort of path carved out for the rest of the family. So there was no question of me going down the pits. My father[1] really was a remarkable man. Very ambitious for us children, and had taught himself, although I was told that he had no schooling and earned his living first of all at nine. In his youth I think there was very little public education, and by the time I remember him very clearly he could help me in my homework from the grammar school. He seemed to know the whole of his Shakespeare. He knew his Bible pretty thoroughly and he taught himself enough trigonometry, mathematics and so on to pass his exam as a manager for the coal mine. So I think it was he who really helped the family. He was absolute boss, a complete Victorian tyrant. I got on with him, but at the same time one had to keep away from his chair in the corner of the room, I remember. And homework, everything else, was done on the kitchen table after the meal was cleared away. His little corner was absolutely sacrosanct. Nobody was allowed to nudge him or bump him in any way whatever. I had a great respect for Father. I knew that his opinions had real foundation. For instance, when I came to want to be an artist, he said, 'First become qualified as a teacher like your brother and sisters have done and then change to art if you wish. Be sure that you have some living in your hand.' Well, this was very intelligent and very sensible, but by the time I got to that age I knew that I wasn't going to be a teacher, that I was going to study art.

Freeman 1964, p.32

2 Moore's father, Raymond Spencer Moore, c.1908

He was a kind of Victorian father. He had his own chair near the coal fire – miners got their coal at a very nominal cost – and nobody had to touch him as they went past. If we accidentally kicked his foot or something, he'd go for us, not physically but [and he imitated growling imprecations]. If he didn't like some food my mother gave him, he would say 'I'll throw this back of fire.' My mother would say 'All right, go on.' He never did. She called his bluff.

Berthoud 1987, p.22

[1] Raymond Spencer Moore (1849-1922).

My father was a miner at the time of a very long coal strike. During that time, he did odd jobs, mended shoes, any job at all. He was good with his hands. He was politically active and used to hold meetings in our front room. It was, I suppose, about the setting up of a kind of trade union. It must have been 1906 or thereabouts.

We had a very thin time, but my father was unbelievably resilient and ambitious for his children. He had had to learn everything himself, from books and so on. He had had no help from his parents so he had a terrific struggle to do what he did. But he had tremendous hopes for his children and he believed in education and he made all of us go in for exams to get to the local secondary school, as it was called then; it became a grammar school later.

I failed the first time that I took them. And I said to my father, I've failed because you make me learn the violin – I hated the noise it made – I don't do my homework because I have to do all that practice. So he agreed. I stopped the violin. I failed the exams a second time, but my father said he would give me one last chance to pass or he would make me take up the violin again. I passed on the third attempt and gave up the violin for ever.

I wasn't frightened of my father, but we were brought up to respect him; it was the Victorian idea of the family and he was the head of it. He was the boss and he expected absolute, complete control. Without my knowing it – I didn't know it – he was a marvellous man. He'd had to work down the mines when he was eight or nine – as children did in those days. Somehow, he'd got himself out of mining and he determined that his children would, too.

Hedgecoe 1986, p.11

I was the seventh of eight children, you see, so she [my mother][2] needed tremendous physical stamina. She worked from morning till night till – well, till we'd all gone out into the world and she was over seventy. And that's what a sculptor needs, too – that physical stamina, real physical energy.

Russell 17 December 1961

3 Mary Moore, c.1908

You know, whenever I see this figure[3] I am reminded of a boyhood experience that contributed towards the conception of its form. I was a Yorkshire miner's son, the youngest of seven, and my mother was no longer so very young. She suffered from bad rheumatism in the back and would often say to me in winter, when I came home from school: 'Henry, boy, come and rub my back.' Then I would massage her back with liniment. When I came to model this figure which represents a fully mature woman, I found that I was unconsciously giving to its back the long-forgotten shape of the one that I had so often rubbed as a boy.

Roditi 1960, pp.183-4

[2] Mary Moore, née Baker (1858-1944).
[3] *Seated Woman* 1957 LH 435.

Not just her shoulder but her whole back down from the shoulder blades with the skin close to the bone, to the fleshy lower parts. I had a strong sense of contrast between bone and flesh. I was seven or eight at the time.

Spender 1978, p.22

Often people don't, but I find that [female] backs are beautiful – although they don't have a lot of incident on them, like the front of a figure.

The Mystery of Henry Moore, produced, directed and written by Harry Rasky, Canadian Broadcasting Corporation, Toronto 1985

Without consciously setting out to do that, they've turned out that way [matriarchal women] merely because that's the basis of my own upbringing and relationship to my own mother. She was to me the absolute stability, the rock, the whole thing in life that one knew was there for one's protection. If she went out I'd be terrified she wouldn't return. So it's not surprising that the women have this kind of feeling and that the kind of women I've done in sculpture are mature women rather than young.

John Heilpern, 'The Master Touch', *Observer Magazine* 30 April 1972, p.37

At home, we lived a communal life, we were never much alone. We lived, mostly, in one downstairs room. It was a very homely, matey, crowded way of living. You saw a lot of people; there was a lot going on.

I was, next to my sister Elsie, the youngest member of my family. Elsie was very keen on athletics running. She always came first. In some ways I blame myself – I encouraged her to go faster and faster and train harder and harder and then she died of heart failure. It upset me for years. So, after that, the family poured their affection on to me. I was the youngest and they all looked after me and helped me. My eldest brother, Raymond, liked drawing and I used to get him to draw for me when I was a small child.

I had a grandmother whom I used to have to go and see every Saturday or Sunday down in the town. I hated it. I had to go up a long flight of steps and there was a dreadful smell. I had to go and kiss her and to me she was terribly revolting. But there we were, it was part of the pattern of life. That was Castleford.

Hedgecoe 1986, p.14

Castleford

I lived in Castleford, apart from being in the army, until I suppose I was 22 years old. One of the first and strongest things I recall were the slag heaps, like pyramids, like mountains, artificial mountains. There were pit heaps all over – the great waste, the unburnable rubbish. We played about in them, and got very dirty.

We lived in Roundhill Road all the years I was a child and growing up.[4]

4 A typical Yorkshire slag heap

---

[4] The small, terraced house at 30 Roundhill Road was demolished in 1974.

5 30 Roundhill Road, Castleford

I remember the street and I can see the sun just managing to penetrate the fog, and the coal heap at the end, it's all very familiar. There were seven of us children in that one little house, no bedroom to yourself. In fact, there were three or four in one bed!

I think people place much too much emphasis on my early life, on the coalmining background. My upbringing was very normal as with the majority of children in this country. Writers and critics love to link one's early life to the present almost as if one hasn't changed.

Ibid., p.10

Our road led to Glasshoughton Colliery and very early in the morning, quite often, one would be wakened by the miners all tramping to work in their clogs. This might be at half-past four in the morning. In the wintertime this always sounded to me very strange and weird, coming up to a crescendo of clogs and then dying away.

Hall 1966, p.28

I had a happy childhood, full of physical enjoyment and exercise. I enjoyed all the games and the fights as well. I fought one boy with my hand tied behind me – I said I could beat you one-handed. You had to stand up for yourself, it was daft if you didn't. Then you were just made a scapegoat. We were brought up to be very independent.

Hedgecoe 1986, p.21

In the mining area where I was brought up, you had to look tough and manly, which meant you had to have a girlfriend. If you didn't, you were thought cissy. As a little boy there was the girl next door, Millie. I was only about eight or nine and we played together. If you got to about ten or eleven and didn't have a girlfriend, you were looked upon as if there was something wrong with you. When I got to about twelve I remember falling for a girl. I walked on air from Castleford to Pontefract and on to Ferrybridge because I'd kissed her.

Ibid., p.18

We used to play games in the back streets – hoops and marbles and so on. There were two or three different types of marbles that I enjoyed very much indeed. There was one game called Ringy in which you drew a circle with a stick in the coal dust that was thick and black on the street. The circle was about ten feet in diameter with a hole in the middle just big enough for a marble to go in. You played from outside of the circle and it took practice to get it into the hole. You had a permanent dark, blistered knuckle. It looked very bad but you got used to it. It was a game that taught you to control things with your hands – a sculptor would be no good if he couldn't use his hands.

Ibid.

Well, there was one game which we called piggy, which in the North in those days was quite a well-known game, in which people pitted themselves against others. In piggy you have a little round ball of wood which you can hit with a stick that has a kind of bottle-shaped piece of wood at the end, and as the ball flies in the air the batsman hits it and then the other person whom you are playing against has to stride out the number of strides to get to the ball from where you struck it. But you can also set a number. Say that you've hit it a long way. You may say, 'I'll give you fifty for that.' And if it is under fifty, you've lost your fifty and he wipes the score out. Anyhow, to play this you shape a piece of wood, which is called the piggy, about four inches long. You point each end so that when you hit that end it jumps in the air. And you have a piece of stick and then you hit the piggy with your stick.

Carroll 1973, p.32

Near where we lived in Castleford there was a quarry, and we used to play about with the clay and make what we called touchstone ovens, little square boxes with chimneys and a hole at the side, and we'd fill these with rotten wood and light it and blow on the fire to warm our hands in winter. And sometimes we'd decorate them with drawings.

Russell 17 December 1961

In Castleford, where I was born, there are what are called sand holes. They're caves where the sand has been excavated and they run into the side of certain hillsides, quite a long distance, and you can get lost in them. Now these had a fascination for me, and as boys we would take a reel of cotton many yards long and go into the caves. But one wouldn't go further than the cotton because it was dark. You wouldn't know your way back. In those days there weren't flash lamps, so one only had a match or something, and the matches were these brimstone matches. And the caves always had this fascination for me, these holes did. Digging into something always had this fascination for me. So I think it's not so much Archipenko, because the Archipenko hole is a decorative one. I mean he makes a hole in a breast instead of a fullness, but the hole acts the same.

Carroll 1973, p.37

What is a cave? A cave is a shape. It's not the lump of mountain over it.

Lake 1962, p.45

As children we would go to the slaughter house every Wednesday. You could stand at the door and see them fell the cow, the sheep, or the bull ready for the butcher. It was done with an axe with a point on one end and blade on the other. Two or three men would get hold of the halter around the bull's neck, put the rope through a ring in the wall in the slaughter house. And those men would pull the animal gradually towards them with its head right up so that it couldn't move it. It was in this position that they started to butcher with the pointed end of the axe and felled the bull so it was unconscious and then they'd stab it and let the blood run out and so on. One used to go and watch that every week. It was a gruesome sight but we'd say, 'Let's go and watch the kill.' It was an excitement. People got reputations, the butchers, for being worthy. Sometimes they didn't hit the right part of the skull to go into the brain, they didn't kill it. But then they would stab it as it lay down. It was a well known thing, I wasn't the only one that watched.

Hedgecoe 1986, p.21

We never went away on holidays, but we went walking or bicycling – not far, say the two or three miles to Pontefract. We would go blackberrying or collecting chrysalises. And I loved fishing in streams and pools and in old clay quarries.

Half a mile outside Castleford, you would be in lovely countryside. There was a great contrast between the weekdays when you would play in the streets and the weekends when the countryside was what mattered. The back streets which were so grimy and muggy and dirty made one love the country. I knew I liked the countryside, but I was most conscious of the contrast.

Ibid., p.32

6 Alabaster effigies of Lionel, Lord Welles and his wife, probably late fifteenth century, St Oswald's Church, Methley

Methley Church,[5] just outside Castleford, contains the first real sculptures I remember. I was very impressed by these recumbent effigy figures, particularly by the simplicity of the woman's head. The female figure is always more simple than the male, less muscles and wrinkles. It was this and the almost Egyptian stillness of the figure that appealed to me, as well as the hands coming away from the body.

Ibid., p.26

In Yorkshire in Adel Woods just outside Leeds, there was a big rock amongst many that I've called Adel Rock [fig.1]. That influenced me quite a bit.[6] For me, it was the first big, bleak lump of stone set in the landscape and surrounded by marvellous gnarled prehistoric trees. It had no feature of recognition, no element of copying of naturalism, just a bleak, powerful form, very impressive. It was the local beauty spot, so to speak, and I knew it from a child. And much later, when I was a student, I would visit it with friends. We would picnic and draw and play around. It was an exciting place for me, Adel Woods.

Ibid., p.35

Yorkshiremen

Well, like all Yorkshiremen, one thinks that Yorkshire is a wonderful place. And we all think, too, that Yorkshiremen have special characters – very

[5] St Oswald's Church, Methley, one and a half miles west of Castleford, was built in the twelfth century with fourteenth- and fifteenth-century alterations. Moore also admired the carved corbels, representing grotesque human beings and animals, which are thought to date from the mid-fourteenth century.
[6] For the influence of Adel Rock on the 1959 bronze *Two Piece Reclining Figure No.1* LH 457, see p.289.

strong, hard-working characters – so probably one takes over something of the general idea of a Yorkshireman. Also, thinking of this little town [Castleford], within a mile and a half of the centre of the town there were five coal mines, three glass works, chemical works, potteries. In fact it was an absolutely intense industrial area. And yet within a mile or two of the centre of the town you came into country that was being farmed. I often spent the winter months as a town boy, playing town games in the streets, but when the good weather came my summertime would often be a kind of country life. Quite a few of my friends were either the sons of farm labourers or of farmers themselves. So I had both in my youth, both town and country, and this I am very pleased about. But also, too, I think life was a little bit tougher in the North of England than it is in the South – perhaps a little bit like the seed potatoes that are used in the South of England but which mostly come from Scotland. That is, you bring the seeds from the North to the South, and they do better in the South because they've been cold-bred, as it were, in the North.

Carroll 1973, p.31

Becoming a Sculptor

I think I was probably about eleven when I first decided I wanted to be a sculptor. I remember quite clearly the instant. As a boy, at school, I liked the art lessons, I liked drawing. I used to get my elder brother to draw horses and other things for me from as early as I can remember. But the little incident that clinches the thing in my mind was that our parents used to send me and my younger sister to Sunday school on Sunday afternoons – to get rid of us I think mainly – and the Sunday school we went to was a Congregational chapel although we were Church of England. The superintendent every Sunday used to give a talk which always had some little moral. And one Sunday he told us about Michelangelo carving the head of an old faun in the streets – in his studio in the streets of Florence – and that a passer-by stood watching Michelangelo carving this head. And after watching two or three minutes he said to Michelangelo, 'But an old faun wouldn't have all its teeth in.' Michelangelo immediately, said the superintendent, took his chisel, knocked out two of the teeth, and there, he said, was a great man listening to the advice of other people even though he didn't know them. Now this story didn't stick in my mind for its moral but merely that there was some-one – Michelangelo, a great sculptor. So instead of saying, as most boys might, that one wanted to be an engine-driver and so on, this pinpointed something in my mind and I knew from then onwards.

Freeman 1964, p.32

I had always wanted to become a sculptor – at least since I was about ten. However, my first art teacher at Castleford upset me a great deal; she said I drew figures 'with feet like tassels'. I recall exactly what she referred to: figures with feet in the air, like early Gothic drawings – suspended in the air, not connected with the earth. This upset me terribly. But she was succeeded by a Miss Gostick[7] who became my ally in the argument with my father which persisted from my fourteenth to my eighteenth year.

Sweeney 1947, p.182

School

7 Alice Gostick's pottery class, Castleford Grammar School, c.1919. Moore is in the front row (right), with Alice Gostick and Raymond Coxon behind her

I loved school. When I got to the secondary school, Alice Gostick came to teach art. She was one of the biggest influences on the direction I took. She had travelled a lot and been to Florence and London. She encouraged me and the other two boys who were interested in painting and drawing – Albert Wainwright and Arthur Dalby. We would compete with each other for doing the poster for the school play. Miss Gostick encouraged all three of us – she lent us books and introduced us to pottery. She would ask us up to tea and all of this was very different from life at home.

But even before all this, even at elementary school, I wanted to draw. The drawing lesson was on Friday afternoon, the very last lesson of the week. The teacher was tired, the kids were all thinking of the weekend, but for me it was the lesson of the week. I drew everything and anywhere, animals, trees and then figures. The figure was always important, animals too, as they were living things, but I always came back to the human figure.

Hedgecoe 1986, p.28

The grammar school was mixed and you could stay there till you were seventeen or eighteen. For morning prayers we stood in rows, all of the girls in front of me. I could have told all the girls of that school from the legs downward.

Ibid., p.21

Literature

At one time I thought I wanted to write, I wrote little plays and essays. I thought then that poetry was the biggest and most marvellous of human activities. But, actually they're all the same. Poetry and sculpture are both about people trying to express their feelings about life, about nature, about their response to the world.

Ibid., p.35

Bhataryan. […] Dead! Narayana, my sister, dead, Naryana, my little sister whom I loved more than myself … And I shall never again know the peace in your gentle speech, your flowing hair, never again know the touch of your kind fingers, the smooth soothing softness of your cheek, your companiable closeness has left me. I shall see no more the glittering gladness in your eyes, nor hear the light laughter of your voice, whose smile was sweet like the

---

[7] Alice Gostick (1873-1960); see Moore's letters to her on pp.40-1.

opening buds of a lotus plant, and now you are dead ... (*Pause –
music begins softly – gradually swelling.*) The music of the singing
moon – my mother, Zabibi and my sister Narayana calling me to
where the big red moon sings for all time, where a gentle wind
plays sweet tunes among the waving grass for all time, where
palm trees wave and fishes swim in fresh blue waters, where the
gods smile for all time, where laughter reigns for all time – [...]

Narayana and Bhataryan[8] 1916 (?);
typescript in Leeds City Art Galleries

Art is a kind of reaction to life and this reaction helps others to live. I owe
a lot to the influence that literature had on my life: Tolstoy, Dostoevsky,
Stendhal formed a secret part of me. Their works help one to understand,
to grow up, to change; algebra or electronics do not change one, I do not
think so.

Lorenzo Papi, 'Incontro con Henry Moore', *La Nazione*, Florence
22 September 1968

Well to begin with as a young person, novelists had the biggest influence,
probably they have had the biggest influence on my life because I think the
influence you have when you are young and when you are an adolescent
at that period is probably the most indelible of all – and from the novelists
that I absorbed and lived in their worlds one by one as a schoolboy around
thirteen or fourteen, – it was Sir Walter Scott, more than Dickens – it was
never Dickens for me. I mean I read David Copperfield and so on but
Walter Scott, the kind of Romantic world that he made – After Scott, well
I read some of the ordinary popular schoolboy books like Treasure Island,
Henty, and so on but those were not as real and definitely did not mean
as much as the Scott, – after that the Russian novels – I mean reading
Dostoevsky and Tolstoy, – one lived in their worlds particularly Dostoevsky
– one lived in that world for as long as the novel lasted. Then after the
Russians came Thomas Hardy – I read every single novel of Thomas Hardy.
After Thomas Hardy came some of the French novelists and D.H.
Lawrence – one lived in his world for a period and for me all those have
coloured my life even more than what painting and sculpture have done.

In conversation with Orde Levinson and David Mitchinson,
23 October 1977; typescript in HMF Library

I think that people with a gift for words have had the biggest influence of
all our past, like Shakespeare, like ... to me, this gift of words is the one
quality that animals don't have. [...] But the one thing that we've got that
allows us to exchange ideas and help each other are words. And in that sense

---

[8] *Narayana and Bhataryan: A Play by Harry Spencer Moore* was performed at Castleford Grammar School,
possibly as early as 1917 but more likely in 1920. Moore acted the part of Bhataryan, and designed the front
and back covers of the programme. The death of his youngest sister Elsie (1901-16), see p.33, must surely
have influenced the plot of this play.

I admire literature and the gift for words in a person more than I do some-body who dances well, somebody who even does sculpture well.

In conversation with Huw Wheldon, c.1983

Teaching

While I was still at the grammar school, I took student teacher training. I taught for two days a week and went to school for the rest. That was from sixteen to eighteen.

Hedgecoe 1986, p.28

I think this was the most miserable period of my life. I was too young to know when the children were going to make fun of me and pull my leg and do their little stunts … the girls were infinitely worse than the boys. They knew just how to make a boy of seventeen embarrassed in all sorts of ways. They'd weep and cry and sob …

John Read, Henry Moore: One Yorkshireman Looks at His World, BBC, London 1967

Army 1917-19

At eighteen, I got called up. I tried to get into the Artists' Rifles because I thought it would be full of artists. But they were full and had a waiting list so I joined the Civil Service Rifles instead. I was in the army from 1916 to 1918[9] and I used to draw trees, flowers, huts, ruins. I drew the people picking lice off their clothes. It was very good experience.

I went to France and we won the battle of Cambrai – only forty-two of us came back out of the 400 who went out. I was not horrified by the war, I wanted to win a medal and be a hero.

Hedgecoe 1986, p.29

Hazeley Down, Winchester[10]

I don't know how to thank you for the letter, cigarettes & chocs, you really are <u>the</u> best friend I have away from home. I have something horrible to tell you – I haven't done any sketches of any account, the time seems to slip by wonderfully down here I don't know how I shall face you when I come home.

From a letter to Alice Gostick, early 1917

8 Private H.S. Moore in the 15th London Regiment of the Civil Service Rifles, 1917

France

The noise even during only a small 'strafe' is hellish (I hope I haven't shocked you, but that's the only word which effectively describes it.) Worse, however than all the 'strafing' is the small amount of sleep one has in the

---

[9] Moore was in fact called up in February 1917 and demobilised in February 1919.

[10] Hazeley Down Camp, near Winchester, Hampshire, was an army training unit where Moore spent at least a month in early 1917.

front line (Between 3 & 4 hours per night, sometimes less) The sleep we did get was in all our clothes & our equipment, in little cubby holes dug into the sides of the trenches. When not sleeping at night we're doing fire step sentry, 2 at a time, one looks over the top whilst the other sits near him on the fire step ready for any emergency. If one likes to let one's imagination run ahead one can be quite convinced that the barbed wire posts are forming fours, or advancing in line towards your trench the only thing to do in that case is to divert one's gaze to some other object & its ten to one that will also become animated, however you've to put up with it (unless the other sentry also thinks they are Huns) until the hour's duty is up.

From a letter to Alice Gostick, 6 October 1917

[…] for me the First World War passed in a kind of romantic haze of hoping to be a hero. Sometimes in France there were three or four days of great danger when you thought there wasn't a chance of getting through, and then all one felt was sadness at having taken so much trouble to no purpose; but on the whole I enjoyed the Army. I was the youngest in the regiment at first, and it was a bit like being back in the family. After I was gassed at Cambrai I was in hospital for three months and it still affects my voice at times, but as they made me a PT instructor afterwards I suppose I must have got pretty fit again.

Russell 17 December 1961

When I came out of the army, I went back to teaching and no longer found the discipline such a problem as I had as a boy of seventeen. Having been a physical training instructor in the army, I now knew how to exercise control. Then the educational authorities gave help to those people who had had their educations interrupted by the war. I applied for an army grant and was given one. This was what enabled me to go to Leeds School of Art.

Hedgecoe 1986, p.31

It was in those two years of war that I broke finally away from parental domination which had been very strong. My old friend, Miss Gostick, found out about ex-servicemen's grants. With her help I applied and received one for the Leeds School of Art. This was understood from the outset merely to be a first step. London was the goal. But the only way to get to London was to take the Board of Education examinations and to win a scholarship.

Sweeney 1947, p.182

Leeds School of Art 1919-21

I spent my first year at Leeds taking the drawing examination and, the following year, I asked the Principal, a person named Hayward Ryder, if I could take the Board of Education's examination in sculpture. It created a bit of difficulty because, since there wasn't a sculpture school, they had to set one up. They appointed a sculpture teacher, called [Reginald] Cotterill, who had just come down from the Royal College of Art. He had been in the Army before that, and so he was probably twenty-six or twenty-seven. For a whole year, I was Cotterill's only full-time student, and he looked after me like a child. He was always breathing down my neck, but, in a way, this was a help because I got through the two-year course in one year, as well as winning a Royal Exhibition, which was at that time the only way of getting into the Royal College of Art. Cotterill was an intelligent person, and a good teacher. He did have part-time students, and even classes, but I was his one real care. Later, he became Head of York School of Art.

Hedgecoe 1968, p.33

While I was at Leeds, I lived at home in Castleford and I used to catch the 8.20 train every morning, running from home to the station.

I was a very conscientious student and it was terribly important to me to get high marks because I knew, without them, I would never get the scholarship to the Royal College of Art. One had to take exams – drawing and sculpture – and there were other subjects which I worked on for the scholarship, like anatomy and history of art.

After I'd been at Leeds for about a year, Barbara Hepworth came to the school.[11] When she arrived, she was just going to do an art school course, like the foundation course of today, and she would have become a drawing teacher in a secondary school. I became a bit sweet on her and we went out together. Through my influence, she changed and wanted to be a sculptor.

We had to draw from men at college. We weren't allowed to have female models at first because of Victorian prudery. I can remember the first time we had a female model – what excitement there was! It was considered very daring in those days. To me a female figure is of more interest. The difference is not aesthetic, it's real. A woman has a different function, she is softer, she doesn't have the boniness. It isn't that men and women grow up differently, they are born different.

Hedgecoe 1986, p.31

Old Pearson.[12] He was a very good teacher in an academic sense. He'd teach you all he knew. He had very strict rules of what was a good drawing. It wasn't a good drawing if you didn't shade at 45 degrees. If you got an angle of 80 degrees or 30 degrees or something other than 45 degrees he would

---

[11] Barbara Hepworth (1903-75) enrolled at Leeds School of Art in September 1920. Moore's patronising account of Hepworth's ambitions and of his role in influencing her to become a sculptor is contradicted in *Barbara Hepworth: A Pictorial Autobiography*, Adams and Dart, Bath 1970, p.11: 'At the age of seven, her [Miss McCroben, Headmistress of Wakefield Girls' High School] lecture and slides of Egyptian sculpture fired me off, and when I approached her at 15 years and said I could not go on with academic training as I wished to be a sculptor, she was the one who said "You can sit for a scholarship to Leeds next week!"' For Moore's tribute to Hepworth after her death, see p.153.

[12] Walter B. Pearson, a former student from the Royal College of Art, was the drawing master at Leeds School of Art. His primary objective was to help his students pass the Board of Education examination and move on to study in London. Both Moore and Hepworth were awarded scholarships to the Royal College of Art.

criticise it. He'd learnt what the Inspector wanted, and insisted on a style of drawing which he'd found was successful with them. He taught me enough of that in one year to pass the exam.

In conversation with Roger Berthoud, 7 March 1983

There was a time at the College of Art in Leeds when I was a bit troubled by not liking the sculpture which the teachers there expected us to like. We were set to draw from the 'antique' such things as the *Boy and Goose*, which is a late Roman copy of the Greek work, and we had to draw the *Discobolus*. I didn't have the slightest bit of interest in those sculptures, and there was a stage in the first week or two at the school when I thought, 'Well, is it me that doesn't know what sculpture is? Is there something wrong with me that I don't like these pieces?'

Now I know that I was quite justified in not liking them because, besides being not very good pieces of sculpture in themselves, they'd been white-washed every year for twenty years and had a thick coat, nearly a quarter of an inch, of whitewash on top of them, which was blurring all the sensitivity and the form. But still we were expected to draw them. Often students in the provinces don't know that they're being asked to appreciate something which in itself is no good anyhow. I think that having been brought up on bad things, having been shown bad things in the school, made one immediately recognise the good things. And it was rather the relief of discovery.

Did the bad versions of classical sculpture for a time spoil good classical sculpture for you?

Yes. There was a period when I tried to avoid looking at Greek – and Renaissance – sculpture of any kind; when I thought that the Greek and Renaissance were the enemy and that one had to throw all that over and start again from the beginning of primitive art. It's only in the last ten or fifteen years that I've begun to know how wonderful the Elgin Marbles are.

Hall 1960, p.114

I was very glad I didn't go to an art school till I was twenty-one. Art schools then, and especially in the provinces, had a terribly closed, academic out-look. When I got to Leeds School of Art in 1919 there were students who'd gone there at fourteen or fifteen, as you could in those days, and any excitement or freshness they might have had had been deadened and killed off by humdrum copying from the antique, just making very careful stump-shaded drawings with no understanding whatever of form. […]

Also I'd had the luck to know Michael Sadler,[13] who was then Vice-Chancellor of Leeds University, a man who had bought Cézanne and

---

[13] Sir Michael Sadler (1861-1943) was Vice-Chancellor of Leeds University 1911-22. His very large collection included at various times works by Gainsborough, Turner, Constable, Corot, Renoir, Gauguin, Van Gogh, Matisse, Augustus John, Nash, Nicholson, Hepworth and Moore. He also collected African sculpture. In 1937 Sadler sent funds enabling The Museum of Modern Art, New York, to acquire Moore's 1934 Pynkado wood *Two Forms* LH 153, see pp.82 and 255.

Gauguin before 1914, and translated Kandinsky, and really knew what was going on in modern art.

Russell 17 December 1961

In those days the museum in Leeds had no work later than the Victorian period. The main work in Leeds that I remember was Lord Leighton's *Return of Persephone* at the top of the steps. But Sir Michael Sadler had a Gauguin, a wonderful Gauguin, and other things. It was the Gauguin and a few ones like that which impressed me most. It opened up a world that was other than the Victorian, academic, art-school world.

Carroll 1973, p.35

Actually Roger Fry's *Vision and Design* [1920] was the most lucky discovery for me. I came on it by chance while looking for another book in the Leeds Reference Library. Fry in his essay on *Negro Sculpture* stressed the 'three-dimensional realisation' that characterised African art and its 'truth to material'. More, Fry opened the way to other books and to the realisation of the British Museum. That was really the beginning.

Sweeney 1947, p.182

London and Kent 1921-40

For the first year I was in a dream of excitement. When I rode on the open top of a bus I felt that I was travelling in Heaven, almost, and that the bus was floating in the air. And it was Heaven all over again in the evenings, in my horrid little room in Sydney Street, when I could spread out the books I'd got out of the library and know that I had the chance of learning about all the sculptures that had ever been made in the world.

With my £90 a year in scholarships I was one of the real rich students at the College, and I had no worries or problems at all except purely and simply one's own development as a sculptor. And, as to that, there were a whole lot of things that one found out for oneself very simply and easily. Once you'd read Roger Fry, the whole thing was there. I went to the British Museum on Wednesday and Sunday afternoons, and saw what I wanted to see.

Russell 17 December 1961

The British Museum

So when I came to London my first visit to the British Museum was like a starved man having Selfridges grocery department all to himself.[14]

Unpublished notes for *Unit One* 1934, HMF archive

London

Yesterday I spent my second afternoon in the British Museum with the

---

[14] This sentence forms part of Moore's answer to question 8 in a questionnaire sent to members of Unit One: 'Do you ever seek inspiration in museums or picture galleries?'

Egyptian & Assyrian Sculptures – An hour before closing time I tore myself away from these to do a little exploring and found – in the Ethnographical Gallery – the ecstatically fine negro sculptures – and then just on closing time I discovered the Print room containing the Japanese things – a joy to come. How wonderful it is to be in London (says country-bred Harry.)

From a letter to Jocelyn Horner,[15] 29 October 1921

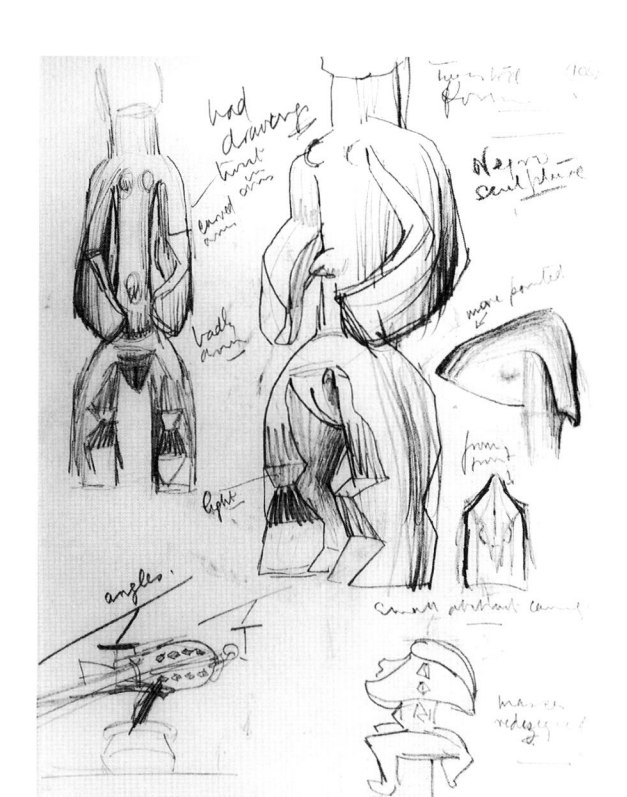

9 *Studies of Sculpture in the British Museum*, page 105 from Notebook No.3 1922-24 HMF 123 recto, pencil, 224 x 172mm (8⅞ x 6¾in). The Henry Moore Foundation: gift of the artist 1977
The Mumuye funerary ancestor figure is discussed and illustrated on p.107.

One room after another in the British Museum took my enthusiasm. The Royal College of Art meant nothing in comparison. Every Wednesday, Saturday, and Sunday I would go to the British Museum. But not till after three months did things begin to settle into any pattern of reality for me. Till then everything was wonderful – a new world at every turn.

That is the value of the British Museum: you have everything behind you; you are free to try to find your own way and, after a while, to find what appeals to you most. And after the first excitement it was the art of ancient Mexico that spoke to me most – except perhaps Romanesque, or early Norman. And I admit clearly and frankly that early Mexican art formed my views of carving as much as anything I could do.

[15] The sculptor Jocelyn Horner was Moore's contemporary at Leeds School of Art. Two letters to Jocelyn and two to her mother Mrs Horner from the early 1920s are known to have survived.

But my aims as a 'student' were directly at odds with my taste in sculpture. Already, even here a conflict had set in. And for a considerable while after my discovery of the archaic sculpture in the British Museum there was a bitter struggle within me, on the one hand, between the need to follow my course at college in order to get a teacher's diploma and, on the other, the desire to work freely at what appealed most to me in sculpture. At one point I was seriously considering giving up college and working only in the direction that attracted me. But, thank goodness, I somehow came to the realisation that academic discipline is valuable. And my need to have a diploma, in order to earn a living, helped.

I now understand the value of an academic grounding: modelling and drawing from life. All sculptors of the great periods of European art could draw from life, just as well as the painters. With me, at one moment, it was just touch and go. But finally I hit on a sort of compromise arrangement: academic work during the semester, and during the holidays a free rein to the interests I had developed in the British Museum. Mixing the two things enabled one to continue drawing from life as I have always done. And it also allowed me to win my travelling scholarship to Italy on academic grounds.

Sweeney 1947, p.183

You see, what was important to me, and to any provincial student, was to have access to the periodicals which reproduced the work of one's own contemporaries. So I often combined my weekly and sometimes twice-weekly visits to the British Museum with a visit for half an hour to Zwemmer's bookshop, where I browsed through the books. I hadn't enough money to buy them, my grant was so small. Zwemmer[16] was here only last week and I reminded him of this. I said 'You never bothered. You never stopped me. I used to look at the books until I didn't need to buy them because I knew all that was in them.' But we got to know each other, and he published the first little book on me. And his bookshop was also, of course, a wonderful library.

Carroll 1973, p.36

Royal College of Art 1921-24

My first few months at College had rid me of the romantic idea that art schools were of no value and I'd begun to draw from life as hard as I could.

A sculptor needs to be able to understand and see three-dimensional form correctly, and you can only do that with a great deal of effort and experience and struggle. And the human figure is both the most exacting subject one can set oneself, and the subject one knows best. The construction of the human figure, the tremendous variety of balance, of size, of rhythm, all those things, make the human being much more difficult to get right, in a drawing, than anything else.

It's not only a matter of training – you can't understand it without being

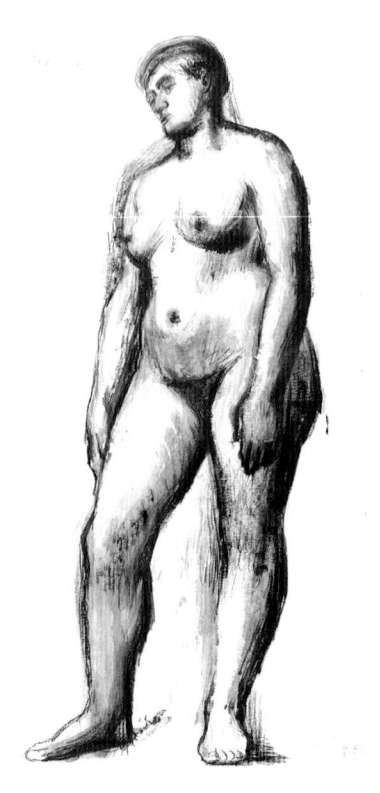

10 *Standing Figure* 1923 HMF 173, pencil, chalk, watercolour and gouache, 407 x 210mm (16 x 8¼in). Private collection

[16] For Moore's tribute to Anton Zwemmer, see p.94.

emotionally involved, and so it isn't just academic training: it really is a deep, strong, fundamental struggle to understand oneself as much as to understand what one's drawing.

And so I had a double goal, or double occupation: drawing and modelling from life in term-time and daytime, and the rest of the time trying to develop in pure sculptural terms – which for me, at that time, was a very different thing from the Renaissance tradition.

Russell 17 December 1961

Till Sir William Rothenstein[17] became Principal, in the year I went up as a student, it had been just a training college where teachers taught students to become teachers and teach more students, and so on for ever. But Rothenstein brought an entirely new outlook into the College. He'd known Degas, and he'd known Rodin, and he didn't regard the College primarily as a teachers' training college.

Not only that, but he would ask one or two of us students in on Sunday evenings, when he kept open house. He had an enormous and very distinguished circle of friends, and I remember meeting Walter de la Mare, for instance, and the then Prime Minister, Ramsay MacDonald.[18]

In fact, meeting MacDonald was another bit of education for someone like me. I remember being left alone with him and standing waiting for him to begin the conversation. He did say one or two words to me, and I remember feeling that it was all perfectly ordinary and natural. I wasn't awed, or anything, and so Rothenstein gave me the feeling that there was no barrier, no limit to what a young provincial student could get to be and do, and that's very important at that age.

Ibid.

At the Royal College of Art, where I arrived in 1921, the stone carving instructor was Barry Hart. He was almost the same age as I was, and had been appointed to teach the art of carving purely and simply because his family were professional stone carvers. They were not sculptors, but they could, by using pointing machines, copy sculpture. The Royal Academicians would send them the plaster cast of a highly finished realistic portrait bust which had first been modelled in clay with eyebrows, eye lashes and nostrils in detail. This type of work demanded the precise use of a pointing machine which would take measurements to within one thousandth of an inch. This procedure was, of course, one of the reasons why the work of the Royal Academy was so uninspired and dead. Had we students been allowed to carve more freely there might have been more quality of stone about our work. Derwent Wood was a Royal Academician and Head of the Sculpture Department of the Royal College. He believed that it was impossible to produce an absolutely correct copy of an existing model for sculpture without

[17] For Moore's tribute to Rothenstein, see p.92.
[18] Ramsay MacDonald (1866-1937) was Britain's first Labour Prime Minister. He was in office from January to November 1924, and from 1929 to 1931; from 1931 to 1935 he headed a National Coalition government.

using a pointing machine, and since an identical copy was what he wanted, we were only taught how to carve in that way. We were given classical sculptures to copy and no original carving was permitted. I believed that I could copy faithfully without using the pointing machine and I persuaded Barry Hart to let me try to carve my piece freely. Although he himself could handle a hammer and chisel remarkably well, he still didn't believe it was possible and I had to make false points in pencil on the marble so that, when Derwent Wood came round, he would think I was using the pointing machine.

Hedgecoe 1968, p.33

Another tutor at the college was Leon Underwood.[19] He had a private school, too, in Hammersmith and I used to go there two or three nights a week. I couldn't have paid because I didn't have any money, only the £80 a year scholarship money.[20] He was a good teacher, though a bit hard. He insisted that drawing was terribly important and you had to know the laws of light falling on a solid object and reflecting it back to the human eye; and that being translated into a two dimensional representation. You're not born with this understanding, you have to learn it, you have to be taught it.

Hedgecoe 1986, p.45

Except for Rothenstein there was only one teacher I learned anything from – Leon Underwood, then a young painter, new on the college staff, with a passionate attitude towards drawing from life. He set out to teach the science of drawing, of expressing solid form on a flat surface – not the photographic copying of tone values, nor the art-school imitation of styles in drawing.

The Times 2 November 1967

Partly for practical reasons I did my 'monthly comp.' as a painter. The subject on one occasion in my first year was Night. My composition showed the influence of some Etruscan sculpture I had admired in the British Museum. It was criticised very adversely by the Professor of the Architecture department, Beresford Pyte [Pite]. Eventually he arrived in front of my painting and for several minutes spotlighted his violent dislike of it. 'This student,' he said, 'has been feeding on garbage.' That Friday afternoon I could not work, but wandered around Hyde Park to work off my hurt feelings. I almost decided I would leave the college and study on my own.

But on the Monday morning Rothenstein sent for me and said: 'Moore, do not take what happened on Friday too much to heart, you will often meet this kind of criticism throughout life.' He talked to me like a father.

Ibid.

[19] The sculptor Leon Underwood (1890-1975) was a drawing instructor at the Royal College of Art 1920-23. In June 1923, after he resigned from the RCA, he was persuaded by Moore, Coxon and others to teach life drawing at his studio in Girders Road, Hammersmith.
[20] Moore usually gave the figure as £90.

Most of my friends were in the painting school, the small number of students in the sculpture school took no interest in painting, and not much in drawing, either, they were mainly interested in the craft side of sculpture. My closest friend was Raymond Coxon,[21] with whom I shared rooms in Chelsea, and later, a studio in Hammersmith. Other friends were R.V. Pitchforth, Barnett Freedman, Percy Horton, Eric Ravilious and Edward Bawden, all painters. With me in the sculpture school was Barbara Hepworth, whom I looked upon as a kind of young sister, as she was four or five years my junior in age. [...]

They were happy and productive years. I think I got strength from fighting the academic restrictions and prejudices. It was a preparation for meeting the widespread philistine atmosphere which prevailed in England up to 1940 towards the so-called Modern Art.

Altogether I owe a tremendous lot to the college. Above all, the many years of modelling and drawing from the figure (and of teaching life-modelling and drawing, which demands nearly as intense observation as doing it one's self).

Ibid.

Travels

Stonehenge 1921

Soon after settling into my digs, a tiny bedroom in Sydney Street, Chelsea (it must have been towards the end of September or early October 1921), I decided one weekend to go and see Stonehenge. I took the train to Salisbury arriving in the early evening, found a small hotel but by this time it was getting dark. After eating I decided I wouldn't wait to see Stonehenge until next day.

As it was a clear evening I got to Stonehenge and saw it by moon-light. I was alone and tremendously impressed. (Moonlight, as you know enlarges everything, and the mysterious depths and distances made it seem enormous.)

I went again the next morning, it was still very impressive, but that first moonlight visit remained for years my idea of Stonehenge.[22]

Henry Moore: Stonehenge, introduction by Stephen Spender,
Ganymed Original Editions, London 1974

Paris 1922[23]

In my first year at College, Raymond Coxon and I thought we'd like to see some original Cézannes, and so we asked if we could go to Paris for

---

[21] The painter Raymond Coxon (1896-1997) met Moore, Hepworth and Edna Ginesi ('Gin') at the Leeds School of Art. All four went to the Royal College of Art where they were known as the 'Leeds table'. Coxon and Ginesi, who was also a painter, were married in 1926, with Moore as best man.
[22] See the 1972-73 Stonehenge lithographs, p.298.
[23] Moore first visited Paris in 1922, not in 1923 as often stated in published chronologies.

Whitsun week. Rothenstein said, 'Yes, and I'll give you some introductions,' and he did give me one to Maillol, in fact, which I was too shy to use. I got to the door and I thought, 'Well, he's working and he won't want to be bothered,' and so I turned away.

But we did go to see the Pellerin collection, and what had a tremendous impact on me was the big Cézanne,[24] the triangular bathing composition with the nudes in perspective, lying on the ground as if they'd been sliced out of mountain rock. For me this was like seeing Chartres Cathedral.

Russell 17 December 1961

Visit to Charles Rutherston 1923

Wighton, Norfolk

Charles Rutherston, (The College Principal's brother,)[25] to whom probably you remember I told you I sold two of my things – invited me to spend a few days with him at his house in Bradford – that I might have a good opportunity of seeing his collection.

He has probably one of the most important collections (outside museums) of ancient Chinese Art in England – besides which he has examples of Negro, Scythian, Siberian, Archaic Greek & Egyptian Art – three or four Epstein busts, about the same number of busts by Dobson – several Eric Gill carvings & most of his woodcuts – & an unknown quantity of paintings & drawings by contemporary artists – French & English – So that you can guess how much I enjoyed & saw in those four days. Oh & I've forgotten his library, which contains books of reference on almost every known art.

From a letter to Jocelyn Horner, August 1923

Wells, Norfolk

He [Charles Rutherston] must be rolling in money & yet I don't think he's tremendously happy – If I were in his position I should take myself into a country district in England, somewhere like Wighton or Walsingham, & stay there until I'd found & wedded one of these richly formed big limbed, fresh faced, full blooded country wenches, built for breeding, honest, simple minded, practical, common sensed, healthily sexed lasses that I've seen about here – but of course we don't know, there may be insurmountable obstacles that make him not free to take such a course –

From a letter to Raymond Coxon, early August 1925

[24] *The Large Bathers* 1906, now in the Philadelphia Museum of Art, see fig.47.
[25] Charles Rutherston (1866-1927) was the brother of Sir William Rothenstein, Principal of the Royal College of Art, through whom he met Moore. Rutherston was the first collector to acquire Moore's sculpture; by 1923 he had purchased *Head of a Girl* 1922 (fig.85) and *Standing Woman* 1923 (fig.86). He introduced Moore to Dorothy Warren, at whose London gallery Moore's first one-man exhibition was held in 1928, see p.55.

Travelling Scholarship 1925

France

Paris[26]

Dear Old Sven[27]

You were right about Paris, its a dull hole, nothing of any great interest seems to be going on, & the place itself hasn't the variety of London. – I've given up all the notions I had of wanting to settle down here for a few months or a year – no a week is enough –

We've made one discovery though, you remember Rothy[28] giving me the address of a museum which I lost, well we've found it – The Musée Guimet, containing mostly Indian sculpture. There's one room in particular, a real stunner, and one figure in it (or rather a cast – I'd give anything to see the original) a standing male nude, that is one of the finest pieces of sculpture I've ever seen – I've managed to get hold of photographs of most of the best ones; when I've had the pleasure of these reproductions for a little while & when I begin to get stocked out with others I'll send 'em along for you to enjoy – Upstairs in the Musée Guimet are some heads (sculptures & paintings) from Antinoe – Greco-Egyptian I believe – They remind me of the ones in the National – (& those two in the Mond collection at the Tate) – there are about 15 paintings & about fifty heads in the round – all very wonderful – big & full of character, intensely alive – & some remarkably realistic, like Rembrandt – You mustn't fail to see 'em Sven next time you trot over to Paris. – I think on my way back I shall spend four or five days making drawings of them & of the Indian sculptures –

Apart from the Musée Guimet the only other place in Paris is the Louvre – and that's no better, if as good, as our National – We've spent most of our time in the Louvre – the new experience I've made is Mantegna, – but Italy I believe is the place for him – Oh I suppose you know they've got photographic reproductions of many of the best things in the Louvre – I haven't bought any, but intend to on my return journey, if by then you've not been again to Paris, let me know what reproductions you'd like and I'll try to get them – It has just come into my mind that any how I might have sent you a repro. of Ingres Turkish Bath rondel – it would have made up for the lack of nudes on the wall of 3 Grove studios – We might go to the Louvre again tomorrow, if so & the repro-stalls are open I'll get one & send it on to you.

We are leaving Paris tomorrow night by the 10.20 for Turin – we shall probably have a day there and then on to Genoa, a day there & then on to Pisa, & from there to Rome – we shall therefore, probably arrive in Rome, sometime in the middle or towards the end of next week – if its not too

---

[26] Moore visited Paris in 1925 en route to Italy, on a Royal Academy of Art travelling scholarship awarded the previous year.
[27] Raymond Coxon's nickname.
[28] Sir William Rothenstein.

much trouble Sven will you send on the Baedaker & photographs to me c/o Messrs. Cook & Son/54 Piazza e Sedra [dell'Esedra]/Rome. Has Gin[29] left Rome for Florence yet – I've written to Bob telling him when I'm likely to arrive in Rome & I enclosed a little note for Gin –.

Dawson[30] is alright, he seems better away from the Freedman clique – but I think in a week or a fortnights time I shall have had enough of him & shall quietly steal off one day – We've drawn two evenings at Colarossi's, but on each occasion the model wasn't very inspiring – I wish to goodness you were here with me instead of Dawson –

I'll write again from Rome – telling you of what I find in Turin, Pisa & Genoa – & any repros worth collecting, I'll collect for you – Remember me to everybody – [...]

Yes remember me to all the women –:– my opinion of the Paris women is lower than ever. – Let me have any news when you've some minutes to spare – Cheerio – I'll drink your health in Haut-Barsac at tomorrow's dinner.

From a letter to Raymond Coxon, 7 February 1925

Italy

Florence

I have until now been moving with the speed of an American tourist – the first week of being out – spent in Paris – has sunk into the very distant past, but the Guimet Museum (the Indian sculptures in the entrance hall, and the room on the ground floor – and the sculptures and paintings from Antinoe[31] stands out like – like cypress trees in an Italian landscape – Paris itself I did not like – and after the Louvre and the Guimet Museum the few exhibitions of contemporary work which I saw seemed almost rubbish.

I've made stops at Genoa, Pisa and Rome, before coming on here to Florence. In Italy the early wall paintings – the work of Giotto, Orcagna, Lorenzetti, Taddeo Gaddi, the paintings leading up and including Masaccio's are what have so far interested me most. Of great sculpture I've seen very little – Giotto's painting is the finest sculpture I met in Italy – what I know of Indian, Egyptian and Mexican sculpture completely overshadows Renaissance sculpture – except for the early Italian portrait busts, the very late work of Michelangelo and the work of Donatello – though in the influence of Donatello I think I see the beginning of the end – Donatello was a modeller, and it seems to me that it is modelling that has sapped the manhood out of Western sculpture, but the two main reasons are, don't you think, the widespread avoidance of thinking and working in stone – and the wilful throwing away of the Gothic tradition – in favour of a pseudo Greek – I believe that even mediocre students at college or anywhere, had they been lucky enough to have entered a sculptor's workshop, later would most

[29] Edna Ginesi (1902-2000), see note 21 above.
[30] Norman Dawson was a college contemporary who had won the painting department's equivalent scholarship (Berthoud 1987, p.77).
[31] In *Modern English Painters*, this line reads: 'and the sculptures and paintings from [indecipherable] stands out like ...'. In James 1966, p.37, the editor has correctly supplied 'Antinoe' as the indecipherable word (see Moore's letter to Coxon, p.51).

probably have been doing work which we should now admire – in Italy of the 14th century, in one small town of 20 or 30 thousand inhabitants there must have been living and working at the same time 50 or 60 painters each of whom were he doing his same work now would be accounted a genius! … The only hope I can see for a school of sculpture in England, under our present system, is a good artist working carving in the big tradition of sculpture, who can get the sympathy and admiration of students, and propagate good as Dalou and Lanteri spread harm.

I have been seeing rather than doing until now – and I think I have seen examples of most of the Italians – Giotto has made the greatest impression upon me (perhaps partly because he's the most English of the primitives). My present plans are, the Giottos at Assisi, and at Padua, then out of Italy via Ravenna and Venice and on to Munich – from Germany home via Paris so that I can finish up at the Guimet Museum.

11 Moore in Rome, 1925, with Eric Ravilious (top left), Norman Dawson (bottom left) and Mr and Mrs Robert Lyon

I am beginning to get England into perspective – I think I shall return a violent patriot. If this scholarship does nothing else for me – it will have made me realise what treasures we have in England – what a paradise the British Museum is, and how high in quality, representative, how choice is our National Collection – and how inspiring is our English landscape. I do not wonder that the Italians have no landscape school – I have a great desire – almost an ache for the sight of a tree that can be called a tree – for a tree with a trunk.

Letter to William Rothenstein, 12 March 1925;[32] quoted in John Rothenstein,
Modern English Painters, Volume 2: Lewis to Moore, Eyre and Spottiswoode,
London 1956, pp.314-15

[32] In *Modern English Painters,* this letter is incorrectly dated 12 March 1924, a mistake repeated in James 1966, p.38.

There, although I came almost immediately to the Masaccios in Santa Maria del Carmine,[33] I was no more able to use the frescoes directly for my work than I was able to make an accurate copy of the Chacmool from a halftone reproduction. Still, as I see it now, both were to have an equally lasting influence....

Sweeney 1947, p.183

Perhaps that's what makes Picasso's work often seem capricious: a conflict between an interest in the approach illustrated by archaic art and the art of primitive peoples and a respect for the Mediterranean tradition. At any rate, as I look back, I am very conscious of such a conflict throughout my own work, particularly since I went to Italy first in 1925 on a travelling scholarship. Before that time I had associated Classical and Renaissance art with academism and those plaster casts I had to copy at the Leeds School of Art and in the Royal College of Art in London. In fact when I learned that my travelling scholarship should be spent in Italy I at once pleaded to have it re-arranged for Paris. But nothing could be done; no financial arrangements could be made to permit it; I had to go to Italy against my will. But thank goodness now I did go.

For about six months after my return I was never more miserable in my life. Six months' exposure to the masterworks of European art which I saw on my trip had stirred up a violent conflict with my previous ideals. I couldn't seem to shake off the new impressions, or make use of them without denying all I had devoutly believed in before. I found myself helpless and unable to work. Then gradually I began to find my way out of my quandary in the direction of my earlier interests. I came back to ancient Mexican art in the British Museum. I came across an illustration of the 'Chacmool' discovered at Chichen Itza in a German publication[34] – and its curious reclining posture attracted me – not lying on its side, but on its back with its head twisted around. Still the effects of that trip never really faded. But until my *Shelter Drawings* during the war I never seemed to feel free to use what I learned on that trip to Italy in my art – to mix the Mediterranean approach comfortably with my interest in the more elementary concept of archaic and primitive peoples. I feel the conflict still exists in me. And I ask myself is this conflict what makes things happen, or will a synthesis eventually derive? And does all date from this conflict which developed in Italy? –

Ibid., pp.180, 182

Teaching at the Royal College of Art 1924-31

The first two or three years of teaching your own subject is as much a way of learning for the teachers as for the students themselves. I remember I used to be very surprised quite often at the things I discovered while teach-

---

[33] See Moore's ultimate praise of the Masaccio frescoes on pp.155-6.
[34] Walter Lehmann, *Altmexikanische Kunstgeschichte*, Verlag Ernst Wasmuth, Berlin 1922, plate 45. See p.97, note 2.

ing, the actual sentences, the words … after a few years of teaching then I think it isn't a very good thing, because there comes a stage when you have to repeat things that you think are fundamental in the training of a sculptor. They become a deadening thing.

Hall 1966, p.59

First One-Man Exhibition 1928

You were thirty when you had your first show, weren't you?

Yes, it was at the Warren Gallery [London]. Dorothy Warren[35] was a remarkable person with tremendous energy and real verve, real flair. […]

She'd shown D.H. Lawrence's paintings, hadn't she?

That's right. I remember all the excitement of that, and the police raiding the show, and so on. She sold £90 worth of my things – thirty drawings at £1 each, several to Epstein, several to Augustus John, and Henry Lamb – it was mostly other artists, and established ones, who bought, and that was a great encouragement to me. I sold several sculptures, too, but in my first four or five shows it was the drawings that kept me going, not the sculptures, and the other artists who bought.

Was there real antagonism to the sculptures?

Well, there was an article in the *Morning Post* that said that it was 'immoral', or something of the sort, that a man like me should be teaching the young, and there was one professional body that actually called for my resignation, and one of my colleagues at the College who said, 'Either Moore goes, or I go.' But Sir Will sent for me and said, 'I know your teaching is all right. What you do as an artist is your own affair, and I don't even want to see it.'

So that was all right, and there were things like Alfred Barr's first visit to the studio in 1932 or 1933,[36] when he liked a piece that Michael Sadler then gave to The Museum of Modern Art in New York – things like that made one forget all the rest.

Russell 17 December 1961

Irina[37]

I first saw Irina when I was a student at the Royal College – she was a student, too – and I saw her coming across from the Common Room where

[35] Dorothy Warren (Mrs Philip Trotter) was the niece of Lady Ottoline Morell and the goddaughter of Henry James. She was introduced to Moore by Charles Rutherston, see p.50, note 25.

[36] Barr met Moore in 1928 and visited him again in 1935 and 1936. He borrowed *Two Forms* 1934 LH 153 for his 1936 exhibition *Cubism and Abstract Art* at The Museum of Modern Art, New York, see note 13 above. See also p.82.

[37] Irina Radetsky was born in Kiev in 1907. She and Moore were married on 29 July 1929; Mary, their only child, was born in 1946. Irina died at home in Perry Green in 1989. For her charming reminiscences on her life, see Stephen Spender, *In Irina's Garden*, photographs by David Finn, Thames and Hudson, London 1986, pp.45-53.

12 Henry and Irina Moore on their wedding day, 29 July 1929

we used to have lunch at ninepence a time. I met her at a dance at the College and more or less took her out for the evening, not realising she was at that time unofficially engaged. Leslie, her fiancé, was sitting there and I didn't realise he was anything to do with her and ignored him. Afterwards, I walked her back to Kensington Station and poor old Leslie came with us – Irina and I walking together on the pavement, Leslie dragging his feet in the gutter.

Hedgecoe 1986, p.152

Before then I had argued with all my friends that really artists shouldn't get married, they should be married to their art. After all Michelangelo wasn't married, Beethoven wasn't married and so on, all the examples of really good artists who weren't married; but after meeting Irina, I began to say Rembrandt was married, Bach had twenty children and so on. All this attitude changed, and within six months we were married.

In conversation with Roger Berthoud, 4 July 1978

After getting married I moved from the digs I was in – I had rented in advance 11A Parkhill Road, so when Irina and I were back from our honeymoon we went straight there. It was near other friends. Barbara and Jack Skeaping[38] when they were married – in fact I think they found that 11A was to let and told me about it. There were a few others in the area, like Ivon Hitchens,[39] who was living in Adelaide Road.

Ibid., 22 July 1982

Irina has always been a tremendous inspiration, my most valuable constructive critic. Of course, it made a difference, the fact that I married a painter, Irina was trying to do the very same thing that I was and so she knew the problems I was faced with.

Irina knows what she likes of what I do, and she tells me. I take notice of it, too. She has kept my feet on the ground, she has made the reality of life easier for me. It's to do with sympathy, joining in, being interested. She even moved the stones with me.

Hedgecoe 1986, p.152

I remember once looking through some drawings with Irina, thinking some of them were rather poor, and beginning to tear them up. I held each one up and asked her what she thought. I might say, 'I don't think it's good,' and she might say, 'Oh no, keep that.' Then I might say of another one, 'I think this is not so bad,' and she would say, 'No, I don't like that, that can go.' Between us we got worked up into a frenzy, because there is great pleasure in destruction especially in tearing up a thing you have done; tearing it in half. We ended up with a pile on the studio floor. We must have destroyed a thousand drawings. It was good for the spirit.

Hedgecoe 1968, p.49

Barfreston, Kent

She's garden mad – whenever we go for a walk I'm made to take a small garden trowel & a large paper carrier (plain) & we go in whatever direction the horses have taken carting the harvest – & the garden is getting that healthy smell to it.

From a letter to Edna and Raymond Coxon, 3 September 1933

I can't imagine what it might have been like if I hadn't been happily married, and to Irina with her temperament, such as it is, in that she is not overwhelmed by flattery and public … she keeps my feet on the ground, and has this real practical common sense.

In conversation with Roger Berthoud, 18 October 1982

[38] Barbara Hepworth and her first husband, the sculptor John Skeaping (1901-80), had moved to 7 The Mall Studios, Parkhill Road, Hampstead, in early 1928.
[39] The painter Ivon Hitchens (1893-1979) was a founding member of the Seven and Five Society, see p.162, note 36. During the 1930s Hitchens lived in Adelaide Road not far from the Moores. He did a painting entitled *Henry Moore Carving the Leeds 1929 Reclining Figure in his studio in Parkhill Road, Hampstead c.1930* (Leeds City Art Gallery).

I am likely to say yes to people. She thinks through before committing one-self to something which is quite a big affair and which I would treat lightly. Oh no, she – without Irina, I don't know what.

Ibid.

Kent

13 Burcroft, Kingston, near Canterbury

Jasmine Cottage at Barfreston, our first country cottage. We used to go there for weekends and summer holidays and right next door we had this beauti-ful example of Romanesque architecture.[40] The sea, Shakespeare Cliff and the country in between made a big impact on me. A good half of my year's work was done in the country during these holidays. In London I was teach-ing two days a week and seeing a lot of our friends. Thus I would save up ideas for the holidays. I had this wonderful desire always to get back to Barfreston, and later to Kingston, particularly in the summer when I could work fourteen to sixteen hours a day.

Hedgecoe 1968, p.68

My wife and I first bought a cottage in Kent in 1931. We chose Barfreston, I think, because my sister Betty had married a school-teacher and was living quite close by. The Barfreston cottage was very small and had no real garden so in 1934 we bought a house with a fairly large plot of land at Kingston. This house was called Burcroft and we lived there practically all the time although we still had a flat in Hampstead. Kingston is close to Canterbury so we used to go in to Canterbury every Saturday to do our shopping. It's a city I like very much and it has a marvellous cathedral.

Burcroft had quite a lot of land attached to it so my assistant[41] and I

14 Bernard Meadows (right) with Moore and Michael Wickham moving *Reclining Figure* 1939 LH 210 (see fig.99) at Burcroft, 1939

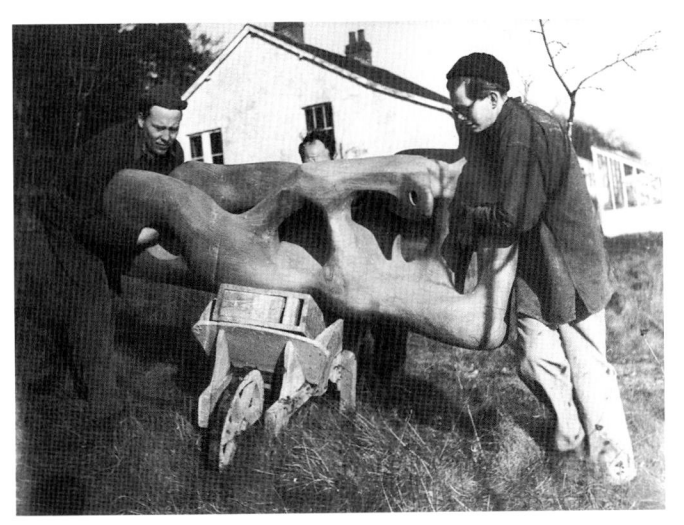

[40] The twelfth-century church of St Nicholas, Barfreston, has a prodigious display of Romanesque carvings around the south doorway of the nave.
[41] The sculptor Bernard Meadows (b.1915) worked for Moore from 1936 to 1940, from 1946 to 1948 and at various times during the 1950s. He was Professor of Sculpture at the Royal College of Art 1960-80, and Acting Director of the Henry Moore Foundation 1983-88. See also p.235, note 27.

were able to carve out of doors eight, nine or even ten hours a day. We would get up very early in the mornings and throw buckets of cold water over each other to make sure we were really awake. Some days we used to go down to Dover by car and swim before lunch.

Living at Burcroft was what probably clinched my interest in trying to make sculpture and nature enhance each other. I feel that the sky and nature are the best setting for my sculpture. They are asymmetrical, unlike an architectural background with its verticals and horizontals. In a natural setting, the background to a sculpture changes if you move only a very small distance.

Henry Moore, Arts Centre, Folkestone 1983 (n.p.)

The cottage had five acres of wild meadow. Here for the first time I worked with a three or four mile view of the countryside to which I could relate my sculptures.[42] The space, the distance and the landscape became very important to me as a background and as an environment for my sculpture. I particularly remember a windmill on the skyline.

Hedgecoe 1968, p.93

Any bit of stone stuck down in that field looked marvellous, like a bit of Stonehenge.

Hall 1966, p.83

15 Stones in the garden at Burcroft, photographed by Moore c.1936

War

After war was declared I continued for a time to live at Burcroft, although it was made a restricted area. I was very fond of the cottage and was working well there.

Chelsea School of Art, where I was teaching two days a week, was attached to the Chelsea Polytechnic and we were informed that the Poly was instituting a course in precision toolmaking. Graham Sutherland[43] and I volunteered for this course and we were told to be prepared to start at any moment.

As a result Irina and I left Burcroft and went to live at my studio at 11A Parkhill Road. Shortly afterwards we accepted the offer of No.7, Mall Studios from Ben Nicholson and Barbara Hepworth, who had decided to evacuate to Cornwall because of their children.[44]

[42] The setting in Moore's 1939 drawing *Sculptural Object in Landscape* HMF 1441 was inspired by the view from Burcroft.

[43] See p.184.

[44] In March 1932, following the break-up of her marriage to John Skeaping, Hepworth lived with Ben Nicholson (see p.161) at 7 The Mall Studios. They were married in November 1938, and moved to St Ives in late August 1939. According to letters from Moore to Hepworth, it seems that he took over 7 The Mall Studios in late October 1939 because he could no longer afford the rent of £130 a year for 11A Parkhill Road. He agreed to pay £75 a year for No.7, and wrote that he probably would not use it as he was working at his cottage in Kent. Moore took it on as a sort of insurance that at the end of the war there would be a good studio for him to go back to: 'We're sorry for your sake you've had to give it up …', he wrote to Hepworth in late October or early November 1939. 'But I'm glad it's us who are to have it, so that it stays, as it were, in the family.' I am grateful to Sophie Bowness for this information.

Every day I expected to hear from Chelsea Polytechnic that the course was about to begin. Consequently there seemed to be no point in starting work on a new sculpture and so I concentrated on drawings. Then came the Battle of Britain, and I was still waiting to hear from the Polytechnic when the blitz began.

Hedgecoe 1968, pp.132-3

Kingston, Kent

My Chelsea teaching is over & seems it wont start again during the war, & there'll be little likelihood of any sales anywhere, so in 4 or 5 months time when our funds have run out, I'll have to look for some sort of paid job. But to see financially that far ahead we count ourselves lucky, & in having this cottage where I can go on working as usual.

I'm a couple of months over the present military service age limit. But if the war goes on for long, the limit wont stay at 41, I'm sure. Having been in the trenches in the last war, not for anywhere near as long as you were, but long enough not to want it twice in a lifetime – I hope it won't come to that. But I hate Fascism & Nazism so much that if the war gets closer & more intense, & that grows into a main issue, the state of mind to go on quietly working might not be possible to keep up, & apart from necessity one might willingly seek to take some part in it.

From a letter to Herbert and Ludo Read, 9 October 1939

Much Hadham, Herts.

The night-time in London is like another world – The noise is terrific & everything seems to be going on immediately over one's own little spot – & the unreality is that of exaggeration like in a nightmare.

But what doesn't seem like a cinematograph reel to me, are the queues, before four o'clock outside some of the Tube Stations, of poor looking women & children waiting to be let in to take shelter for the night – & the dirty old bits of blankets & clothes & pillows stretched out on the Tube platforms – Its about the most pathetic, sordid, & disheartening sight I hope to see.

From a letter to Arthur Sale,[45] 10 October 1940

At the outbreak of the war I had a studio in Devon [Kent], not far from Dover. And for the first months of the war I continued to work there undisturbed. In fact, up to the fall of France there were no difficulties in doing sculpture just as before. During those first months, however, nothing happened in the art world of London, no exhibitions or anything of the sort. Then the code gradually became 'to live as usual'. And in 1940 I exhibited

[45] Arthur Sale (1912-2000), English scholar, poet and Fellow Commoner at Magdalene College, Cambridge, met Moore at the *International Surrealist Exhibition* in London in 1936. They corresponded between 1939 and 1962, but most frequently during the early years of the war, when they exchanged views on pacifism, Nazism, Fascism and politics.

the large reclining figure in elm wood [fig.99], which now belongs to Elizabeth Onslow-Ford,[46] and several small lead figures at the Leicester Galleries. But when France fell and a German invasion of England seemed more than probable, like many others I thought the only thing to do was to try to help directly. I moved back to London and applied at the Chelsea Polytechnic for training in precision-tool making. But the training classes were so few in proportion to the numbers of applications that several weeks went by and I heard nothing. Still I felt it was silly to start a large sculpture when at any moment I might have to give it up. So I took up drawing. Months went by, waiting; I went on drawing. Then the air-raids began – and the war from being an awful worry became a real experience. Quite against what I expected I found myself strangely excited by the bombed buildings, but more still by the unbelievable scenes and life of the underground shelters. I began filling a notebook with drawings – ideas based on London's shelter life. Naturally I could not draw in the shelter itself. I drew from memory on my return home. But the scenes of the shelter world, static figures (asleep) – 'reclining figures' – remained vivid in my mind, I felt somehow drawn to it all. Here was something I couldn't help doing. I had previously refused a commission to do war pictures. Now Kenneth Clark saw these and at once got the War Artists Committee to commission ten. I did forty or fifty from which they made their choice. The Tate also took about ten.[47] In all I did about a hundred large drawings and the two shelter sketchbooks in the Museum Exhibition. I was absorbed in the work for a whole year; I did nothing else.

Then at Herbert Read's suggestion I undertook to do drawings of miners at work in the coal mines – 'Britain's Underground Army', as they were called – another commission of the War Artists Committee. I went to my home town of Castleford and spent two or three weeks in all down the mine. Yet I did not find it as fruitful a subject as the shelters. The shelter drawings came about after first being moved by the experience of them, whereas the coal-mine drawings were more in the nature of a commission coldly approached. They represent two or three weeks of physical sweat seeing the subject and that number of months of mental sweat trying to be satisfied carrying them out.

Sweeney 1947, p.184

Hertfordshire 1940-86

Perry Green, Much Hadham

We came here in 1941 [1940], when my studio in London was made unusable by a bomb falling nearby and it happened that we were not in London that weekend. We were staying in Much Hadham with friends only two or

[46] The 1939 *Reclining Figure* is now in the Detroit Institute of Arts; see p.259.
[47] The War Artists' Advisory Committee purchased four Shelter drawings in 1940 and a further thirteen in 1941, of which eight were presented to the Tate Gallery in 1946.

three hundred yards across from here in a little park called South-End.[48] We could see that there was a raid going on because it is near enough to London as the crow flies – only about twenty miles. The friends we had been staying with tried to persuade us to stay a little longer, but I said I was doing the Shelter Drawings and had to get back. We left them on the Monday morning in the little Standard Coupé that we had in those days, and for which I had a small petrol ration, being a war artist. When we got to Hampstead, the road leading to our studio was cordoned off by the police because of an unexploded bomb. A policeman said, 'You can't go this way. Where do you live?' I said, '7 Mall Studios,' and he said, 'Oh, they're flat to the ground,' with almost a kind of enjoyment in the devastation. So we had to go all the way round, taking about five minutes and imagining all the time that our studio was flat to the ground. However, he had mistaken it and it was Park Hill Studios that had the direct hit, but it was near enough our studio for it to be made unusable, with the windows and doors blown in. In those days you couldn't possibly get a house repaired within six or seven months but we had to have somewhere to live. I rang our Much Hadham weekend friend and said, 'We would like to come back as you were suggesting.'

Levine 1978, pp.25-6

16 Hoglands, Perry Green

At Much Hadham,[49] we discovered that we could lease half of a house called 'Hoglands'. The owner was away at the war and his wife and children were living in the other half. A month or so later the wife decided to go and live with her mother and offered to sell us Hoglands. I had just been offered £300 by Gordon Onslow-Ford for the big 1939 elmwood 'Reclining Figure' and this happened to be exactly the deposit required on the house. We have lived at Hoglands ever since.

I used to go to London two days a week spending the nights in the Underground and coming up at dawn. Then I would return to Hoglands and spend two days sketching.

Hedgecoe 1968, p.140

Much Hadham, Herts.

We're here at a village called Much Hadham, in Hertfordshire. Do you know this part? its surprisingly pretty & unspoilt for so near to London (27 mls). I think we may stay here for some time. Our Hampstead studio had another nearby bomb cutting off the gas & water, & making a mountaineering job of climbing over debris to get into the place, so we've taken a house here that happened to be to let – or rather it's half a house, but self-contained & Irina has the full use & control of the very neglected garden, which she's enjoying playing about in & trying to put into order – although it will be a

---

[48] The Moores were staying with Leonard Matters and his wife at a house called Fiddlers Brook, South-End, about a quarter of a mile south of Perry Green, see following note. Matters, a journalist and writer, had been Labour MP for the Kennington Division of Lambeth from 1929 to 1931.

[49] Although Moore almost always referred to living in the village of Much Hadham, Hoglands is in fact in the hamlet of Perry Green, about a mile away.

long time before there can be any results from her efforts, & by then we may no longer be here.

It's easy to get to London & I go up once or twice each week when there's anything to be seen to – & perhaps also out of morbid curiosity, & a strange subdued excitement there is being in London now. […]

We're beginning to feel more or less settled down here & I've got back to some drawing & am enjoying it. I've joined the Home Guard here, & go out on Night duty patrolling the country lanes twice a week. My battle-dress uniform is very warm, but the trousers are six inches too long & the tunic too tight under the arms. As I was a bayonet instructor for a time in the last war I'm told I shall be asked to instruct our squad in it – But I shall make an awful mess of it, I've forgotten it all.

From a letter to Jane Clark, 3 November 1940

Studios

Hoglands Maquette Studio

My little studio is a very important 'habitat' for me. It is where I am most personally isolated, and that's probably why I like it so much.

Hedgecoe 1968, p.496

17 A profusion of Moore's original plasters, interspersed with found objects in Hoglands Maquette Studio

I am always very happy there. I like the disarray, the muddle and the profusion of possible ideas in it. It means that whenever I go there, within five minutes I can find something to do which may get me working in a way that I hadn't expected and cause something to happen that I hadn't foreseen.

Ibid., p.266

Plastic Studio

This studio dates from when I was asked to do a sculpture for the Lincoln Center in New York [LH 519] about fifteen years ago. I knew the site was

18 Moore cycling past the Plastic Studio in 1964, with the original plaster for the Lincoln Center *Reclining Figure* (see fig.82)

going to need a larger work than any I had done before – even larger than the Unesco *Reclining Figure* [fig.126]. I knew that it was going to take me more than the summer to do it, and that I would have to work through the winter. Yet I realised that a big sculpture intended to live out-of-doors permanently is better if actually made out-of-doors. Light out-of-doors comes of course from the sky, it is an all-round light, it is not the directional light which you get in a room with windows. So I built this studio large enough for the Lincoln Center sculpture, and yet so that I could use it as though it was out-of-doors. The construction is something like a Meccano Set, covered with transparent plastic material allowing the light to be virtually identical with outside, even in winter. In summer, when it is too hot, the sides can be taken out. Since 1963, this studio has been a tremendous asset to me. All my large sculptures have been made in this studio.

Levine 1978, p.36

Gildmore Graphics Studio

When our housekeeper moved into Gildmore, the house next door, I used its studio for my drawing and lithography. I painted the walls white and put a carpet on the floor, which has made it a pleasant place to work in. By putting screens in, I can hang my lithographs, to see if I need to do any further work on them. I couldn't have done this in the old days, when I had to clear a space in my sculpture studio.

Ibid., p.63

Irina's Garden

Irina loves the garden and she works as hard in it as I do in the studio. I give her practically no help, except perhaps now and then I wheel a heavy barrow to the rubbish dump. Irina has changed five acres of ground of barbed-wire chicken runs, rhubarb patches, piggeries, etc., into a simple and excellent setting for my sculpture, which is a great help and asset. Without that piece of ground I cannot imagine how I could have produced some of the large sculptures that I have done in the last ten years. If a large sculpture has to be made in a studio it would be impossible to get away from it, and I would tend to work on its surface rather than on its bigger architectural forms. In our garden I can place the sculptures and see what they look like from a distance and in all weather conditions.

Hedgecoe 1968, p.393

I think the fact that we have lived here since 1941 [1940] was very fortunate for me and for the development of my work. Gradually we were able to acquire further areas where I can place and relate my sculptures to the landscape. A local farmer friend grazes his sheep in these fields, which I like very much, because sheep are just the right scale to contrast with my sculptures – horses or cows are too big in scale. So, working on pieces like the *Sheep Piece* [LH 627], and planning a sculpture for the small hill on the horizon, have been a great help in making sculptures to be seen in the open air.

Levine 1978, p.43

This small hill on the horizon is man-made. When I acquired the ground it was a pyramid of waste gravel. But you cannot put a sculpture on a pyramid if the point is too small, so I had a bulldozer and shaped it into a small hill (sometimes mistaken for a pre-historic barrow). Now I want to put a sculpture there. The sky is the perfect background for sculpture, because you are contrasting solid, three-dimensional form – the sculpture – with its opposite, the sky, which is space, with no distractions. A cast of *Three Piece Reclining Figure: Draped* [LH 655] will be tried out on the hill. This hill is first seen from three or four hundred yards away, and therefore a sculpture there needs to be of some size.[50] The first things I tried on the hill were too small – from a distance they just looked as though there could be a stray sheep that had got there.

Ibid., p.40

19 The bronze *Large Reclining Figure* 1984 LH 192b on the hill at Perry Green

Family Events

Mother's Death[51]

She had such a dignity, such an eternity feeling about her, that to me it was beautiful but terribly, terribly moving; terribly, but beautiful in a way that you could almost look at it like a work of art. There's something about a dead

---

[50] The bronze sculpture finally chosen for the hill, *Large Reclining Figure* 1984 LH 192b, approximately 9 metres in length, was an enlargement of the 1938 lead *Reclining Figure*, only 33cm long, which Moore had photographed against the landscape at Burcroft, see fig.67.
[51] Mary Moore died in May 1944, aged eighty-six, in a nursing home in Woking, Surrey.

body which is statuesque. It's like a sculpture. The foreheads are cold. If you touch a dead forehead it's like touching marble. So in that sense death to me has a remarkable dignity.

John Heilpern, 'The Master Touch', *Observer Magazine* 30 April 1972, pp.30, 33

Mary's Birth[52]

The theory that the work of an artist or a novelist is directly attributable to his personality is a romantic one. An artist's gift is that he can project his imagination. Balzac, for example, carried away on his imagination could write continuously for days and nights on end, living in his mind the lives of his characters. It doesn't mean that if you write about sorrowful things you are in reality miserable. And yet, of course, an artist uses experiences he's had in life. Such an experience in my life was the birth of my daughter Mary, which re-invoked in my sculpture my Mother and Child theme. A new experience can bring to the surface something deep in one's mind.

Hedgecoe 1968, p.173

20 Moore and his daughter, Mary, at Perry Green, Easter 1951

Exhibitions

The Museum of Modern Art, New York 1946

Of course, I spent a good deal of time at the museum helping with the installation of my show but there was also a hectic round of socialising. Curt

[52] Mary, the Moores' only child, was born on 7 March 1946.

[Valentin][53] was a pretty good drinker and I remember an evening with e.e. cummings in Greenwich Village where a smashed table landed on his foot. But in the morning he would rise early with the day's programme worked out for me. He would see to it that some flowers were sent to anyone I had seen the night before to thank them for their hospitality, and he would straighten out all sorts of engagements I had gotten all muddled up. Somewhere along the line I met a lot of top artists I had not known like Arshile Gorky, Jackson Pollock, and Mark Tobey.

Seldis 1973, pp.75-6

Before leaving England I knew that I wanted very much to see the Barnes Collection in Pennsylvania because I had heard how fabulous it was with its 80 Renoirs and so on. In fact I was carrying an introduction to Dr. Barnes[54] from my friend Kenneth Clark. When I got to New York one of the first things I told Alfred Barr was that I wanted very much to see the Barnes Collection. He said: 'don't show or send any letters of introduction from museum directors or critics. Barnes just hates them. It would be much better if you tried to contact him personally.' And so I thought, this is the only thing to do. Next day I was somewhere in the museum with Dorothy Miller[55] discussing some details of the exhibition when she received a phone call from René d'Harnoncourt who said 'I know that Henry wants to see the Barnes Collection. Barnes is just about to come to my room now. I've had a message that he's coming to see me right away. Why don't you ask Henry to come into my office in a few minutes so that I can introduce them to each other.' So Dorothy and I went down there a few minutes later, and sure enough, there was René and Dr. Barnes with two of his bodyguards who looked like Chicago gangsters. D'Harnoncourt said 'Dr. Barnes, may I introduce Henry Moore.' And I said 'I'm so pleased to meet you, Dr. Barnes, because I was about to write to you since I would love to come, if I may, and see your fabulous collection.' And for about a minute there was dead silence. Then he said 'such exaggerated flattery makes me sick.' I was taken aback and didn't say a word in reply. Even his bodyguards looked aghast. So did everyone else in the room except Barnes, of course, who let another minute go by – it seemed more like five minutes to us – and then he said, 'well, when would you like to come?' I said, 'well, anytime you like because I really do mean I want to see your collection. What I said was true. I have heard fabulous reports about it.' He then looked at his diary and he picked the exact day of the opening of my exhibition and said, 'come on the 17th.' At first I was a bit startled but told him, 'all right, Dr. Barnes, I'll come providing that I can get back here by seven o'clock because the opening of my exhibition is on the same day.' He said, 'I'll see to it.' So I went there on that day and

---

[53] Moore's New York dealer; for his tribute to Valentin see p.92.

[54] Dr Alfred Barnes (1872-1951) established the Barnes Foundation in 1925 at Merion, Pennsylvania, outside Philadelphia.

[55] Dorothy Miller succeeded James Johnson Sweeney after he resigned as director of painting and sculpture at MOMA shortly before Moore arrived in New York on 1 December 1946. See Seldis 1973, pp.73-4.

he sent someone to the station at Philadelphia to meet me and from then on in he couldn't have been any nicer. He went around the whole collection with me. Then he let me wander about while there was some session going on with a number of students. He asked me whether I would say a few words to them. I agreed as long as it was only a sentence or two to tell them how pleased I was to be there and how lucky they were to have such a long time to visit and study the collection. And then he gave me lunch, presented me with one of his books on Renoir and a bottle of whisky. He put me back on the train himself, certainly in time for me to be back at the hotel to change for the opening. So, this is my Dr. Barnes story.

Ibid., pp.77-8

Venice Biennale 1948

For the 1948 Venice Biennale – the first one after the war – the British Council decided to have just my sculpture and Turner paintings which was a very sensible thing. But I doubt that one would have won the Biennale sculpture prize that year without the real groundwork and the real impetus that The Museum of Modern Art retrospective provided. Really the foundation where the international side of one's career is concerned – that international thing happened through The Museum of Modern Art exhibition.

Now I notice in counting up that a good three-quarters of my work is in America. At least two-thirds of what I consider to be my most successful earlier drawings were all disposed of to Americans by Curt Valentin. And then, in more recent years there has been the development of the Moore Centre in Toronto[56] and many large public displays of my sculptures throughout the United States.

Ibid., p.67

Refusal of a Knighthood

Much Hadham, Herts.

Thank you for your letter of December 1st.

I am very honoured indeed by the Prime Minister's[57] suggestion that he should submit my name to His Majesty the King for the honour of a knighthood.

I find it very difficult to explain why I feel unable to accept this very great honour.

I have been trying to consider how I myself should feel if I were addressed as 'Sir Henry', every day, even in my workshop, and I cannot help thinking that it would somehow change my conception of myself, and with it the conception of my work.

I have tried to think too, of how my name would fit in among those of the painters and sculptors who have actually received this honour, and I feel that my name might seem rather an anomaly on this list.

[56] The Henry Moore Sculpture Centre, Art Gallery of Ontario, Toronto; see p.76.
[57] Clement Attlee (1883-1967) was Labour Prime Minister from 1945 to 1951.

I also feel that such a title might tend to cut me off from fellow artists whose work has aims similar to mine.

I do hope that the Prime Minister will believe that my reasons for feeling unable to accept this honour do not detract in any way from the great pleasure and gratitude which I felt on learning of his very kind intentions.

Letter to 10 Downing Street, 5 December 1950

Travels

Greece 1951[58]

My first visit to Greece came late in life – it was in 1951, when I was fifty-three – and I thought before going that I knew about Greek art, because I'd been brought up on it, and that I might even be disappointed. But not at all, of course. I'd say that four or five of my top ten or twelve visual experiences came in Greece.

For example, Mycenae had a tremendous impact. I felt that I understood Greek tragedy and – well, the whole idea of Greece – much, much more completely than ever before. And Delphi, though I did find it had a slight touch of theatricality, as if the eagles were flying round to order, and Olympia, with the idyllic sense of lovely living that you get there, and of course the whole of the Acropolis. That too had something I hadn't at all foreseen.

In fact I would say that the Parthenon now is probably much more impressive than when it was first made. You feel the spaces much more, and the openings, and the fact that it's not solid throughout and that the light comes in makes it into a piece of sculpture and not, as it was before, a building with four external sides. It's completely spatial, now – a different object altogether. And the Greek landscape was another revelation to me – that stark, stony quality, with the feeling that the sea may be round the next corner. I can understand why they were sculptors – the stone just had to be used, it was the one thing they had to hand.

Was it a revelation, too, to see your own sculptures in Greece?

The Greek light is, as everyone says, something you can't imagine till you've experienced it. In England half the light is, as it were, absorbed into the object, but in Greece the object seems to give off light as if it were lit up from inside itself. But I think that the element of light can be over-emphasised. The northern light can be just as beautiful as Greek light and a wet day in England can be just as revealing as that wonderful translucent Mediterranean light. I really don't think that Mediterranean light is the only light, by a long chalk.

Russell 24 December 1961

21 Moore in front of the Temple of the Wingless Victory, the Acropolis, Athens, 1951

[58] Moore visited Greece at the time of the British Council exhibition of his work in Athens.

At Delphi you have to work from one temple to another. But the Greek landscape is a terrific affair. The Parthenon is really sculpture in landscape. Greece! I think their landscape is their body. They come upon the sea just round the corner everywhere. I think they have a sense of their landscape like of their own bodies. You don't have to be told there that landscape is important. All their siting is marvellous …

Spender 1978, p.26

Well, if one were asked for the ten visual greatest experiences, three or four of them would come from Greece. I mean there would be Mycenae, with the lion, the tombs there and so on, the Parthenon, Delphi – which no novel can convey, the romantic, poetic, heavenly something that Delphi has. I mean a few of the others that I've mentioned would be the Sistine chapel of Michelangelo, would be the Altamira caves[19] that one's seen, and there must be a few that I haven't seen – I bet the Grand Canyon would be … all these, but three or four of my most exciting experiences visually come from Greece.

Interview with Edwin Mullins, Kaleidoscope, BBC 27 June 1978

Mexico 1953[60]

It must be very exciting for you to be in Mexico … It is the one country in the world which I have always wanted to visit most. And one day I will certainly do so.

Pre-Columbian Mexican sculpture has been the most important single influence in my own sculpture – I should love to see it, in its own environment.

From a letter to Mathias Goeritz, 9 January 1950

Mexico was the place I had always wanted to see. The week there was one of the most exhilarating and rewarding weeks I have ever spent. It was quite as interesting as my visit to Greece.

Britain and the São Paulo Bienal 1951-1991, British Council,
London 1991, p.63

The present-day architecture of Mexico was one of the most pleasant surprises for me during my stay in this country. I knew already that Mexico regarded itself as being advanced in terms of modern architecture, but I never imagined the profusion of architectural works, and of such artistic quality …

I saw the University City – surely the most extraordinary enterprise to be seen in any country! This would not be possible in Europe at the present

---

[19] Henry and Irina Moore went to Altamira, Cantabria, in northern Spain while on a motoring holiday with Raymond and Edna Coxon in the late summer of 1934.
[60] Moore went to Mexico after attending the exhibition of his work at the second São Paulo Bienal, Brazil. He met the great muralists Siqueiros, Tamayo and Rivera and saw the latter's collection of pre-Columbian art.

time. I saw many things that I found beautiful, such as the Stadium, the Faculty of Humanities, etc. Others seemed to me formally of less interest, but it is their splendid conjunction that matters. […]

I don't understand the desire to subscribe consciously and at any price to what is called 'the integration of the plastic arts'. That the architect should produce good architecture, as many in Mexico have done, and that sculptors and painters on their side should produce good sculpture and good paintings – this will lead to a greater harmony, provided that the common denominator is the high quality of the work …

I personally don't believe that architecture can achieve a human expression as deep or as moving as painting or sculpture; for example, I don't think that one could find an architect whose work could be compared in depth of feeling with Picasso's painting *Guernica* …

22 Rufino Tamayo and Moore at the Pyramid of the Feathered Serpent, Xochicalco, Mexico, 1953

Of course, the most beautiful architecture in Mexico, where all arguments cease and where man becomes mountain, is the Pyramid of the Sun at Teotihuacán …

I would love to come back to Mexico and to get to know this great country better and, if possible, to work in it.

'Henry Moore dice' (Henry Moore speaks), *Arquitectura México*, Mexico City
March 1954, pp.3-4 (translated from the Spanish)

Italy: Querceta and Forte dei Marmi

I first went to Querceta, near Forte dei Marmi in Italy, in connection with the Unesco sculpture.[61] Querceta is a little village which lies beneath the mountain called Altissimo, part of the famous marble mountain range behind Carrara. Altissimo is for me a most fascinating and exciting place. It is where Michelangelo spent two years of his life quarrying marble. Altissimo

[61] *Unesco Reclining Figure* LH 416 was commissioned in 1956 and executed in 1957-58.

is owned by a firm called Henraux, who deal in stone from all over the world. It was they who supplied the Roman travertine which was used on the Unesco building in Paris and, when I decided that the Unesco sculpture was to be a carving and not a bronze, it seemed right to use the same stone. The Unesco sculpture was to be so big that the cost of sending the stone to England would have swallowed up the whole of my fee. Therefore I went to the mountain, instead of the mountain being sent to me. To do the Unesco sculpture meant that I was in Italy intermittently for nearly a year. I would go over for three or four weeks, work on the stone and, because I hated being away from home and from Irina and Mary, who was then only a child, I would come home for a month and then go back again. Whilst I was in England, I would leave the straightforward roughing out of the stone to two of Henraux's stonemasons.

On some of these visits Irina and Mary came with me. It was a holiday for them, being so near the sea, and because they enjoyed it so much, after the Unesco sculpture was finished we continued to go there every year for two or three weeks. I find I have become so used to working continuously that, after a week off, I am conscience-stricken and I stop enjoying myself. The solution is to go to Henraux's and do a bit of carving each morning.

Three years ago an Italian painter friend sold me his cottage and now the three of us can go to Italy every summer for at least two months.[62] Irina and Mary have a lovely holiday, and I work in the mornings and join them in the afternoons for the Italian sunshine and warm bathing.

Hedgecoe 1968, p.416

Forte dei Marmi has changed a great deal. When I first went, there was hardly anybody on the beach. Now in summer it is rather crowded. But we don't mind this so much, for in England we live quietly in the country at Much Hadham, and don't lead a very social life.

Originally I had intended having a studio at the cottage, but because handling large pieces of stone is very difficult, I find that it is much easier to work in a room given to me in Henraux's stone-yard, where I can have all the facilities of their cranes. So what was to have been my studio has become my sleeping quarters for any of Mary's friends who visit us in the summer.

Our routine every day is to get up around seven-thirty, have a very simple breakfast in the garden of coffee and fruit. I try to get to Henraux's not later than ten and work until one o'clock, before joining Irina and Mary on the beach. I can be with them by ten past one and have my morning bathe. We leave the beach probably by quarter to two and do whatever shopping there may be. By three we have finished lunch and, following the Italian custom, we take it easy until four-thirty or five. Just occasionally I go back to the stone-yard for an hour or two. At other times, I may do a little drawing in my sketchbook. In the evening we go out for a meal. These months in Italy always pass very quickly.

Ibid., p.435

[62] Moore purchased the cottage at Forte dei Marmi in 1965.

... the staggering work it must have been for Michelangelo to get these marbles down from here. There is a tremendous feeling of scale that you get here, more than anywhere else.

Look at this sheer, steep quarry wall. It's as if the whole of a skyscraper has been sliced up vertically. The men scrambling up that little ladder are so dwarfed in scale that the whole picture reminds me of Paul Klee.

Last year we came to look for just the right kind of marble for a piece of mine that is now being finished down below. I was looking for white marble, but not so white that it would not be marked at all. I wanted it to have some bit of nature in it, some natural markings. Even so, one of the blocks we finally chose had to be abandoned since a bad vent was found in it as it was being cleaned up. So the crew had to start out all over again. Driving over these roads, made by Henraux in more than a century's time, one begins to understand what a staggering amount of man's effort has gone into getting at this marble.

23 Moore at the Henraux marble quarry in the Carrara Mountains, mid-1960s

It's very dangerous work now. But just think how very much more dangerous and difficult all this must have been in Michelangelo's time. That greyish space you see up there is the quarry where he worked. The very best marble is always found at the highest points. That's where the greatest geological pressures occurred millennia ago after an unimaginable number of shellfish that had once rested at the bottom of the sea had been volcanically pushed up into the mountains and solidified.

And the colours. One can find marble that is completely black and marble that is completely white and nearly every colour in-between. It's simply terrific.

Seldis 1973, pp.24, 26

Florence Exhibition 1972[63]

Much Hadham, Herts.

My dear Mayor,

I want to tell you how happy it makes me to have been invited to hold this exhibition of my work in your great city.

I have loved Florence since my first visit in 1925, as a young student spending a five months' travelling scholarship to Italy. – It was the most impressionable stage of my development – Out of the full five months, I stayed three months in Florence. At first it was the early Florentines I studied most, especially Giotto, because of his evident sculptural qualities.

24 Sculptures on the terrace of Forte di Belvedere, overlooking the city of Florence

[63] The exhibition was held at the Forte di Belvedere from 20 May to 30 September 1972.

Later Masaccio[64] became an obsession, and each day I paid an early morning visit to the Carmine chapel before going anywhere else … Towards the end of my three months, it was Michelangelo who engaged me most, & he has remained an ideal ever since.

I have made many subsequent visits to Italy, of course, & always to Florence. For the last seven years my family & I have made our home in Tuscany for two months every summer, where I work on my marble sculptures, – & when I need refreshing in spirit, in little over an hour from our house, I can be in Florence surrounded by the great paintings & sculptures I love.

And so my close relationship with Florence grows, & I feel it is my artistic home – Therefore, this opportunity to hold an exhibition at the Forte di Belvedere, I accept with gratitude, but also with some apprehension!

No better site for showing sculpture in the open-air, in relationship to architecture, & to a town, could be found anywhere in the world, than the Forte di Belvedere, with its impressive environs & its wonderful panoramic views of the city. – Yet its own powerful grandeur and architectural monumentality make it a frightening competitor for any sculpture – and so I know that showing my work here would be a formidable challenge, but one I should accept. I knew also that to realise the exhibition I must count on a lot of generous help from others.

May I, Mr Mayor, thank you & your committee, & all those who have given so much time and effort to make this exhibition possible.

Undated letter to Luciano Bausi, reproduced in *Mostra di Henry Moore*,
Il Bisonte Editore/Nuovedizioni Enrico Vallecchi, Florence 1972, p.17

Homage to T.S. Eliot,[65]
Globe Theatre, London 13 June 1965

While I was working on 'The Archer' [fig.134] which was destined for Toronto, I was asked to paint a backcloth for T.S. Eliot's memorial programme which was to take place on a Sunday evening at the Globe Theatre. Since I could not stop work on the sculpture for a month, it was suggested that 'The Archer' would be even better for the purpose than a backcloth.

The original plaster was so heavy that it could not have been moved without cutting it into several pieces, and so I decided to take a plaster cast of it with a skin a quarter of an inch thick, weighing one tenth of the original. Incidentally, that is why there are two plasters of 'The Archer'.[66]

On the Saturday evening after the theatre had closed, the plaster arrived by road and we just managed to squeeze it through the door with two inches to spare, and on to the stage by the following morning. All the next day we worked on the stage-lighting until we were happy with it.

[64] See p.155.
[65] For Moore's tribute to Eliot see p.85.
[66] Neither of the plasters has survived.

On the Sunday night, the programme began with an overture, lasting three or four minutes, which had been specially composed by Stravinsky. Then the curtain went up and the sculpture, which I had placed assymetrically on the stage and had left its natural white colour, very slowly made one complete revolution in silence. Throughout the evening while Laurence Olivier, Paul Scofield and many others read extracts from Eliot's poetry, we changed the position and the lighting of the sculpture.

It was my first experiment in using real sculpture on the stage instead of fake pictorial scenery, and it was a moving experience. If I ever worked for the theatre again, I think I would use real three-dimensional sculpture and not a pictorial illusion. I am sure there is a future use for real sculpture in the theatre.[67]

Hedgecoe 1968, p.487

The Henry Moore Sculpture Centre, Art Gallery of Ontario, Toronto[68]

25 The unveiling of *Three Way Piece No.2: (The) Archer* 1964-65 LH 535 in Nathan Phillips Square, Toronto, 27 October 1966

To make a bronze sculpture you first have to make the piece in some other material. In my case it has been sometimes in clay, but mostly in plaster. These are not plaster casts; they are plaster originals. That is, they are built up in the plaster. Later I cut them down or add to them, continually altering them until I am satisfied they are ready to be cast. They are the actual works that one has done with one's own hands. At one time I used to destroy these because of what happened to someone like Rodin, who didn't destroy his originals nor leave clear instructions as to how many pieces should be in an edition of each bronze. I remember Curt Valentin telling me once that there were something like eighty casts for one particular Rodin sculpture, most of them made after Rodin died. To prevent this, just as an etcher will score the original plate, a sculptor will break the original terracotta or plaster or whatever material he has made his original in. This was my practice until about ten years ago.

Then someone – a friend who works at the Victoria and Albert Museum – came out one day just as we were breaking up some plasters and said, 'But why do that, because sometimes the original plaster is actually nicer to look at than the final bronze.' He was right because sometimes an idea you've had and that you've made in the original material or plaster can suit it better than what the final bronze may do. Especially to begin with it was difficult for me sometimes in the early stages of making a bronze to visualise for sure just what the plaster I was doing would look like in bronze. But I've learned by now to know that I can change the patina of bronzes and I can visualise very easily what kind of final result there will be in the bronze as I make it in the plaster. So, this led to the idea of not destroying the plasters, leaving me with

[67] See p.227.
[68] The Moore Centre houses the largest public collection of Moore's sculpture, drawings and prints. For an account of Moore's close ties with Toronto, see Alan G. Wilkinson, *Henry Moore Remembered: The Collection at the Art Gallery of Ontario in Toronto*, Art Gallery of Ontario/Key Porter Books, Toronto 1987, pp.3-21.

a great many of them that I would not sell but wanted to find proper homes for. The Tate's new extension will not be built for some years, nor would I want to give them all the plasters. It was this situation that made me receptive to giving them to Toronto when the idea of a possibility for a Moore Centre there was first broached to me the spring after the 1966 October unveiling of the *Archer* in front of the new city hall.[69] There had been a lot of controversy over it there. The then-Mayor Philip Givens strongly defended it. With all the debates on it in the newspapers and everywhere it became the best-known piece of sculpture – easily – in Canada. People were saying 'what is it? What does it mean?' Since this all took place during the re-election campaign, the Mayor lost the election by a few votes. He was very nice and wrote to me during that time saying that if the controversy over my sculpture had any part in his losing the election, he was very proud of it. He met me when I went there in March 1967.

It was at that time I also met the collector Sam Zacks, who unfortunately died recently. He had very fine modern and primitive things. Among others I met was Bill Withrow, the director of the Art Gallery, and a number of art patrons including Allan Ross and Mrs J.D. Eaton. It was Sam Zacks who took the lead in making the necessary financial arrangements through public and private funds to provide housing for the plasters and other works I was willing to give them. I remember his coming here with Edmund Bovey, who succeeded him as chairman of the trustees, architect John C. Parkin, and Withrow. We all went all around London together to see the different museums so that I could show them what was right or wrong with them as far as the display of sculpture is concerned. When I was eventually

26 Alan Wilkinson, Mary Moore, Henry Moore and William Withrow in the Moore Gallery at the Art Gallery of Ontario, October 1974

[69] Moore did not visit Toronto for the unveiling of *Three Way Piece No.2: (The) Archer* 1964-65 LH 535 in October 1966, as is often stated in published chronologies. See Wilkinson 1987, pp.9-11.

shown the model for the building, I could see that my ideas about that very important subject had been followed.

This Moore Sculpture Centre is only part of that museum's overall expansion, including space for the very fine collection that Sam and Ayala Zacks have donated. As far as I am concerned, it will display my plasters and some of the bronzes. But there will also be a theatre where lectures on sculpture generally will be given and a library of all books on sculpture that are available. It will also house a very large slide collection of sculpture of all periods. We have signed a general agreement on the whole matter. I think that the people concerned in Toronto will do everything very well and seriously.

Seldis 1973, pp.222-4

Much Hadham, Herts.

It is going to be a long time before all of us here at Hoglands forget the Toronto Experience.

We have, more or less, settled back to the old routine, but we go on talking about Toronto.[70]

From a letter to Alan Wilkinson, 8 December 1974; reproduced in Wilkinson 1987, p.xiv

The Henry Moore Foundation[71]

The Foundation has two or three main purposes. One is to help the appreciation of sculpture generally because I remember that as a young sculptor, there was nothing; there wasn't a single piece of sculpture in my home town – a church two or three miles away did have some little Gothic heads on the arches of the doors and windows. Leeds Art Gallery had nothing of any value. Another purpose is to look after my own work after I'm gone: probably exhibit it and also keep some of my things in suitable places in nature.

Myron Brody, 'Henry Moore: An Interview', *Forum*, Kansas City, Missouri March 1981, p.7

Summing Up

It is impossible to turn to a single influence in any work of art, it can only come by the development and experience of a lifetime combined with all these influences. And then it is only the truly great artists who can emerge to create their own individual style. Then with the artist's own ideas and abilities one hopes that an added vitality will be embraced within the work

[70] In October 1974 Henry, Irina and Mary spent ten days in Toronto and attended the official opening on 26 October of stage one of the Art Gallery of Ontario's expansion programme, which included the Henry Moore Sculpture Centre. Members of Moore's staff – John Farnham, David Mitchinson, Michel Muller and Malcolm Woodward – were there to help with the installation.
[71] For an account of the formation in 1977 of the Henry Moore Foundation and its evolution, see *Celebrating Moore: Works from the Collection of The Henry Moore Foundation*, selected by David Mitchinson, Lund Humphries, London 1998, pp.11-66.

he produces. But nobody can say where that added force comes from other than that it comes from within the artist himself.

When I've finished a sculpture and through it expressed my ideas, emotions and feelings, then I can look and philosophise about the reason for doing a particular piece. But it would never be exact. Who is to tell if an experience which occurred yesterday, or ten years ago, or a lifetime ago was an influence or not? I can't.

Hedgecoe 1986, p.181

Great original talent cannot be quantified, although the question of heredity and environment must be involved.

This doesn't mean necessarily that someone in your family was a direct link and had shown a similar talent. But if it did, it doesn't have to be your father or your mother or your brother or your sister. It could have been your father's grandfather, or his grandfather's father, stretching back many centuries. And then it could have been a latent talent that had never been developed.

On the other hand, the environment in which you have been brought up, your experiences, the people who have encouraged you and helped to teach you the language of your discipline – these influences must play a major part in your understanding and in your aspirations, especially in your formative years.

The great artists that I admire have a life-giving power in their work that extends beliefs and understanding beyond normal perceptions. Michelangelo, Tintoretto, Rembrandt, Rubens, Cézanne, Rodin and some others have this quality in their work. I would like to think that in my own work some of this vital force has been imprisoned, independently from the object it represents, so that other people can be aware and sense it. But how it gets there would be impossible to explain. Nor should it need explanation. It is enough that our senses are enriched.

Ibid., p.149

Happiness is to be fully engaged in the activity that you believe in and, if you are very good at it, well that's a bonus. An artist's raw material is what he has seen and done so I still have to refresh my eyes every day. It is not enough to sit in my comfortable chair surrounded by outstanding examples of fine art. Although it is difficult, I have to go out every day for a drive, to see nature, the countryside, the trees, the sky, to be renewed and refreshed. The drawings I make reflect my love of nature.

Even now, at the age of 87, it is necessary to go out for a drive each afternoon because it refreshes my vision.[72]

Ibid., p.175

27 Moore with Frank Farnham and 'Charlie', c.1985

---

[72] Moore died at home in Perry Green on 31 August 1986, a month after his eighty-eighth birthday.

28 Roland Penrose, Moore and Peter Gregory in Venice for the XXIV Biennale, 1948

CHAPTER TWO

FRIENDS AND COLLEAGUES[1]

<u>Friendship</u>

Ray [Raymond] Coxon / Herbert Read / Peter Gregory / K [Kenneth] &
Jane Clark / Philip & Cecily [Hendy] / Bob & Lisa [Sainsbury] / Maurice –
Ruth [Ash] / Con [Constantine] Fitzgibbon / David S. [Sylvester] / Roland
Penrose / Ivon Hitchens / Ben & Barbara [Nicholson and Hepworth] /
Curt Valentin / Bernard Meadows –[2]

Unpublished notes late 1950s (?), HMF archive

Alfred Barr

*Alfred H. Barr (1902-81), the American art historian and administrator, was the first
director of The Museum of Modern Art, New York, 1929-43. He organised more than a
hundred exhibitions at MOMA. Moore's* Two Forms *1934 LH 153 was shown in his
1936* Cubism and Abstract Art, *and acquired by MOMA the following year. Among
Barr's most influential books are* Picasso: Fifty Years of his Art *(1946) and* Matisse:
His Art and his Public *(1951).*

29 Moore with Alfred Barr, looking
through *Large Torso: Arch* 1962-63 LH 503
at The Museum of Modern Art, New York,
September 1965

Much Hadham, Herts.

I've just got a letter from Bill Paley,[3] inviting me to dinner at his home
on March 12th, & to the Reception afterwards for you at the Museum of
Modern Art.

I have replied to him that I'm terribly sorry that its impossible for me to
come to New York at that date, because of work pressure and an unchange-
able engagement in London on 13th March.

But I want to tell you, Alfred, how much I would have liked to be there,
to join with all your friends in showing you how much we admire & love you
– & to thank you for all the wonderful work you have done.

You are a great man, – <u>all of us are incalculably in your debt.</u> You made
a great museum (to begin with, single handed.) – The whole world of mod-

---

[1] Moore's tributes to his artist friends Epstein, Hepworth, Nicholson, Piper, Richards and Sutherland
appear in Chapter Three.
[2] Apart from letters, no special tributes by Moore to some of his closest friends, namely Raymond Coxon,
Philip and Cecily Hendy and Bernard Meadows, have come to light.
[3] William S. Paley was Chairman of the Board of The Museum of Modern Art, New York.

ern Painting & Sculpture praises you. I am very grateful Alfred, for your part in my life – beginning when you first came to my Hampstead Studio early in the 1930's & when through you Michael Sadler[4] presented the first of my works (TWO FORMS – Pynkado Wood [fig.92]) to the Museum.

That began, with you & with the Museum, a lasting relationship, which I value enormously.

Thank you Alfred for all your wonderful work, for your deep devotion & love of art, for your great scholarship, & for being the man you are.

Please give my love to Marga & may I wish all future happiness to you both –

Letter to Alfred Barr, 19 February 1973

John Desmond Bernal

The Irish-born physicist J.D. 'Sage' Bernal (1901-71) was a researcher at Cambridge (1927-37) and became Professor of Physics (1936-63) and first Professor of Crystallography (1963-68) at London University. A pioneer in the field of X-ray crystallography and molecular biology, he had a lifelong interest in art. In 1937 he contributed an article to Circle: International Survey of Constructive Art.

We saw quite a lot of each other in the early thirties; we met in a small, isolated group – Solly Zuckerman,[5] Sage Bernal and other friends – battling against the Philistines. Sage would talk about mathematical analysis, and graphs and shapes which could not be defined, yet he found that we sculptors were doing that kind of thing instinctively. It was a most exciting time.

Tribute to John Desmond Bernal in his Seventieth Year, by Artists and Scientists,
Queen Elizabeth Hall, London 1971

Kenneth Clark

The British art historian Kenneth Clark (1903-83) was Director of the National Gallery, London, from 1934 to 1945. He and his wife Jane became close friends of the Moores in the late 1930s, and acquired a number of sculptures and an important collection of Moore's drawings. Among Clark's best-known books are Landscape into Art *(1935),* The Nude *(1955) and* Civilisation *(1970), the latter based on his popular television series of the same title. His book on Moore's drawings was published in 1974.*

[...] now K and Jane, we first met them when they lived in Portland Place. [...] it must have been '29 or '30, but I think he already owned one or two of my things that he'd bought from the Leicester Galleries [...][6] But I

---

[4] See p.43, note 13.

[5] Solly Zuckerman (1904-93), the South African-born British zoologist and educationist, joined the faculty of Oxford University in 1934. From 1955 to 1977 he was Honorary Secretary of the Zoological Society of London. He wrote the introduction to Moore's 1981-82 album of etchings *Animals in the Zoo*. Lord Zuckerman OM represented HM The Queen at the 'Service of Thanksgiving for the Life and Work of Henry Moore OM, CH' at Westminster Abbey on 18 November 1986.

[6] Moore's first exhibition at the Leicester Galleries was held in 1931. According to Berthoud, 'the evidence suggests that Kenneth Clark had entered Moore's life in early 1938' (Berthoud 1987, p.157).

remember us going round there to Portland Place and being tremendously impressed by the pictures that he owned at that time too – and then the friendship grew very, very steadily […] and perhaps the closest period came at the beginning of the war […]

In conversation with Véra and John Russell, c.1961

I think perhaps the contact [with Graham Sutherland], the very definite contact, was Kenneth Clark. K Clark at that time was a very great influence and help to my generation and the generation a bit younger. He helped secretly, without people knowing. He supported some of the artists, I know. He gave a private income to one or two, he gave them money, and even people other than artists. Who was it told me the other day: Bryan Robertson[7] said he suddenly got a cheque for three or four hundred pounds from him because they talked together and K Clark realised he had ambitions to write about art; […] and I think a good deal of our meeting was around and with K, because he admired Graham's work and bought it and appointed him as a war artist before me.

In conversation with Roger Berthoud, 24 July 1979

30 Moore at the British Museum with Kenneth Clark, 1958

[7] Bryan Robertson (b.1925) was director of the Whitechapel Art Gallery, London, 1952-68. Among the major exhibitions which he organised there were Turner, Mondrian, Pollock, Rothko (see p.184), Hepworth, and in 1960, *Henry Moore: Sculpture 1950-60*.

Kingston, Kent

I've been wondering since I wrote to you about the price of the large re-clining figure,[8] whether you might think I have put a price that's too high on it, that I've been greedy about it. And I should hate to believe you were thinking anything like that.

I've so much else to thank you for, the great help for example you gave in so many ways towards making my recent drawing show a success, & I owe so much to your help & friendliness during the last year or two, that of course I'm ready to meet your ideas about it all, & so should be glad if you'd write & tell me what you think the price should be from your point of view as buyer for The Contemporary Art Society. – Perhaps you had thought it would be about half its exhibition figure, i.e. £250.

We're here at Kingston. I'm working on the large wooden reclining figure [LH 210]. The weather hasn't been so good until today, but today its worth being in the country.

Letter to Kenneth Clark, 8 April 1939

Kingston, Kent

I read your Leonardo book[9] with tremendous enjoyment. I didn't think any-one outside a practising artist could have the insight you show in what you write about the individual works. I hope that National Gallery work & all the other work you do, wont mean a long time will pass before you write more books as enlightening and stimulating. I was still reading it when the war began. The whole spirit of it, the values & mental attitude it creates, – is just what we mustn't let the war destroy or dim.

With our warmest regards to you both & the children

From a letter to Kenneth Clark, 1 October 1939

Nancy Cunard

Nancy Cunard (1896-1965) was the daughter of Sir Bache Cunard and his American-born wife Lady (Maud) Emerald. Imperious, brilliant and opinionated, she grew up in the safe aristocratic world of pre-First World War England. In addition to her espousal of worthy causes she founded the Hours Press, which published fine editions of poetry. Nancy Cunard was painted by Kokoschka and Wyndam Lewis, sculpted by Brancusi, and photographed by Man Ray and Cecil Beaton.

Outwardly Nancy Cunard did not correspond with the mental picture I had formed of her from my previous knowledge of her activities connected with many worthwhile and often unpopular causes, her support for the Negro in America, for the Republicans in the Spanish civil war, for example. I

---

[8] Moore is discussing the 1938 Hornton stone *Recumbent Figure* (fig.98) that on Clark's recommendation was bought by the Contemporary Art Society and presented to the Tate Gallery in 1939, the first work by Moore to enter the collection.

[9] Kenneth Clark, *Leonardo da Vinci: An Account of his Development as an Artist*, Cambridge University Press, London 1939. Moore's copy of this book is inscribed 'Henry Moore from K.C.'

expected a more militant physical presence. Instead, there was this elegant, sensitive woman whose very bone-structure seemed finer and more delicate than any one else's. She conveyed an immediate impression of gentle intensity. She had an abundance of nervous energy, and no matter how long you were with her, you were conscious of a burning enthusiasm, a perpetual giving-out whatever subject (and her range was enormous) came under discussion.

She had an innate feeling for sculpture, developed through her long familiarity with examples from early and primitive civilisations and her expert knowledge of African ivories. She had indeed a rare appreciation of form-meaning whether in man-made sculpture or in the kind of unusual *objet trouvé*[10] she discovered and describes with such lyrical aptness in the letter quoted here, written when she was so desperately ill.

She was a dear, sweet, generous person one was always delighted to see and one feels enriched to have known.

Nancy Cunard: Brave Poet, Indomitable Rebel 1896-1965, edited by Hugh Ford, Chilton Book Company, Philadelphia, New York and London 1968, p.287

T.S. Eliot

Thomas Stearns Eliot (1888-1965), poet, critic and dramatist, was born in St Louis, Missouri, and settled in England in 1911. The Waste Land, *his most famous early poem, was published by Leonard and Virginia Woolf at the Hogarth Press in 1922. His plays include* Murder in the Cathedral *1925,* The Family Reunion *1939 and* The Cocktail Party *1950. His great philosophical poem* The Four Quartets *was published in 1944. Eliot was awarded the Nobel Prize for Literature in 1948.*

I think I first met T.S. Eliot in the thirties – at the time of the formation of the Group Theatre – when in a bare room next to Leicester Square Tube Station I remember vividly a Sunday Night (rather amateur) performance of Sweeney Agonistes.

But I only began to know him well after the last war, because we shared two or three close friends among them Peter Gregory the publisher. When he formed the Gregory fellowships at Leeds University he asked Herbert Read, Bonamy Dobrée,[11] T.S. Eliot & myself to select these fellows a poet, a painter & a sculptor to be chosen each year.

Over choosing the painter & the sculptor Eliot was ready to defer to the rest of us, but over choosing the best young poet to fit the fellowships requirements – I was amazed at the time & consideration Eliot had already given before the meeting – perhaps reading & assessing the work of ten or fifteen young poets & going into their background & potentialities – & the discussions we had taught me much about his attitude to the writing of poetry.

[10] This refers to a small stone given by Cunard to Moore, which she called 'Henry Moore's Ring' (see *Nancy Cunard: Brave Poet, Indomitable Rebel*, pp.228-9).
[11] Bonamy Dobrée was Professor of English Literature at the University of Leeds from 1936 to 1955.

No trouble seemed too much for him to take to help the younger poets.

Tom Eliot was a wonderful man to have known. What struck me always was his unpretentiousness – In spite of being the most famous poet, the most respected, the most written about (& in my opinion the greatest poet of this century) he put on no airs – no act of 'I'm the great man I am' – because like all men of real gifts, he had no need to – his achievements spoke for themselves.

What to me he proved, was that a poet or an artist is first a person who searches into himself, who tries to use all his gifts, intellectual as well as instinctive, & does not just exploit the talent that comes easiest to him.

But above all what I felt most strongly in his company was his deep sincerity – that inside him was a hard core of integrity – He was not effusive not outwardly full blooded not wetly warmhearted – rather he was dry like a hard grain of human wheat – but a grain you knew could germinate – & did, in his poetry.

I think I'm very very lucky to have known so true a man & so great a poet.

Unpublished notes for *Monitor*, BBC 12 January 1965; HMF archive

E.C. Gregory

E.C. 'Peter' Gregory (1887-1959), the British collector, patron and philanthropist, was chairman of the publishing firm Lund Humphries. He was an early patron of Moore, whom he met in 1923, and of Hepworth, Nicholson and Sutherland. In 1943 he established the Gregory Fellowships at Leeds University which were offered to painters, sculptors, composers and poets. Gregory helped to found the Institute of Contemporary Arts, London, in 1947.

I should like to add my personal tribute to the memory of my good friend Peter Gregory [see fig.28]. Although I knew him well for 30 years, it was during the last 15 years that we spent most time together, either in this country or, very frequently, travelling abroad. He was the ideal travelling companion, never ruffled or moody or upset by difficulties: and perhaps, even more important, ever fresh and anxious to visit any place or site or building or gallery that might contain objects of beauty. In Greece, in Italy (where we went to the Etruscan sites together), in the New World, Peter, though no longer a young man, was always ready to set off, regardless of comfort or convenience, if he believed that there was something worth seeing at the other end.

And this quality of enthusiasm that he possessed in so wonderful a degree was apparent in his very fine collection of paintings and sculptures, a collection that is known only to a few, since he never made use of it to further his own position or to gain renown for himself.

When first I knew him, I was an unknown sculptor. At that time there were very few, less than half a dozen, collectors of modern sculpture in this country. Charles Rutherston, like Peter Gregory, a Bradford man, introduced us, for he had imparted his own enthusiasm for sculpture to Gregory. He immediately joined that very small group of men who were prepared to encourage modern sculpture. The debt that I owe him is enormous. It is thanks to Peter Gregory and a very few others of his sort that young sculptors in this country can nowadays anticipate that their work may be of interest to their compatriots.

Nor was his interest in the work of artists limited to his own or my generation. That splendid vitality and ability to perceive beauty never deserted him. To the end of his life he was able to show enthusiasm and understanding for painters and sculptors even half a century younger than himself. He was always open to new ideas and directions. His heart remained young, and he was at all times ready to help those whose work he admired or who, he felt, needed the various forms of help that he could give. He gave his help quietly – unobtrusively, and for the right reasons.

He died so far away.[12] I and other of his friends are arranging that a memorial service be held for him, probably in about three weeks' time. We are also arranging that an exhibition of his collection be held at the Institute of Contemporary Arts for which he did so much. This collection alone shows the breadth of understanding and the qualities of perception of a man who was to me, as to so many others, a deeply loved friend.

The Times 19 February 1959

There are, perhaps, two main types of art collection. There is the collection which is done for a purpose, and the collection that grows, as it were naturally, that is in fact a part of the collector's life. Peter Gregory's was emphatically of the second sort.

I first met him in 1923, in Bradford his home city, at the house of Charles Rutherston. Rutherston was my first patron. My relationship with Peter was different. Indeed it must have been nearly ten years before he bought any work of mine, for in the first years of our acquaintanceship – an acquaintanceship that grew slowly into what was to be the closest friendship of my life – he was only slightly interested in what is loosely called 'modern' art. As director of Lund Humphries,[13] the printers, he had as artistic adviser McKnight Kauffer. Before that, and in the twenties his taste ran to painting and sculpture which had already received the approval of distinguished critics. But even in those distant days he was a man who showed interest and curiosity. He chose as his friends painters and writers who were often unaccepted or even unknown. And slowly, gradually he acquired an appreciation of original talent that is seldom to be encountered in Yorkshire businessmen.

And this, I think, is the essence of Peter Gregory's collection. It grew, as his understanding of the arts grew. He was never 'fashionable'; he bought

[12] Gregory died in West Africa.
[13] Lund Humphries published the six-volume catalogue of Moore's complete sculpture, and is currently, in association with the Henry Moore Foundation, publishing the catalogue of the complete drawings, also in six volumes.

where he chose. The reasons for his choice were often as much in the artist as in the work of art. If he felt that a young, unknown painter or sculptor was sincere, serious and talented, he would buy – as much to help the young artist as to add to his collection. That will explain why there is a certain unevenness in the works here shown: and an examination of the dates at which many of these works passed into his hands will show that he frequently bought from artists who only later achieved fame and fortune. There is no need to say what an enormous help such generous perspicacity is to young artists. It is rare, at any time: it was almost non-existent a generation ago.

As the years went on, Peter Gregory's feeling for painting and sculpture became both more self-assured and bolder. Some collectors will go on buying the works of their contemporaries all their life. With him the development was in the opposite direction: the man who at thirty had admired accepted artists was, at seventy, buying pictures and sculpture which some would call extreme *avant-garde*. His mind and appreciation were, in fact, constantly growing more supple. He was not bound to any particular school or tradition of painting. This inevitably gives to this collection a certain heterogenous quality.

What is here shown, then, is part only of a collection that was made not for a purpose, but rather one that grew as a man grows. There are few men who have done so much, so modestly for young living artists. That was Peter Gregory's life, and this exhibition is therefore his artistic biography.

The Gregory Collection, Institute of Contemporary Arts, London 1959, n.p.

Julian and Juliette Huxley

The British biologist and humanist Julian Huxley (1887-1975) carried out important research in many fields of biology, including ecology, ethnology and genetics. He taught zoology at King's College, London (1925-35), and was Secretary of the London Zoological Society (1935-42). From 1946 to 1948 he served as the first director-general of Unesco. Juliette Huxley studied sculpture under John Skeaping.

Since the Unesco days, one has seen Julian and Juliette regularly, they'd quite often drive out here with little bits of bones or information. I mean they knew that I was very keen on bone structure, and Julian asked me to go and see on one occasion the skull of an elephant,[14] which was the most wonderful sculptural object. But this kind of thing, which was always an excitement, and I mean the postcards one gets from them in different parts of the world are always very exciting, and he's always full of new experiences to tell one about. Oh, it's just that one has been very fortunate in having such an alert, alive and terrifically interested person as a friend.

Sir Julian Huxley: A Portrait of the Scientist on the Occasion of his Eightieth Birthday, BBC 22 June 1967

[14] It was Juliette Huxley who said to her husband, 'I think I will give my elephant skull to Henry' (Berthoud 1987, p.347), although Moore often said that Julian Huxley had given him the skull. However, in his discussion of the Elephant Skull etchings Moore gives Juliette full credit for the gift, see p.296.

Henry Morris

Henry Morris (1889-1961) was the chief education officer for Cambridgeshire from 1922 to 1954. He advocated radical curriculum reforms and new social and architectural ideas in school design and function.

I first met Henry Morris, I think at Jack Pritchard's Lawn Road flats in Hampstead, when Gropius[15] because of Hitler left Germany, I suppose around 1933. Henry Morris later on asked Gropius to design Impington Village College, and it was then that Henry Morris approached me about a piece of sculpture for Impington. We talked and discussed it, and I think from that time dates my idea for the family as a subject for sculpture. Instead of just building a school, he was going to make a centre for the whole life of the surrounding villages, and we hit upon this idea of the family being the unit that we were aiming at. He at first fired me by the idea of the whole of Impington, and his idea that painting and sculpture … that there should be places for concerts, for music – that the whole of the arts should be integrated into life. This led, as I said, to thinking that a family group would be the right theme.

Henry Morris was a terrific fighter for carrying out his projects, and against all opposition, but he always hoped and went on hoping. When we met, he had a little maquette of a family group I had done for him on his mantelpiece, and whenever I visited him he'd say, 'We'll still carry that out, Henry. One day we'll do it.' As I say, eventually it was carried out, but by one of his disciples, not by him.

Farewell Night, Welcome Day, BBC 4 January 1963

Herbert Read

Herbert Read (1893-1968), the British art historian, critic and poet, championed the modern art movement in England. From 1922 to 1931 he worked in the ceramics department of the Victoria and Albert Museum, where he met Moore in about 1929. During the 1930s he lived close to Moore, Hepworth and Nicholson, whom he described as forming 'a nest of gentle artists'. In 1934 he wrote the first monograph on Moore, and in 1965 the more comprehensive Henry Moore: A Study of his Life and Work. *Read was editor of* Unit One *(1934), and in 1936 he helped to organise the* International Surrealist Exhibition *in London.*

I've known Herbert Read intimately for forty years. He was one of my oldest and very dearest friends. His death is a great sadness to me personally and a great loss to the world of literature and the world of art, not only in England but in countries all over the world where his books are read and his gentle influence felt. His work helped to change the whole situation for art in this country. For example his book *Education Through Art* [1943] altered the whole balance of our educational system and showed younger people

---

[15] See p.273.

how important art should be in our lives. Indirectly it certainly helped to produce the large number of gifted artists who have made England count in the international scene. But quite apart from the effect of his books, he gave his time unstintedly, both at an official level and to individual artists in whom he saw promise. At a time when English art life was beset by provincial attitudes and a narrow small mindedness, he consistently promoted a philosophical world view. Yet as a fellow Yorkshireman I never failed to find in his character, and in his actions, the authentic ring of our native county. Herbert Read had a great impact on the world of art, but I believe that his most lasting achievement will be found to lie in his own creative writing, in his *Collected Poems* [1926 and 1946], in his novel *The Green Child* [1935] and in the account of his childhood in Yorkshire, which is called *The Innocent Eye* [1933]; these words will live, but on this very day of his death, what I feel most strongly is that I have lost a wonderful friend and beautiful human being.

Malahat Review, Victoria, BC January 1969, p.31;
from a BBC broadcast of 12 June 1968[16]

31 Herbert Read (left) with Moore and André Lhote at the British Council Gallery, Champs Elysées, Paris, 1945

[16] The tribute was broadcast on the day of Read's death.

I have never met anyone who was more loyal to the things and the people that he believed in, or more generous with his time, or more self-sacrificing in the way that he would put aside his own concerns to help others.

I remember that just after he had his first operation he read an article in which Shelley was attacked as a poor poet and a bad man. Herbert got off a terrific letter in reply, and when it was published and I congratulated him he said 'Yes, I wrote that with four radium needles in my tongue.' In those conditions I should only have been concerned with myself, and here was Herbert provoked into writing by his love for what he believed in.

In a more general way I think that his 'Education Through Art' was one of the really influential books. It changed the whole art-situation in this country – and in other countries, too – by insisting on the part that art should play in education, and particularly in elementary and primary school. In his and my youth, 'art' in schools meant half an hour on Friday afternoon. But 'Education Through Art' helped to change all that, and I believe that if we have an exceptionally large number of gifted young artists today it is partly thanks to Herbert's having prepared the ground.

He had an almost German thoroughness in everything that he did, and he was aware of what was being written and done in other countries at a time when many people in the English art-world were narrow-minded and provincial. He kept up with his English friends – with T.S. Eliot, for instance, whom he had been seeing every other week since Imagist days – but he also kept up with a wide international circle. He was not at all gushing or effusive – in fact he was uncommonly silent – but when he and I were at some party abroad, as we often were, I would look round the room and find him in a corner with people who had got on to his quiet sociability and recognised him as a really remarkable man.

In the 1930s he was invaluable to us all in the way that he could see both sides of any situation and act as a link between all the different things that were going on. I think that fundamentally he was a romantic, and nearer to poetic or surrealist painting than to abstraction or constructivism, but he never wrote from prejudice of any kind. In politics he was an anarchist, but the gentlest anarchist one will ever know and the best explanation of what the anarchist philosophy really is, as against the popular idea of it. If anyone wanted to prove that an anarchist was not a bomb-throwing destroyer, Herbert was the man to do it.

He was an artist himself, in his poems and in 'The Green Child' and the autobiographical fragment called 'The Innocent Eye', and he knew what artists were all about. I remember in 'Art Now' [1933] a quotation he'd taken from Lenin, about how artists were a special sort of person and easily damaged and that the State should leave them alone. The Russians haven't lived up to it, but that was how Herbert thought it should be.

He got through a fantastic amount of work, as a critic and historian, as a publisher, and as a selfless committee-man, but the part of him that will live for ever is his own creative writing. He loved Yorkshire, and the moors, and the beautiful house he bought towards the end of his life, and he was always a Yorkshireman in his speech. He was proud of the connection but, more than that, he just loved it and I couldn't imagine him going abroad and living there for any reason whatsoever. This was one of the things, but only one of them, that made him a wonderful friend and a beautiful human being.

The Sunday Times 16 June 1968

William Rothenstein

The British painter, draughtsman, printmaker and teacher William Rothenstein (1872-1945) studied at the Slade School, London, and at the Académie Julian in Paris, where he became a close friend of Whistler and was encouraged by Degas. He was best known for his portraits of the famous, although in later life he became more renowned as a teacher than as a painter. Rothenstein was Principal of the Royal College of Art from 1920 to 1935.

I was fortunate in arriving at the Royal College of Art the same time that Will Rothenstein (late Sir William Rothenstein) became the new principal, September 1921.[17] The college was pretty much in the doldrums. It had become a place to train teachers, to train teachers, to train teachers and so on – something eating its own tail, having no real contacts with the outside world, or with the real world of painting and sculpture.

Rothenstein, who believed that teaching art should not be a career in itself, shook up the college in many ways and gradually changed many of the old staff. He had lived in Paris for some years – he knew personally the French impressionist painters including Degas. He knew most of the writers of his time. Max Beerbohm was his intimate friend. He brought this air of a wider more international outlook into the college. There is no doubt that I gained much through Rothenstein being principal of the college.

The Times 2 November 1967

The further my Royal College of Art days recede, the more I realise that William Rothenstein was wonderfully good to me – and the more surprised I am that he should have troubled to help, and believe in, the raw Yorkshire student who came to the Royal College of Art, from Leeds.

And more and more I appreciate that Will Rothenstein was a great idealist and a unique man.

Sir William Rothenstein 1872-1945: A Centenary Exhibition,
Bradford City Art Gallery and Museums, Bradford 1972

Curt Valentin

Curt Valentin (1902-54) was born in Germany and settled in the United States in 1936. The following year he opened the Buchholz Gallery in New York, which in 1951 was re-named Curt Valentin Gallery. He played an important role in introducing twentieth-century German artists to the American public, most notably Beckmann, Feininger and

[17] See p.47.

Kirchner. He was passionate about modern sculpture, and showed the work of Rodin, Arp, Lipchitz and Moore.

I first got a letter from Curt Valentin in 1942 from America asking if I would have an exhibition of drawings with him.[18] His name was then unknown to me, but the letter was a very nice one, and unlike my usual practice I answered the same day, accepting. By the next morning's post I got another letter from New York, this time from an art dealer, well known to me, also asking me to have an exhibition. If both letters had come the same day, or if I had not for once answered promptly, I should no doubt have accepted the offer of the well known dealer. I have been continually thankful for my luck ever since.

Curt Valentin has been my sole agent in America since that time. But it was not until I came to New York for my exhibition at The Museum of Modern Art in December, 1946, that I got to know him in person. It is from then that I began to count him as my friend as well as my dealer. I spent a month in New York, he looked after me as if I was a near relative. Every morning at 8.30 a.m. he telephoned my hotel to know my programme, my problems, and in what way he might help throughout the day. I marvelled that such a busy man could show so much thoughtfulness. Since then our friendship has yearly grown stronger.

32 Moore with Curt Valentin in the Top Studio, Perry Green, *c*.1950

In addition to our twelve years of correspondence I saw him at least twice every year, in the summer and again in December. For the last six years he spent every Christmas day here at Much Hadham with me and my family.

His death has been a terrible shock to me.

[18] The exhibition *Henry Moore: 40 Watercolors & Drawings* was held at Buchholz Gallery Curt Valentin, 32 East 57th Street, New York 11-29 May 1943.

As a dealer he will not be easily replaced, for no one will be both such a good business dealer and at the same time have such ideals and taste in art. Certainly there will be no dealer with a more burning love for sculpture. All other art dealers I know have twenty exhibitions of painting to every one exhibition of sculpture … He will be a great loss to the cause of contemporary sculpture.

He treated his Gallery as an artist should his work. He kept as true as he could to his ideals and made no compromise for the sake of financial success. He sold only the work of artists he believed in. This helped to make him unique as a dealer and to give his opinion such authority.

He kept to only a few artists and these he called his 'boys'. They were his family and he looked after them and felt towards them like a father. I have had personal proof any number of times, that no trouble was too great for him to take on their behalf.

To try to work out why one loved him so much is not easy. He was naturally shy, and never demonstrative. Walking by his side he would, on rare occasions, rest his hand on one's shoulder – only for a brief moment – but to me it expressed a deep warmth and affection.

I begin to realise all the more now that he is dead how much he meant to me. How much, all the time, one unconsciously counted on his steadfast support, on him being there, tirelessly working for the cause of the painters and sculptors he believed in.

I loved him very deeply and shall miss him terribly.

Letter to Jane Wade,[19] 13 September 1954; quoted in *Artist and Maecenas: A Tribute to Curt Valentin*, Marlborough-Gerson Gallery, New York 1963, p.14

Anton Zwemmer

Anton Zwemmer (1892-1979), bookseller, publisher and art dealer, was born in Holland and settled in London in 1914. In 1922 he opened Zwemmer's bookshop in Charing Cross Road, which played an important role in spreading awareness of modern art in England between the world wars. The Zwemmer Gallery, located in Lichfield Street adjacent to the bookshop, opened in 1929. Important exhibitions there in the 1930s included Dali's first one-man show in Britain (1934), the final exhibition of the Seven and Five Society (1935) and Henry Moore Drawings *(1935), the first show devoted entirely to Moore's drawings.*

I discovered Zwemmer's bookshop in October 1921, in my first term at the Royal College of Art. I was a provincial student, raw from Yorkshire. That first year in London was the most tremendous exhilaration for me. No doubt the British Museum contributed most of all to my great excitement and education – but the art books I found in Zwemmers had a great share too.

Charing Cross Road is between the British Museum and the National Gallery, and so it was easy to combine weekly visits with a 'call-in' at

[19] Curt Valentin's assistant.

Zwemmers. These calls would sometimes, quite shamelessly, last an hour. Having only my scholarship grant I couldn't afford to buy a book unless I was sure it was one I would want to consult continuously – but looking at a coveted book week after week it often became unnecessary to buy it, so most times I would walk out with no purchase. But nobody bothered.

As the years went by I made a friend of Mr Zwemmer himself – so much so that in 1934 he published the first small monograph on my work.[20]

Then came the more intimate visits to the bookshop, when I would be invited to his upstairs office, and be given the surprise of seeing the latest Picassos, Rouaults, or Braques which he'd have bought in Paris a few days previously. And I vividly remember him at a party given by Peter Gregory of Lund Humphries when he was the gayest of guests.

Later came the opening of the Zwemmer Gallery [1929]. In those days the dealers' galleries in London where a young artist could show his work were very few, nowadays they seem numberless, and increase every day. But at that time a new gallery was a great event. I was very happy to be given an exhibition of my drawings there in 1936 [1935].

There are a few individuals in every age and country, whose vision and vitality, applied in a particular sphere have immense influence. I could mention eight or nine such individuals (apart from artists themselves) whose efforts during my lifetime have helped to change the whole climate of the English art world. Some of these I am very happy to count as my close friends, and one of them is Anton Zwemmer, whose 70th birthday we now celebrate.

I would like to thank him deeply for all he has done, and to wish him a very happy birthday.

Anton Zwemmer: Tributes from Some of his Friends on the Occasion of his 70th birthday, privately printed (Percy Lund, Humphries), London and Bradford 1962, pp.19-21

---

[20] Herbert Read, *Henry Moore, Sculptor: An Appreciation by Herbert Read*, A. Zwemmer, London 1934.

33 Toltec-Maya Chacmool figure AD900-1000, limestone,
length 148cm (58¼in). Museo Nacional de Antropología, Mexico City

CHAPTER THREE

ART AND ARTISTS

Ancient, Medieval and Primitive Art

Pre-Columbian Sculpture

For the Mexicans, stone was almost their bread and butter.

In conversation with Huw Wheldon, *c*.1983

Mexican Sculpture[1]

Toltec sculpture is the connecting link between Mayan (which is mostly in relief & highly decorative) & Aztec sculpture. Toltec is rather florid & conventionalised. Aztec sculpture became more & more a style of its own & very distinct from Mayan. It reflects the character of the Aztecs in its vigorous simplicity, power, almost fierceness. I prefer Mexican to Mayan sculpture. Mexican stone sculptures have largeness of scale & a grim, sublime, austerity, a real stoniness. They were true sculptors in sympathy with their material & their sculpture has some of the character of mountains, of boulders, rocks & sea worn pebbles.

Unpublished notes *c*.1925-26, HMF archive

Chacmool

The last [Chacmool] is about as good a piece of sculpture as I know.[2]

Ibid.

First of all, I didn't see the real one. I saw a small reproduction, probably only two inches big, in an 'Orbis Pictus' series,[3] edited by a German art writer or critic or editor, and these reproductions were in Zwemmer's bookshop. I can see them now. They were black. There was one on Negro sculp-

---

[1] This extract is the last paragraph of four pages of notes on 'Mexican Sculpture', written on Royal College of Art headed notepaper. The essay is followed by a note to an unidentified student or colleague about several books on Mexican sculpture which Moore plans to send, one of which ('No III Mexico') is clearly Ernst Fuhrmann, *Mexico III*, Folkwang-Verlag, Hagen and Darmstadt 1922. Moore's copy of this book is inscribed 'Henry Spencer Moore 1923'.

[2] This comment, which appears at the end of four pages of notes on 'Negro Sculpture' (see extract below), refers to plate 45 in Walter Lehmann, *Altmexikanische Kunstgeschichte*, Verlag Ernst Wasmuth, Berlin 1922, which is an illustration of the Chacmool carving in the Museo Nacional de Antropología, Mexico City. This is the first written reference to the Chacmool, which was, Moore told me, 'undoubtedly the one sculpture which most influenced my early work'.

[3] This refers to Lehmann's book in note 2 above.

ture, one on Mexican sculpture, one on Egyptian sculpture, and so on. And all these I knew. And in one of them was this small reproduction of the Chac Mool. It was the pose that struck me – this idea of a figure being on its back and turned upwards to the sky instead of lying on its side, which is a different sort of idea from the Renaissance or Greek reclining figure, which is usually on its side. And this gave me all sorts of chances of making variations on that.

Carroll 1973, p.38

Why did the Chacmool have such a tremendous impact when you first saw it?

Its stillness and alertness, a sense of readiness – and the whole presence of it, and the legs coming down like columns.

Wilkinson 1977, p.80

African Sculpture

Negro Sculpture[4]

In sculpture it [their religion] produced the fetishes & love-charms – the idols which were the images of chiefs & gods, of good & evil spirits; & the carvings of women, long breasted, heavy legged, of cylindrical form, symbolic of fertility & production. These female figures & the phallic male figures are the intense expression of thousands of years of earthy prostration before sex. Their idols & fetishes, sharp, pointed, conical, are the intense expression of deep-seated-dread of the unknown.

The Negroes (until spoiled by contact with European ideas)* undoubtedly possessed high sculptural genius. Their carvings show them to have had a wonderfully fertile invention of abstract forms. […] But their unique claim for admiration is their power to produce form completely in the round. Most other periods of sculpture only rarely produced works completely in the round, & reached that stage through a relief conception being taken round to the other side & freed from its background. – Negro sculpture is completely in the round, fully-conceived air-surrounded form. –

Stone was difficult to obtain but wood was plentiful, therefore negro sculpture is mostly wood carving. This no doubt made it easier for them to produce form completely in the round; wood being of a stringy fibrous construction the negro sculptor was able when he wished to free arms, in places well from the body, to have a space between the legs to have long necks, etc. without weakening his figure to breaking point –

(Sculpture in stone can be completely in the round without carving it into free arms, thin necks supporting huge heads etc – but the negroes'

---

[4] This extract includes almost all of the four pages of notes on 'Negro Sculpture'. At the end of the essay, Moore wrote to an unidentified student or colleague: 'The illustrations in the Negro book which are most satisfying to me are on pages 6, 13, 14 &15, 18, 22 & 23, 32 & 33, 36 & 37, 54 & 55, 62, 66 & 67, 71, 76 (this is a very good one) 94 & 96'. He is almost certainly referring to Carl Einstein, *Negerplastik*, Kurt Wolff Verlag, München 1920.

wood sculptures can teach us their lesson & make us more conscious when a stone sculpture fails in full form realisation.)

*They now carve men in top hats, silly, formless works – their tradition has gone; except in some very few out-of-the way untouched tribes.

Unpublished notes *c.*1925-26, HMF archive

This Exhibition presents the first comprehensive survey of primitive African Sculpture in this country.

Since artists such as Picasso, Matisse, Modigliani, Derain and Epstein first began to get excited about it thirty years ago, the interest in Negro sculpture has steadily increased. Many exhibitions have been held on the Continent, and museums have begun to realise the aesthetic value of their primitive sculpture collections, of which the finest is to be seen at the British Museum.

Negro Sculpture played a great part in the birth of cubism, and has had a powerful influence on all contemporary painting and sculpture. It has helped the artist to realise the intrinsic emotional significance of shapes as distinct from their representational values, and has freed him to recognise again the importance of the material in which he works.

Practically all African sculpture is carved in wood. The main qualities of wood are its cylindrical form and upward growth, and these have their influence on the carvings. Like the growing tree of which they had been part, the forms are upward and vertical, and the heavy, bent legs are as their roots, and connect them with the earth.

The distinguishing quality of most primitive art is the intense vitality which it possesses, because it has been made by a people in close touch with life, who felt simply and strongly, and whose art was a means of expressing vitally important beliefs, hopes and fears. Negro sculpture is essentially religious and cannot be detached from the tribal gods, priests and ancient rituals. When civilisation destroyed these things, it also destroyed their Art.

These carvings have a serious and pathetic power – a bigness and monumental simplicity born of the racial patience in bearing life with all its terror and mystery.

The works are dominated by the two main preoccupations of the negro's life, sex and religion, which are often interwoven, but which are to be seen separately in the love charms and the fetishes.

Foreword to *Primitive African Sculpture*,[5]
The Lefevre Galleries, London 1933

The skill as carving is immense it is not that they [African sculptors] were unable to imitate natural proportions & shapes – but that they did not try to – it never entered their heads to do it [...]

[5] The foreword is unsigned. It was Moore's inscription 'Notes on Negro Sculpture for catalogue of Lefevre Gallery Negro Sculpture Exhibition', in a notebook in the HMF archive, which led to his identification as the author.

9/10ths or more of the worlds sculpture has not had meticulous copying of nature as its main aim. –

But as always, it was the artist who was the first to see in them a new thing – a new plastic conception – an artistic worth – a value as art – their importance as art.

Unpublished notes for the foreword to *Primitive African Sculpture* 1933

Mesopotamian Art[6]

In the last thirty years or so many factors have worked together to call for a review and a revaluation of past periods of art. Easier means of communication and travel, more scientific and systematic conduction of excavations, the development in photographic reproduction, better arrangement and showing of collections in museums, the breakdown of the complete domination of later decadent Greek art as the only standard of excellence – the interplay of such factors as these, together with the work of the important artists of the last thirty or forty years, in their researches and experiments, has enlarged the field of knowledge, interest and appreciation of the world's past art.

M. Christian Zervos has now produced two of his series of volumes devoted to the great periods of art. His first volume, *L'Art en Grèce*, appeared a few months ago; the second volume, *L'Art de la Mésopotamie*, has just appeared.[7] Both set a new standard for books on art, in the selection and quality of the works reproduced and in the size and number (close upon 300) of superb photographs of sculpture.

The present volume covers the period of Mesopotamian art from earliest times up to the time when the Sumerian race was absorbed by the Semites, that is up to the beginning of the Babylonian dynasties. Most scholars and critics writing about Mesopotamian art have either neglected the sculpture of the earlier and greater Sumerian period or else have lumped it together with the later Babylonian and Assyrian work, which (except perhaps for a few isolated pieces) is much inferior. The Sumerian period, as M. Zervos says, cannot be interpreted through the decadent art of the Babylonians and Assyrians, with their materialist and militarist society, their love of the sumptuous and the colossal, their luxurious palaces and temples.

The Sumerians were an agricultural and pastoral people, and they had their poets and perhaps scholars – astronomers and learned men. Their art dates from the birth of civilisation, so that most of the work reproduced in *L'Art de la Mésopotamie* was made between 5,000 and 4,000 years ago. But it is not necessary to know their history in order to appreciate and respond to these works of art. We need to look at them as sculpture, for once a good piece of sculpture has been produced, even if it was made like the palaeo-

---

[6] For a later statement on Mesopotamian art, see p.109.
[7] Christian Zervos, *L'Art en Grèce*, Editions Cahiers d'Art, Paris 1934, and *L'Art de la Mésopotamie*, Editions Cahiers d'Art, Paris 1935.

lithic 'Venuses' 20,000 years ago, it is real and a part of life, here and now, to those sensitive and open enough to feel and perceive it.

For me, Sumerian sculpture ranks with Early Greek, Etruscan, Ancient Mexican, Fourth and Twelfth Dynasty Egyptian, and Romanesque and Early Gothic sculpture, as the great sculpture of the world. It shows a richness of feeling for life and its wonder and mystery, welded to direct plastic statement born of a real creative urge. It has a bigness and simplicity with no decorative trimmings (which are the sign of decadence, of flagging inspiration). But for me its greatest achievement is found in the free-standing pieces – sculpture in the round, which is fullest sculptural expression – and these have tremendous power and yet sensitiveness. The sculpture of most early periods, even when carved from a block and not from a slab, is not fully realised form, it is relief carving on the surface of the block; but these Sumerian figures have full three-dimensional existence.

And in Sumerian art (as perhaps in all the greatest sculpture and painting) along with the abstract value of form and design, inseparable from it, is a deep human element. See the alabaster figure of a woman which is in the British Museum and reproduced here [see fig.40], with her tiny hands clasped in front of her. It is as though the head and the hands were the two equal focal points of the figure – one cannot look at the head without being conscious also of the held hands. But in almost all Sumerian work the hands have a sensitiveness and significance; even in the very earliest terracotta figures, where each hand seems no more than four scratches, there is a wealth of meaning there.

Except for the impressions from Sumerian seals which are all placed at the end, and which are remarkable for their vitality and flicker of life, the reproductions in this book are arranged chronologically, and so one can observe the changes that occur as the period proceeds. From the beginning to the end there is astonishing virility and power. Perhaps the Gudea period (about 2400 B.C.) can be called the peak of Sumerian art. Soon after then it seems to fall quickly, and from bare sculptural statement moves towards decorative and linear stylisation. In many of the earliest works (around 3000 B.C.) there is a richness, a tenderness and fullness. The Gudea period (which 'A Governor of Lagash' beautifully represents) is baldly powerful with a tense, held-in tightness, of conserved energy.

And throughout the whole period, the Sumerian artist shows understanding of the possibilities and limitations of whatever material he uses. Clay, being soft, is modelled, and is worked quickly, and allows a freedom of treatment. So that the terracottas have spontaneity and ease. Stone by its resistance gives to the carvings more hardness, power and precise exactness. And there is a difference between the free-standing sculpture and the reliefs. Their sculpture in the round is still and static, no physical movement or action is attempted, for one of the essential facts about a block of stone is its weight and immovability. But in their reliefs we find actual movement and action portrayed – for work in relief is akin to drawing, and it is an easy attribute of line to flow and move.

34 *Gudea, Ruler of the City State of Lagash*, Neo-Sumerian *c.*2125-2025BC, black diorite, height 75cm (29in). Copyright © The British Museum, London

The photographs in *L'Art de la Mésopotamie* are by M. Horacio Coppola, and they cannot be overpraised. As a substitute or as an introduction to the actual sculptures good photographs are very useful. In illustrated books on sculpture the photographs should be the best possible and well reproduced, or the book loses half its value. Most people, I think, respond more easily and quickly to a flat image than to a solid object (this may partly explain why sculpture seems to be a more difficult art to appreciate than painting). I have often noticed that people, after seeing a good photograph of a piece of sculpture which until then they had more or less ignored, find their interest in the original greatly increased.

The real appreciation of sculpture comes from seeing and comprehending it in its full three-dimensional volume, but if a photograph leads people to see the original, then it has been of value.

Some of the photographs in M. Zervos' book are many times larger than the original works. To see a piece one knows to be only 2 or 3 inches high, looking several times its real size comes as a great surprise – but I think it is legitimate to use any means which help to reveal the qualities of the work. A further justification for these enlarged photographs is that they may draw attention to very fine small pieces which, exhibited in a crowded collection, can easily be overlooked. Another point raised by these small figures seen suddenly enlarged four or five times, is the importance of size in sculpture. These small figures, seen so much bigger, take on an extra importance and impressiveness, and are a proof that size itself has an emotional value. But size alone should not in sculpture become of main importance. There is a limit at which the control of the unity of the parts to the whole becomes physically too difficult – and when the love of size becomes a love of the colossal it results in insensitiveness and vulgarity.

About one-third of the reproductions in M. Zervos' book are of works in the British Museum, and help us to realise what a wonderful selection of the world's sculpture we have there. It is only recently that the Mesopotamian works have been collected in one room and shown so that they can now be well seen. A central position has been given to the very fine upper portion of the figure already mentioned, 'A Governor of Lagash', acquired by the Museum two or three years ago. But the effect of this figure has been ruined by the way it has been abominably mounted on a wooden stand which is a kind of reconstruction of the remainder of the figure.

The Listener 5 June 1935, pp.944-6

Primitive Art

The term 'Primitive Art' is generally used to include the products of a great variety of races and periods in history, many different social and religious systems. In its widest sense it seems to cover most of those cultures which are outside European and the great Oriental civilisations. This is the sense in which I shall use it here, though I do not much like the application of the word 'primitive' to art, since, through its associations, it suggests to many people an idea of crudeness and incompetence, ignorant gropings rather than finished achievements. Primitive art means far more than that; it makes a straightforward statement, its primary concern is with the elemental, and its simplicity comes from direct and strong feeling, which is a very different thing from that fashionable simplicity-for-its-own-sake which is emptiness. Like beauty, true simplicity is an unselfconscious virtue; it comes by the way and can never be an end in itself.

The most striking quality common to all primitive art is its intense vitality. It is something made by people with a direct and immediate response to life. Sculpture and painting for them was not an activity of calculation or academism, but a channel for expressing powerful beliefs, hopes, and fears. It is art before it got smothered in trimmings and surface decorations, before inspiration had flagged into technical tricks and intellectual conceits. But apart from its own enduring value, a knowledge of it conditions a fuller and truer appreciation of the later developments of the so-called great periods, and shows art to be a universal continuous activity, with no separation between past and present.

All art has its roots in the 'primitive', or else it becomes decadent, which explains why the 'great' periods, Pericles' Greece and the Renaissance for example, flower and follow quickly on primitive periods, and then slowly fade out. The fundamental sculptural principles of the Archaic Greeks were near enough to Phidias' day to carry through into his carvings a true quality, although his conscious aim was so naturalistic; and the tradition of early Italian art was sufficiently in the blood of Masaccio for him to strive for realism and yet retain a primitive grandeur and simplicity. The steadily growing appreciation of primitive art among artists and the public today is therefore a very hopeful and important sign.

Excepting some collections of primitive art in France, Italy and Spain, my own knowledge of it has come entirely from continual visits to the British Museum during the past twenty years. Now that the Museum has been closed, one realises all the more clearly what one has temporarily lost – the richness and comprehensiveness of its collection of past art, particularly of primitive sculpture, and perhaps by taking a memory-journey through a few of the Museum's galleries I can explain what I believe to be the great significance of primitive periods.

At first my visits were mainly and naturally to the Egyptian galleries, for the monumental impressiveness of Egyptian sculpture was nearest to the familiar Greek and Renaissance ideals one had been born to. After a time, however, the appeal of these galleries lessened; excepting the earlier dynasties. I felt that much of Egyptian sculpture was too stylised and hieratic, with a tendency in its later periods to academic obviousness and a rather stupid love of the colossal.

The galleries running alongside the Egyptian contained the Assyrian reliefs – journalistic commentaries and records of royal lion hunts and battles, but beyond was the Archaic Greek room with its lifesize female figures, seated in easy, still naturalness, grand and full like Handel's music; and then

35 Moore at the British Museum in 1981 admiring *A Court Official and his Wife*, Egyptian, late eighteenth dynasty *c.*1340BC

near them, downstairs in the badly lit basement, were the magnificent Etruscan Sarcophagus figures – which, when the Museum reopens, should certainly be better shown.

At the end of the upstairs Egyptian galleries were the Sumerian sculptures, some with a contained bull-like grandeur and held-in energy, very different from the liveliness of much of the early Greek and Etruscan art in the terracotta and vase rooms. In the prehistoric and Stone Age room an iron staircase led to gallery wall-cases where there were originals and casts of Paleolithic sculptures made 20,000 years ago – a lovely tender carving of a girl's head, no bigger than one's thumbnail, and beside it female figures of very human but not copyist realism with a full richness of form, in great contrast with the more symbolic two-dimensional and inventive designs of Neolithic art.

And eventually to the Ethnographical room, which contained an inexhaustible wealth and variety of sculptural achievement (Negro, Oceanic Islands, and North and South America), but overcrowded and jumbled together like junk in a marine stores, so that after hundreds of visits I would still find carvings not discovered there before. Negro art formed one of the largest sections of the room. Except for the Benin bronzes it was mostly woodcarving. One of the first principles of art so clearly seen in primitive work is truth to material; the artist shows an instinctive understanding of his material, its right use and possibilities. Wood has a stringy fibrous consistency and can be carved into thin forms without breaking, and the Negro sculptor was able to free arms from the body, to have a space between the legs, and to give his figures long necks when he wished. This completer realisation of the component parts of the figure gives to Negro carving a more three-dimensional quality than many primitive periods where stone is the main material used. For the Negro, as for other primitive peoples, sex and religion were the two main interacting springs of life. Much Negro carving, like modern Negro spirituals but without their sentimentality, has pathos, a static patience and resignation to unknown mysterious powers; it is religious and, in movement, upward and vertical like the tree it was made from, but in its heavy bent legs is rooted in the earth.

Of works from the Americas, Mexican art was exceptionally well represented in the Museum. Mexican sculpture, as soon as I found it, seemed to me true and right, perhaps because I at once hit on similarities in it with some eleventh-century carvings I had seen as a boy on Yorkshire churches.[8] Its 'stoniness', by which I mean its truth to material, its tremendous power without loss of sensitiveness, its astonishing variety and fertility of form-invention and its approach to a full three-dimensional conception of form, make it unsurpassed in my opinion by any other period of stone sculpture.

The many islands of the Oceanic groups all produced their schools of sculpture with big differences in form-vision. New Guinea carvings,

---

[8] Moore is almost certainly referring to the carved corbels, thought to be mid-fourteenth century, in St Oswald's Church, Methley, see p.36, note 5.

with drawn out spider-like extensions and bird-beak elongations, made a direct contrast with the featureless heads and plain surfaces of the Nuknor [Kukuoro] carvings; or the stolid stone figures of the Marquesas Islands against the emasculated ribbed figures of Easter Island. Comparing Oceanic art generally with Negro art, it has a livelier, thin flicker, but much of it is more two-dimensional and concerned with pattern making. Yet the carvings of New Ireland have, besides their vicious kind of vitality, a unique spatial sense, a bird-in-a-cage form.

But underlying these individual characteristics, these featural peculiarities in the primitive schools, a common world-language of form is apparent in them all; through the working of instinctive sculptural sensibility, the same shapes and form relationships are used to express similar ideas at widely different places and periods in history, so that the same form-vision may be seen in a Negro and a Viking carving, a Cycladic stone figure and a Nuknor wooden statuette. And on further familiarity with the British Museum's whole collection it eventually became clear that the realistic ideal of physical beauty in art which sprang from fifth-century Greece was only a digression from the main world tradition of sculpture, whilst, for instance, our own equally European Romanesque and Early Gothic are in the main line.

Primitive art is a mine of information for the historian and the anthropologist, but to understand and appreciate it, it is more important to look at it than to learn the history of primitive peoples, their religions and social customs. Some such knowledge may be useful and help us to look more sympathetically, and the interesting tit-bits of information on the labels attached to the carvings in the Museum can serve a useful purpose by giving the mind a needful rest from the concentration of intense looking. But all that is really needed is response to the carvings themselves, which have a constant life of their own, independent of whenever and however they came to be made, and remain as full of sculptural meaning today to those open and sensitive enough to receive it as on the day they were finished.

But until the British Museum opens again books and photographs must be a substitute, so far as they can, for the works we are unable to see in the round; and the above reflections have been prompted by an excellent, solid little book called *Primitive Art* [1940], by L. Adam, which has just appeared, with thirty-six photogravure reproductions and numerous line drawings in the text. It is within everyone's reach in the sixpenny Pelican series, and if it receives the attention it deserves, it should bring a great many extra visitors to the British Museum when its Galleries reopen. Dr. Adam does not regard primitive art in the condescending way in which it used to be regarded, *i.e.*, as if the real aim of the artist had been naturalistic representation, and that though he hadn't yet learned how to do the job convincingly, he could be praised every now and then for making some pretty good shots at it. Even so, in spite of Dr. Adams' general sensibility to his subject, the very high praise he gives to the portrait heads from Ite may perhaps be regarded as an indication that this prejudice still lingers, and it is no doubt as a further con-

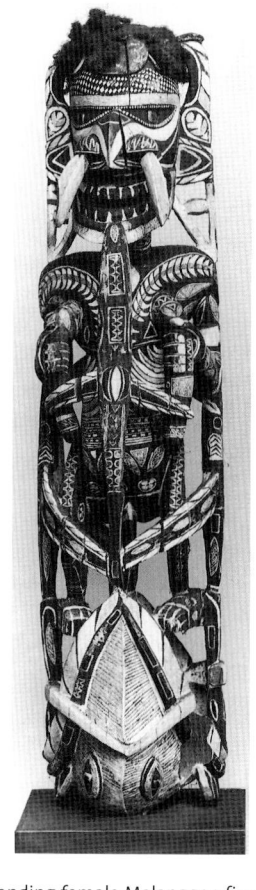

36 Standing female Malanggan figure, painted wood, height 106.7cm (42in), collected in New Ireland by H.H. Romilly in 1883 and presented to the British Museum in 1884 by the Duke of Bedford. Copyright © The British Museum, London

cession to it that the reproduction of one of these heads has been chosen for the cover of the book.

The Listener 24 April 1941, pp.598-9

Tribal Sculpture:
A Review of the Exhibition at the Imperial Institute[9]

Do you think that it is possible to distinguish among these exhibits the elements that are the contribution of original inspiration as opposed to the mechanical reproduction of traditional forms? How is one to tell whether to ascribe to a particular primitive sculpture the status of an original work of art or that of a competent copy comparable, say, to one of van Meegeren's copies of Vermeer?

Looking at these sculptures, for example those from the Chamba, Ashani and Okuni tribes of Northern Nigeria, I think that even where a traditional form is followed fairly closely, there are many subtle touches which a poor artist would have missed. All these pieces have been selected for their quality, and practically every one of them has the 'flicker' of originality. Of course, it is difficult often to say whether the artist merely recognised these touches and copied them or whether he thought of them himself – but the Chamba figure seems to me to have been conceived by an individual, and I should think that it has a special rhythm and set of proportions, and a unique expression in the head, for example, not to be found in any other Chamba figure.

How far do you feel that these sculptures show domination of the artist by his material?

I should say, on the contrary, that the material is dominated by the artist in almost every case. The soapstone figures from Sierra Leone have a quality of stoniness about them because the artists have avoided the more deeply carved and slender forms which are easily possible in wood, but they show a mastery of the possibilities of stone; they are not just incised lumps of stone – but have forms fully realised in the round. In most of the wood carvings the sculptor has imagined something which has no relation to the original form of the tree trunk. In the Bali elephant mask from the Cameroons the artist has imagined a shape – everything a child would re-member about an elephant – which could not possibly have been suggested to him by the block of wood from which he started.

The imagination of the artist has been equally free in the Okuni ante-lope mask with long slender horns, or in the complicated Akumaga mask from the Jukun, or the great ram head from Owo in which the neck and breastbone have been carved down to a deep, narrow, wedge-shaped form of astonishing power.

Do you think that the static, four-square qualities of most of these works are to be re-garded as restrictions inhibiting the artist's genius or rather as a useful discipline which

[9] The exhibition *Traditional Art from the Colonies*, sponsored by the Colonial Office, was held during the Festival of Britain in 1951. William Fagg, the distinguished scholar on African art and Honorary Editor of *Man*, interviewed Moore during a visit to the exhibition.

assists its expression? In fact, is 'primitive' art to be regarded as limited, when compared to 'civilised' art?

The only piece of primitive sculpture I can call to mind which represents actual physical movement is the Borneo dancing figure from the British Museum, in this exhibition, which I well remember from my earliest visits to the Museum. But I do not think that representation of movement is at all necessary to the finest sculpture, or that its absence is a crippling restriction upon the artist; there is so much else left for him to do. (In fact, most of the finest carved sculpture of the past, of all periods and styles, is static.)

As to the 'four-square' posture of most primitive figures, I think that this *is* a limitation on the artist. But even then there is a tendency to avoid exact symmetry: the Chamba figure has a definite twist in it, and the life-size figure of a woman from Bekom in the Cameroons has its folded hands placed to the left of the centre line of the body.

Is it possible from a study of the sculptures themselves to discern where the carver has transcended the religious or magical basis of the sculpture and produced what is, to all intents and purposes, art for art's sake?

I feel certain that this never happens in primitive art. A man must have something more than an intellectual interest in art before he can produce a work of art. All of these works seem to me to be based on much more than just aesthetic impulses. I do not think in fact that any real or deeply moving art can be purely for art's sake.

To what extent can you correlate high finish, smoothness of surface, with a particular kind of form? Or, to what extent is the high polish of some styles essential to their nature as works of art?

Some pieces, such as the warthog mask from the Nafana of the Gold Coast, must certainly have been conceived with a highly polished surface, and would look unfinished without it. But all these masks and figures show some finishing on at least the salient surfaces – even the masks of the Kalabari Ijo. Though the adze marks are still visible on many medium-sized pieces, they are usually softened by partial finishing. On big sculptures like the Urhobo village fetish rough adze marks are left, but they are in scale with the carving as a whole.

High polish brings out the special quality of some materials – but finish and high polish in sculpture is often a matter of the size of the work. If the work is small and the sculptor wants to show subtle shapes or small refinements of detail he must have 'finish'– but on a large piece definition of shape can be got without it.

Which sculpture would you select as showing the best use of the special qualities of wood?

The Chamba [Mumuye] figure seems to me one of the best from this point of view. The carver has managed to make it 'spatial' by the way in which he has made the arms free and yet enveloping the central form of the body. A rather similar effect can be seen in the large Owo ram head, with its great

37 Mumuye funerary ancestor figure, Northern Nigeria, wood, height 47.6cm (18¾in). Copyright © The British Museum, London

forward-curving horns framing the head and breastbone. But very many of the sculptures show a good use of the special qualities of their particular wood.

How can we counteract the impact of European aesthetic concepts on the tribal artists? How would you set out to convince a school of tribal artists of the value of their traditional style, as compared with the European concepts of photographic realism which threaten it? Is there any hope for the preservation of these primitive values?

I do not believe that it is any use to try to keep primitive art going or to shield the African artist from outside influences. All that we can do is to see that all the good tribal sculpture is preserved from destruction so that it can be put on show in wonderful exhibitions like this – here and in the colonies – to teach young artists what real vitality is. Nowadays artists have a greater opportunity than ever before of studying all the great traditions in the history of art, and working their way through them until they find their own style; at first, they may imitate Picasso, or primitive art, or the painters of the Renaissance, but eventually, if they have it in them, they will find their own way. So with the young African artists. What they have to learn from tribal art is not how to copy the traditional forms, but the confidence that comes from knowing that somewhere inside them there should be the vitality which enabled their fathers to produce these extraordinary and exciting forms.

Man, The Royal Anthropological Institute, London July 1951, pp.95-6

Cycladic Sculpture

Much Hadham, Herts.

I've found some pieces of mine which might not be completely irrelevant, if seen near the wall case you showed me, containing that beautiful selection of Cycladic pieces – I love & admire Cycladic sculpture. It has such great elemental simplicity (I'm sure the well-known Cycladic head in The Louvre influenced Brancusi, & was the parent of his sculpture, that simple oval egg-shaped form he called 'The Beginning of the World'). The Cycladic marble vases are remarkable inventions, seen just as sculpture in themselves – & the thinness, looked at from the side, of the 'standing' idol figures, adds to their incredible sensitivity.

The white two-form sculpture I call 'Moon Head' is one of several recent 'Knife-Edge' sculptures I've made – which have all come about through my interest in thin bone forms – for example the breast bones of birds – so light, so delicate & yet so strong – But I can also think that my 'Knife-Edge' sculptures may be unconsciously influenced by my liking for the sharp-edged Cycladic idols.

From a letter to Lord Eccles,[10] (?) June 1969; reproduced in
Henry Moore at the British Museum, British Museum Publications,
London 1981, p.13

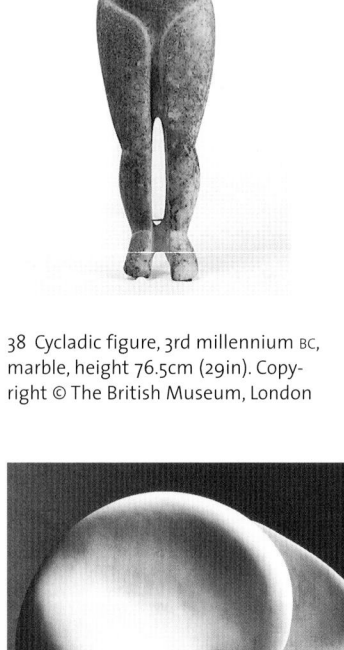

38 Cycladic figure, 3rd millennium BC, marble, height 76.5cm (29in). Copyright © The British Museum, London

39 *Moon Head* 1964 LH 522, porcelain, height 30cm (12in)

[10] In this letter to the chairman of the Trustees of the British Museum, Moore agreed to his 1964 porcelain *Moon Head* being exhibited with Cycladic sculptures in October 1969.

Mesopotamian Art

It is my profound conviction that the testimony of the past must not be ignored. A knowledge of our history can be of great use in our life; all human activity is conditioned by this past, without which man would have to start all over again from the beginning. We all owe something to our parents, as they do to their parents; this debt goes back to the beginning of man. Human history is of immense value through the light it sheds on our nature and character. The more we know about man's past responses to life, his customs, habits, efforts, achievements, and failures, the better off we are. Today we have at our disposal the most diverse technical means to gain a more profound knowledge of the world around us, as well as of the world of the past. Improved means of communication, greater possibility of travel, archaeological excavations carried out with the most advanced techniques, the development of photography – all facilitate the relationship between man and his world while opening up unlimited horizons. Certainly direct contact with nature and the monuments of the past can never be substituted by films or photos, but then neither can we see everything in a lifetime. Thus, films, books, and photos help us enormously to establish a relationship with works and countries which would otherwise be inaccessible.

I have never been to the Grand Canyon, for example, but through films and photographs I can get, all the same, a deep emotional impact from this marvel of nature. The same holds true for me over Mesopotamia, which I have never visited. My first contact with Mesopotamian art occurred when I saw the works exhibited in the British Museum. I was fascinated and moved by the monumentality of the tiny statuette of a Sumerian woman, in which the tiny head and tensely held hands seem to contrast with the large body. It is just this relationship of proportions (or disproportions, to be more exact), between parts and the whole, which produces the sense of monumentality.

When I discovered this small figure I was very excited, because at that time I was struggling to get this difference in size of the parts of the sculptural whole in my own work. For if a work is just as it is in nature, one part is not more important than another. But if, for example, the head is very large, then the expression is concentrated there; and if it is small, the body becomes more important in the meaning of the sculpture. (Michelangelo always reduced the heads of his pieces.) This realisation of a Sumerian woman taught me much. Certainly the tiny hands make the head important, but they also give a soft feminine quality to the piece: they are the spirit of the work.

The great architectural and monumental remains, as well as the small sculptures of Mesopotamian civilisation, all have the same emotional impact, the same force; I get a similar feeling of grandeur from large and small forms alike. In Mesopotamian art there is a unity of sculpture and architecture, a strong relationship between the two; both arts are fused. The great masses that man has sculptured or organised in architectural space cannot but strike all men in some way. I think that deep in all of us there still exists

40 *A Female Worshipper* from Lagash, southern Iraq, Sumerian, early dynastic period *c.*2900BC, brown limestone, height 22cm (8½in). Copyright © The British Museum, London

something primitive which is impressed by large monumental blocks of stone, as also by mountains. In fact, in ancient civilisations we find an almost religious reverence for large boulders of stone isolated in the desert or projecting out from the sea. An example of this is Stonehenge in England. Nobody knows for certain how or why it was built, and we do not understand its 'meaning', but its mysterious, monumental presence fascinates us.

This same sense of awe of the grandiose is to be found in Mesopotamian art. It reveals a richness of feeling for life, welded to a direct plastic statement born of a real creative urge. There is a bigness and simplicity about it, with no decorative trimmings. But for me its greatest achievements are its freestanding pieces – sculpture in the round. These pieces have tremendous power combined with great sensitivity. Much of the sculpture of ancient periods, even when carved from blocks and not from a slab, is not in fully realised form; often it is a relief carving on the surface of a block. But the Sumerian figures have a full three-dimensional existence. And in Sumerian art (as perhaps in all the greatest sculpture and painting), along with the abstract value of form and design, inseparable from it, there is a deep human element.

Architecture and sculpture both deal with the relationship of masses. In practice, architecture is not pure form expression; it also has a functional or utilitarian purpose, which limits it as an art of pure expression. And sculpture, more naturally than architecture, can use organic rhythms. Aesthetically, architecture is the abstract relationship of masses. If sculpture is limited to this, then in the field of scale and size, architecture has the advantage; but sculpture, not being tied to a functional and utilitarian purpose, can attempt more freely the exploration of the world of pure form. It seems to me that a perfect synthesis of sculpture and architecture is expressed in the picture of the corridors of Yazilikaja reproduced in this volume. In the procession of figures sculptured in the rock, the rhythm of men walking is wonderfully portrayed. I can imagine myself among these stones and sensing a marvellous natural life force. This is beautiful architecture, real stone architecture, where the material, the stone, has contributed to the form, so that it becomes sculpture – or rather, sculptured architecture. It also strongly expresses the importance and seriousness of ceremony and ritual. The Lion Gate at Boghaz Köy, in particular, gives me the monumental sense that large works in stone can give. It reminds me of Stonehenge: it has the same power.

I hope I have succeeded in at least partially transmitting my emotions and feelings upon seeing the Mesopotamian world, both directly at the British Museum and through the photographs in this fine volume. Above all, I want the reader to see in these great works the testimony of a distant past which belongs to all of us, since it is an integral part of human history.

Lucienne Laroche, *The Middle East*, foreword by Henry Moore,

Cassell, London 1974, pp.7-8

Romanesque Sculpture

Perhaps the single period in past art which I love most is the Romanesque – when sculpture and architecture had such complete unity and religious sincerity.

Of Romanesque art in England I think of Durham Cathedral, the crypt of Canterbury, also Chichester.

I first visited Chichester Cathedral as a young Yorkshire sculpture student in the early 1920's. It was a big surprise to come upon the two reliefs in the south quire aisle; THE RAISING OF LAZARUS and CHRIST ARRIVING AT THE HOUSE OF MARY AND MARTHA. I had not known of them even from photographs. I stood before them for a long time. They were just what I wanted to emulate in sculpture: the strength of directly carved form, of hard stone, rather than modelled flowing soft form.

A year or two later I got the same satisfaction and sustenance at Malmesbury when first seeing the tympanum and reliefs in the porch of the Abbey. For me the Chichester and Malmesbury sculptures are the two finest and most complete works of Romanesque art in England – and equal to the greatest French examples.

In the Chichester sculptures there is deep human feeling. I think the sense of suffering and tragedy is chiefly given through the heads. Look particularly at the head of Christ in the RAISING OF LAZARUS. The eyebrows and the eyes are sloped steeply downwards from the centre line of the face expressing intense grief.

And in the mourning heads of Mary and Martha there is the same tragic feeling. These two heads should be studied on their own, photographed life-size – or casts made of them – and examined as we do with close-up details of old master paintings so that we respond to their strong sculptural quality and deep religious sincerity.

Chichester Nine Hundred, Chichester Cathedral, Chichester 1975, p.11

41 *The Raising of Lazarus*, detail, c.1125, carving in the south aisle of Chichester Cathedral

General Statements on Art

The Royal Academy of Arts

1. Do you ever submit your work to the Royal Academy? If not, why not?

2. What useful purpose, if any, do you think the R.A., as at present constituted, serves?

3. In the event of your answering Question 1 in the negative, what reforms, if any, in the Royal Academy would lead you to submit your work to it for exhibition?

1. No. The sculpture at the R.A. is of an even lower standard than the painting – when it is not incompetent it is purely commercial. It is badly presented and overcrowded. I find sufficient opportunities for exhibiting without sending to the R.A.

2. No; unless catering for popular taste is a useful purpose.

3. It is impossible to expect the R.A. to judge with understanding or sympathy the work of artists more alive to contemporary growths and movements. By forming from, say, the New English, the London Group, and the 7 and 5 Society, a selection committee who would control a modern section to the Academy, exhibitions more representative of present-day art might be produced.

Architectural Review June 1931, p.189

I must admit I have had a prejudice against the Royal Academy ever since as a young artist I knew their attitude towards certain artists who were trying to perhaps change things a bit. And in my lifetime the Royal Academy has taken an attitude towards certain artists which I think is very bad. For instance, they made no protest when the Epstein figures on the medical building in the Strand [were destroyed][11] and they were some of the best works that Epstein had done. One would have expected that the Royal Academy would have protested against this, that they would have taken the side of an individual artist [...]. They were appealed to but they did nothing. [...] You see when people say, as they have said to me: 'Well if the so-called what, not progressive – I don't know what word to use – artists won't come into the Royal Academy, how can it get better?' If you have what you think is a contaminated river, you don't make it pure by pouring in a bucket of clean water; you only dirty the clean water.

Interview with Mervyn Levy, *Kaleidoscope*, BBC 4 May 1973

Abstraction

Abstraction & Surrealism

The conflict between the theories of surrealism & of pure abstraction leads many to look upon one as black & bad & the other as white & good.

Yet it seems to me that a good work of art has always contained both abstract & surrealist elements – just as it has both classical & romantic elements (order & surprise?).[12]

An artist should use all his powers, when he picks up a brush or chisel he does not cease to be a reasoning being – & the intellectual ordering & designing of the work within its medium, & its critical control will be necessary, but the subconscious perhaps plays a greater part in the creation of the fullest works of art.

Surrealism is widening the field of contemporary art & is giving more freedom to the artist (& perhaps what is not unimportant, – stretching the appreciation of the public.)

Abstraction, is re-establishing fundamental laws; bringing back form to painting & sculpture.

There are many products of surrealism which I personally dislike, –

[11] In 1907-8 Epstein carved eighteen over-life-size figures for the British Medical Association Building, Strand and Agar Street, London. For an account of the removal and partial destruction of the Portland stone statues and the involvement of the President of the Royal Academy of Arts, see Evelyn Silber, *The Sculpture of Epstein*, Phaidon Press, Oxford 1986, p.123.

[12] Variations on these two sentences appear in Moore's 1937 *Listener* article 'The Sculptor Speaks', see p.197.

chaotic jumbles, paintings that are badly mixed salads of literary fancy; pornographic shock stuff, and the echoes of the nineties (Beardsley) decadence – But equally unimportant to me are the empty decorations produced in the name of abstraction.

Unpublished notes for 'The Sculptor Speaks' 1937, HMF archive

I do not see why an artist should have to be a complete surrealist or a complete abstractionist.

Ibid.

Surrealist element of surprise & the inevitable unity & order of abstraction.

Ibid.

Decoration & Abstraction

There can be two kinds of (abstract) painting (& sculpture) One which is 'easy to look at', tickles the visual pallet, & is pleasant tasteful decoration, & the other which is much more, a charged-up concentration. They are the results of two very different (attitudes in the artist.)

One, to make a pleasing harmony of nice shapes & colours, designed & ordered within the given area; – An exercise in taste & two dimensional design, producing at its best, lovely decoration.

With the other attitude the artist also aims at ordering & relating forms & colours within his space, (& added to the two dimensional design is a three dimensional vision (though not necessarily a 3 dimensional illusionist technique)) But there is a keyed-up tension within him, & forms & colours must be created & ordered to the satisfaction & expression of this powerful emotion. (He may even use forms & colours which in themselves, taken from their context, are harsh & unpleasant.)

Such work will get its meaning from the unified & total effect of its colour & form & not by literary reminiscences of its parts. But its unity will also have a surprise within it & a life of its own. And this for most people may make it too intense, to hang upon the wall of a living room, there to serve as a distinguished decoration or as a restful pleasing change to the eye.

(How easy a picture or sculpture is to live with is no criterion of its value as a work of art. I might prefer to live in a modern service flat with one discrete pale picture on the wall than to live say with Michelangelos Sistine Chapel paintings always around me – & should I therefore say that the picture in my flat because it is comfortable & pleasing to live with was the product of a greater mind than that which produced the Sistine Chapel paintings?)

Ibid.

Abstract Art

Abstract Art
For me the aim of pure abstraction forbidding the artist using so much mental & human & visual experience that it can never have the fullness &

richness of meaning that art with a human reference with human drama has […] say Gothic & Romanesque sculpture, or Masaccio's painting. Its doubtful anyhow whether there can be purely abstract art divorced from any associational or representational element – The painters who make this their aim find that to make their point of view be taken as anything more than design or pleasant decoration, have to use such words as vitality, tension & power & talk about equivalents for Greek skies & effects like deer passing through woods, apparently admitting they cannot get away from associations with life.

(I myself in my work tend to humanise everything, to relate mountains to people, tree trunks to the human body, pebbles to heads & figures, etc. –)

To cut out & make a taboo any organic representational element or human reference & then say the artist has gained freedom, seems as silly as locking yourself up in a small cell & saying 'now I know where I am – this is freedom – freedom from the outside world'.

Unpublished notes for 'Art and Life' 1941, HMF archive

A purely abstract work (unless it is no more than the simple decoration of a given space) has a subconscious content – An artist like Mondrian in his continued preference for rectilinear design is perhaps only to be explained by his subconscious make up –

Unpublished notes for 'The Sculptor Speaks' 1937, HMF archive

A straight line, a pure curve, solid geometrical forms, a perfect sphere, cone, cylinders, cubes, are thought to be beautiful – (Plato) but they can best be made by machines, not artists – Art shows the fallible, human, variations from the perfect.

Unpublished notes late 1950s (?), HMF archive

Of course, some people set up a distinction between abstract and figurative and try to separate good from bad on that basis. It's a false distinction, in any case, and generally an emotional one. Take Poussin, for instance. He's like a juggler, not with two or three balls, but with twenty, and keeping them all going. He is doing something much more difficult, and in that sense he has greater ability as an abstract artist when he keeps his figures and their relationships than Mondrian has when he reduces everything to squares and rectangles.

Lake 1962, p.45

People say 'Are you trying to be abstract?' thinking then that they know what you are doing though, of course, they don't understand what the devil it is all about. They think that abstraction means getting away from reality and it often means precisely the opposite – that you are getting closer to it, away from a visual interpretation but nearer to an emotional understanding. When I say that I am being abstract, I mean that I am trying to consider but not simply copy nature, and that I am taking account of both the properties of the material I am using and the idea that I wish to release from that material.

Hedgecoe 1986, p.87

Art and Eroticism

PETER WEBB: What role does eroticism play in your work?

HENRY MOORE: As I do my work I am not conscious of erotic elements in it, and I have never set out to create an erotic work of art. My work is mainly intuitive. But of course it is true that almost any sculptured form can be seen as erotic and can arouse erotic associations in the mind of the viewer; in nature many simple things, the petals and stamen of a flower, can become erotic forms to some eyes. I have no objection to people interpreting my forms and sculptures erotically, relating my figures to erotic imagery in their own thinking. Part of the excitement of sculpture is the associations it can arouse, quite independent of the original aims and ideas of the sculptor. But I do not have any desire to rationalise the eroticism in my work, to think out consciously what Freudian or Jungian symbols may lie behind what I create. That I leave for others to do. I started to read Erich Neumann's book on my work, *The Archetypal World of Henry Moore* [1959],[13] in which he suggests a Jungian interpretation, but I stopped halfway through the first chapter, because I did not want to know about these things, whether they were true or not. I did not want such aspects of my work to become henceforth self-conscious. I feel they should remain subconscious and the work should remain intuitive. Perhaps the associations it can arouse are all the stronger for that very reason. Anyhow, for me, making my sculpture is an intuitive process without any conscious intention to create erotic images

Peter Webb, *The Erotic Arts*, Secker and Warburg, London 1983, pp.378-9

Art and Science

[...] art is different from science in this way. Science has usually a practical purpose. Art is like individuals. I mean, if Shakespeare didn't write *Hamlet*, there wouldn't be anybody else come along and write it. If Michelangelo hadn't painted the Sistine Chapel, nobody else would come along and do it. But if Einstein hadn't discovered the slight differences in Newton's theory, somebody else would do it. If we didn't send a man to the moon now, somebody else in two hundred years will. And this is the difference – art is something like creating another individual, almost. In that way, it's more unique, and for me is more special, more a miracle of life, than science.

Interview with Edwin Mullins, *Kaleidoscope*, BBC 27 June 1978

Art and the Subconscious

The subconscious plays a great part in art, that is to say that in conceiving & realising a work a great deal happens which cannot be logically explained

[13] See p.142.

– the mind jumps from one stage to another much further on without there being traceable steps shown between – preferences for one shape over another which cannot be explained – sudden solutions which cannot be followed step by step – in a word – inspiration.

Unpublished notes for 'The Sculptor Speaks' 1937, HMF archive

Classical and Romantic Elements in Art

The classical tendency	The romantic tendency
order	surprise
unity	variety
design & formal relations for their own sake	content & expression
conscious, intellectual, logical, calculated	intuitional, emotional, imaginative
symmetrical	asymmetry
static	dynamic
squareness, – rectilinear	curves & roundness
geometric	organic & biomorphic
hardness, tenseness	flowing softness
ordered shape, abstract non-representational	surrealist

My work may be balanced on the second side [the romantic tendency] but it also contains some of the other elements – but I believe it has some element of order & unity, some design, even [?] balance & abstract qualities, some tenseness.

When its all classic, its too obvious & cold & deadly perfect, when its all romantic, its too loose uncontrolled wildly chaotic & shapeless – But in my opinion – Gothic sculpture – Mexican, all primitive sculpture, Shakespeare, Beethoven, Tintoretto, El Greco, Rubens, Michelangelo, Masaccio, are all more romantic than classic.[14]

Unpublished notes 1937, HMF archive

Conflict: Tough and Tender

I feel the conflict still exists in me – but not causing me any difficulty in working, as it did immediately after returning from Italy [1925], – in fact I ask myself is this conflict what makes things happen? For it seems to me now that this conflict between the excitement & great impression I got from Mexican sculpture & the love & sympathy I felt for Italian art, represents two opposing sides in me, the 'tough' & the 'tender', & that many other

---

[14] In response to Moore's article 'The Sculptor Speaks' in *The Listener* 18 August 1937 (see p.193), Stanley Casson's letter 'Romanticism in Modern Sculpture?' appeared in *The Listener* on 25 August. Moore in turn responded in six pages of handwritten notes, of which this extract deals with the last two sentences of Casson's letter: 'Mr Moore concludes with the statement that "all good art has contained both classical and romantic elements". That may be true, but it is certainly not true of the work of Mr Moore.'

artists have had the same two conflicting sides in their natures ... Blake for example was torn between the two – his <u>tender</u> 'Songs of Innocence' & lyrical watercolours – & his <u>tough</u> muscular 'Nebuchadnezzar eating grass'. Goya could make beautifully tender portraits of children, & yet painted the violent 'Satan devouring a child' (on his own dining-room wall)! Shakespeare wrote 'Romeo & Juliet' & 'Macbeth' & 'King Lear'. (But we easily accept double sympathies in literature – & realise that Shakespeare's tragic & violent side was all the richer & deeper because he had the tender side!) Michelangelo's art shows conflict – the bombastic insensitive swagger of his 'David', & the slow lazy melancholy of 'Night' & 'Day'. Only at the end of a long life, in his greatest & last works are these qualities mixed to become a noble rich-blooded maturity of strength mingled with melancholy. –

And as I've suggested, what conflicting attitudes don't we find in the work of today's greatest painter, Picasso – (in his so-called 'sweet & sentimental' blue period, (& his Greek vase loveliness) – in the violent recent work.)

And really I see no difficulty in appreciating both sides & finding them in the same artist.

Perhaps an obvious & continuous synthesis will eventually derive in my own work – I can't say – I can only work as I feel & believe at the time I do the work. I can't consciously force it to come.

Undated notes 1950s (?); reproduced in Will Grohmann, *The Art of Henry Moore*,
Thames and Hudson, London 1960 (n.p.)

The Hidden Struggle

There is one quality I find in all the artists I admire most – men like Masaccio, Michelangelo, Rembrandt, Cézanne. I mean a disturbing element, a distortion, giving evidence of a struggle of some sort. It is absent, of course, in all late Greek, Hellenistic art and in painters like Botticelli in his pre-Savonarola period, or in Raphael; although I find traces of it in the last. Look at his details – the face of Plato or that of Aristotle in the 'School of Athens' at the Vatican, for instance. There it is again.

The classical style has a pleasing quality, a happy fixed finality is its aim – a resolved world. Rembrandt, on the other hand, shows in every painting marks of an unending struggle, as though he were being impelled all the time to solve something. (Van Gogh is another matter. His art, great as it is, grows from a weakness, we have to admit it. It is panicky when compared to Rembrandt.) Rembrandt had an undisputable success as a portraitist of the Amsterdam burghers. But it did not satisfy him; he wanted something deeper. He wanted to achieve the impossible.

Great Art is Not Perfect
Here the disturbing element comes in. It is instructive to know that Rembrandt copied Mantegna, whose art is the extreme opposite of his own. Why did he do so? Because he was conscious that his own art lacked the classical element. He was aware of the opposite, and that makes him greater.

Cézanne, too, wanted to do the impossible. His art was always disturbing (one of his last works was almost a Rembrandt. The picture is now in the National Gallery).[15] When we ask ourselves whether Cézanne really underwent a change, the answer must be: No. His late 'Bathers' have still the disturbing quality which we find already in the large romantic Baroque compositions he began with. One cannot change one's nature. Artists try to debate all the time what they do, instead of seeing that there is something in the opposite. No one really knows anything unless he knows also the opposite.

I personally believe that all life is a conflict; that's something to be accepted, something you have to know. And you have to die, too, which is the opposite of living. One must try to find a synthesis, to come to terms with opposite qualities. Art and life are made up of conflicts.

I think really that in great art, i.e., in the art I find great, this conflict is hidden, it is unsolved. Great art is not *perfect*. Take the Rondanini Pietà, one of the greatest works of Michelangelo. It is not a perfect work of art. There is a huge arm remaining from the earlier statue which was later changed into the Pietà. It has nothing to do with the composition. Nevertheless, it was left there.

Perfectionist art does not move me. Chinese painting is unsatisfactory to me. I can appreciate it and find it very pleasing and decorative, even beautiful, but something is missing. At the Chinese exhibition in Venice in 1954 I realised more strongly than ever before the conscious aesthetic and effectivist point of view which determined these works and which empties them of conflict. Try to compare, in your mind, some of the late Chinese works with Rembrandt. Rembrandt never started from this. His aim was not the perfect brush stroke arrived at by continual hand practice. For me this is just where the difference lies between art and craft.

All that is bursting with energy is disturbing – not perfect. It is the quality of life. The other is the quality of the ideal. It could never satisfy me. The crystal which is an ideal in life can hardly change this general rule.

It is the same quality of disturbance, which makes one distrust things too easily achieved. I always have a distrust of something I can do easily. X once showed me a big picture and remarked with pride 'I did it in half an hour.' If I had done something as easily as that, I would have felt unhappy.

The average person does not want to be disturbed by art. What he asks from art is the entertainment value of the cinema. When the modern artist turned away from his entertainment function, he found himself isolated. The Greeks, up to the fifth century B.C., did not want only to please. The 'Parthenon' sculptures are not perfectionist sculptures. If you put a Parthenon figure against one of the sixth century B.C. you'll find that they are of the same spirit. Compare it with the work of a hundred years later, and one realises what a wealth of content the Parthenon still had. Not the sweetness and emptiness into which it degenerated later on.

All primitive art is disturbed, or an experience of power, not per-

[15] *An Old Woman with a Rosary*, probably 1896.

fectionist. You may come to certain periods when the primitive element seems to have gone altogether as, say, in the outward calm of Piero della Francesca, but in him, in spite of his sophistication and conscious mastery of art, there is also a disturbing element. It is present in all true art, as it is in life. Classical detachment doesn't try to solve enough.

The Character of Our Time

This disturbing quality of life goes hand in hand with the disturbing quality of our time. The temporal emphasises the perpetual. I put it into words – because people criticise. They do not understand the basic character of their age. They want to escape. Many of them expect of art perfect craftsmanship, artefacts. They have become, through education, used to other standards. Never once did I want to make what I thought of as a 'beautiful' woman. This does not mean that I don't want beauty in what I do. Beauty is a deeper concept than perfection or niceness, or attractiveness, sweetness, prettiness. To me, 'beautiful' is much more than that. I find a bull more beautiful than a frisking lamb ('How beautiful!'), or a big fleshy beech-tree trunk more beautiful than an orchid.

I do not really want to play the role of the obvious disturber. The bogyman business I leave to the Grand Guignol, to others. The crime and horror-comic line is theirs. I don't want to produce shocks. After Surrealism nobody should be upset that a head of one of my sculptures is different from the rest. Could we not say the same of Chartres, or of many primitive works? In Chartres Cathedral, the bodies are like columns and the heads are realistic. No one reproaches them for disunity of style.

I willingly accept what I try to bring together. In the heads of my 'King and Queen' [fig.122] or in the head and body of my 'Warrior' [LH 405], some mixture of degrees of realism is implicit. But we got used to this mixture in Chartres, and we shall get used to it again. I do not suggest that I have intentionally done it. I did not say: 'Now, I'll make the head different' – it is just that in the head part I could focus, in essence, the intention of the entire figure. A bull-like though docile, a strong though battered, being; suffering – the cleft down the middle of the skull – a resignation but still a defiance. By contrasting the head to the natural structure of the rest, the whole idea of the figure is pointed out – it is these contrasts which do it.

Many of my contemporaries, even some great ones, want to produce a perfect world in life. They see it as an ideal at which life has to aim. To me, it is a life which I do not want. Consequently, I do not consider our age to be worse than others. I would not want to transplant myself to another period. I could not even imagine it. For life, every period is a terrible period. Lots of people argue and would probably say that the artist today is in a deplorable position. We are sorry for the poor fellow! There is no unified structure in society for him to fit into. Because they think that life and thought were unified in Gothic times, therefore, every artist of the Gothic era necessarily produced great works of art. They did not and they could not. Only a few are great. Works of art are not done so easily. I don't believe that the really important contributions were done easily by anybody.

Besides, what is valid socially and spiritually for the visual arts must be equally valid for music and poetry. The human spirit expresses itself now through one art, now through another – for this twenty years poetry will be good and somewhere else for a hundred years painting will flourish. There is Beethoven in the late eighteenth and early nineteenth century, or Shelley, but around them no painters. One cannot argue that society is spiritually unable to produce great painting but able to produce great poetry and music. Society is bad for all or for none.

The Public Cannot Have Any Say

I don't believe in crying out at the artist's lot. I don't believe in decrying conditions today. ('My goodness if only we had lived in the past, we could have done much better!')

No art has ever existed, and no artist has ever created, out of real despair. To be an artist is the opposite of being in a state of despair. To be an artist is to believe in life. Would you call this basic feeling a religious feeling? In that sense an artist does not need any Church and dogma.

We all think that art and society now are torn apart. But I believe that in other periods the relationship was an individual relationship; it was not based on a State decree. If you can admit that a novelist can produce a great novel without being commissioned, say Dickens, Tolstoy, Flaubert, Stendhal – if one admits that theirs are works of art, why should one accept the case for the visual arts to be different?

Cézanne, by all the arguments, should have had everything against him. He had enough money to be lazy, or to go on modestly working in isolation, but no commissions, no public use. We must say however: it is certainly better that he was not commissioned. If he had been, we might not care for Cézanne. To-day, in Sweden, the arts are patronised. They are the pet of society. But how much happens there artistically?

Then again, they say that great works of art need a religious belief. This was the unifying bond in former times and it is gone. To-day you can base your art only on life itself. All right. When did Rembrandt create his greatest works? When he was old and cut off from society. And Goya's boldest fantasies were produced in isolation, in protest, when he was deaf and sick. Either the society argument is valid, then a Rembrandt, a Goya, etc., cannot happen. Or it is bunk. The artist is a human being. He has to live; that is understood. We have to live in this world. This fact does not change my argument.

Society, the public, cannot have any say in art. Because they cannot work it out. It is a bit of a mystery what happens there.... It disturbs, it is interesting. In poetry there is something which is not easily explainable. If it were, it would be like the public monuments in squares – one passes and does not look.

The Observer[16] 24 November 1957

[16] This article was headed 'Based on material from a work in preparation by Dr J.P. Hodin, "Conversations with Henry Moore"'. Hodin visited Moore at Perry Green in 1957 and based several articles on his interviews.

Modern Sculpture

The work of the sculptors of my age & somewhat older – Brancusi – Arp – Lipchitz – Laurens – Giacometti – has gradually – has approached a freedom & moved into space, compared with the sculptors of earlier period – Rodin – Maillol – & the young sculptors of today all have the tendency to work with space – to model rather than carve – but it is very necessary in my opinion to have been able to get the refinement & completeness of a single form before going on to space form with no body –

Unpublished notes *c.*1951, HMF archive

From when would you date those advances? What, for instance, would you say was the first modern sculpture?

I'd say it was a general contribution. Rodin and Medardo Rosso cleared the way. Then Brancusi, at one end of the scale, simplified form, got people to look at shape again for its own sake, and made a martyr of himself, really, for a single form, for the egg, or the egg-form, as the basis of a sculpture. And then much later a man like González with his welding brought a lot of

42 Alberto Giacometti, Ossip Zadkine, Moore, Karl Hartung and Antoine Pevsner in the garden of the Musée Bourdelle, Paris, *c.*1961

disparate elements together and made one single unified thing out of it. He was working from the opposite direction.

Then there were isolated pieces like Picasso's 'Glass of Absinthe' in 1914. Picasso realised that you could make poetry out of objects that everyone else had passed over, and that is one of the fundamental inspirations of modern art. Then there was the idea of the found object, the re-interpretation of natural forms, the use of materials discarded from ordinary life. And then again there was, in my case, the possibility of seeing in the British Museum what had been done in sculpture in the whole history of mankind.

This new friendship, if you could call it that, between art and anthropology has been of fundamental importance to twentieth-century art. We know that Epstein and Derain and Picasso and Braque were influenced before 1914 by the Negro sculptures which are now in the Musée de l'Homme in Paris, and anyone who knows that museum and knows modern art can find evidence as he goes round it that some artist has been round before him. For instance, González must have known that Negro figure that has the butcher's hooks and bits of chain hanging from its hat, and a skirt made of a bit of waste tin. That's the sort of thing that opened his eyes and taught him to look around.

You don't feel that all this hunting for new sources, new materials, new combinations has made the traditional ones obsolete?

Walter Gropius once told me that he had a man to lecture at the Bauhaus, in the 1920s, who told the students that oil-painting and carving were worn-out, Stone Age procedures, and that the artists of the future would use the materials of their own day – plastics and so on, I suppose. And this so depressed the students that most of them gave up work altogether till they noticed that Klee, who'd also been at the lecture, had just gone on painting as before, and then they recovered and thought it might be all right, after all.

And of course, like all liberations, the liberation from conventional materials has its over-done, destructive, gimmicky side. If an artist feels more free, more alive, with new materials, then his work may benefit. But a second-rater can't turn himself into a first-rater by changing his medium, or his style. He'd still have the same sensitivity, the same vision of form, the same human quality, and those are the things that make him good or bad, first-rate or second-rate.

Russell 24 December 1961

Painter–Sculptors

Picking up your point about the interplay of painting and sculpture, do you think that there are any recent painters who have had the authentic three-dimensional instinct? Any painter–sculptors, for instance?

Oh yes – Picasso, for one. His sculptures are really three-dimensional – unlike those of, say, Braque, who does a painter's sculptures and gives them a two-dimensional quality. Picasso uses an object in its complete reality. He really aims to understand the form completely. Daumier is another who could draw in a three-dimensional way and had no difficulty in transferring his concepts into sculpture.

I think the same thing applies to a great extent to Matisse. Matisse was tremendously influenced by sculpture – Rodin had a very strong effect on him – and that makes Matisse's sculpture real. He was interested in it right from the start. It wasn't just a painter having his fun. Degas was another who could do sculpture because he had a tremendous understanding of the human figure and just used the knowledge he'd gained in painting and drawing in a solid way. But I doubt if someone like Puvis de Chavannes could have done sculpture. He'd probably have made reliefs.

Russell 11 November 1962

Surrealism

I can remember a little note – because I used to take a little notebook with me in those days [Paris, 1920s], and sketch things or draw things – but I remember in it: 'Beware of Chirico.[17] It will lead to the wrong path.'

Interview with Edwin Mullins, *Kaleidoscope*, BBC 27 June 1978

I find myself lined up with the surrealists because Surrealism means freedom for the creative side of man, for surprise & discovery & life, for an opening out & widening of mans consciousness, for changing life & against conserving worn out traditions, for variety not a uniformity, for opening not closing –

Unpublished notes for 'The Sculptor Speaks' 1937, HMF archive

I welcomed Surrealism at that time. Actually, before the Surrealist exhibition in London took place, I had met Breton, Eluard, Giacometti and so on in Paris. I liked certain of the surrealist artists, but I liked some of their ideas too, and to me it was an antidote to absolute pure abstraction, which I have never completely and absolutely believed in, and which I don't think Herbert [Read] did, and I saw the Surrealist thing as – and this I think is why Herbert was so involved in it, it's really the kind of romantic side of the artist's functioning – how he works, what happens in doing his work – this subconscious, this something which you can't explain, and I've always thought that that's there and it has to be there. At the same time, one believes, I believe, that as men we are given brains and we should use them, that whatever you've got you should use, so that in comes the other side. But there was at that time such a, probably in England, a danger of just the purely constructivist, abstract people getting the stronger influence than I felt was necessary. So that the Surrealist thing, for me, was this bringing back a balance.

Interview with Basil Taylor, *Recollections of Herbert Read*, BBC 4 December 1977

[17] The Italian surrealist painter Giorgio de Chirico (1888-1978).

Well one knew that Surrealism was stretching the frontiers – or whatever you call them, the barriers really – of art generally. One knew that their belief in the subconscious and the irrational was a part of art. But I also knew that Poussin and people like that were very intellectual and very controlled [?], so I was never really a full Surrealist. I remember Breton saying that he would like to claim Mondrian as a Surrealist, and in fact the Surrealists wanted to claim anything that they knew was good as being part of Surrealism.

Interview with Edwin Mullins, *Kaleidoscope*, BBC 27 June 1978

Art and Society

Art and Life

Part of a discussion between V.S. PRITCHETT, GRAHAM SUTHERLAND, SIR KENNETH CLARK, and HENRY MOORE

V.S. PRITCHETT: In the last discussion of this series[18] there was one point which rather bothered me; Bell seemed to be longing for an artist to paint air-raid damage without expressing any human emotion – exactly as if he were Canaletto painting buildings which had been ruined centuries ago. When we spoke of literature, Read seemed at one point to have something very much like the same sort of view. Sutherland, you have done a good many pictures of war damage; do you approach your subject in this way?

GRAHAM SUTHERLAND: I can't say that I do. It's the force of the emotion in the presence of such a subject which determines and moulds the pictorial form that one chooses. The kind of emotion which one feels may vary. For instance, the forms of ruin produced by a high explosive force have a character of their own, but the effect which they have on one's emotions will vary according to one's mood. One day one will feel moved by the purely explosive character of one's subject and wish to get rid of this sensation in a picture. At another time, the sordidness and the anguish implied by some of these scenes of devastation will cause one to invent forms which are the pictorial essence of sordidness and anguish – dirty-looking forms, tormented forms, forms which take on an almost human aspect, forms, in fact, which are symbols of reality, and tragic reality at that. In either case, the point is, I think, that the forms which the artist creates, according to his inner capacity, will transcend natural appearances. To quote Maritain such an art will recompose its peculiar world with that poetical reality which resembles things in a far more profound and mysterious way than any direct evocation could possibly do.

SIR KENNETH CLARK: Yes, of course, Sutherland, your pictures of war damage and Moore's shelter drawings are rather peculiar in modern art in that you had a really moving tragic subject which is within the range of almost anyone's experience. It hasn't been common in painting for the last

[18] The series was called *The Living Image*; part of the previous discussion between Clive Bell, Herbert Read and V.S. Pritchett, entitled 'What to Look for in a Picture', was published in *The Listener* 16 October 1941.

fifty years or so for an artist to treat such subjects, and he had to express his feelings about life less directly – in landscape, shall we say, or in still life. I suppose Delacroix was almost the last painter who could deal successfully with a great dramatic subject – except perhaps Rouault. One can't go into the reasons without telling the whole story of nineteenth-century painting; but there it is. And I suppose Picasso's great tragic symbolic picture of Guernica marks pretty clearly and appropriately the end of the nineteenth-century tradition.

PRITCHETT: You seem to be assuming, Clark, that art *is* concerned with ordinary human emotions about life. But as you said just now, Bell seemed to take an entirely opposite view.

CLARK: Yes, I know I did, and I confess I read Bell's remarks with a kind of incredulous respect – what one feels for someone else's religion. Well, I must come clean, I suppose, and confess that I think art has everything to do with life; it is, if one can venture a sort of definition, a concentration of human emotions and experiences communicated in a controlled and intelligible manner through an appropriate medium.

PRITCHETT: Well, that's started hares enough to give us plenty of exercise, I think. Moore, some of your work looks to the average man, I should say, fairly remote from human experience.

HENRY MOORE: What you mean, I take it, Pritchett, is that the average man, who's got very little time to look at sculpture and painting, looking at sculpture such as mine, would find some work puzzling and strange. I think this is natural, because for over twenty years I, like most artists, have been thinking all day long about sculpture and painting, and if after all that I only produced something which the average man, who has very little time to think about it, would immediately recognise as something he would have done if he'd had the technical experience, then I think that my time would not have been very profitably spent. I think that is true of the past too, and that all good art demands an effort from the observer, and he should demand that it extends his experiences of life.

CLARK: Yes, but, Moore, there is this difference in the past – that up to about 1830, the patrons of art were in much closer touch with the artists and themselves had a tradition of taste and of understanding, so that they could follow an artist's new inventions and changes of direction much more easily than the average man nowadays, who visits an exhibition only two or three times a year, if that.

MOORE: To come back to the other point: I agree that artists being human beings, human experience is the only experience we have got to work from. Even the most abstract artists of all who want to divorce their work from any representational element, when they want to show that their work is more than design or pleasant decoration have to use such words as vitality, power, or tension; or they have to make analogies to Greek skies or effects like deer passing through woods, and when they do this, they seem to me to admit that they can't get away from associations with life.[19]

---

[19] See notes on Abstract Art, p.114, for another version of this sentence.

PRITCHETT: Then do you think that an art, as it succeeds in becoming abstract, loses its value?

MOORE: No, I think abstract art is valuable. It teaches people the language of painting. In my own work I have produced carvings which perhaps might seem to most people purely abstract. This means that in those works I have been mainly concerned to try to solve problems of design and composition. But these carvings have not really satisfied me because I have not had the same sort of grip or hold over them that I have as soon as a thing takes on a kind of organic idea. And in almost all my carvings there has been an organic idea in my mind. I think of it as having a head, body, limbs, and as the piece of stone or wood I carve evolves from the first roughing-out stages it begins to take on a definite human personality and character. From then on one begins to be critical – satisfied or dissatisfied with its progress – in a deeper way than from only a sense of pleasant shape or formal design, and a more active relationship gets going, which calls upon the same sort of feelings one has about people in real life. And to bring the work to its final conclusion involves one's whole psychological make-up and whatever one can draw upon and make use of from the sum total of one's human and form experience.

PRITCHETT: So in all your work, even the most abstract, there is ultimately some human reference, both to the forms of the human body and to the emotions. Now Sutherland, do you think that can be applied to landscape?

CLARK: Before Sutherland answers from the landscape-painter's point of view, I would like to give the historical point of view, I mean the point of view of the artist, because it is relevant I think. And that is that the art of landscape did develop comparatively recently in the history of painting precisely because it took a long time for the old painters to realise that landscape could be made to express all the qualities of moral grandeur and human destiny and so forth, which they thought a great picture ought to contain. I do believe that great landscapes must be painted with a pervading sense of human values; they can't be just records of a tract of country, but of the emotions which that particular scene allows the painter to express. That's why to my mind, a painter must know his landscape intimately. He must belong to it, and it to him. And the idea that an English painter can take a holiday in Provence and paint a great landscape there seems to be a complete fallacy.

SUTHERLAND: I thoroughly agree with Clark about the English painter in Provence. A painter must be part of his landscape to find the best in it. As the ground reflects sky, and sea reflects land, each appearing to be part of the other, so must the painter learn to recognise himself, as it were, both materially and spiritually in the landscape and the landscape in himself.

CLARK: Yes, in a way it's a Wordsworthian relationship with nature, isn't it?

MOORE: Yes, Wordsworth often personified objects in nature and gave them the human aspect, and personally I have done rather the reverse process in sculpture. I've often found that by taking formal ideas from landscape, and putting them into my sculpture I have, as it were, related a human figure to a mountain, and so got the same effect as a metaphor in painting.

SUTHERLAND: Yes, I thoroughly agree about that. Personally I find that practically all the figurative elements are contained in landscapes. In a sense the landscape painter must almost look at the landscape as if it were himself – himself as a human being. As a landscape painter goes on with increased experience of his subject he will tend to find that the forms and qualities which start him off, excite his ideas and stimulate his emotions, are the more rare and hidden forms. And I'm interested in looking at landscapes in this way, so that the impact of the hidden forms develops in my mind. Later again I feel the necessity to break the whole thing up, break up the whole elements of landscape, separate all these elements. Then out of that reservoir, I find that certain elements leave a decided and permanent mark on my enthusiasm and on my excitement, and form in themselves subjects for pictures. Thus follow forms which, because of the excitement connected with their discovery, assume in their pictorial essence what one might call a certain strangeness.

CLARK: Yes, Sutherland, I'm sure that is one reason why some people might find your pictures rather hard to understand, but I believe there's another reason why all good artists, or nearly all good artists, seem to distort, or at any rate to re-arrange nature. And that is, in addition to his feelings about life and what he sees, every artist has inside him a few controlling rhythms, so to say, and those controlling rhythms are really him, and it's to those he has to make his vision of the external world conform, if he is to make it truly expressive. I would say that even the greatest artists have quite few forms, or rhythms or chords of colour, whichever it may be, which they feel to be completely expressive. Take two of the greatest draughtsmen who have ever lived – Leonardo and Michelangelo; well, Leonardo used the same forms – the same poses and gestures – the figure pointing back over its shoulder and so forth in his very first work that he did in his last. And as to Michelangelo, there's an amusing instance – he drew a figure of Tityus lying on a rock, and the form pleased him, so he turned the paper over and he traced the figure through and made it into a Christ rising from the tomb. Thus showing that even for Michelangelo a really coherent and expressive form wasn't a thing to be wasted.

MOORE: I agree that everyone has a sort of individual form vision. In all the greatest artists the seeds of this form vision has been present even in their early work, and to some extent their work has been a gradual unfolding of this rhythm throughout. In their later work it becomes more concentrated, that's all. It's something the artist can't control – it's his make-up. All the same I think that he ought not to go on repeating it, he ought to be fighting against it. He ought not to sell himself his own idea over and over again. Or it should become so instinctive in him that he's not worried about it. In Michelangelo it was so instinctive that he was free to think about the other things that interested him. The less conscious you are of your own individual form rhythm, the more likely it is, I think, to get richer and fuller and develop.

SUTHERLAND: I should say that this inner life which we've been talking about must be constantly refreshed by visual experience. A painter cannot create out of nothing, as it were, so he must be continually gathering material from his experience of things seen. If he fails to nourish these conceptual ideas by familiarising himself with the ways of nature he will dry up and fail to produce. But I feel that it is always the idea of nature, transcending nature and forming reconstructed and recreated images, *via* the heart and mind of the artist which is the thing that is worth while.

CLARK: I'm not much impressed with the claim that an artist may have an inner life which is incomprehensible to everybody. We are members one of another. But it is true that certain of the greatest artists have made great leaps ahead of their contemporaries, and for a time only a few people have been able to follow them.

PRITCHETT: Wouldn't you say that in the last few years the artists have made greater leaps ahead of their contemporaries than ever before – or at least that some artists have been painting further away from ordinary visual experience than ever was known in the history of the past?

CLARK: Yes, I think that by and large that is true, and there seem to me to be two reasons for it. One is that just as language can be degraded by popular use and thoughtless use, so the realism of the nineteenth century degraded the realistic style of painting till it became like the lowest form of journalese, and then some violent form of purification became necessary, and that form of purification was the abstract movement. And the second reason is that as the painter became more and more cut off from his patrons and began to paint for himself, and for a few friends, a few fellow artists, so he became more interested in specialised problems of picture-making, design and composition, and in the realising of his own inner vision and he didn't try to carry with him the section of informed opinion that had previously constituted his body of patrons.

SUTHERLAND: I thoroughly agree with that. Then I think there's also the effect of photography. I think that's had a very definite effect on painters, because people have been made much more familiar with appearances. Painters are always feeling the need for experiment, and the need for working away from known facts, and therefore the photograph has done away with three-quarters of what they were originally asked and what they originally set out to do.

PRITCHETT: Do you mean that the main purpose of the artist up to the invention of photography was in fact imitation?

MOORE: That would be, I think, to take too narrow a view. There have been other times at which it has not been the first aim of the artists to reproduce the visible world. In fact, if you took the whole history of art you would find that artists have only made the representation of the visible world their chief aim for a relatively short time, round about the Mediterranean countries. I think one of the main difficulties people have over so-called modern art is that they don't know enough about the whole history of the world's art.

PRITCHETT: Yes, I agree. But isn't it possible that all the so-called 'primitive' art in the world doesn't imitate nature simply because the artists were not capable of doing so?

MOORE: I think it couldn't have been their chief aim at all these times, because once it did become their chief aim, as with the Greeks, within a hundred years they had achieved an almost perfect representation of human form. And it's not that they didn't have technical skill enough, because the degree of technical skill in what used to be called 'primitive' arts – that is to say, non-representational arts – is very high indeed.

PRITCHETT: If you say the chief aim was not representational in this sense, then what do you think it was?

CLARK: Well, let's say for the sake of argument that all art in its beginning is concerned with religion or at any rate with the magical nature of imaginative experience. The Greeks, who thought of their gods as looking like human beings, developed an art in which there was naturally a very close representation of nature, and of human beings, but in other civilisations, where the religion was more mysterious, the art was more symbolic. Art had to employ more abstract symbols.

PRITCHETT: And what's a symbol in this sense?

CLARK: Let's say the pictorial equivalent of an idea.

PRITCHETT: Well, there's another question that I'd like to ask, and that concerns the relation of the artist and society. Do you think that there is a sense in which an artist reflects the society which has produced him? He may be expressing himself, of course, but isn't he also society expressing itself? If this is so, it ought to follow, I think, that the best art will arise at times when the relationship between the artist and society is most vital and mutually refreshing.

CLARK: Yes, the artist cannot escape from his time. He cannot fail to reflect the society that produced him. Even if he thinks that he has chosen to live, as the saying goes 'in an ivory tower', that's probably only because his digestion is too weak to allow him to assimilate contemporary life or perhaps because the society of his time is so disintegrated as to be incapable of assimilation. Recent art really has shown very clearly the conflict and the lack of unity of purpose in recent society. But there are also in art more subtle reflections of social and intellectual currents as – to take rather an erudite instance – when Correggio by shifting the vanishing point of his perspective outside the picture frame seemed to anticipate the Copernican revolution.

The Listener 13 November 1941, pp.657-9

Art and Religion

I believe that art in itself is akin to religion, art is, in fact, another expression of the belief that life is worth living – and that is what religion is basically about. I go further and say that artists do not need religion for art is religion in itself. If one believes that life is significant, and everyone who does not commit suicide has this feeling, then one is religious in one's art. It is much more important to have good art in the churches and good artists working for churches than to ask a practising Christian who is a bad artist to produce a work for the church. What he will do is not religious art. All good art is religious but not all good art is suitable for placing in a church. I would not put a Boucher in a church but I could put a Watteau there. And certain works by Klee, or Picasso and Braque and abstractions by Soulages and others. Matisse in his chapel has got that kind of innocence which is like the pure innocence of an adolescent girl of fourteen. He imparted a purity to his work which is the kind of thing that Christ meant when he spoke of the children as something holy.

J.P. Hodin, 'Quand les artistes parlent du sacré',
Vingtième Siècle, Paris December 1964

There was a period when the Church was the greatest patron of the arts, but in the last two or three hundred years the Church has gradually abandoned the good artists in favour of those who have been taught to produce religious art for its own sake. One knows from the so-called religious art shops connected with the Roman Catholic Church and the Church of England that the standard is terribly poor – sentimental, sweet and sloppy. Religion no longer seems to provide inspiration or impetus for many artists. And yet all art is religious in a sense that no artist would work unless he believed that there was something in life worth glorifying. This is what art is about. There is of course a difference between a work of art which is contemplated for a church and one which is intended for a house, a museum or a street. It was this difference that caused me all the trouble and the doubts about doing the Northampton 'Madonna and Child' [fig.107]. The same doubts remain over my doing any work for the Church.

For example, I have been asked to do a Crucifixion, but this would make me have the same misgivings all over again. In my work each sculpture usually grows out of the last one, without any conscious programme. Thus the Glenkiln Cross [see fig.125] is a crucifix, although I didn't deliberately set out to make it that. It was an upright motif idea which developed into a worn-down rudimentary cross.

If I agreed to do a subject from someone else's suggestion, it would mean stopping work on whatever else I was doing. This is the reason why I dislike and refuse commissions.

However, the Crucifixion is such a universal theme that I may attempt it one day. Everybody thinks more often of death as they grow older, unless they are too occupied or too extrovert. An artist can't be either. When you are young you don't think so realistically about death. Now I often think about it.

Hedgecoe 1968, p.164

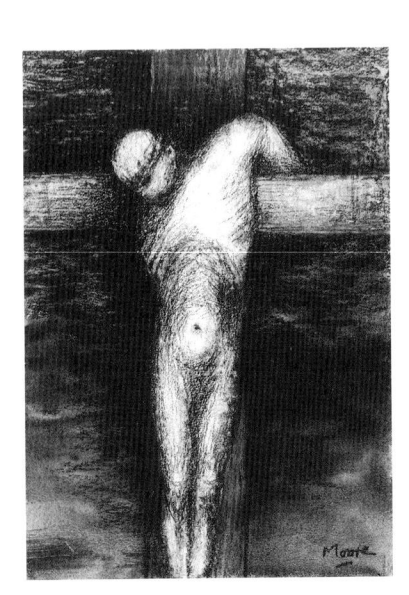

43 Moore did attempt the subject of Christ on the cross towards the end of his life in several drawings, including *Crucifixion* 1982 HMF 82(442), wax crayon, charcoal, pencil, watercolour wash and ink wash, 355 x 253mm (14 x 10in). Private collection

Art and Politics

Artists & Politics
Politics, of course, concern us all, but until recent years it might have been possible, in more stable political & economic surroundings, for a good artist

to live & paint away, completely unconcerned with politics. But today no person sensitive to contemporary events & with any ideals can remain aloof & just disinterested.

(Though the artist may leave politics alone, thinking they are no real concern of his, politics may not leave the artist alone, as recent events in other countries have shown.)

Apart from all other political, social & economic questions which concern us all equally, for example, the danger to peace everywhere, by crazy nationalist pride & hatred, there is one which is an obvious particular concern of all artists, scientists & writers, that is freedom of individual expression.

The artist (& scientist & writer) must have freedom to work in whatever direction his mind & sensibility lead him. His whole existence is towards the finding of new truths & values, & though new truths & new vision are often uncomfortable, especially to those in power, they are among man's most important achievements.

In England the artist, writer & scientist still have a great deal of freedom. But in some countries their freedom has completely gone. We cannot be indifferent. For the threat to intellectual freedom is greater in the world now than at any time during the last two or three centuries. The freedom we have was gained by the continuous struggles of past generations. Every attempt at the curtailment of freedom of ideas must be fought by us all.

Unless he is prepared to see all thought pressed into one reactionary mould, by tyrannical dictatorships – to see the beginning of another set of dark ages, – the artist is left with no choice but to help in the fight for the real establishment of Democracy against the menace of Dictatorships.

Unpublished notes *c*.1936-39, HMF archive

My greatest sympathies lie towards Communism. I imagine every decent (moral, intelligent) person nowadays is more socialist than anything else.[20]

Unpublished notes for *Unit One* 1934, HMF archive

Sir, – The announcement of a mass demonstration to be held in Leeds next Sunday, under the title of 'Collective Security – the People's Answer to Dictators', should cause us all to pause and consider our own position in relation to the present critical condition of the world.

We are witnessing to-day in Europe, in Africa, in Asia, three large-scale wars which are being carried on, despite the deeply shocked protests of the whole civilised world, with an inhuman totalitarian ferocity which may well make us despair.

With the ruthless destruction of life goes the systematic obliteration of all those civilised creations of science, of art, of education, of the institutions of social betterment, of the very instruments of civilised government, which centuries of human endeavour have established.

[20] This is one of Moore's two answers to question 16 in the questionnaire sent to members of Unit One: 'Have you any political convictions of a party kind (conservative, fascist, communist)?'

But the evidence of the decay which is attacking the very roots of civil-isation does not end with the victims of wars. Great countries in Europe have destroyed within their borders the whole concept of the freedom of the individual in the social, economic and political structure. Brute force and the imminent fear of torture and death have been set up as the keystone of national organisation. Instead of peaceful negotiation between free sovereign States, the last decade has seen example after example of terms dictated by ultimatum, invasion and war, in defiance of treaties, agreements and assurances freely made. Lessons taught by Great Powers have not been missed by the smaller.

We are confronted to-day with a world situation in which it is our own civilisation, our own freedom and well-being, our own democratic faith which is in danger. The dictatorial Powers are rapidly gaining strategical advantages in Europe which will make the defence of our principles infinitely more difficult, if not impossible. France is being surrounded; our own line of communication with the Colonies and the Dominions, both by the Mediterranean and the African coast, is being menaced.

Are we to stand aside while these forces complete the wreck of our civilisation?

Whatever our political differences I suggest that the conclusion is forced upon us that it has become immediately urgent for the peace-loving Powers to agree upon collective action to defend any country which becomes the victim of aggression, to present to the menace of the dictators the firm resolve of the democratic powers to put an end to defiance of the law and to re-establish the authority of civilised obligations between States.

If that is our desire, it also becomes a duty to take every opportunity of demonstrating it to our own Government. We have such an opportunity in Leeds, under an all-party banner on April 3. I sincerely hope that that demonstration in favour of Collective Security as the people's answer to dictators, will be in accordance with the urgency of the time, and one of the greatest that Leeds has ever undertaken.

Letter to The Yorkshire Post, 31 March 1938

Artists in Wartime

Kingston, Kent

I was in the trenches in the last war, & so all the more don't want to shoot or be shot at, again. And like every other sane person I hate war & all it stands for. But I can't say with complete certainty that there aren't some-things I might find myself ready to fight for, & so I can't call myself a wholly consistent conscientious objector. I'd be glad if I could, for I respect greatly the real pacifist point of view, and I'm glad to know that you are a C.O, & will have the courage to remain so.

I think this war need not have come – if we'd had a better government & a different attitude to Russia. Now its here, I think its more or less the same set up as in 1914, that is it's largely an Imperialist war again, but with this difference that in place of the Kaiser & the old German militarists there is the more reactionary & barbaric regime of Hitler & the Nazi Party. And now the war's started, – if Fascist Germany wins, then I think most of the civil liberties in Europe, would go; there'd be less freedom of expression & a poor chance for the existence of the kind of painting, sculpture, literature, music, architecture, that I believe in. – Although no one can say there's democracy in England in the real sense of the word, & although British Imperialism has a pretty bloody record, I hate Fascism & Nazism & all its aims & ideology so intensely, that I don't think I could refuse to help in trying to prevent it from being victorious. However, when the time comes that I'm asked, or have got to do something in this war, I hope it will be something less destructive than taking part in the actual fighting & killing. There ought to be ways of being used even as a sculptor, – in making of splints etc, or jobs connected with plastic surgery, – though the most likely thing I suppose is camouflage work. But until I'm prevented from doing so, my idea is to go on working just as I am, for as long as its possible, or our finances last out.

From a letter to Arthur Sale,[21] 8 October 1939

WILLIAM ZORACH: I was wondering – how do artists feel over there, about carrying on during the war. Do you feel that artists should put aside their own work for the time being, or enter some needed branch of war activity, or do you feel that it is more important for them to continue their work and try to keep the spirit of art alive during this conflict?

MARY ADAMS: Well Mr. Zorach, we have here in the studio – Henry Moore – sculptor and artist, whose work was always appreciated by, what perhaps I should call the Inner Temple – but the war has brought to him an audience far larger and his sculptures and his drawings, in particular of 'Forms in Shelters' and 'People in Coal-Mines', have brought him very great appreciation now. May I introduce him to you.

HENRY MOORE: This is Henry Moore, answering William Zorach. I can't, of course, answer for all British artists, I can only answer personally your question. For me I find it's a necessity to work anyhow – that is if I take a holiday for too long it's just that I get dissatisfied and unhappy and un-settled, and I should say that generally all artists work out of necessity and that to have to work is just part of their make-up. Anyhow, the one thing I personally want to do is to carry on working, and I feel it's important that as many artists as can do, should carry on painting and drawing and carving in wartime, as during peacetime. Anyhow, after all, one of the most important things we're fighting for, I take it, is to keep freedom of expression, of which art is an important part. Therefore to want to stop one of the very things we're fighting for would, I think, be a great mistake and a drastically short-viewed policy. […]

ZORACH: […] And here's another question I'd like to ask:– Do you think

[21] See p.60, note 45.

133

war, with its tremendous upheaval and emotional human experience, will produce a new or great art expressions? Or will it destroy what art expression has been developed in contemporary life? I'd like to get your point of view on that, Mr. Moore.

MOORE: […] I think neither; I don't think that great upheavals and human war experience is needed to produce new and great expression in art. War might perform a very useful service in giving artists a subject matter, whose significance is commonly shared and so help to narrow the gap between the artists and the general public, but I believe that 90% of the subject matter of art is permanent and fundamental to life at all periods.

ZORACH: I agree with you absolutely.

MOORE: And that it shouldn't need the stimulus or general upheaval or war for the good artist to respond and react to life. After all, the sun shines, the seasons change, the relationship of men and women continues, shapes and colours go on existing, and art is men's expression of response to these things, which remain permanent and fundamental.

Answering You No.69 (Two-Way Series No.8),[22] BBC 15 and 16 November 1942; typescript in HMF library

In answer to the second part of the question, I don't think that the war will destroy what has already been developed in contemporary art – Unless as was pictured in some pre-war novels, which I don't think will come true, the evil & destructive powers so continue & prevail, that at the end, the struggle to remake & maintain the necessities of life would occupy all the efforts of the remaining few. I do believe the war will test & challenge some of the experiments & directions of contemporary art, which will only be all to the good. And it may hasten the development of a new movement or quicken the end of a dying one, but I don't think that war itself makes new movements – so I can see no reason to think that the war will destroy what has already been developed in Contemporary Art. To take the last war as an example of what I mean, cubism was begun fore the 1914-1918 war & it emerged further developed, & continued on at the end of the war.

Unpublished notes for *Answering You* 1942, HMF archive

Auschwitz Monument[23]

The choice of a monument to commemorate Auschwitz has not been an easy task. From the very beginning it was obvious that the commemoration

[22] This extract is taken from a radio discussion between speakers in London and New York. Mary Adams was the master of ceremonies in the London broadcasting studio, where Kenneth Clark was among the seven participants. William Zorach (1887-1966), the Lithuanian-born American sculptor, was one of five speakers in the New York studio.

[23] Moore was President of the Jury of a competition for a monument to be erected on the site of the Auschwitz–Birkenau concentration camp. The jury met for the first time in Auschwitz in April 1958, and out of the 426 designs sent in they selected seven for the second stage of the competition. The jury met again, this time in Paris, in November 1958, where Moore made this announcement. In 1959 the jury selected a winner (Moore was not present), but the project was not realised at this time because it violated a 1947 law on the inadmissability of changes to the camp grounds. In 1961 the International Auschwitz Committee prepared a new plan for a monument, which was unveiled in 1967.

of Auschwitz must present problems almost insoluble both to the artists and to the jury.

Essentially, what has been attempted has been the creation – or, in the case of the jury, the choice – of a monument to crime and ugliness, to murder and to horror. The crime was of such stupendous proportions that any work of art must be on an appropriate scale. But, apart from this, is it in fact possible to create a work of art that can express the emotions engendered by Auschwitz?

It is my conviction that a very great sculptor – a new Michelangelo or a new Rodin – might conceivably have achieved this. The odds against such a design turning up among the many *maquettes* submitted were always enormous. And none did. Nor were any of the purely architectural – or predominantly architectural – projects fully satisfactory.

There were, in the end, three projects, all of which were judged good, but none of which was considered entirely adequate. The jury considered that its primary task was not to award a prize, to decide which of these three was the best, but rather to ensure that the finest possible monument be built at Auschwitz.

With this end in view, a unanimous decision was reached: the three best teams have been asked to submit, if possible in collaboration, but if necessary singly, a new project or new projects. A final judging will take place [in] 1959. The jury will meet again to decide whether one of these projects is worthy of its approval, and if so which.

The three teams, each designated by the name of the team's leader, are as follows:

Hansen: His approach to the problem is considered exceptionally brilliant. But the alterations that he would make to the site are regarded as being unacceptable to the former inmates of Auschwitz. His design also lacks an emotional focus which, in the opinion of the jury, might well be supplied by a plastic element.

Lafuente: His sculptural element is highly praised. Nevertheless this team's almost exclusive concentration on a single element of the Auschwitz tragedy – the sealed trains – is considered to be too limited a concept.

Vitale: The architectural talent of this team is recognised. It is nonetheless considered that in this case the sculptural element lacks the strength necessary to express the full force of the emotions evoked by Auschwitz, and also that his projected cutting of the camp into two would alter excessively the nature of the site.

It is the jury's hope that after more work has been done by one or more of these highly commended teams, a project will emerge with the dignity, the emotional intensity and the artistic merit worthy of so important and unusual a memorial.

Auschwitz Monument, International Auschwitz Committee, Vienna 1958

The Sculptor in Modern Society

I have been asked to address you as a sculptor and it might therefore be appropriate if I began by trying to give you some idea of my own attitude to the art I practise. Why have I chosen to be a sculptor – or why has the art of sculpture chosen me as an exponent of its special aims? If I can answer that question satisfactorily I may be in a better position to answer some of the specific questions which are before this conference.

Some become sculptors because they like using their hands, or because they love particular materials, wood or stone, clay or metal and like working in those materials – that is they like the craft of sculpture – I do. But beyond this one is a sculptor because one has a special kind of sensibility for shapes and forms, in their solid physical actuality – I feel that I can best express myself, that I can best give outward form to certain inward feelings or ambitions by the manipulation of solid materials – wood, stone or metal. The problems that arise in the manipulation of such materials – problems of mass and volume, of light in relation to form and of volume in relation to space – the problem of continually learning to grasp and understand form more completely in its full spatial reality – all these are problems that interest me as an artist and which I believe I can solve by cutting down, building up or welding together solid three-dimensional materials.

But what is my purpose in such activity? It might, of course, be merely a desire to amuse myself, to kill time or create a diversion. But then I should not find it necessary, as I do, to exhibit my sculpture publicly, to hope for its sale and for its permanent disposition either in a private house, a public building or an open site in a city. My desire for such a destination for my work shows that I am trying, not merely to express my own feelings or emotions for my own satisfaction, but also *to communicate* those feelings or emotions to my fellowmen. Sculpture, even more than painting (which generally speaking, is restricted to interiors) is a public art, and for that reason I am at once involved in those problems which we have met here to discuss – the relation of the artist to society – more particularly, the relation of the artist to the particular form of society which we have at this moment of history.

There have been periods – periods which we would like to regard as ideal prototypes of society – in which that relationship was simple. Society had a unified structure, whether communal or hierarchic, and the artist was a member of that society with a definite place and a definite function. There was a universal faith, and an accepted interplay of authority and function which left the artist with a defined task, and a secure position. Unfortunately our problems are not simplified in that way. We have a society which is fragmented, authority which resides in no certain place, and our function as artists is what we make it by our individual efforts. We live in a transitional age, between one economic structure of society which is in dissolution and another economic order of society which has not yet taken definite shape. As artists we do not know who is our master; we are individuals seeking patronage, sometimes from another individual, sometimes from an organ-isation of individuals – a public corporation, a museum, an educational authority – sometimes from the State itself. This very diversity of patronage requires, on the part of the modern artist, an adaptability or agility that was not required of the artist in a unified society.

But that adaptability is always in a vertical direction, always within a particular craft. One of the features of our industrialised society is special-isation – the division of labour. This tendency has affected the arts, so that a sculptor is expected to stick to his sculpture, a painter to his painting. This was not always so – in other ages – the Middle Ages and the Renaissance, to mention only European examples – the artist's talent was more general, and he would turn his hand, now to metalwork or jewellery, now to sculpture, now to painting or engraving. He might not be equally good in all these media, and it is possible that we have discovered good reasons for confining our talents within narrower bounds. There are certainly painters who would never be capable of creating convincing works of art in three-dimensional forms, just as there are sculptors who could not convey the illusion of three-dimensional space on a two-dimensional surface. We know now that there are specific kinds of sensibility, belonging to distinct psychological types, and for that reason alone a certain degree of specialisation in the arts is desirable.

The specialisation, due to psychological factors in the individual artist, may conflict with the particular economic structure of society in which the artist finds himself. Painting and sculpture, for example, might be regarded as unnecessary trimmings in a society committed by economic necessity to an extreme utilitarian form of architecture. The artist might then have to divert his energies to other forms of production – to industrial design, for example. No doubt the result would be the spiritual impoverishment of the society reduced to such extremes, but I only mention this possibility to show the dependence of art on social and economic factors. The artist should realise how much he is involved in the changing social structure, and how necessary it is to adapt himself to that changing structure.

From this some might argue that the artist should have a conscious and positive political attitude. Obviously some forms of society are more favour-able to art than others, and it would be argued the artist should on that account take up a position on the political front. I would be more certain of his duty in this respect if we could be scientifically certain in our political analysis, but it must be obvious, to the most superficial observer, that the re-lation between art and society has always been a very subtle one, and never of the kind that could be consciously planned. One can generalise about the significant relationship between art and society at particular points in history, but beyond describing such relationships in vague terms such as 'organic' and 'integrated', one cannot get near to the secret. We know that the Industrial Revolution has had a detrimental effect on the arts, but we cannot tell what further revolution or counter-revolution would be required to restore the health of the arts. We may have our beliefs, and we may even be actively political on the strength of those beliefs; but meanwhile we have to work, and to work within the contemporary social structure.

That social structure varies from country to country, but I think that broadly speaking we who are participating in this Conference are faced with mixed or transitional economies. In my own country, at any rate, the artist has to satisfy two or three very different types of patron. In the first place there is the private patron, the connoisseur or amateur of the arts, who buys a painting or a piece of sculpture to indulge his own taste, to give himself a private and exclusive pleasure. In addition there are now various types of public patron – the museums or art galleries that buy in the name of the people: the people of a particular town, or the people of the county as a whole. Quite different from such patrons are those architects, town-planners, organisations of various sorts who buy either from a sense of public duty, or to satisfy some sense of corporate pride.

This diversity of patronage must be matched by a certain flexibility in the artist. If I am asked to make a piece of sculpture for (1) a private house, (2) a museum, (3) a church, (4) a school, (5) a public garden or park, and (6) the offices of some large industrial undertaking, I am faced by six distinct problems. No doubt the Renaissance sculptor had similar problems, but not of such a complexity; whereas the medieval sculptor had to satisfy only one type of patronage – that of the Church. Flexibility was always demanded by the function and destination of the piece of sculpture, but that is a difficulty which the artist welcomes as an inspiration. The difficulty that might cause the modern artist some trouble is due to the shift, at a moment's notice, from the freedom of creation which he enjoys as an individual working for the open market of private patrons to the restrictions imposed on him when he accepts a public commission. It is usually assumed that if sufficient commissions were forthcoming from public authorities, all would be well with the arts. It is an assumption that takes no account of the fact that the tradition of modern art is an individualistic one – a craft tradition passing from artist to artist. We have only to look eastwards, beyond the Iron Curtain, to see that State patronage on an authoritarian basis requires quite a different tradition – a tradition in which the State that pays the artist calls the tune, in other words, determines the style. I am not making any judgement of the relative merits of the two traditions, but I think it should be made quite clear that the transition from private patronage to public patronage would mean a radical reorganisation of the ideals and practice of art. We have to choose between a tradition which allows the artist to develop his own world of formal inventions – to express his own vision and sense of reality; and one which requires the artist to conform to an orthodoxy, to express a doctrinaire interpretation of reality. It may be that in return for his loss of freedom the artist will be offered economic security; it may be that with such security he will no longer feel the need to express a personal philosophy, and that a common philosophy will still allow a sufficient degree of flexibility in interpretation to satisfy the artist's aesthetic sensibility. I think most artists, however, would prefer to feel their way towards a solution of this problem, and not to have a solution imposed on them by dictation. The evolution of art cannot be forced – nor can it be retarded by an obstinate adherence to outworn conventions.

We already have considerable experience in the State patronage of art, even in countries which are still predominantly individualistic in their economy. I have myself executed various pieces of sculpture for public authorities – schools, colleges, churches, etc. – and although I have had to adapt my conception to the function of the particular piece of sculpture, I have been able to do this without any surrender of what I would regard as my personal style. Such pieces of sculpture may meet with violent criticism from the public, and I might be influenced, perhaps unconsciously, by such criticism. That is my own look-out, and I do not suggest that the artist should be indifferent to such criticism. But the public is also influenced by the work of art, and there is no doubt that the public authority which has the vision and the courage to commission forward-looking works of art, the work of art with what might be called prophetic vision, is doing more for art than the public authority that plays for safety and gives the public what the public does not object to. But can we rely on such courage and initiative in public bodies in a democratic society? Isn't there a primary duty in such a society to make sure that the people have the interest and eagerness that demand the best art just as surely as they demand the best education or the best housing? It is a problem beyond the scope of this address, but not beyond the scope of Unesco – the renewal of the sources of artistic inspiration among the people at large.

I turn now to technical matters more within my special competence as a sculptor. When sculpture passes into the public domain, the sculptor is then involved, not merely in a simple artist–patron relationship, but also in a cooperation with other artists and planners. The piece of sculpture is no longer a thing in itself, complete in its isolation – it is a part of a larger unit, a public building, a school or a church, and the sculptor becomes one artist in a team collaborating in the design as a whole. Ideally that collaboration should begin from the moment the building is first conceived, and neither the planner of the town nor the architect of the particular building, should formulate their plans without consulting the sculptor (or the painter if he too is involved). I mean that the placing of a piece of sculpture, in a public square, on or in a building, may radically alter the design as a whole. Too often in modern building the work of art is an afterthought – a piece of decoration added to fill a space that is felt to be too empty. Ideally the work of art should be a focus round which the harmony of the whole building revolves – inseparable from the design, structurally coherent and aesthetically essential. The fact that the town planner or the architect can begin without a thought of the artists he is going to employ to embellish his building shows how far away we are from that integral conception of the arts which has been characteristic of all the great epochs of art.

Assuming that such cooperation is sought and given from the beginning of an architectural conception, then there are many considerations which the sculptor must bring into play. He will want to consider both external proportions and internal spatial volumes in relation to the size and style of sculpture that might be required – not merely the decorative function of sculpture in relation to formal quantities, but also the possibility of utilitarian functions. Utilitarian is perhaps not the right word, but I am thinking of the didactic and symbolic functions of sculpture in Gothic architecture, inseparable from the architectural conception itself. The sculptor will also want to consider his own materials in relation to those to be employed by the architect, so that he can secure the effective harmony or contrast of textures and colours, or fantasy and utility, of freedom and necessity as one might say.

These are perhaps obvious rights for a sculptor to claim in the conception and execution of a composite work of art, but nothing is such a symptom of our disunity, of our cultural fragmentation, as this divorce of the arts. The specialisation characteristic of the modern artist seems to have as its counterpart the atomisation of the arts. If a unity could be achieved, say in the building of a new town, and planners, architects, sculptors, painters and all other types of artist could work together from the beginning, that unity, one feels, would nevertheless be artificial and lifeless because it would have been consciously imposed on a group of individuals, and not spontaneously generated by a way of life. That is perhaps the illusion underlying all our plans for the diffusion of culture. One can feed culture to the masses, but that does not mean that they will absorb it. In the acquisition of culture there must always be an element of discovery, of self-help; otherwise culture remains a foreign element, something outside the desires and necessities of everyday life. For these reasons I do not think we should despise the private collector and the dealer who serves him; their attitude to a work of art, though it may include in the one case an element of possessiveness or even selfishness; and in the other case an element of profit-making, of parasitism, nevertheless such people circulate works of art in natural channels, and in the early stages of an artist's career they are the only people who are willing to take a risk, to back a young artist with their personal judgement and faith. The State patronage of art is rarely given to young and unknown artists, and I cannot conceive any scheme, outside the complete communisation of the art profession such as exists in Russia, which will support the artist in his early career. The present system in Western Europe is a very arbitrary system, and entails much suffering and injustice. The artist has often to support himself for years by extra artistic work – usually by teaching – but this, it seems to me is preferable to a complete subordination of the artist to some central authority, which might dictate his style and otherwise interfere with his creative freedom. It is not merely a question of freedom. With the vast extension of means of communication, the growth of internationalism, the intense flare of publicity which falls on the artist once he has reached any degree of renown, he is in danger of losing a still more precious possession – his privacy. The creative process is in some sense a secret process. The conception and experimental elaboration of a work of art is a very personal activity, and to suppose that it can be organised and collectivised like any form of industrial or agricultural production, is to misunderstand the very nature of art. The artist must work in contact with society, but that contact must be an intimate one. I believe that the best artists have always had their roots in a definite social group or community, or in a particular region. We know what small and intimate communities produced the great sculpture of Athens, or Chartres, or Florence. The sculptor *belonged* to his city or his guild. In our desire for international unity and for universal cooperation we must not forget the necessity for preserving this somewhat paradoxical relation between the artist's freedom and his social function, between his need for the sympathy of a people and his dependence on internal springs of inspiration.

I believe that much can be done, by Unesco and by organisations like the Arts Council in my own country, to provide the external conditions which favour the emergence of art. I have said – and it is the fundamental truth to which we must always return – that culture (as the word implies) is an organic process. There is no such thing as a synthetic culture, or if there is, it is a false and impermanent culture. Nevertheless, on the basis of our knowledge of the history of art, on the basis of our understanding of the psychology of the artist, we know that there are certain social conditions that favour the growth and flourishing of art, others that destroy or inhibit that growth. An organisation like Unesco, by investigating these laws of cultural development, might do much to encourage the organic vitality of the arts, but I would end by repeating that by far the best service it can render to the arts is to guarantee the freedom and independence of the artist.

Unesco, International Conference of Artists, Venice 1952; typescript in HMF library

On Critics and Art Criticism

There is a difference between literary criticism and art criticism in the sense that literary critics are working in their own medium. In their literary criticism, Baudelaire, Coleridge and Eliot really knew what they were about because they were poets, whereas very few art critics are practising artists. Therefore they are more inclined to make stupid errors.

Hedgecoe 1968, p.352

It is a pleasant change to find a critic accusing me of being too close to nature –[24]

Unpublished notes 1937, HMF archive

Most critics (including Adrian S & David S)[25] approach sculpture from a painters point of view (thats why they are often suckers for relief sculpture

[24] This comment refers to Stanley Casson and his letter in *The Listener* 25 August 1937, see note 14 above.
[25] Adrian Stokes (1902-72), the painter, poet and writer on art, architecture and aesthetics, reviewed Moore's exhibition at the Leicester Galleries (*The Spectator* 10 November 1933). The art critic and curator David Sylvester (1924-2001) worked as Moore's part-time secretary in 1944. He curated the 1951 and 1968 Moore retrospective exhibitions at the Tate Gallery, London.

– they find it impossible to get away from their liking for not destroying [?] the picture plane, why often they get their opinions studying photographs of sculpture & not the sculpture itself – why they retain a flat picture of a sculpture in their minds –

Unpublished notes late 1950s (?), HMF archive

But when the book[26] came out I began to read the first chapter. After halfway through it I gave it up because I don't want to know what makes me tick. […] I don't want to be influenced by what critics think because often they don't know. And anyhow they are making it up.

In conversation with Joseph Darracott, Imperial War Museum, London 1976

Every great artist can be criticised destructively taking the opposite qualities to what he possesses as being the only important qualities – e.g. Rembrandt, seen from hard classical architectual construction, can be shown to be sentimental, only an illustrator etc etc – Michelangelo – lazy slowness rather than sad melancholy. – El Greco – eye rolling melodrama.

Unpublished notes c.1951, HMF archive

Beauty – To everybody it means something different – The word is usually employed to avoid the issue of precise expression – its the most misleading, misused, muddle-headed word in art criticism.

Unpublished notes late 1950s (?), HMF archive

Artists

Heinrich Brabender (*c.*1475–*c.*1538)

Some time in the mid-1970s I visited Münster in connection with the purchase of two of my sculptures by the Landesbank. One, an outdoor work [LH 580], was to be sited on the grounds outside the new Bank building, and the other was presented by the Bank to the Münster Museum [LH 491a]. While I was there, Dr. Paul Pieper, who was then the director of the Museum, kindly took me on a tour of the collection, which I enjoyed very much. As I walked through the galleries I came across the sculptures which had been produced in the sixteenth century for the exterior of the cathedral in Münster, and was greatly impressed by them. I asked who they were by and was surprised to hear a name that I hadn't known before, Heinrich Brabender. I wanted to obtain a book about his work so that I could learn more about him, but was told there was none to be had. It seemed to me this was wrong and that the world should know of this outstanding sculptor. That is how the idea for this book came about, with comments which I promised to write, expressing my appreciation, as a fellow sculptor, for Brabender's remarkable work.

[26] Erich Neumann, *The Archetypal World of Henry Moore*, Pantheon Books, New York 1959.

In discussing the book with Dr. Pieper, I suggested that Brabender's work not be shown through standard academic photographs, representing, as they usually do, straight front or side views. A sculptor would like to see his work photographed in a different way, at least that's the way I feel about my work. To do the right kind of book on Brabender's sculpture, new photographs ought to be taken with the eye of a sculptor. I suggested that David Finn, whose photographs of sculpture I like, might be interested in photographing all of Brabender's work in a way that would show what a fine sculptor he was. I am very pleased that David Finn did become interested in the project and that after several years, the work has been finished, Dr. Pieper has written a scholarly text, and the book can be published.

The first sculpture by Brabender that I saw was the monumental 'Entry Into Jerusalem' in the Münster Museum and it was that work which made me realise that he was a great sculptor. I was moved by the remarkable human expression in the faces, the dignity, aristocracy, nobility of the figures, the feeling for form one finds in the skeletal structure of the arms and legs, the beautiful arrangement of details. The figures are organised into a fine composition, marvellously posed into a good, simple, monumental design in which the whole work functions. There's a fine sense of the material, an interpretation of life in stone. The work has a remarkable presence. I knew I had come across a truly distinguished sculptor.

As one moves on to the other groups in the museum, one finds the same remarkable qualities. The sculptor was clearly a man who observed nature closely, as in the stubble on a man's chin, the details of an ear, the wrinkle in the skin. But what simplicity there is in it all! If you study the work carefully, you can see how Brabender takes drapery in one big swoop as a sculptural abstraction, and how that makes a marvellous contrast with the realism of the face. One is so simple and the other so detailed, the whole effect is beautiful.

And what a sense of humanity! One of the sculptures I like best is the figure of a woman with her remarkable eyes looking downward in a kind of tragic sorrow. Even the top of the hat, where it has been broken off, looks fine. Luckily, the damage to the sculpture has not hurt the design.

One feels the great quality of the work in the fragments as well as the full figures. In the torso of the crucified Christ, for instance, one feels the wound and the blood coming out translated into extraordinary sculptural terms. It is a real gash, a deep wound.

The work in the Münster Museum which impressed me so much was from Brabender's mature years, when he was in his 50s and 60s. I have now seen photographs of his earlier works, some of which I find competent, but not outstanding. In the early years, in his 20s and even 30s, Brabender was, I believe, a good but not a great sculptor. In that respect he was far different from one of his contemporaries, Michelangelo, who produced his 'David' while he was only in his 20s. Brabender began, as I see it, as an able but somewhat naive Westphalian sculptor who rose from obscurity to execute some great works in his later years.

44 Heinrich Brabender, *Christ's Entry into Jerusalem*, c.1512-5, limestone, height 240cm (94½in). Westfälisches Landesmuseum für Kunst und Kulturgeschichte, Münster

In Brabender's early works, as in the Blomberg tomb, one can see hints of outstanding sculptural qualities. The drapery in the figures, for instance, has strength in the design, but it doesn't have the variety or sensitivity or the personal vision of the mature sculpture.

When one examines later works, one can see the growing development of the artist. 'The Madonna' relief in Münster which Brabender did when he was about 40 years old is a beautiful work, although it still follows what must have been the traditional style of the period. Brabender's true originality is not yet apparent.

When one comes to smaller works done in the later period which Brabender completed after 'The Entry Into Jerusalem', one finds all the force and originality of his later years. The photographs of details – faces, hands, feet – in these sculptures are especially lovely. I find the expressions on the faces very moving, even though they are very small. I don't care much for the decoration in the Philippus-Jakobus altar, where I find too much elaborate detail, particularly in the branches. However, I feel some of the features, such as the skull with the roots of the tree coming through it, are very strong.

I did not see the 'Madonna' which is located in Paderborn, but judging from the photographs, it is a fine work, although not as moving as some of Brabender's other sculptures. Here one can see the sculptural carving of the folds and the excellent design of the figures. The details are remarkable, and the natural lighting in the photographs seems especially good.

The Lubeck sculptures are among Brabender's most impressive works. There is a superb unity in the way the figures are grouped. In 'The Last Supper', for instance, the folds of the garments are carefully designed to make a horizontal pattern across the scene, which gives a rhythm to the whole work. In another, the details of feet and hands, the table, chairs, the tub of water in which Christ is washing the apostle's feet, are all excellent. I know these sculptures were damaged during World War II, and I wonder about some of the restorations, particularly the noses on some of the faces which seem too shiny or the wrong shape. But the work as a whole is very human, very tragic and surprisingly modern.

The large work of Petrus and Paulus in Warendorf is one of Brabender's last works. It seems strong to me, well designed, with good details, but somewhat mannered. A more moving work of his last years, at least for me, is the 'Christ Before the People' in Münster. I think the faces are marvellous, as good as those in the 'Entry Into Jerusalem', although, of course, much smaller. And even though the work is damaged, it has a fine composition. I think this is one of Brabender's best sculptures.

I am glad that I could be helpful in bringing the work of Heinrich Brabender to the attention of those interested in sculpture. He had a unique vision to contribute to the world and he deserves to be known widely.

My interest in seeing the book published has enabled me to get to know Dr. Paul Pieper who has visited me several times in Much Hadham to discuss the project with me and to go over the photographs. He has been most helpful in explaining the historical background of Brabender's life and I have enjoyed the friendship which has developed through our common interest in Brabender's work.

I am also pleased that David Finn found Brabender's sculpture as moving as I did, and that he was able to make several trips to Münster and other places in Westphalia to photograph all of the work. His photographs accomplish exactly what I hoped they would, and effectively present the monumental and human qualities of Brabender's great work.

Draft, dated 28 January 1980, for Moore's introduction to Paul Pieper,

Heinrich Brabender: ein Bildhauer der Spätgotik in Münster,

Coppenrath Verlag, Münster 1984

Constantin Brancusi (1876-1957)

Since the Gothic, European sculpture had become overgrown with moss, weeds – all sorts of surface excrescences which completely concealed shape. It has been Brancusi's special mission to get rid of this overgrowth, and to make us once more shape-conscious. To do this he has had to concentrate on very simple direct shapes, to keep his sculpture, as it were, one-cylindered, to refine and polish a single shape to a degree almost too precious. Brancusi's work, apart from its individual value, has been of historical importance in the development of contemporary sculpture. But it may now be no longer necessary to close down and restrict sculpture to the single (static) form unit. We can now begin to open out. To relate and combine together several forms of varied sizes, sections and directions into one organic whole.[27]

From 'The Sculptor Speaks', *The Listener* 18 August 1937

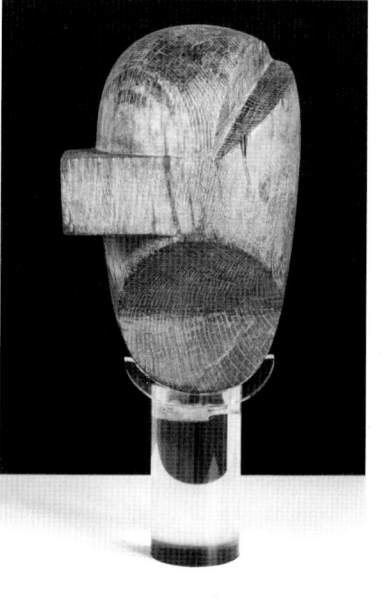

45 Constantin Brancusi, *Head* 1919-23, wood, height 29cm (11in). Tate, London; © ADAGP, Paris and DACS, London 2002

46 Brancusi, Moore, Frank McEwen (British Council), Herbert Read and Paul Eluard at the British Council Gallery, Champs Elysées, Paris, 1945

[27] In order to have Brancusi represented in this section among the artists whom Moore admired, this extract has been taken from 'The Sculptor Speaks', where it also appears on pp.194-5.

47 Paul Cézanne, *The Large Bathers* 1906, oil, 208.3 x 251.5cm (82 x 99in). Philadelphia Museum of Art: purchased with the W.P. Wilstach Fund

Paul Cézanne (1839-1906)

Sometimes, the impression of seeing something for the first time is immense. A great work, for instance Cézanne's *Bathers* [fig.47], the big triangular bathers, will always stand out clearly in my memory. I went to Paris several times when I was a student, but the Cézanne was the big event. He brought painting back from straightforward copying of nature to picture making, into using the mind as well as just taste. I think photography was playing an important role at this time in that its ability to copy with accuracy freed the painter to explore other ideas.

Cézanne's figures had a monumentality about them that I liked. In his *Bathers*, the figures were very sculptural in the sense of being big blocks and not a lot of surface detail about them. They are indeed monumental but this doesn't mean fat. It is difficult to explain this difference but you can recognise a kind of strength. This is a quality which you see only if you are sensitive to it. It's to do with the full realisation of the three-dimensional form; colour change comes into that too, but not so importantly as human perspective.

Bathers is an emotional painting but not in a sentimental way. Cézanne had an enormous influence on everyone in that period, there was a change in attitudes to art. People found him disturbing because they didn't like their existing ideas being challenged and overturned. Cézanne was probably the key figure in my lifetime.

Hedgecoe 1986, pp.150-1

HENRY MOORE: Well, it's the only picture I ever wanted to own.[28] It's a Cézanne and the joy of my life. I saw it about a year ago in an exhibition and was stunned by it. I didn't sleep for two or three nights trying to decide whether to … To me it's marvellous. Monumental. It's only about a foot square, but for me it has all the monumentality of the bigger ones of Cézanne. The first – the very first composition I saw of Cézanne's was in

[28] *Three Bathers* c.1873-77, see fig.149.

1921, on a visit to Paris, when I had an introduction to M. Pellerin and there in the entrance hall of his house was the big triangular composition 'The Bathers'. For me, that represents the most ambitious, the biggest effort that Cézanne made in all his life. This one that I have has to me just as monumental a sense.

In this kind of composition I think that Cézanne was trying to compete with all the things he admired. He was trying to do all he knew in it. In some of his things he was trying to learn, trying to find out, and to reduce his problems to a single one. But in this, he is competing with everything in picture-making that he knew about.

It's not perfect, it's a sketch. But then I don't like absolute perfection. I believe one should make a struggle towards something one can't do rather than do the thing that comes easily.

Perhaps another reason why I fell for it is that the type of woman he portrays is the same kind as I like. Each of the figures I could turn into a piece of sculpture, very simply.

HUW WHELDON: Not slips of girls.

MOORE: Not young girls but that wide, broad, mature woman. Matronly. Look at the back view of the figure on the left. What a strength – what a … almost like the back of a gorilla, that kind of flatness. But it has also this, this romantic idea of women. Four lots of long tresses, and the hair he's given them.

WHELDON: I imagine that 'romantic' is not a word, is it, that could be applied to your work?

MOORE: Oh no, not at all, – I think I have a very romantic idea of women.

WHELDON: Your earlier point about perfection. Do you want the struggle made clear to you in the final product?

MOORE: Well, I don't expect the problem to be solvable and so easy. In fact that's the thing about Cézanne: he was ready to pit himself against all that he admired, against the old masters. He wasn't satisfied with impressionism. He said, 'I want to make impressionism an art of the museum, which it isn't' – which means that when he went to the museums and saw Rubens and El Greco, Tintoretto, he knew there was something missing, something not wide enough – broad enough – deep enough – in impressionism. That is, his life was one monumental struggle and aim to extend himself and painting and art generally.

Monitor: An Anthology, edited by Huw Wheldon, Macdonald, London 1962, pp.21-2

Salvador Dali (1904-89)

I remember going to a Surrealist meeting at which Salvador Dali was the speaker.[29] We all sat there for about 25 minutes or so and nothing happened,

---

[29] Dali gave a lecture at the New Burlington Galleries, London, during the *International Surrealist Exhibition* (11 June to 4 July 1936), in which Moore had exhibited four sculptures and three drawings. Dali wore an old-fashioned diving suit. The heat in the gallery was so great that he had to be rescued; when the helmet was unscrewed, Dali was found to be unconscious.

just an empty stage. Everyone was getting fed up and starting to leave when suddenly there was an enormous bang and a great puff of smoke and, as it cleared, there was Dali standing in a diver's suit with a diving helmet, giving his lecture. Anything for publicity. We had already met him before he was well known, before he started being odd. He had come to our studio in Hampstead.

Hedgecoe 1986, p.72

Donatello (*c.*1386-1466)

For me he is one of the greatest, of course. If one had to play the game of naming the ten greatest, he'd certainly be along with Michelangelo, Rembrandt, Leonardo, Titian. [...] I think that what relates all the people that I have talked about is their great humanity, is the fact that they love life, understand the tragedies and the miseries and so on, but give to other people this enjoyment and belief that life is a marvellous, wonderful thing and worth living.

Chronicle: Italian Breakthrough, BBC 1978

On Donatello's *David*

It's perfect. It's like a beauty contest. It's like the Miss World. It's marvellous but it's giving you a kind of superficial perfection whereas Michelangelo, and Donatello in his great works, was not. This was his work when he was trying to prove to everybody how good he was. It's all such observation of life, but you can't all the time be producing your best masterpiece. Some are better than others and ... you have to have, not a fallow period, but ... less tension on some occasions than others.

Ibid.

On Donatello's *Gattamelata*

This is an affirmation that life can be marvellous, that life can be full of achievement and of glory and as such it expresses it by the pose of the horse, the pose of the rider, his face, everything in it is this singing of a glory of life, the singing of a glory of living and of power. Look at the feet of the rider – such decision and power, such absolute assurance. This is really a pent-up lump of energy. Here he's using all his great human experience and his sculptural experience, his knowledge to make what I think is one of the greatest equestrian statues the world has produced.

Ibid.

On Donatello's *Magdalen*

He loved hair. We know how different a woman can make herself look by a different hair-do and Donatello knew that he could play with hair and get it to do things, and in this Magdalen the hair coming down over the forehead repeats some of the lines in the sides of the mouth and of the skin being stretched over the starved cheekbones. But the hands then have this gentle,

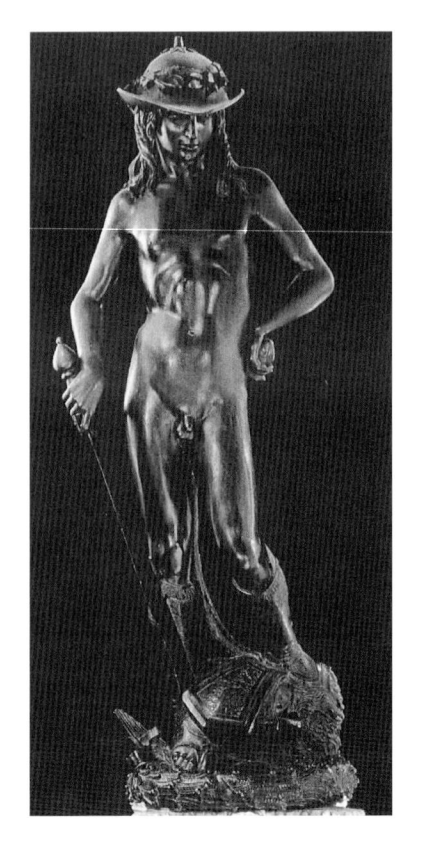

48 Donatello, *David* c.1440, bronze, height 158cm (62in). Museo Nazionale del Bargello, Florence

almost appealing, asking people to be sympathetic and if one looks at the feet, the feet are almost clutching the rock that she is standing on. The feet have got expression almost like hands.

Ibid.

Jacob Epstein (1880-1959)

I first met Jacob Epstein (who died last week, aged 78) in the mid-1920s, a time when I was unknown and he was the most famous sculptor in Britain, and I have two reasons to be grateful to him, both in a way personal, but one more personal than the other. He bought works of mine, before ever I had had an exhibition, and he showed an excitement in my work, as he did in everything else that he liked or loved, which was characteristic of the man, and which is perhaps not found as often as one might hope in the attitude of a famous artist towards his juniors.

This vital quality, this engagement of himself – I remember that on one occasion he jumped into a taxi with a piece of sculpture of mine he had just bought from me, even though I did not regard it as completely finished, because it was his and therefore he wanted it then and there – was perhaps one of the most attractive qualities of the man. He was strong and immediate in his likes, and also in his dislikes.

And this immediacy and strength drew forth a similar response. In the years before and just after the first world war, while he was perhaps the sculptor most admired by the perceptive, he was undoubtedly the most loathed by the philistines.

*   *   *

And that is the second, and slightly less personal, cause for my feeling of gratitude towards Epstein. He took the brickbats, he took the insults, he faced the howls of derision with which artists since Rembrandt have learned to become familiar. And as far as sculpture in this century is concerned, he took them first.

We of the generation that succeeded him were spared a great deal, simply because his sturdy personality and determination had taken so much. Sculpture always arouses more violent emotions than, say, painting, simply because it is three-dimensional. It cannot be ignored. It is there. And I believe that the sculptors who followed Epstein in this country would have been more insulted than they have been had the popular fury not partially spent itself on him, and had not the folly of that fury been revealed.

Why he should have aroused such anger it is hard now to see. His Strand figures, carved in 1908, which in 1937 were removed from the façade of the building which had belonged to the British Medical Association, were in the direct tradition of European sculpture, and show more strongly than any other influence that of Rodin – at a time when Rodin was universally admired. His Oscar Wilde, which shows a strong Mexican combined with a certain Sumerian–Assyrian influence, may have been tarred in Paris in 1912 for reasons not solely deriving from the work itself. Indeed, apart from his Paris period just before the first world war, when he was seeing a great deal of Modigliani and others (I am thinking of his 'Rock Drill' period), he was scarcely an innovator, let alone a revolutionary.

* * *

He was a modeller, rather than a carver. To put it in other terms, his was a visual rather than a mental art, and with him the emphasis was on subject rather than on form. He was an intensely warm man, who in his work transmitted that warmth, that vitality, that feeling for human beings, immediately. His master was Donatello, rather than Michelangelo; and in Rembrandt, whom he also studied most carefully, it was the direct and personal warmth that affected him perhaps more than the formal side.

It was this quality of Epstein's, I think, that produced his greatest work, which I believe to have been his portraits (particularly his portraits of men, whom he saw with a greater objectivity than that which a man of his direct and personal vision could turn upon women) and also such pieces of sculpture as his 'Madonna and Child', one of his best and last works, that is now in Cavendish Square. Of the sculptor's media, his was surely clay.

Artists tend, perhaps inevitably, to be egotistical. Epstein was no exception, and there is nothing that he made that is not redolent with his own personality. But egotism is not synonymous with selfishness. And few men can have loved sculpture purely for its own sake more than Jacob Epstein. The wideness of his sympathies is shown in his own fine collection of sculpture, which included Negro, Egyptian, Chaldean work as well as much else – and in his collecting he was even more appreciative of carving than he was of modelling.

He was a broad-shouldered, fine, sturdy man. Insults and misunderstanding, which dogged him all his life, hurt him of course, but he shrugged them off. In his old age he even came to resemble Rembrandt physically. His warmth and his vitality and his courage will not be quickly forgotten.

We have lost a great sculptor.

The Sunday Times 23 August 1959

The portrait heads. Well, I think he was a very gifted portraitist. He was a very good draughtsman. I mean he could draw from life and from nature, so he had this gift for doing portraiture. Oh yes, and working from the model. He was a very figurative artist. But you see Epstein had a kind of type of women, and he turned all the portraits of women into an Epstein type. And for that reason, when I knew the person that he was doing, if I'd seen the original, the female ones, the women, I would find that he had turned them into his own kind. But with the men he didn't, he looked much more objectively in the male portraits. And for that reason I prefer the male portraits to the female ones, to the women.

Interview with Colin Ford, *Kaleidoscope*, BBC 5 November 1980

49 Jacob Epstein, *The Rock Drill* 1913, bronze, height 70.5cm (27¾in). © Tate, London 2002

Henri Gaudier-Brzeska (1891-1915)

I wonder if many artists have been affected by a book about art criticism as you have been by Roger Fry's Vision and Design. *Have any other works of art criticism affected you so greatly?*

No. But another book that I found a great help and an excitement was Ezra Pound's book on Gaudier-Brzeska.[30] This was written with a freshness and an insight, and Gaudier speaks as a young sculptor discovering things.

Interview with Donald Hall 1960; quoted in James 1966, p.49

Another help to me was the appearance of Gaudier-Brzeska, who really changed his work because of Epstein. They met, it's recorded in one of the books on Gaudier-Brzeska, I think, that Gaudier, when he'd attempted two or three [sculptures?], went to some exhibition where he met Epstein, and he admired what Epstein had done and he was introduced to Epstein. And Epstein then was a strong believer in direct carving: he was the first in England to believe that something carved out of stone and evolved in that direct way was better than modelling, and when he was introduced to Gaudier, the first question Epstein said is 'Do you carve direct?' And Gaudier being a bright young fellow said yes, but he hadn't done it. But he said yes, and Epstein said, 'Oh, I'll come to your studio next Sunday then.' Now this was Tuesday I believe, or Monday, and Gaudier went out to the stoneyards and got all the blocks of stone, the bits of stone, the lumps of stone that were going, and he put them in the studio and he did a little bit of carving on each of them, so when Epstein came on Sunday he believed that he was a direct carver – which he wasn't!

In conversation with Huw Wheldon, *c.*1983; HMF library copy

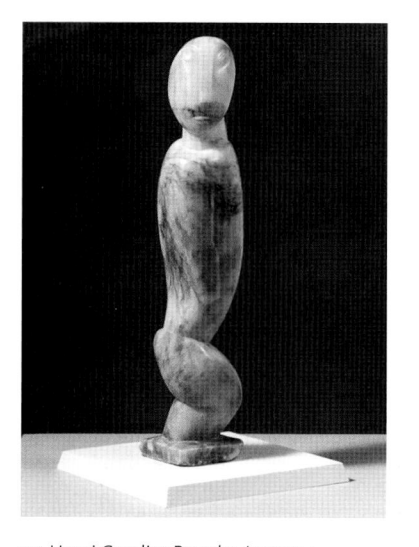

50 Henri Gaudier-Brzeska, *Imp* 1914, alabaster, height 40.6cm (16in). Tate, London

Alberto Giacometti (1901-66)

After this visit to Picasso's studio to see *Guernica* in progress,[31] we all went back and had drinks at the French restaurant, wherever it was, sitting at tables outside, and I sat between Breton and Giacometti – this was '36, '37. We were talking about art in general – again, they could talk a little bit of English, Breton could, and I could understand French – and […] somehow the conversation turned to Maillol, and it became a kind of argument between Breton and Giacometti about Maillol. And Breton was saying that Maillol was a very poor artist, second rate or what, and Giacometti was trying to say that Maillol was a very good artist; and I was appealed to, sitting between them, for my opinion. I realised that this was a kind of father and son situation, in which the son was trying to break the dominance, the domination of the father, because one knows that Giacometti had been greatly influenced by Breton's ideas, and under that influence Giacometti produced some remarkable, imaginative and more Surrealist kind of works than he

---

[30] Ezra Pound, *Gaudier-Brzeska: A Memoir*, John Lane, London and New York 1916.
[31] See p.166.

might have done without the influence and friendship of Giacometti [*sic*, i.e. Breton]. [...] I could see that here I was sitting between this desire of Giacometti to begin to not be dominated by ... which made him argue. And one knows that later Giacometti broke this domination, and he became completely interested again in the figure, he became figurative – he did nothing in the end but portraits of his brother and so on, and all very ... not realistic, but interested in life, in nature, and not so much in the dream or in the fantasy. This was interesting, too, to be in on the emergence of a very good artist like Giacometti into his own work, because all young artists have to be influenced, but there comes a time when an artist begins to have his own direction, and likes to follow it in spite of other people, as he should do.

In conversation with David Mitchinson, Margaret McLeod, Ian Barker and others, *Henry Moore on Spain and Henry Moore Interview c.*1981; HMF library

And there are still sculptors with plenty to say in the traditional materials, aren't there?

Giacometti, for one. In his surrealist period he showed a remarkable poetic imagination in things like his 'The Palace at 4 a.m.' – *poetic*, I mean, not literary – and later, when his feeling for Etruscan and Egyptian art came together with his understanding of, and particular excitement about, Cézanne, he produced something very specially his own: a reality of the wraith, as it were. In Giacometti's work the armature has once again become the life-line of the sculpture, and also he's brought back to sculpture a nervous sensitivity which the 'pure carving' side of sculpture can lose sight of altogether. There had been a danger, when Giacometti was developing, of sculpture becoming just a matter of craftsmanship.

Russell 24 December 1961

He wanted to make a thing like a spring onion.

In conversation with Huw Wheldon, *c.*1983; HMF library copy

We have just lost a great artist with a profound sensibility – a unique human being. Giacometti knew and appreciated the artistic tradition stretching right back to ancient times and including such art as Egyptian and Etruscan sculpture, and reaching right up to the great masters such as Cézanne. This knowledge was combined with the precise observation of nature. He created his own poignant and personal world. I love his sculpture and his painting but above all it is his drawings which move me most. The greatest note of consolation that one can find with his death comes from the fact that he was present in London last summer and saw the large exhibition,[32] so marvellously installed by David Sylvester, which was dedicated to his work. He was thus able to clearly recognise fully his success and see how his art was appreciated in England and what it meant to the English public.

Lettres Françaises, Paris 20-26 January 1966, p.12 (translated from the French)

[32] Tate Gallery 1965.

Mathias Grünewald (1460-1528)

[...] I'd forgotten Grünewald's Isenheim altarpiece, which I saw for the first time last year at Colmar. That was like the Rondanini Pietà of Michelangelo, or like Shakespeare almost, in the most absolute and beautiful human tenderness that Grünewald manages to mix in with the awe and the misery of it all.

Russell 24 December 1961

Barbara Hepworth (1903-75)

Barbara Hepworth was born in Wakefield, in Yorkshire, and I was born in Castleford, just eight miles away. So perhaps you ought to think of us as two Yorkshire people who went to the same college. I went to the Leeds School of Art in 1919. It was in my second year that Barbara Hepworth came to the college, though not to do sculpture;[33] she was 17 years old and a very pretty girl. We were always like a younger sister and an older brother.

The School had no sculpture department when I first went there: at first I was the only pupil who wanted to do sculpture and so the sculpture department was set up for me. Sculpture was not a popular art form in England in those days. People today don't quite realise what a huge difference came about during and after the Second World War. The art situation has changed completely. This is very important when you remember the sort of work Barbara Hepworth has done.

And of course when we came to London, to study at the Royal College of Art, Barbara Hepworth and I and a few Yorkshire students, on county grants, you could have counted the people who were interested in collecting sculpture on the fingers of one hand. Modern art in general, too, was very little appreciated.

I suppose we were a kind of little Yorkshire influx. Most of us had never been to London before, so we hung together a good deal. And of course it was very fortunate that William Rothenstein was appointed Principal just in the year when Barbara Hepworth and I arrived: his family had lived in Yorkshire too, and I suppose he had a sort of understanding and sympathy for us and the way we felt. And he changed the College completely. It used to be a place where teachers taught teachers who became teachers and taught teachers who taught teachers, rather, you know, like a snake eating its own tail. Rothenstein was horrified. 'What arrogance,' he used to say to people who wanted to just become art teachers, 'how can you presume to want to teach what you don't know?'

And Rothenstein was already a man who'd moved far beyond the closed-in world of the provincial art school. He used to give dinner-parties on Sunday evenings and ask one or other of us students in for coffee. We would meet people like Eliot and Yeats.

As for the world we made our professional beginnings in, I remember

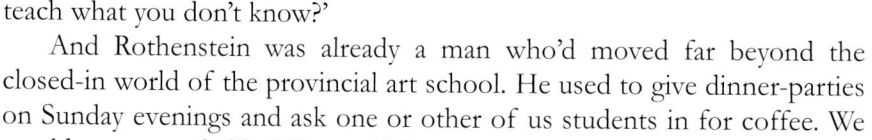

51 Barbara Hepworth, *Figure of a Woman* 1929-30, stone, height 53cm (21in). Tate, London © Sir Alan Bowness

---

[33] Hepworth did go to Leeds School of Art to study sculpture; see p.42, note 11.

that at the first Paul Klee exhibition in London in the early Thirties, at the Mayor Gallery, there were about 40 watercolours, the average price was about £30, and not one was sold. At my first exhibition in 1928 there were only about £90's worth of sales. Because there was so little interest in modern art, the few of us who were intense about it acquired a kind of force, confidence – a pioneering, Messiah-like spirit. When you put a tight lid on a kettle you develop quite a head of steam.

When in 1934 Freddie Mayor exhibited a Picasso still life which cost £150 a few of us decided that we'd try and collect £5 each from thirty people, or £3 each from fifty people, buy the picture and present it to the Tate. You know what the Tate was like in those days: the Director had only recently refused a Cézanne as a gift from somebody. Anyway, all we managed to collect was £9.

And then Paris was a regular place of pilgrimage. It was the absolute centre of the art world, which it no longer is. I went first in 1922, and afterwards every year, sometimes twice, for a week or a fortnight. We'd go in small groups, three or four of us, often including Barbara, and after doing the rounds of the galleries we thought we'd better do some work, so we used to buy one-franc tickets for those 'croquis classes' in those little academies in Montparnasse, for a two-hour sitting. You drew your model in one hour, then again in half an hour, then in ten minutes, then in five and finally in one. Perhaps the result wasn't always very good, but it was very good practice. The people who came to these classes sometimes looked much more interesting than the models, who were often awful. We even had some businessmen at these classes, I suppose that was their chance to see a nude model.

When I got married in 1929 my wife and I lived near Barbara in Hampstead; she was already married to another sculptor, John Skeaping. He had the most wonderful facility with his hands as a carver, and Barbara Hepworth learned a great deal from him technically. We had wonderful times with them. My wife and I would go over and we would have long discussions or play skittles; shove-ha'penny was another great game of ours. Jack built a little pond in the garden with goldfish in it, and we used to have competitions to see who could catch more goldfish. They never came to any harm though: they'd bite on the worm but never actually get caught on the hook, so we could always throw them back again.

Gradually Hampstead became a colony of the arts – Paul Nash, Mark Gertler, Roland Penrose, Herbert Read, Breuer from the Bauhaus, Mondrian. And Geoffrey Grigson started 'New Verse' up there.

When the Surrealist exhibition was held Barbara was by then married to Ben Nicholson,[34] they were strongly against it, though I felt, and feel, that there needn't be the sort of division in art that sprang up then. And Ben had also been much influenced by Mondrian. He was devoted to abstract art and

[34] The *International Surrealist Exhibition* was held in London in 1936; Hepworth and Nicholson were married on 17 November 1938.

she became much more interested in the abstract form. But for me, the essence of sculpture has always been the human figure. Still, of course, one kept in touch and one met and one's paths crossed. They went to live in St Ives. She had children, triplets – but that didn't stop her from working. She was a woman of great dedication and perseverance and bravery. And you must always remember that sculpture was a very uphill fight for anyone then, and especially for a woman.

We mustn't think of the terrible way she died. We must look back on the good days of the past. We have lost a most remarkable artist and a wonderful woman.

The Sunday Times 25 May 1975

52 Moore, Barbara Hepworth and Naum Gabo at the opening of a display of four works given by them and Ben Nicholson in memory of Sir Herbert Read at the Tate Gallery, 10 March 1970

Masaccio (1401-28?)

The old masters I admire. If I were asked to give a list of ten amongst them would certainly be Masaccio whom on my travelling scholarship as a young [sculptor?], I used to visit every morning, before going anywhere else I went and looked in the little Brancacci Chapel […]

But the 'Tribute Money' and the other pictures in the chapel bowled me over completely because he was the first artist, the first one really, to get weight, to make sculpture in painting really, to get the reality that sculpture can have into painting. But also too, what he could do and what he did, he fitted in with my beliefs and attitude to sculpture and the fact that he did it not by jumping around, not by action, not by battle scenes and so on, I mean, the 'Tribute Money' is just twelve people or thirteen, whatever number there are, standing in a row with just something happening between two of them that gives a kind of Greek ominous tragedy […]

In conversation with Juliet Wilson, 1979

53 Masaccio, *The Tribute Money* 1427, fresco. Brancacci Chapel, Santa Maria del Carmine, Florence

If you had one work of art to live with, which would it be?

Perhaps I would move into the Brancacci Chapel in the church of Santa Maria del Carmine in Florence. It's a small chapel, painted by Masaccio. It has scenes from the life of St. Peter – the tribute money, healing the sick, baptising and distributing alms with St. John, raising the son of Theophilus – and, of course, the expulsion of Adam and Eve from the Garden of Eden. It's like seeing the essence of a person's point of view. It expresses such an understanding of human nature.

Interview with Milton Esterow, 'Mr Moore, what use is what you're doing?'
Art News, New York October 1982, pp.110-11

Michelangelo (1475-1564)

The Michelangelo Vision

DAVID SYLVESTER: Your generation of *avant-garde* artists tended to react against Renaissance art. I know that you yourself as a student were especially interested in things like Pre-Columbian and African art. Where did you see Michelangelo in relation to this?

HENRY MOORE: I still knew that as an individual he was an absolute superman. Even before I became a student I'd taken a peculiar obsessive interest in him, though I didn't know what his work was like until I won a travelling scholarship and went to Italy. And then I saw he had such ability that beside him any sculptor must feel as a miler would knowing someone had once run a three-minute mile.

Take the *Moses*. The way he builds up a mass of detail yet keeps the same vision and dignity throughout it – it really is staggering that anyone should do that out of such an intractable material as marble. There's an ability to realise his conception completely in the material and to find no restrictions or difficulties in doing it. You look at any of the parts and it's absolutely perfect: there's no hesitation – it's by someone who can do just what he wants to do. But later his technical achievement became less important to him, when he knew that the technical thing was something he could do without worrying.

I do dislike in some of his sculptures, like the figures of *Night* and *Day*, the kind of leathery thickness of the skin. You feel that the bodies are covered with a skin that is half an inch thick rather than a skin such as you see in the Ilissus of the Parthenon. The skin there is exactly skin thick, whereas in some of Michelangelo's middle-period sculptures there's a thick leatheriness that looks to me a little bit repellent. Nevertheless in a work like the *Night* there's a grandeur of gesture and scale that for me is what great sculpture is. The reason I can't look at Bernini, or even Donatello, beside him is his tremendous monumentality, his over-life-size vision. What sculpture should have for me is this monumentality rather than details that are sensitive.

SYLVESTER: Do you ever find yourself put off by that high polish on his marble?

MOORE: Sometimes. But in the *Night* or the *Moses* you'd lose something without that high polish. In some of his works he used contrast between a highly finished part and a part that is not so finished, and this is something one likes.

I would say that all young sculptors would be better if they were made to finish their early works to the very utmost. It's like a singer learning to sing higher than he can readily go, so that he can then sing within his own range. In the same way, if you can finish a sculpture, later you can afford to leave some parts unfinished. And for me Michelangelo's greatest work is one that was in his studio partly finished, partly unfinished, when he died – *The Rondanini Pietà*. I don't know of any other single work of art by anyone that is more poignant, more moving. It isn't the most powerful of Michelangelo's works – it's a mixture, in fact, of two styles.

It must have been started at least ten years before his death and at some stage was probably nearly finished throughout, in the style that the legs are in still. Then Michelangelo must have decided that he was dissatisfied with it or wanted to change it. And the changing became so drastic that I think he knocked the head off the sculpture. Because, if you look at that arm,

54 Michelangelo, *Rondanini Pietà*, between 1552 and 1564, marble, height 192cm (75⅝in). Castello Sforzesco, Milan

which hangs there detached from the body of Christ, you see that it ends less than halfway up the biceps, yet this brings it nearly level to the shoulder of the existing figure. So the figure must originally have been a good deal taller. And if we also see the proportion of the length of the body of Christ compared with the length of the legs, there's no doubt that the whole top of the original sculpture has been cut away.

Now this to me is a great question. Why should I and other sculptors I know, my contemporaries – I think that Giacometti feels this, I know Marino Marini feels it – find this work one of the most moving and greatest works we know of when it's a work which has such disunity in it? There's a fragment – the arm – of the sculpture in a previous stage still left there; here are the legs finished as they were perhaps ten years previously, but the top re-carved so that the hand of the Madonna on the chest of Christ is only a paper-thin ribbon.

But that's so moving, so touching: the position of the heads, the whole tenderness of the top part of the sculpture, is in my opinion more what it is by being in contrast with the rather finished, tough, leathery, typical Michelangelo legs. The top part is Gothic and the lower part is sort of Renaissance. So it's a work of art that for me means more because it doesn't fit in with all the theories of critics and aestheticians who say that one of the great things about a work of art must be its unity of style.

SYLVESTER: It has been called by some historians a wreck – which seems obtuse.

MOORE: It does to me, because it's like finding the altered work of all old men a wreck. I think the explanation is perhaps that by this time Michelangelo knew he was near death and his values were more spiritual than they had been. I think also he came to know that, in a work of art, the expression of the spirit of the person – the expression of the artist's outlook on life – is what matters more than a finished or a beautiful or a perfect work of art.

I'm sure that had he taken away the nearly detached arm we should find it less moving because that part is near the new part. And undoubtedly, in my opinion, had he re-carved the legs to have the same quality as the top, the whole work would have lost its point. This contrast, this disunity of style, brings together two of the Ages of Man, as it were.

SYLVESTER: It's not great in spite of its disunity but because of it?

MOORE: For me it's great because the very things that a lot of art writers would find wrong in it are what give it its greatness. There's something of the same principle in his unfinished *Slaves* – so-called unfinished: I don't think they're unfinished, because though Michelangelo might have gone on a bit more, I can't conceive that he would ever have wanted to finish them in the high way he finished other works.

Here again it's that same contrast – a contrast between two opposites, like the rough and the smooth, the old and the new, the spiritual and the anatomic. Here in this *Pietà* is the thin expressionist work set against the realistic style of the arm. Why should that hand, which scarcely exists, be so expressive? Why should Michelangelo, out of nothing, achieve that feeling of somebody touching another body with such tenderness? I just don't know. But it comes, I think, from the spirit. And it seems to me to have something of the same quality as the late *Crucifixion* drawings.

SYLVESTER: They are certainly the other works by Michelangelo to which *The Rondanini Pietà* relates. For one thing, they have the same stark up-and-down movement.

MOORE: Yes, I think that towards the end of his life he was someone who knew that a lot of the swagger didn't count. His values had changed to more deeply fundamental human values.

SYLVESTER: By the way, the arm that remains from the earlier state echoes the vertical movement of the group.

MOORE: Yes, that's maybe why he left it and didn't want to lose it. He wasn't dissatisfied. But I think there was no such conscious kind of design. I think that the parts he disliked he would alter and the parts he didn't dislike he'd leave.

And this is how artists work. It isn't that they work out – at least I don't – a theory, like saying 'This is upright and I'm going to leave it because it fits in with my new thing.' It's because you *see* it fits in that you leave it – you're satisfied with it. It's that you work from satisfaction and dissatisfaction. You alter the things that don't seem right and you leave the things that are more right to go on with sometime later.

SYLVESTER: But why does this kind of simplicity in Michelangelo produce such a different effect from the kind you get in archaic forms of sculpture?

MOORE: Well, I think that if you do the opposite of something which you have a full experience of doing, the seeds of the previous thing will still be there. That is, nothing is ever lost, nothing is ever missing. The *Crucifixion* drawings are very simplified, without the twisting and turning of the earlier Michelangelo, yet they have a slight movement, a slight hang and turn that gives a sense of agonised weight. All his past experience is in them.

This is the kind of quality you get in the work of old men who are really great. They can simplify; they can leave out. Even someone like Matisse can just sit in his bed, ill and sick, nearly dying, and with a pair of scissors and so on he can cut out things – and why they're so good is because of the past history of Matisse. There's this little difference that he makes which some young man trying to imitate him would never make. And that's why I'd say that in the *Crucifixion* drawings and in *The Rondanini Pietà* there's the whole of Michelangelo's 89 years' life somewhere. This *Pietà* is by someone who knows the whole thing so well that he can use a chisel like someone else would use a pen.

Also, there is a fact, and for me a strange fact, about the really great artists of the past: in some way their late works become simplified and fragmentary, become imperfect and unfinished. The artists stop caring about beauty and such abstract ideas, and yet their works get greater.

SYLVESTER: You've emphasised the fragmentary character of this *Pietà*, and likewise you prefer the so-called unfinished *Slaves* to the finished

55 Michelangelo, *Christ on the Cross between the Virgin and St John*, between 1538 and 1557, chalk, 40.7 x 27.7mm (16 x 10⅞in). Copyright © The British Museum, London

ones. Now this is very much something that modern taste likes: the fragment. But we'd like to think that this was something more than a fashionable cult.

MOORE: Yes, I'm pretty sure it isn't that. You see, I wouldn't call the *Crucifixion* drawings that we've been admiring fragmentary and unfinished. I think they have about them a wonderful existence in space. The figure on the Cross, the two figures at the side of the Cross – there is an atmosphere round them: they're realised tremendously in space, they're not sketches in the sense that they're just the beginnings of something which if it were carried further would have meant more.

SYLVESTER: But what is it that makes you like the unfinished *Slaves* better than the finished ones?

MOORE: I prefer them because they have more power in them, to me, much more power than the finished ones. That one in the Louvre is much too weary and sleepy and lackadaisical.

SYLVESTER: Well, it's meant to be dying.

MOORE: I know, but I mean you can have a thing that's dying and yet it has the vitality of the sculptor in it.

SYLVESTER: Maybe the more finished works are often less sympathetic just because they express Michelangelo's fantasy more clearly and we find certain things in his fantasy repellent. For instance, that leathery skin in the figure of *Night*. With the unfinished *Slaves*, you don't refer them back in a literal way to life in the same way as you do the *Night*.

MOORE: No. And when one compares her breasts to a real woman's breasts, one finds them unpleasant. And I think in some of Michelangelo there can be a kind of melancholic lazy slowness. I admire that, but I don't like it, and that's perhaps why when he hasn't arrived at that, like in the unfinished *Slaves* – where that can't come in because he hasn't had the time to put it in – they appeal to one more.

But one still admires *Night*. I mean, this is still an unbelievable pose. The whole attitude of the figure, the grandeur, the magnificence of the conception is still a wonderful thing. In all his work – early, middle, late – there's no sculptor of more ability. He could do anything he wanted.

The Sunday Times Magazine 16 February 1964, pp.18, 20-2

Michelangelo has the biggest reputation of practically any artist there has ever been. I don't know of any since him who touch on that true greatness. He wasn't, of course, recognised as the great man that he was until some long time after his death.

The unfinished sculptures impressed me most of all. They taught me what happened in his mind. When you see only the finished thing you don't know how it was arrived at. To see something that's not highly finished, or not had an enormous amount of time spent on it, you learn more about the person's methods and thinking.

Hedgecoe 1986, p.150

[Michelangelo] is just superhuman [...] you know it's like someone being able to run a three-minute mile when [everybody] else can do only four minutes.

Interview with Aline Saarinen,
NBC TV Today: Henry Moore Report, NBC, New York 1970

Michelangelo for instance has a kind of lazy heavy ponderous slowness as though slowly turning in thick treacle –.

Unpublished notes *c.*1951, HMF archive

You see, Michelangelo liked nude men. I mean, even when he makes the women, they've got skin like rhinoceros, really, I mean, in certain ways I dislike Michelangelo's women.

In conversation with Juliet Wilson, 1979

Joan Miró (1893-1983)

Miró was a lovely person, a very, very sensitive and sympathetic friend, and I think there's such an appreciation of the joyful side of life, and of a kind of childish – not childish, but childlike freshness of appreciation of the world. Of course he's one of the greats.

In conversation with Huw Wheldon, *c.*1983; HMF library copy

Ben Nicholson (1894-1982)

Of course we knew Ben when he lived next door to us in the Mall (studios). Irina knew how to deal with Ben best. She would say: 'Now Ben, when you're bored and you want to go home, don't hesitate, go!' He was that type. He was so self-centred that if the conversation was about something he wasn't interested in, he couldn't bear it. But he was a good artist of course.

In conversation with Roger Berthoud, 18 October 1982

56 Moore and Miró at Perry Green, 1973

MAURICE DE SAUSMAREZ: The years from 1933 to 1939 in the art of this country were a remarkable six years don't you think?

HENRY MOORE: Yes, but I think it was only the development of what had been prepared some time before. If I were trying to explain it historically, I would begin with Roger Fry and Clive Bell importing Post Impressionism, with later the counter ideas of Wyndham Lewis, with *BLAST* and the Vorticist movement, and people like that, all leading up to the period of the thirties. A great deal of what was done then in England was a sort of 'catching-up' on what had been initiated mainly in Paris in the twenties and earlier. And for me Paris in the thirties, my meeting with Picasso, Giacometti, Paul Eluard and André Breton was far more important than Unit One[35] and other episodes here. Unit One was really only a gather-

35 See p.191, note 5.

ing together of English talent which had got its chief sustenance, not from England but from outside.

DE SAUSMAREZ: And yet, in talking with Naum Gabo, he referred to the situation then in Paris as being hostile to constructivist artists and that, coming to England, he had found a group and a situation with which he could establish real links.

MOORE: I'm sure that is true. There were so few artists in London in the early thirties that there were no deep jealousies. Someone like Gabo could come and contribute something, but in Paris there were the giants, Picasso, Matisse, Braque, Mondrian, Kandinsky and other big names, and an artist like Gabo might have been having a rather lonely time of it – I think this may be what made the English scene such a contrast and attractive to him.

Then in Paris there were individuals like Jean Hélion (who was a close friend of both Mondrian and Léger); he provided a link with the English group. I liked him enormously. At that time he was someone who had to have a theory, a directional system to work on; he was perhaps more convinced in an intellectual way about abstract art than Nicholson or anybody else in England. Nicholson's conviction comes, not from theory and argument, but purely from what he feels he likes, and from an inner direction. He's very able to give justifications and throw light on what he's doing, but he is not what one would call an intellectual, whereas Hélion had about him the stamp of the intellectual, and this I think is what led him, after the war and the experience of being a prisoner, to revalue his attitude to art and life in general and to reject abstract art.

DE SAUSMAREZ: I suppose you got to know Ben Nicholson in the Seven and Five Society[36] didn't you?

MOORE: Well it must have been then, but you know I can't remember ever exhibiting with that group, because, by that time, I'd begun to have my own exhibitions, and to have enough sculpture every two years for an exhibition at the Leicester Galleries, I needed to gather together and retain my work. I often found I didn't have work available for other shows. But I should say it was about 1930 that I got to know Ben, because I was married in 1929 and I remember that when someone had proposed me as a member of the Seven and Five my wife, Irina, took photographs of my work down to Chelsea for the meeting at which I was to be elected.

DE SAUSMAREZ: But I don't suppose you were ever a great one for attending meetings, so that you probably didn't see much of Ben at the meetings of the society?

MOORE: No, I only began to meet him frequently after he came to know Barbara Hepworth well and came to live in Hampstead in one of the Mall Studios. I had been living in a studio very near there, in Parkhill Road, since

---

[36] The Seven and Five Society, a progressive group of British artists originally made up of seven painters and five sculptors, was formed in 1919. Ivon Hitchens and Leon Underwood were among the founding members. Nicholson joined in 1924, Skeaping, Hepworth and Moore in 1931; Moore exhibited with the group the following year. The Seven and Five Society disbanded after their final exhibition at the Zwemmer Gallery, London, in October 1935.

my marriage. The Seven and Five was being transformed at that time from what had been a rather mixed and muddled group of seven painters and five sculptors – though where they got five sculptors from in those days I don't know. I can't remember there being that many, unless one went to the Royal Academy. The few sculptors outside the R.A. – Epstein, Gill and Dobson – weren't members of the Seven and Five; John Skeaping might have been.

DE SAUSMAREZ: During this period in the thirties would a sculptor's keenest interests lie abroad?

MOORE: Well, as far as I was concerned, mine didn't lie abroad so much as in the British Museum. If I had to say what things helped me most I would say, the British Museum, in learning what world tradition in sculpture was, my academic study of Life modelling and drawing and absolute obsession with the human figure, and my interest in natural forms.

But Paris, of course, did mean a lot to me – it was in those days the undisputed world capital of modern painting and sculpture. Starting from 1923 [1922] I made trips to Paris once or twice every year – and got to know what was going on there, from Cézanne and Cubism onwards. I think most of my contemporaries here had contact with Paris – many of them living there for long periods.

DE SAUSMAREZ: Do you recall any aspects of Nicholson's working situation at that time or anything that might throw light on his ways of working then?

MOORE: 'Experimental' artists in England were having a terribly thin time. It was natural and necessary for those of us with like aims and sympathies to know each other and to be friends – you couldn't help it, it was like the situation of a foreigner in another land finding people he could talk to in his own language. And we sometimes went on holidays together – I remember there was a summer holiday, maybe the summer of 1930, when a group of us spent a fortnight at Happisburgh on the Norfolk coast – there's a photograph of the party reproduced somewhere, with Ben, Ivon Hitchens, Barbara Hepworth, Jack Skeaping and two friends of Skeaping's, and Irina and me.[37] I remember it was very good weather, and it was there that we found ironstone pebbles which are hard enough and also soft enough to carve. Some were already beautifully simplified shapes.

So it was natural we all knew each other, but that didn't mean that we were not critical of each other's work, or divided in our directions – some surrealist, some abstract, and so forth. For example, in Unit One, in spite of its name, the people in it were so critical of each other's work that, after a year and a half, they decided to resolve the situation by a vote. Unless each member got more than half the total votes of the membership, he would automatically resign; when the voting was completed, I was the only one left in the group!

DE SAUSMAREZ: So, eventually, you alone were Unit One!

MOORE: But to go back to Nicholson, I remember very clearly the architect

[37] See fig.57 overleaf. Skeaping does not appear in this photograph.

57 Ivon Hitchens, Irina and Henry Moore, Barbara Hepworth, Ben Nicholson and Mary Jenkins, Happisburgh, Norfolk, 1931

Bobby Carter with his wife and children one Saturday morning coming away from 7 Mall Studios with a small Nicholson work under his arm. I could see the whole family was very elated, and I'm sure Ben was very pleased that somebody was buying a picture, because it would be very interesting to know whether, up to the war, Ben could have lived on what he got from his paintings. I couldn't have lived only on selling my sculpture, I depended on my two days' teaching each week, and I don't believe that Ben and Barbara could have managed on sales of their work alone. Now this gave a common sympathy, because we were all in the same boat, in a philistine unappreciative world. In a sense I enjoyed it, because when people said there had never been any English sculpture and never would be, which is what was often said, it acted rather as a challenge, than otherwise.

DE SAUSMAREZ: Nicholson started to produce his white reliefs in 1934. Do you think this might have had some connection with his being then in closer touch with sculptors?

MOORE: It may have been that having a few sculptors around indirectly prompted him to translate the Mondrian influence into carving, but he has always been a very good craftsman and to do that kind of thing would have been a quite natural direction.

DE SAUSMAREZ: And of course it does relate essentially to the idea of two-dimensional screens moving back in a controlled space.

MOORE: Yes, it's a picture-plane progression – a relief idea allied to painting, a one-directional view.

DE SAUSMAREZ: What would you say you recall most vividly about Nicholson in those days, apart from his work?

MOORE: In a way my biggest contact with Ben was really through his liking of games which I liked. Quite often he would ring up and say 'Henry, what about a game of tennis?' Well, he could make rings round me, despite my having won a competition in the tennis club at Castleford. I don't know whether he ever qualified for Wimbledon but he could well have done so. Ben is a natural ball player – he was an absolute wizard at ping-pong. He actually invented a variation of the game which he demonstrated at Gamage's or somewhere, hoping to patent it. Instead of a net one had a platform about 4 or 5 in wide and used the top of this platform to bounce the ball on to and off. It gave hazards to the game rather like those in a game of fives, one never knew quite at what angle the ball would come off the platform.

DE SAUSMAREZ: Geoffrey Grigson reminded me of another game you used to play on a large sheet of paper.

58 Letter from Ben Nicholson (16 June 1931) showing Moore's 1929 alabaster *Head* LH 73 on the dressing-table in his studio at Bankshead, Cumberland. © Angela Verren-Taunt 2002/All rights reserved DACS

165

MOORE: Ah yes, shut-eye golf. That was introduced and I think invented by Eric Ravilious. On this large sheet of paper you drew an imaginary golf course with a variety of obstacles – e.g. a dog, a tree, a cow, a bandstand, a duck pond and so on – and then you'd put a few extra bunkers in; it was a golf course in plan. Then you put the point of your pencil in hole 1, had a good look at the course and where hole 2 was, and what obstacles lay between, then you had to close your eyes and attempt to draw a line to hole 2, without the line touching any drawn obstacle. Sometimes one did it in one, but more often at one's first shot one's line touched a tree, or a bunker, or ended up far away from the hole – one had to play a second, a third and so on until the pencil point rested plumb in the hole. You could play a nine-hole course, or eighteen holes, and as in real golf the least score was the winner.

DE SAUSMAREZ: Grigson recalls that Ben and you were absolutely prodigious at this game.

MOORE: Well, it's a game that relies on visual memory, a judgement of distances and angles. Ben was an absolute 'natural'. This ability and skill was something that he enjoys enormously, and I'm sure that it comes out in his work – the actual technique, the way that it's done, the splendid craftsmanship, the unerring judgement – I'm sure all this is a great part of the pleasure that he has in working.

In 1930 Ben and I exchanged a work. I gave him a carving in white alabaster of 1929 [fig.58], and he gave me a very beautiful still-life oil, *Jug and playing cards*, also of 1929. We still have Ben's picture hanging where we see it every day, and we continue to get just as great enjoyment from it as ever.

Ben Nicholson: A Studio International Special, edited by Maurice de Sausmarez, Studio International, London 1969, pp.23-4

Pablo Picasso (1881-1973)

Did you get to Spain during the civil war?

No. A whole party of us were going to go – Auden and Spender and Blackett and Bernal and people like that, and Alexander Calder wanted to come along, too – but we weren't allowed to, at the last moment.

Most artists were of the same mind about Spain – I remember that when Irina and I were in Paris in the summer of 1937 Picasso invited a whole lot of us to go along to his studio and see how his 'Guernica' was getting on.[38] There was a big lunch, with Giacometti, Max Ernst, Paul Eluard,

[38] Moore does not mention Picasso's friend and biographer, the surrealist painter Roland Penrose, who wrote: 'In the summer of 1937 Henry and I found ourselves in Paris and we decided one evening to pay a call on Picasso' (*Scrap Book 1900-1981*, Thames and Hudson, London 1981, p.103). Moore recalled an afternoon visit to Picasso's studio, Penrose an evening visit. Penrose, who helped to organise the 1936 *International Surrealist Exhibition* in London, met Moore in the mid-1930s and acquired several important sculptures of his. For another account of the lunch in Paris with Giacometti and his friends, see p.151.

59 Pablo Picasso, *Guernica* 1937, oil, 349.3 x 776.7cm (138 x 306in). Museo Nacional Centro de Arte Reina Sofia, Madrid © Succession Picasso/DACS 2002

André Breton, and Irina and me, and it was all tremendously lively and exciting and we all trooped off to the studio, and I think even Picasso was excited by our visit.

But I remember him lightening the whole mood of the thing, as he loved to do. 'Guernica' was still a long way from being finished. It was like a cartoon just laid in in black and grey, and he could have coloured it as he coloured the sketches. Anyway, you know the woman who comes running out of the little cabin on the right with one hand held in front of her? Well, Picasso told us that there was something missing there, and he went and fetched a roll of paper and stuck it in the woman's hand, as much as to say that she'd been caught in the bathroom when the bombs came.[39] That was just like him, of course – to be tremendously moved about Spain and yet turn it aside with a joke.

Russell 17 December 1961

I'm nearly twenty years younger than Picasso. I didn't go to art school until 1919 and it was 1921 when I first came to London, but by then I did know about Picasso because one knew about Cubism by then. So really all my practising life was as a student, and as a sculptor I have been very conscious of Picasso because he has dominated sculpture and painting – even sculpture as well as painting – since Cubism. You see, it begins with Cézanne, and Cézanne led almost directly through to Cubism, and this then broke down

---

[39] Penrose wrote of this incident: 'As though she had been disturbed at a critical moment, her bottom is bare and her alarm too great to notice it. "There," said Picasso, "that shows clearly enough the commonest and most primitive fear".' (*Scrap Book 1900-1981*, p.103)

the idea, which had been more or less general with everybody, that art was trying to copy nature, that art was representational: the nearer you got to the average person's idea of nature, the better you were. This we know by the discovery … not the discovery, but by the appreciation of primitive arts, Negro sculpture and so on, all this changed. And this one can trace in the life of Picasso, very clearly. So all that leads then to people being open to experiments and to new ideas in painting and sculpture. But right up until the war there was a very definite anti-modern attitude. People forget that so-called modern art was looked upon as Bolshevik, and immoral, and so on. I remember two or three of us, at one time, wanting to have Picasso properly represented – or better represented – in the Tate Gallery (this must have been somewhere round about 1931 or 2), found that there was a painting, a still life, by Picasso in a gallery called the Mayor Gallery … and it was only £150. We thought that if we could get fifty people to give three pounds each we could then present this painting to the Tate Gallery, and as a presentation they wouldn't be able to refuse it. At that time there was a very [...] anti-modern director named [J.B.] Manson, who I think had even refused a Cézanne as a gift. So we sent out a pamphlet, a little cyclostyled pamphlet, appealing for donations of three pounds a time, and we sent out about oh, three or four hundred – we got three replies, one of which was me! So that we got nine pounds towards this. Now this is the kind of situation that there was. Nowadays the young of today don't realise what a different world it is, how novelty, innovation and new, seemingly new ideas are welcomed and can get exhibitions. And of course Picasso, I mean his work has undoubtedly gradually brought people to see and appreciate and to value work which before the war was very difficult to have people appreciate. Now there's no doubt that we've lost by Picasso's death – it's the end of an era, and all the young people who feel or think that they are not influenced by the Picasso generation, that he's irrelevant and so on, it's like a young person saying they don't want anything to do with their father, they want to be against their father, they want to just do the opposite. But they should realise they wouldn't be there if it weren't for their father.

Interview with Elizabeth Blunt, *Kaleidoscope*, BBC 9 April 1973

John Piper (1903-92)

John Piper has been a good friend of mine since my student days at the Royal College of Art, after which we often showed our work in the same exhibitions. He helped to keep going the interest we all had in enlivening the English art scene, which at that time needed help. He has developed a very personal vision and style, and has helped people to see, particularly the architecture around them, with new eyes. I would like to send John my very best wishes for his 80th birthday.

To John Piper on his Eightieth Birthday, 13 December 1983,
edited by Geoffrey Elborn, Stourton Press, London 1983

Giovanni Pisano (1245/50-1314?)

The first time I saw the sculptures of Giovanni Pisano was in 1925 when I visited Pisa on a travelling scholarship from the Royal College of Art. I must only have been able to admire, or try to admire, the sculptures on the façade and those on the top of the Baptistery, with struggle and effort, for when I could only see them at such a distance above me it was impossible to feel the true three-dimensional, face-to-face relationship which I need from sculpture. I wanted to see them as Giovanni made them, because a sculptor cannot work with a long arm and a long chisel from the ground and carve something up in the air; he must carve it in his studio as a man-to-man relationship. It was only after the war, when the big figures from the niches were taken down and put inside the Baptistery, that I saw them near-to, and then I was at once struck by the tremendous dramatic force of what I would call the hallmark of Giovanni's sculptural quality, style, or personality. It was also after the war that I saw properly the smaller life-size figures which, for their preservation, have been removed from the architecture and put into the Pisa Museum. Then I saw in so many of them the thrusting-forward neck, the neck that goes forward at an angle of forty-five degrees or even more (but with the head itself left upright). It has been said that he carved them like that to avoid a squat, foreshortened appearance when the figure was to be seen high up in perspective, but you get the same urgent, thrusting attitude in some of his figures which are meant to be seen at eye-level, such as the Caritas on the Pisa Cathedral pulpit. This thrust, I think, was something Giovanni felt about the urgency of human communication. He simply felt that the figure needed this tremendously potent gesture forward to 'give the message'. These sculptures are absolute presences and they made a lasting, most powerful impression on me.

Not only the figures in the Pisa Museum but, later, the Siena Cathedral façade sculptures proved to me that Giovanni Pisano was a great sculptor in every sense, particularly in the sense of understanding and using three-dimensional forms to affect people, to portray human feelings and character, to express great truths.

The surprising thing was to find how Giovanni had freed himself from his father Nicola. I had been taught and, later, when I was teaching, I repeated that the father of the Renaissance was Nicola Pisano and that Giovanni, his son, was his follower. Nicola, I presume, took his start from Roman sarcophagus reliefs which freed him from the Byzantine stiffness and gave him a naturalistic, more realistic, point of view about sculpture than his predecessors. But Giovanni went further; what he did was really to articulate the individual parts of the human body. I think it was Giovanni Pisano's excitement over articulating the human body in sculpture, *in a way that we know from our own physical experience that it can't articulate*, that made his sculpture new and great; we know that the head is a separate movable unit, the neck is another unit, the shoulders are another, the pelvis is another, the legs can bend at the knees and then bend at the feet. There are about sixteen individual units in the human figure: head, neck, thorax, pelvis, thighs, lower legs, feet, arms and hands all of which can bend at angles to each other. Having these units, you can place them at different angles in space. Take Giovanni's so-called 'dancing figure': look at that forward-thrusting neck, that vertical head; the body sways so that the hips are pushed forward and the legs are held back. I don't think it was meant to be a figure that was actually dancing; I think he was giving energy to the figure by articulating it from inside. His father's sculptures, wonderful as they are, are often very static and rigid. They do not have what I was searching for when I was a young sculptor, the using of real three-dimensional forms poised in space. Nicola Pisano did not use the human body as he used facial expression, and you have to use the body as you use the face if you want really to convey the fullest human meaning. This is something which Michelangelo did later on. He used the body to express his deep philosophical understanding of human nature, human tragedy and everything else. In this Giovanni had been the innovator.

But if I compare Michelangelo's David with Giovanni Pisano's figure of David from the Siena façade, I find that although the David of Michelangelo is an unbelievable, superhuman achievement for a young man of twenty-five, it is very different as an expression of a philosophical outlook on life; it is a marvellously realistic understanding of a young man's body, a body exuding tremendous physical assurance … The David of Giovanni Pisano has behind it an intensity of human understanding, of deep personality; it's like comparing Benedick and Hamlet. The Giovanni Pisano has all the implications of the contradictions, troubles and worries inside its head that Hamlet had, whereas the Michelangelo has no real troubles in its head at all, no unconquerable problems.

I have said that by making the pieces of the human body seem movable and articulated with one another, you give sculpture intensity, but by this I do not mean the portraying of actual physical movement such as walking, running etc. For Giovanni gets drama into his figures when they stand still, as Masaccio did later. In Masaccio's *The Tribute Money* [fig.53] you feel, when Peter hands over the money, that there is a kind of electric charge in the air and this is created not by strong physical action but by a dramatic tension, something that both Masaccio and Giovanni could give in their work. The late Michelangelo has the same thing. In the *Rondanini Pietà* you get an absolute volte-face from his early David, through an almost expressionist antirealistic use of anatomy. It's a change from the Renaissance back to the Gothic. It's as if Michelangelo had come through at the end of his life to something nearer to Giovanni's attitude. It's the huge difference between using anatomy for its own sake and using a knowledge of the human figure to express one's philosophy, one's interpretation of life generally — and this is what surprises me: that Giovanni had done this so early. This is why I think he should be more widely recognised now as the great artist that he is. When you look at Giovanni's relief carvings, it is natural to relate them to Giotto's frescoes. So many people think that Giotto was the forerunner of the Renaissance, that he changed Italian art by using the human figure in a

60 Giovanni Pisano, *David* c.1284, stone. Siena Cathedral façade

plastic way to express human emotions, but Giovanni was doing this earlier; for instance those triangular eyes with which Giotto expressed terrific grief can be found in Giovanni's *Massacre of the Innocents* on the Pistoia pulpit. But all this does not impress me as much as the single figures I first mentioned. For me, it is possible to separate his narrative, his story-telling gift, from his gift for form, which is why to me the single figures are the most exciting.

I want to say something about stone and marble carving as a technical thing. For instance, if you carve a piece of marble freshly quarried, it is much softer than it will be a year or two later. When it is new, it is called 'green' (like a green tree with the sap in it), and a stone used quickly out of a quarry is twice as easy to cut and to carve as stone which has been quarried a few years. I think that having his quarry near Pisa would mean that the marble would be used very soon after being quarried. Then, again, I think Giovanni had better-tempered tools than his predecessors. This would have given him more speed and freedom than his father. He would not have taken half as long to block out a big mass, and then to articulate it into his smaller masses. This could be one of the explanations for his freedom in the use of stone compared to other sculptors before him. Of course there's a difference in the hardness of various stones, but even this relates to its time of quarrying. This applies even to very hard stones like granite. The granite in Cornwall is worked into kerb-stones and cobble-stones immediately it is quarried, and while it is 'green'. Giovanni's marble from San Giuliano wasn't all that hard, which is why his exterior sculptures are so weathered. I don't think we lose anything essential by that weathering. I even think the weathering reveals the big, simple design of his forms more clearly. It probably reduces what we see to what it had been a stage before it was finished, simplifying it back again without the detail.

Nicola Pisano used the drill as part of his studio technique because with the drill you can free the stone so that you are not punching against absolute resistance but against something that will free itself; you open it up like a Gruyère cheese before you cut it away. The drill technique was a very special mark of the Pisano school, but Giovanni used it as an expressive instrument as well as a practical one. He used it to give colour and texture to a surface so that if he wanted to make a beard have darkness, he would so drill it that it would take on a colour and a texture seen from a distance. This is one of the things that amazes me about him, this expressive use of the drill, not simply to make the job easier, but to accentuate its form. If you look at really primitive stone sculpture, such as early archaic Greek or Pre-Columbian work, you will find the drill used, but most of it is what we call 'rubbed sculpture', that's to say that after roughing out the forms with a punch, which breaks and stuns the stone, the craftsman got to work with abrasives, and rubbed the surface down until he got as far as he could beyond the stunning marks, and as smooth as he wanted his surface to be. By these means he got very simplified forms which are thought to be typically 'stone', but people think this because the sculptors did not have tools which could go beyond these simplicities; once you get a drilling technique as expert as Giovanni's you can go deeper into the stone and give it more expression, more colour, texture, light and shade.

But it's wrong to think that form and expression are separate things. For instance, if I put my hand on someone's shoulder, I can put it in a way that seems to be gripping or just gently touching. I may be touching it with affection and gentleness or I may be making some kind of empty gesture. All this is in the intention of the sculptor; it's part of his expression but it's part of form; you cannot separate the two. If you made a sculpture of Adam and Eve and Adam had his hand on Eve's shoulder, you could do it in a way that would show that he loved her or that he was ashamed of her; it's all done by a sensitivity to form, perhaps a greater sensitivity than is needed in dealing *only* with simple geometric abstract shapes – and it's in this way that Giovanni Pisano was a fully developed sculptor. His form, his abstraction, his sculptural qualities were integrated. The human and the abstract formal elements were inseparable and that is what I think really great sculpture should be.

The way Giovanni used and understood marble gave the stone life, the power to live from inside. Michelangelo said once 'the figure is in the stone; you have only to let it out', so that stone sculpture is not man-made but man-revealed. Giovanni let the inside of the stone come out; he freed something from the inside.

Giovanni Pisano's humanism has a quality which is for me the same as Rembrandt's humanism or Masaccio's humanism or the humanism of the late Michelangelo drawings. He was a man who showed in his sculpture the whole situation of the human being. It is, for me, this quality which makes Masaccio and Piero della Francesca and Rembrandt great. If I were asked to choose ten great artists, the greatest in European art, I would put Giovanni Pisano among them. It would be because of his understanding of life and of people. I feel terribly strongly that he was a great man because he understood human beings and if you asked me how I would judge great artists it would be on this basis. It would not be because they were clever in drawing or in carving or in painting or as designers; something of these qualities they must naturally have, but their real greatness, to me, lies in their humanity.

These are the reasons why I wanted a book on Giovanni Pisano to be published. I wanted to convey by it something of the impact his sculpture had on me so that other people could see that they must go and look at that sculpture itself. I well remember going to Pisa one afternoon a few years ago to look once more at the Giovanni Pisanos and I was full of them that evening when I went to dinner with Walter and Eva Neurath[40] at their house at Camaiore. What a shame it was, I said, that there was no book in English, so far as I knew, that gave Giovanni his due. Here was an artist who had done in sculpture things that Giotto and Masaccio would come to do in painting, but it was they who had got the credit for being the fathers of the Renaissance. I said that it seemed a pity that there was no book that tried to show what a great artist in sculpture Giovanni was.

[40] Walter and Eva Neurath founded the art publishing firm Thames and Hudson in London in 1949.

'Why don't we do it?' Walter Neurath asked. 'Why doesn't Thames and Hudson do this? Would you help?'

I have helped as far as I could. I have spent many hours in Pisa and Siena with Michael Ayrton, who has shared my enthusiasm for twenty years and had proved it as long ago as that, by his lecture to the Royal Society of Arts from which his text has grown. Cavaliere [Ilario] Bessi, our photographer, was with us and I showed him in detail exactly what I wanted to bring out in the photographs. I wanted to illustrate that Giovanni Pisano approached the structure of sculpture from inside. Many early sculptors approached form from the outside, rounding it off and smoothing it, but Giovanni was one of the first Italians to feel the bone inside the sculpture and when we looked at the lions on the Pisa Cathedral pulpit and at the wolf in Siena, we could see how the elbow joints pushed out, that there was an inside structure, a skeleton to the sculpture coming out. It is not rubbed down, not sucked, like a sucked sweet, which is made unified because the outside is all smoothed. Looking at that lion and seeing that there were no smooth connections between the forms, I knew how Giovanni had understood the articulations of the figure. I would not easily nowadays give up time and energy to helping with a book, but I feel that in devoting both to this one I am doing something to repay a debt, for we are all indebted to Giovanni Pisano.

Michael Ayrton, Giovanni Pisano: Sculptor, introduction by Henry Moore,
Thames and Hudson, London 1969, pp.7-11

Giovanni Pisano
Compare him with his father Nicola Pisano,[41]
Nicola – all one piece – stiff
Giovanni – Articulates the human figure – so that a pelvis can move in opposition to the thorax – the neck comes out of the body with a thrust of its own – the head is then set on the neck at another angle (not just a continuation of the neck) the legs restore the balance with a rhythm etc. etc.

But all this is not a figure in physical action, not a figure moving off its pedestal, it is static, yet dynamic – it is capable of movement, it is articulated –

But besides all this sculptural originality (experiment) (expression) a greater quality still is the warm, human dignity & tenderness & grandeur – something akin to Masaccio.

Unpublished note late 1950s (?), HMF archive

Rembrandt (1606-69)

In the early portraits of Rembrandt we find all the wealth of human character, a quality which psychologically seen is very satisfactory without conveying the experience of form. In his later portraits, for instance, the one in our

---

[41] Nicola Pisano, active c.1258-78.

National Gallery,[42] the reality of form comes to the fore. One feels that one could touch that forehead, knock on it. It is like a loaf of bread.

In conversation with J.P. Hodin, 12 July 1957

Pierre Auguste Renoir (1841-1919)

Whoever doesn't like those girls doesn't understand what Renoir was trying to do. The two pictures [figs 61, 62] must represent at least three or four months of continuous work at the best period of Renoir's life. A tremendous amount of application went into the painting of them, a great deal of real ambition; they represent a big effort to produce something worthy of the museums.

If you copy nature as it is, as Renoir was mainly doing during his earlier impressionist period, you can't really show the form that underlies appearances. Nature is too complicated, and to make a work of art out of it you have to simplify, to invent a system of vision. In painting, where you have to reduce everything to a flat surface with only colour and texture, you have, above all, to simplify the lighting. Renoir hit on this method of lighting the model, as it were, simply from his own eyes; so that all his surfaces are subject to a logical system of lighting which explains the form. In these pictures he has learned to fit his forms into space. The shapes of these two girls are melted into the background; so that what you see and feel about them comes from inside the forms, not just from the outlines, as it did earlier, in his hard-edge paintings.

And yet these rounded forms have a marvellous, supple rhythm, such as people are apt to associate only with outlines. What one likes about them is that, though they are so monumental, yet, if you compare them, for instance, with Maillol's sculptures, they have none of the stiffness which these are apt to have. They make me realise that Renoir was really a much greater sculptor than Maillol.

And, in addition, what lovely passages there are of delicious painting and wonderful colour! There are so many subtleties in the painting of them which one goes on discovering that I never know which I like the better of the two. One day it's one, another day it's the other.

One could say most of these things if these were 'abstract' pictures. But they are anything but that; Renoir tried to put into them all that he felt about women. The way he dressed them up is a key to this. For me their costumes only emphasise the sculptural grandeur of them, as Rembrandt wanted to do when he dressed up Saskia. Renoir didn't just paint these girls as he saw them about the house, as he did in so many of his smaller, more everyday pictures. When they came into his studio in the morning to pose, they didn't just take off their clothes either. The whole ceremony of getting dressed up would help to make the occasion important.

[42] Moore is almost certainly referring to *An Old Man in an Armchair*, which entered the National Gallery as a Rembrandt but is now thought to be by a seventeenth-century follower. In 1982 Moore executed two charcoal drawings of the National Gallery painting, HMF 82(24) and 82(25). It is possible, although less likely, that he may be referring to Rembrandt's 1669 *Self Portrait at the Age of 63*, also in the National Gallery.

61 Pierre Auguste Renoir, *Dancing Girl with Tambourine* 1909, oil, 1549 x 648mm (61 x 25½in). © National Gallery, London

62 Pierre Auguste Renoir, *Dancing Girl with Castanets* 1909, oil, 1549 x 648mm (61 x 25½in). © National Gallery, London

The pictures represent, I'm sure, a significant episode in Renoir's career, a special effort; that's why I think they are not just ordinary pictures for private collectors, why I believe they are the kind of pictures we should have in the National Gallery.

Statement in support of Philip Hendy, Director of the National Gallery 1961;[43]

quoted in James 1966, pp.187, 189

But besides a personal preference for particular subject matter and composition you also mean of course a personal form vision, for example Renoir & Cézanne both painted compositions of bathers – Renoir has a sinuous flowing snakelike rhythm and Cézanne has a short staccato, stratified rocklike rhythm as though his forms were chopped into their shape by an axe –

Unpublished notes for 'Art and Life', 1941, HMF archive

Ceri Richards (1903-71)

What I always admired about Ceri Richards, right from his Royal College of Art student days, was the way he could draw. More than any other British

---

[43] This statement in support of the purchase of the Renoirs was made when Moore was a trustee of the National Gallery. In the first edition of *Henry Moore on Sculpture* 1966 the statement was dated 1962, but this was changed to 1961 in the revised edition of 1971.

painter of his time he understood three-dimensional form and knew how to express it on a flat surface. His drawing is so assured, so full of energy and virility, that it gives his work a quality that goes way beyond charm. In fact, 'charm' isn't the word for it at all: Ceri's work has authority because of his drawing.

I think it is this ability to draw which gives to his painting the same boldness and assurance, which both Picasso and Matisse show in their painting, because they are both superb draughtsmen. I have a special liking for Ceri's reliefs – works he did around 1932/38 – I find them full of invention, and wit and originality. His work, of course, reveals something of his character as a man. With other people there are little things that one has to excuse, or to take for granted. But with Ceri there was none of that – I never knew him to say a nasty or spiteful thing about another artist – he never showed envy or jealousy, and he was a marvellous enthusiast and appreciator. I never knew anyone who had so few faults, so few blemishes, so little that anyone could dislike. Now that he's gone, I think all of us want to say just that.

Homage to Ceri Richards 1903-1971, Fischer Fine Art, London 1972, p.15

Auguste Rodin (1840-1917)

Rodin died on 17 November 1917, aged 77. Henry Moore was then 19, a soldier serving on the battlefront in France. We began our conversation by talking of his earliest memories of Rodin. Moore has no recollection of learning of Rodin's death, though he was already well aware of the great sculptor's reputation:

I certainly knew about Rodin. I remember my father showing me some photographs of his sculpture, and this may have been as early as 1914. And when I was demobilised in 1919 and went to the Leeds School of Art, I remember making a figure influenced by Rodin, a figure of an old man with a beard. He was very thin and scraggy, but he cracked, because I didn't know enough about armatures. Miss Gostick at Castleford had it in her house, on a shelf, until it disintegrated and fell apart. Then I did another piece influenced by Rodin, a head of a baby, also in 1919.

About this time in Leeds Reference Library I came across Rodin's book called *Art* [1912] – as simple as that – the conversations with Paul Gsell. I read this book with great interest. I remember in it somewhere Rodin saying that when he got stuck with modelling a clay sculpture, he would sometimes drop it on the floor and have another look. Now this was for me as a young sculptor a tremendous revelation of how you can take advantage of accidents, and how you should always try and look at a thing over again, with a fresh eye.

What happened when you got to London, as a student at the Royal College?

I met people who knew Rodin, and that interested me. I remember Eric Maclagan[44] talking about him and to know that somebody like Rodin had

44 Director of the Victoria and Albert Museum from 1924 to 1944.

been in London and had walked these same little streets that I was walking – that was a very real thing for me. And I saw the works that he'd given to the Victoria and Albert Museum, and could study them. I had a great admiration for them at the time, though I never made any conscious study of Rodin.

There's usually a reaction against any great artist shortly after his death, and in Rodin's case this must have affected your generation in particular. I have the feeling that for a long time in the 1920s and 1930s nobody could make very much of Rodin's sculpture. Was this your own experience?

I think we were all influenced by Rodin at first – even Brancusi. And it's true that sculptors were interested in primitive art and that this profoundly altered sculpture. But Rodin himself, somewhere in one of his conversations, pointed to an early Greek or early Chinese sculpture, and said that this was what he would like to start from now. Towards the end of his life, he had come through to this point of view about sculpture.

But it's quite true that when I first went to Paris in the early 1920s I don't think I went to the Musée Rodin. I was much more interested in Cézanne and the Musée de l'Homme. It was the same with Michelangelo – when I won the travelling scholarship from the College, I did my best in the first two months in Italy to avoid seeing Michelangelo.

That's just the opposite from Rodin, because when he went to Italy as a young sculptor, he was tremendously impressed by Michelangelo – as we can see from works like The Age of Bronze *and* St John the Baptist.

I agree, there's no doubt about this, and Rodin owes a tremendous amount to Michelangelo. But you know, if you like something tremendously you may react and think you're against it, but inside you can't get away from it. This is what happened to me over Rodin. Gradually I began to realise that a lot of things one might be using and being influenced by – Negro sculpture for example, which gives you a simplified programme to work on – are, compared with Rodin, altogether too easy. So that as time has gone on, my admiration for Rodin has grown and grown.

In some ways your own personal experience mirrors a change in the general reaction to Rodin. Don't you think it's easier for us to appreciate Rodin today than it was thirty years ago?

I doubt it. Perhaps for the general public, but I don't know about the young sculptors. And there's still that literary, pictorial side to Rodin's work which we find in Victorian painting. This comes out particularly in the carvings, which weren't actually touched by him. Rodin wasn't a carver.

Can you define this Victorian flavour?

Well it consists of the sort of thing you associate with Victor Hugo – what can one call it? – the expression of a philosophical outlook on life, moral, universal …

You don't believe sculptors can be universal?

Oh no, I think they can, but they don't consciously need to be. And Rodin is as universal in his fragments as in the big figures, because he understood the human body so well. This is in my opinion the greatness of Rodin, that he could identify himself with and feel so strongly about the human body. He believed it was the basis of all sculpture. He understood the human figure so well and loved it so much that this is the universal quality in him. And out of the body he could make these marvellous sculptural rhythms. It's interesting that he talks about sculpture being the art of the hole and the bump – all his sayings on sculpture are about physical reactions to it.

I think that perhaps Rodin didn't take the literary meanings of his sculptures as seriously as his contemporaries. He changes his titles all the time, as though he really didn't care what the work was called. It's all a part of the extraordinary interchangeability you find in Rodin. In making the selection for the exhibition we have tried to switch the emphasis to Rodin as a sculptor of the figure or part-figure. I am sure that this is the kind of Rodin sculpture that interests us today.

I think you're quite right. For example, the final grouping of *The Burghers of Calais* is an arbitrary affair. So far as I can follow the history of the commission, Rodin's idea was to make separate figures and place them one by one on the route that the Burghers took. The figures were all made separately, and he put them together afterwards.

But this putting of things together is one of Rodin's most extraordinary qualities. He uses a figure from The Gates of Hell *in one context one minute, and in quite another the next. And then there's the way that he will join separate pieces of the body together in almost arbitrary fashion. He manufactured hands and limbs for possible use on later occasions. Certain plasters – like the* Burghers of Calais *assemblage – show him making something completely strange and original out of all these fragments. And in your torso [fig.63][45] the legs and trunk are taken from quite different works and then joined together.*

I'll tell you where the torso comes from – it comes from Michelangelo, from a drawing in the British Museum, I think.[46] Then the legs came from a striding man – they were done from a model. Rodin turned this striding figure into *St John the Baptist*. There comes the literary addition.

Probably most of us prefer The walking man *without a head and without arms to the figure of* John the Baptist *precisely because it hasn't got that literary association.*

I do, but I don't know how right we are in doing so. It's a problem of today, wanting to begin with the essence. A lot of young artists want to start with a simplified boiled-down soup without ever having had the bones and stock to make it from. I don't think we can do that.

[45] The bronze cast which Moore owned of Rodin's *The Walking Man* is no.7 in the catalogue of the 1970 exhibition at the Hayward Gallery, where it is dated 1877-78. Most scholars now agree that this sculpture was executed *c.*1900. See p.181.
[46] *Study of a Nude Youth*, see p.181.

But can't one argue that some of the very late works, like the Dancers, *are a kind of essential Rodin, when everything else has been distilled out?*

I don't believe that the very late works are always the best. The little figure that we have here on the table (no. 83 in the exhibition)[47] isn't for me as good a figure as the striding man we have upstairs. That has a kind of tension and a hardness and a softness, a contrast of bone, soft flesh and tense muscle. But the later work is softer. I can see how he's done it – he's squeezed soft clay through his hands.

Like many of the drawings, the Dancers *and* The walking man *are all very much concerned with the idea of movement. This is clearly of the greatest importance to Rodin, and it links him with the impressionist painters, just as other aspects of his work link him with the symbolists who were also his contemporaries. But how far do you think that the representation of movement is a proper concern of sculpture?*

This is one of the ways in which my generation does stand for a reaction against Rodin. One of my points is that sculpture should not represent actual physical movement. This is something I have never wanted. I believe that sculpture is made out of static, immovable material.

What about the Balzac *then? Do you think as many do that it's the culmination of Rodin's work, or do you find it less interesting, because it's clothed for one thing?*

No – because underneath one can see that there is the nude figure, and that it's been clothed. It's the same with the *Burghers*. What makes Rodin the great sculptor that he is, is his complete understanding of the body's internal structure, his ability to feel inside into the sculpture. This is so intense – even the late work has got behind it all that other observation and knowledge of the human figure. He couldn't have simplified the *Balzac* – he couldn't have started with the idea of a draped figure. Think of all the studies that he had to make first.

This is something one appreciates only if one visits the other Rodin Museum at Meudon, in the south western suburbs of Paris, especially if one is shown the original moulds for bronze casting still carefully preserved and the plaster casts Rodin used to make of work in progress …

Yes, it was visiting Meudon that made me understand one side of Rodin. Instead of the big official museum, one sees all the original plasters, and I found little terracottas and other small things done by his own hand with a freshness some of the later bronze casts have lost.

Were you not very impressed by seeing the succession of plaster casts Rodin would take of a head or a figure as he worked at it?

---

[47] Catalogue no.83 was called *Study of a Standing Nude* (undated), a cast of which Moore had owned and had given to his daughter, Mary. In Catherine Lampert's catalogue of a later exhibition at the Hayward Gallery, *Rodin: Sculpture & Drawings*, Arts Council of Great Britain 1986, p.215, an earlier cast of the same sculpture is called *Psyche*, and dated 1886. In the context of Bowness's question, however, it is possible that Moore was referring to another small Rodin bronze which he owned, *Dance Movement C* c.1911.

Yes, this was an eye-opener to me. Of course it meant that he could keep his original, and yet alter it, and then go back if he liked to the old one. Usually when you alter something in sculpture, you've lost it for ever. But Rodin's practice of taking casts meant that he could make his alterations and still keep the work that he started from.

Have you ever done this?

I have done it on occasion, yes. Though you can't do it with a carving of course.

There's another aspect of Rodin we haven't mentioned, that is his erotic side. This is something that matters very much for Rodin – he can revel in sensuality in a quite uninhibited way. What is your reaction to this?

It is certainly very important for Rodin, though it doesn't excite or interest me very much, perhaps because one knows the human figure so well. But for Rodin I think this erotic excitement was a part of his rapport with the human figure. And he was unlike Cézanne who had his erotic side but who suppressed it. This doesn't make Cézanne less of a physical artist, and I don't think you ever need this obvious erotic element for a person to understand the human figure. You don't get it in Rembrandt, and I would say that Rembrandt understands the human figure and the human character and the whole of its dignity and everything else.

Are you making a connection between Rodin and Rembrandt?

No, I don't see that at all. I can see a big connection between Rodin and Michelangelo. That is his greatest influence, without any doubt. I should say that he's the one artist since Michelangelo who has understood Michelangelo best. Rembrandt has an entirely different attitude, and he understands human feelings just as deeply as Michelangelo does. But Rembrandt was a painter, and Rodin was a sculptor. He brought sculpture out of the doldrums.

I remember that Herbert Read said somewhere that Rodin re-invented a lost art. Perhaps that's a little extravagant, but it's near to the truth.

Well, it is an exaggeration, because if an art is lost it means that nobody appreciates it, and nobody can again. But I can remember as a young sculptor reading a review of a mixed exhibition when the writer said that he didn't intend to talk about sculpture as it was a dead art, only something to bump into or to knock your head against. Now everything has changed, and I could reel off the names of a hundred sculptors in England alone. So that something very remarkable has happened, and to a great extent it is Rodin who is responsible.

In conversation with Alan Bowness; published in
Rodin: Sculpture and Drawings, Hayward Gallery, London 1970, pp.9-11

Rodin's 'Walking Man' as seen by Henry Moore

Albert Elsen in collaboration with Henry Moore

Rodin's *Walking Man* is a haunting sculpture for artist and art historian. For Henry Moore, 'The *Walking Man* has everything in it that I love about Rodin, especially his wonderful sense of the human figure'. Longer than the seven years he has owned a superb Alexis Rudier cast of this work, Moore has known, admired and reflected on what is certainly one of Rodin's best sculptures. (It is so placed in his home so that he can see it daily.) Although he remembers that only one work he ever did, the head of an old man which was kept by one of his art school teachers, was ever directly influenced by this great artist (specifically *The Old Courtesan*), Moore likes to talk about the many things he learned from such sculptures as the *Walking Man*. [...]

63 Auguste Rodin, *The Walking Man* c. 1900, bronze, height 83.8cm (33in). Formerly in the collection of Henry Moore

Henry Moore studied photographs of the Petit Palais torso,[48] noticed its repetition in the *Walking Man* and then commented on what it was that attracted him to both sculptures. From the beginning of his admiration for

[48] Rodin's *Torso* of 1875-77, bronze, Le Petit Palais, Paris.

the latter sculpture he has been drawn to 'the strongly Michelangelesque quality of concentrated tension, of taut muscles over bone in the upper chest area'. For him no sculptor past or present more than Rodin has so understood the possibilities of treating the figure that were opened up by Michelangelo. Years of observation and reflection on Michelangelo's art lead Henry Moore to believe that a drawing by him such as a *Study of a Nude Youth* in the British Museum, could have inspired Rodin to model this torso. [...]

There are paradoxes about the *Walking Man* which Moore pointed out. As one changes the viewing angle, the figure's weight seems to shift forward or backwards, towards or away from the front foot, which helps to give the impression of motion. (Thus, for those who want to see the sculpture as one of movement, there are many viewing angles.) But, as Moore points out, the figure's feet 'clench the earth'. Imitating the position of the figure with the right foot turned in, he showed how one could not possibly walk in this manner. The toeing-in is for him the result of the model 'striking a pose', which is borne out by Rodin's own recollection that was not known to Moore when he made this point. He liked the ambivalence between the moving and static poses, as the latter is more compatible with his own art. He sees the left leg, for example, as 'dragging', and prefers the angle in which the weight is closest to the front foot. His photographs shows his preferred angles that take in the fullest effect of the torso.

I asked Henry Moore why he should admire Rodin's emulation of an antique ruin and why he should be enthusiastic about a way of work different from his own. He replied that Rodin helped open the eyes of modern sculptors to the fragment, the sketch, the accident, and the importance of much older sculpture that was being ignored. I asked Moore if his own work wasn't intended to give the appearance of ancient or older forms that had survived the elements or been shaped by them as I had so often read. He shook his head. 'It's alright for Rodin but not for me ... I like to use Hornton stone, for example, because it doesn't look new. It doesn't look like white marble or as if you would leave dirty finger prints if you touched it ... I want sculpture that looks permanent and can stand up to nature and ill treatment so that you can still see the shape I put into it. I don't consciously make my work look like a ruin.... In pieces like that for the Lincoln Center [LH 519] I wanted an analogy with stone, to be sure.... But the texture of my work is the result of the inter-action of tools and materials. For example, white marble requires a high finish. I am not trying to imitate eroded forms.'

Since we had concerned ourselves with technical and historical problems relating to the *Walking Man*, I asked Moore to comment on those additional qualities of the work he was enthusiastic about. 'I like its springiness, tautness and energy. Every muscle is braced. It all heaves upward. Rodin has put something of the archaic Greek style into it by widening the thighs and calf towards the top. The forms diverge upwards from the ankle to the knee and from the knee to the top of the thigh. This gives an upward thrust. The leg is not tired and sloppy like a sack. The knees are braced backward and the knee cap is up.'

Having seen how Rodin built up a sculpture synthetically, I reminded Moore of Matisse's criticism that Rodin lost sight of the total effect by concerning himself with details, and asked if he agreed. 'Rodin does pay attention to the whole. His own nature gives the figure unity. The unity comes from Rodin's own virility ... it is a kind of self-portrait.'

Thinking over the influence Rodin had generally exerted on his own work, Moore said: 'Rodin taught me a lot about the body; its assymmetry from every point of view; how to avoid rigid symmetry; where were the flexible parts of the body such as those in the head, neck, thorax, pelvis, knees and so on, and that these axes should not parallel each other. These are ways of giving the figure vitality. Rodin perfectly understood Michelangelo ... Rodin had great sensitivity to the inner workings and balance of the body.... He could make you feel his modelled feet gripping the ground as in the *Walking Man*. Rodin helped give me that insight into empathy, feeling in to his sculptures. In my own works I have to feel the disposition of their weights, where the pressures are, where the parts make contact with the ground ... I like in Rodin the appearances of pressures from beneath the surface ... Rodin may not have been able to make sculpture for architecture, but he certainly knew the architecture of the body.'

For Henry Moore the beauty of the chest area alone would have been Rodin's motive for making the original torso of the *Walking Man*. He believes that Rodin, like Michelangelo, felt that the body could be as beautiful, forceful, dramatic and eloquent as the face, in fact, more so. Knowing how important the partial figure had been in his own art, which I believe is another significant influence of Rodin on his work, I asked Moore if he thought the absence of the head in the *Walking Man* or on a Michelangelo study deprived the figure of its humanity.

'A torso fragment has a condensed meaning. It can stand for an entire figure, just as Rembrandt's *Self-Portrait* can tell me more about his life view than the *Night Watch* with all its figures ... Michelangelo knew that the human body could express the intellect and the highest feelings. Look at Michelangelo's drawings and use of the body. Michelangelo never was a portraitist.... The expression on his faces is no more intense than the rest of the figure. Facial expressions, a smile, a grimace, are not profound. Actors can do those things even with masks. The face shows superficial expressions. Much deeper indications of a person's feelings will be found in action, all movements of the body, how they hold themselves. Look at someone from a distance where you can't see their hands and face. By their movement you recognise who they are. You recognise their spirit by their general rhythms and general proportions.'

One reason why the *Walking Man* is so favoured by Moore over other works by Rodin, such as the series of embracing couples, like *The Kiss* or

Eternal Idol, is its absence of the sentimental and literary. 'The head and hands are important from a literary point of view.' Rodin had himself commented on the expressiveness of his Italian model's *bearing*, and it is this aspect, the carriage of the *Walking Man*, that for Moore gives it spirit and makes the head irrelevant. Both sculptors share aversion to forms that suggest inertia or death. The *Walking Man* speaks directly and eloquently of their common idea of a virile and vital existence for the body, life and sculpture. One of our last conversations ended with Moore's comment, 'You can't believe in energy and not have an optimistic belief in life.'

Studio International July-August 1967, pp.26-30

Mark Rothko (1903-70)

The struggle of the artist is then to put the three dimensionality of the world on to a two-dimensional canvas.

Yes, some of the painters do it well — to me a painter like Rothko is tremendously three dimensional — I mean the depths and the mystery of the thing — when I first saw his work — he came here sometime too, — when I first saw a big collection of his work together, which was at the Whitechapel Gallery [1961] — some of his were like, if at night-time you go out from a bright room into the outside, to begin with you see nothing with your eyes — once you begin to look then some things are nearer and you begin to see — and Rothko's painting is something like that — it's got depth, mystery depth. So I don't see how, two dimensionality can be. I don't think one can imagine two dimensions anyhow. Even a paper has thickness.

In conversation with David Mitchinson and Orde Levinson, 23 October 1977

Graham Sutherland (1903-80)

When I first met Graham, his big influence, his pacemaker was Samuel Palmer.

What sort of a chap was he then?

Graham has always been a very … sensitive — sensitive is the right word, I think — gentle type of … I liked him very much and liked his work. But I wasn't very interested in the kind of contemporary English painting, because I knew the British Museum had much more to teach me than anybody like Paul Nash or whoever it was, who was a bit older than me.

In conversation with Roger Berthoud, 24 July 1979

We would argue every Thursday morning, we'd talk and discuss what was happening in London generally, the exhibitions. And when he first came to Chelsea, Samuel Palmer was his god. I admired the Palmer things, mainly through liking Blake. Anyhow the whole of that period, the few people who thought they were being experimental, modern or whatever you would like to call it, were very few in England, and therefore we knew each other because we were a little band standing up against the Royal Academy domination of art in England. And so the few who were trying to break out from this academic shell all knew each other, all believing the same thing, but with slight differences. But on the whole we were all following the same bent, the same route.

Graham Sutherland: The Last Romantic, BBC 3 May 1982

J.M.W. Turner (1775-1851)

What to me I think is great ... what he did that nobody else did up till his time and even, I think, no one else has done since – people think that he influenced Monet and the Impressionists but in a different way. They did it by light falling on a solid object. For Monet, doing his series of haystacks, in the morning and at different hours of the day, it was the object being changed by the light he was thinking about.

But Turner painted real space for the first time. Space that has almost a solid quality that a fog can have, that smoke can have. And his space is really three-dimensional space. He makes a flat canvas have all the space of miles in it. But it is shaped – the space is as though it is water that is being pushed around, or steam, and this to me is three-dimensional form. He was going for form, because space and form are one of the same anyhow. Unless you can understand what space is in my hand, you don't understand that form and space are one and the same. So, it is not so much in my opinion that Turner painted light, but that he painted space. For me as a sculptor, three-dimensional space, whether it is made of solid stone, or it is made of cloud, or it is made of distance between a few things – it is form. And for me, he is the one person who did this ... Also, too he painted the glories of nature and of life – the sunsets and the sunrises and all this. These are kind of high moments of any painter.

In conversation with Pat Gilmour, 25 March 1975 [49]

---

[49] Most of this material was quoted in Pat Gilmour, *Graphics in the Making*, Tate Gallery, London 1975, p.43.

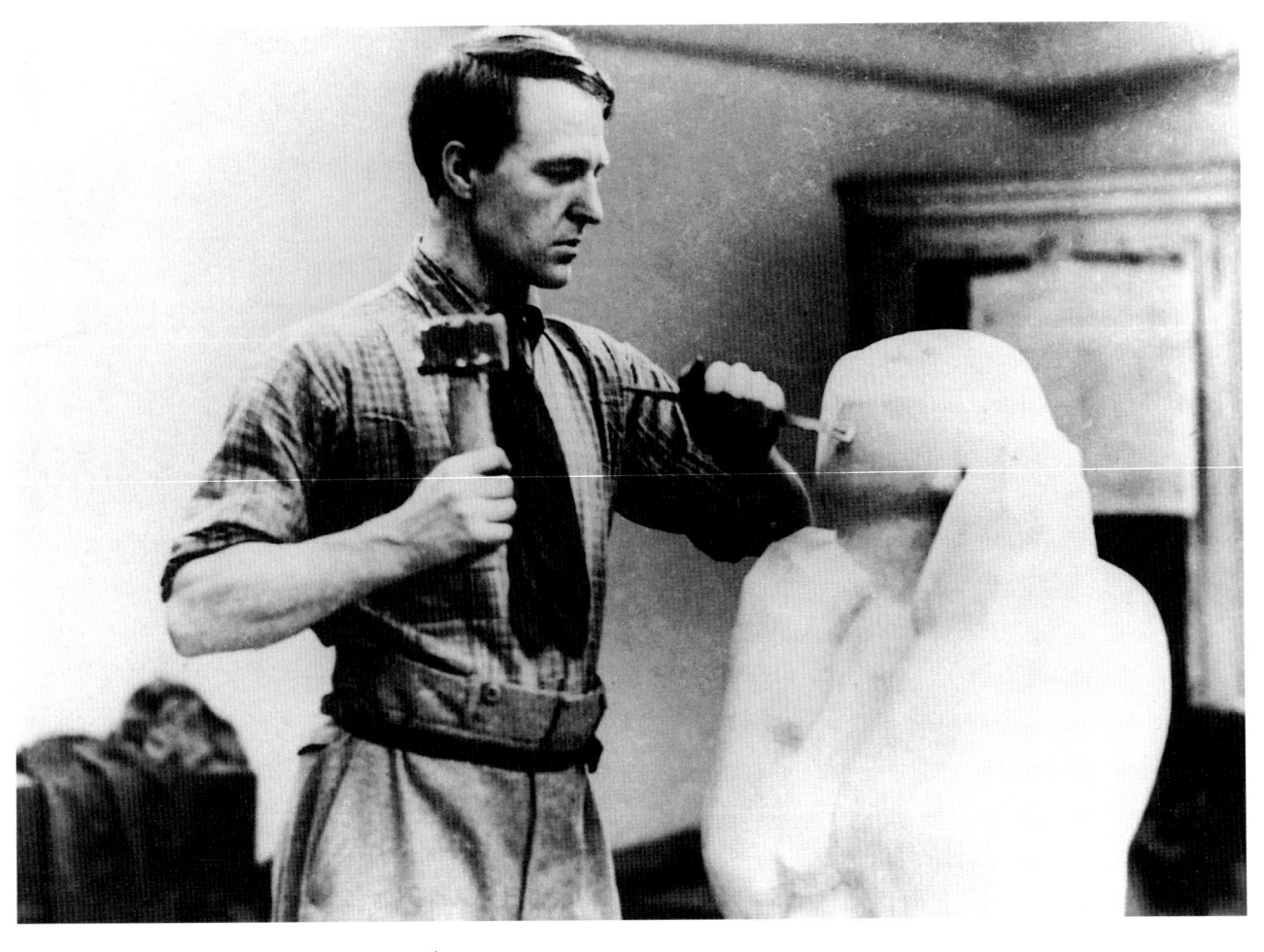
64 Moore carving at 3 Grove Studios, Hammersmith, 1927

Articles and Interviews 1930-37

A View of Sculpture[1]

In sculpture, the later Greeks worshipped their own likenesses, making realistic representation of much greater importance than it had been at any previous period. The Renaissance revived the Greek Ideal and European sculpture since then, until recent times, has been dominated by the Greek Ideal.

The world has been producing sculpture for at least some thirty thousand years. Through modern development of communication much of this we now know and the few sculptors of a hundred years or so of Greece no longer blot our eyes to the sculptural achievements of the rest of mankind. Palaeolithic and Neolithic sculpture, Sumerian, Babylonian and Egyptian, Early Greek, Chinese, Etruscan, Indian, Mayan, Mexican and Peruvian, Romanesque, Byzantine and Gothic, Negro, South Sea Island and North American Indian sculpture; actual examples or photographs of all are available, giving us a world view of sculpture never previously possible.

This removal of the Greek spectacles[2] from the eyes of the modern sculptor (along with the direction given by the work of such painters as Cézanne and Seurat) has helped him to realise again the intrinsic emotional significance of shapes instead of seeing mainly a representation value, and freed him to recognise again the importance of the material in which he works, to think and create in his material by carving direct, understanding and being in sympathy with his material so that he does not force it beyond its natural constructive build, producing weakness; to know that sculpture in stone should look honestly like stone, that to make it look like flesh and blood, hair and dimples is coming down to the level of the stage conjurer.

A limitless scope is open to him. His inspiration will come, as always, from nature and the world around him, from which he learns such principles as balance, rhythm, organic growth of life, attraction and repulsion, harmony and contrast. His work may be comparatively representational or may be as Music and Architecture are, non-representational, but mechanical

[1] This article was headed 'Contemporary English Sculptors: Henry Moore' when it was published in the *Architectural Association Journal*; it was given this title when republished in 1957 in the fourth edition of *Sculpture and Drawings 1921-1948*.
[2] 'Greek spectacles', and several other passages in this article, echo so closely the pronouncements about sculpture by Gaudier-Brzeska as to be almost paraphrases of them; see p.17.

copying of objects and surrounding life will leave him dissatisfied – the Camera and Cameograph[3] have nullified this as his aim. He will want his works to be creations, new in themselves, not merely feats of copying nor of memory, having only the second-hand life of realistic waxworks.

Each sculptor differs in his aims and ideals according to his different character, personality and his point of development. The sculpture which moves me most is full blooded and self supporting, fully in the round, that is, its component forms are completely realised and work as masses in opposition, not being merely indicated by surface cutting in relief; it is not perfectly symmetrical, it is static and it is strong and vital, giving out something of the energy and power of great mountains. It has a life of its own, independent of the object it represents.

Architectural Association Journal May 1930, p.408

On Carving

ARNOLD L. HASKELL: I see that you never model nowadays. I have a delightful bronze of yours, the head of a young girl,[4] that is exceedingly subtle and delicate in its modelling. It gives me increasing pleasure, as I notice fresh beauties in it. Are you concentrating entirely on carving now?

HENRY MOORE: Each sculptor differs in his aims and ideals according to his personality and point of development, and for many reasons I have preferred to work in stone rather than in clay. To begin with, I enjoy the actual physical effort, and I feel happier with a chisel and hammer than when using clay. I think that carving is an admirable discipline for a developing sculptor. His ideas must be definite, and the longer time needed to make a carving trains him to sustain an idea. This is especially valuable today when the tendency is to throw off a work in an afternoon. Each piece of material has a character and construction all its own; you are in touch with a solid mass of reality. I like the power a work gets naturally from the resistance offered by a hard material.

HASKELL: Do you agree with the widely prevalent view that carving as such is a virtue in itself, and that carving alone can be called true sculpture?

MOORE: That is a superstition that has arisen because of the hard fight for the practice and recognition of direct carving, and the sculptors of my generation have to thank Epstein, Gill, and Gaudier-Brzeska for the victory. Nobody now, except for purely commercial reasons, upholds the use of methods such as the pointing machine to produce stone and marble copies of works conceived in clay.

HASKELL: I have long been an enthusiastic admirer of African carving. Purely as an amateur of art I feel that it has taught me a great deal. I would be interested to hear what it can teach the practical carver of today.

MOORE: One great lesson that Negro Sculpture, more than most primitive

---

[3] 'Cameograph' is, according to Philip James (1966, p.57), a word that Moore invented. James says he means the pantograph.

[4] *Head of a Girl* 1923 LH 15.

schools, can teach the carver is the full realisation of form in the round. Too much direct carving nowadays follows the line of least resistance, and, from too great a respect, amounting to fear of the material, remains only relief carving, a smoothed up mass with forms stuck on in relief. By expressing only lines or surfaces it loses sculptural power. The Negro, working chiefly in wood, a fibrous stringy material, could produce form entirely in the round, without too great technical difficulty. He was able to free the arms completely from the body and to have a wide space between thin legs without an appearance of weakness as would have resulted in stone. One of the great problems of stone carving is to find the mean between mere surface scratching, that is, a smoothed-up boulder with decorated surface, and a work that needs a wire fence for its protection.

HASKELL: Michelangelo's dictum was that you could roll good sculpture down a hill without a piece being broken from it.

MOORE: And it is because he conformed to that in his later works that they are in my opinion his best. Perhaps I can explain more clearly some of my ideas about carving by telling you something of my own development.

When I started carving about twelve years ago my work had this limitation of relief. When I became conscious of it there followed a period of experiment, of forcing projections, of making a hole without weakening the composition as a stone construction. This cleared the way to a realisation of block rhythm instead of only linear and surface rhythm. Although sculpture should remain static, it need not be straight up and down like a telegraph pole, but it should have growth and rhythm as a tree trunk has.

During visits to the Norfolk coast I began collecting flint pebbles. These showed Nature's treatment of stone and the principle of the opposition of bumps and hollows. Then I realised that a work loses in interest through having its component forms too similar in size, and I began putting small forms against large forms, enlarging some and reducing others.

As with the flints I have studied the principles of organic growth in the bones and shells at the Natural History Museum and have found new form and rhythm to apply to sculpture. Of course one does not just copy the form of a bone, say, into stone, but applies the principles of construction, variety, transition of one form into another, to some other subject – with me nearly always the human form, for that is what interests me – so giving, as the image and metaphor do in poetry, a new significance to each.

HASKELL: I have heard your work called abstract, symbolical and humanistic. It is of course never possible to label anything in so simple a fashion, but I am interested to hear what you have to say on the human element in sculpture; what is said, as against how it is said.

MOORE: Except to the artist himself, to whom it is of the greatest importance, the theory upon which he works does not matter. What does matter is the attitude of the artist to life, the kind of mind the work reveals. It is, for example, of small consequence in our appreciation of their works that Uccello was obsessed by perspective and Michelangelo by anatomy. A work may show no illogical thinking, yet if it shows a commonplace mind it can be of little value, while if it reveals a unique and personal vision, though it can be open to criticism in other ways, it still will have great value. Also unless a sculptor adds life to his material, whether stone, wood or bronze, in my opinion he has failed no matter what his aesthetic theories. What alone makes Epstein remarkable is his power of imbuing with life whatever he touches, bronze or stone. The primitive mind has a great sense of reality and this quality of vitality is powerfully evident in all primitive sculpture.

To return more concretely to your question. All the best sculpture I know is both abstract and representational at the same time. I do not admire work which is produced as an escape from reality, which is soporific or prettifies merely as an entertainment. Some music (like Chopin's Nocturnes) is an escape from reality, it makes one sit back and go 'soft and mushy'. I prefer the kind which keys one up, – the later quartets of Beethoven, for example. There is sculpture and there is painting of these two sorts.

The primitive simplifies, I think, through directness of emotional aim to intensify their expression. Simplicity as an aim in itself tends to emptiness and monotony, but simplicity in carving, interpreted as lack of surface trimmings, reveals the contrast in section, axis, direction and bulk between different shapes and so intensifies the three-dimensional power in a work.

HASKELL: What do you think of pure abstraction?

MOORE: If you mean just pure geometry, turning subtle shapes into perfect cubes or cylinders, or all curves into sections of a circle then I think that kind of abstract art cannot have great meaning or lasting interest. But if you mean by abstraction the steps away from realistic representation, then it seems to me that most of the world's great art contains a good deal of the abstract.

There are two kinds of artist, the visual and the mental. Velázquez represents the visual, Michelangelo or El Greco the mental. The visual artist reacts to forms, shapes and colours seen, and works often directly from nature, while the mental artist works more from the sum total of his visual experience and composes from his own ideas of nature. Carving is more in keeping with the mental attitude, modelling with the visual.

HASKELL: Renoir and Cézanne both in their work and influence seem to be admirable examples of the visual and mental artist in modern painting.

MOORE: And some artists have shown both sides, as Epstein; the carver of 'Genesis' and the modeller of 'The Visitation'.

HASKELL: How far is the carver bound by his material?

MOORE: The material used for carving should not be forced beyond its natural constructive build, or weakness is the result. At the completion of the work the material should retain its own inherent qualities. Sculpture in stone should look like stone, hard and concentrated. To make stone look like flesh and blood, hair and dimples, is coming down to the level of the stage conjuror.

HASKELL: Isn't carving just because of its materials very closely related to architecture?

MOORE: Most architectural sculpture is relief decoration and not carving in the round, and for that reason I think that a holiday for sculpture away from architecture might be a good thing for sculpture. A man is a sculptor, just because he needs the full reality of concrete form in the round to work with.

New English Weekly 5 May 1932, pp.65-6

Unit One[5]

Each sculptor through his past experience, through observation of natural laws, through criticism of his own work and other sculpture, through his character and psychological make-up, and according to his stage of development, finds that certain qualities in sculpture become of fundamental importance to him. For me these qualities are:

Truth to material. Every material has its own individual qualities. It is only when the sculptor works direct, when there is an active relationship with his material, that the material can take its part in the shaping of an idea. Stone, for example, is hard and concentrated and should not be falsified to look like soft flesh – it should not be forced beyond its constructive build to a point of weakness. It should keep its hard tense stoniness.

Full three-dimensional realisation. Complete sculptural expression is form in its full spatial reality.

Only to make relief shapes on the surface of the block is to forego the full power of expression of sculpture. When the sculptor understands his material, has a knowledge of its possibilities and its constructive build, it is possible to keep within its limitations and yet turn an inert block into a composition which has a full form-existence, with masses of varied size and section conceived in their air-surrounded entirety, stressing and straining, thrusting and opposing each other in spatial relationship, – being static, in the sense that the centre of gravity lies within the base (and does not seem to be falling over or moving off its base) – and yet having an alert dynamic tension between its parts.

Sculpture fully in the round has no two points of view alike. The desire for form completely realised is connected with asymmetry. For a symmetrical mass being the same from both sides cannot have more than half the number of different points of view possessed by a non-symmetrical mass.

Asymmetry is connected also with the desire for the organic (which I have) rather than the geometric.

Organic forms though they may be symmetrical in their main disposition, in their reaction to environment, growth and gravity, lose their perfect symmetry.

[5] Unit One, a group of eleven British avant-garde painters, sculptors and architects, was formed in 1933. The birth of Unit One was announced in a letter to *The Times* by Paul Nash (12 June 1933). Barbara Hepworth and Ben Nicholson were members. In April 1934 the group published *Unit One: The Modern Movement in English Architecture, Painting and Sculpture*, edited by Herbert Read. This was Moore's contribution to the book.

Observation of Natural Objects. The observation of nature is part of an artist's life, it enlarges his form-knowledge, keeps him fresh and from working only by formula, and feeds inspiration.

The human figure is what interests me most deeply, but I have found principles of form and rhythm from the study of natural objects such as pebbles, rocks, bones, trees, plants etc.

Pebbles and rocks show Nature's way of working stone. Smooth, sea-worn pebbles show the wearing away, rubbed treatment of stone and principles of asymmetry.

Rocks show the hacked, hewn treatment of stone, and have a jagged nervous block rhythm.

Bones have marvellous structural strength and hard tenseness of form, subtle transition of one shape into the next and great variety in section.

Trees (tree trunks) show principles of growth and strength of joints, with easy passing of one section into the next. They give the ideal for wood sculpture, upward twisting movement.

Shells show Nature's hard but hollow form (metal sculpture) and have a wonderful completeness of single shape.

There is in Nature a limitless variety of shapes and rhythms (and the telescope and microscope have enlarged the field) from which the sculptor can enlarge his form-knowledge experience.

But besides formal qualities there are qualities of vision and expression:
Vision and expression. My aim in work is to combine as intensely as possible the abstract principles of sculpture along with the realisation of my idea.

All art is an abstraction to some degree: (in sculpture the material alone forces one away from pure representation and towards abstraction).

Abstract qualities of design are essential to the value of a work, but to me of equal importance is the psychological, human element. If both abstract and human elements are welded together in a work, it must have a fuller, deeper meaning.

Vitality and Power of expression. For me a work must first have a vitality of its own. I do not mean a reflection of the vitality of life, of movement, physical action, frisking, dancing figures and so on, but that a work can have in it a pent-up energy, an intense life of its own, independent of the object it may represent. When a work has this powerful vitality we do not connect the word Beauty with it.

Beauty, in the later Greek or Renaissance sense, is not the aim in my sculpture.

Between beauty of expression and power of expression there is a difference of function. The first aims at pleasing the senses, the second has a spiritual vitality which for me is more moving and goes deeper than the senses.

Because a work does not aim at reproducing natural appearances it is not, therefore, an escape from life – but may be a penetration into reality, not a sedative or drug, not just the exercise of good taste, the provision of pleasant shapes and colours in a pleasing combination, not a decoration to life, but an expression of the significance of life, a stimulation to greater effort in living.

Unit One: The Modern Movement in English Architecture, Painting and Sculpture, edited by Herbert Read, Cassell, London, Toronto, Melbourne, Sydney 1934, pp.29-30

Circle[6]

Quotations

1. I dislike the idea that contemporary art is an escape from life. Because a work does not aim at reproducing the natural appearance it is not therefore an escape from life – it may be a penetrating into reality; not a sedative or drug, not just the exercise of good taste, the provision of pleasant shapes and colours in a pleasing combination, not a decoration to life – but an expression of the significance of life, a stimulation to greater effort in living.[7]

2. Architecture and sculpture are both dealing with the relationship of masses. In practice architecture is not pure expression but has a functional or utilitarian purpose, which limits it as an art of pure expression. And sculpture, more naturally than architecture, can use organic rhythms. Aesthetically architecture is the abstract relationship of masses. If sculpture is limited to this, then in the field of scale and size architecture has the advantage; but sculpture, not being tied to a functional and utilitarian purpose, can attempt much more freely the exploration of the world of pure form.[8]

Circle: International Survey of Constructive Art, editors J.L. Martin, Ben Nicholson, N. Gabo, Faber and Faber, London 1937, p.118

The Sculptor Speaks[9]

It is a mistake for a sculptor or a painter to speak or write very often about his job. It releases tension needed for his work. By trying to express his aims with rounded-off logical exactness, he can easily become a theorist whose actual work is only a caged-in exposition of conceptions evolved in terms of logic and words.

But though the non-logical, instinctive, subconscious part of the mind must play its part in his work, he also has a conscious mind which is not in-

[6] *Circle: International Survey of Constructive Art*, edited by Leslie Martin, Ben Nicholson and Naum Gabo, was published in London in 1937. This collective manifesto of Constructivism includes an editorial by Gabo, and essays and statements by painters, sculptors, architects and writers including Mondrian, Moholy-Nagy, Nicholson, Hepworth, Read, Le Corbusier, Gropius and Bernal. Moore did not wholeheartedly embrace pure abstraction and the theories of Constructivism. This was his short contribution to the book.

[7] This sentence has been lifted almost verbatim from the end of the *Unit One* article above.

[8] The wording of this statement on architecture and sculpture is very close to the opening paragraph of Moore's notes on 'The difference between Sculpture and Architecture' (p.242), which were in fact written for but not included in his article 'The Sculptor Speaks'.

[9] The title 'Notes on Sculpture' appears at the top of page 1 of Moore's handwritten text of this article for *The Listener*. However, when it was published in *The Listener* on 18 August 1937, the title had been changed to 'The Sculptor Speaks'. It appeared as 'Notes on Sculpture' in the first edition (1944) of *Henry Moore: Sculpture and Drawings*, and as such in the subsequent five editions of volume 1 of the complete sculpture.

active. The artist works with a concentration of his whole personality, and the conscious part of it resolves conflicts, organises memories, and prevents him from trying to walk in two directions at the same time.

It is likely, then, that a sculptor can give, from his own conscious experience, *clues* which will help others in their approach to sculpture, and this article tries to do this, and no more. It is not a general survey of sculpture, or of my own development, but a few notes on some of the problems that have concerned me from time to time.

Three Dimensions

Appreciation of sculpture depends upon the ability to respond to form in three dimensions. That is perhaps why sculpture has been described as the most difficult of all arts; certainly it is more difficult than the arts which involve appreciation of flat forms, shape in only two dimensions. Many more people are 'form-blind' than colour-blind. The child learning to see, first distinguishes only two-dimensional shape; it cannot judge distances, depths. Later, for its personal safety and practical needs, it has to develop (partly by means of touch) the ability to judge roughly three-dimensional distances. But having satisfied the requirements of practical necessity, most people go no further. Though they may attain considerable accuracy in the perception of flat form, they do not make the further intellectual and emotional effort needed to comprehend form in its full spatial existence.

This is what the sculptor must do. He must strive continually to think of, and use, form in its full spatial completeness. He gets the solid shape, as it were, inside his head – he thinks of it, whatever its size, as if he were holding it completely enclosed in the hollow of his hand. He mentally visualises a complex form *from all round itself*; he knows while he looks at one side what the other side is like; he identifies himself with its centre of gravity, its mass, its weight; he realises its volume, as the space that the shape displaces in the air.

And the sensitive observer of sculpture must also learn to feel shape simply as shape, not as description or reminiscence. He must, for example, perceive an egg as a simple single solid shape, quite apart from its significance as food, or from the literary idea that it will become a bird. And so with solids such as a shell, a nut, a plum, a pear, a tadpole, a mushroom, a mountain peak, a kidney, a carrot, a tree-trunk, a bird, a bud, a lark, a lady bird, a bulrush, a bone. From these he can go on to appreciate more complex forms or combinations of several forms.

Brancusi

Since the Gothic, European sculpture had become overgrown with moss, weeds — all sorts of surface excrescences which completely concealed shape.[10] It has been Brancusi's special mission to get rid of this overgrowth,

[10] This 'extraordinary statement', as Douglas Lord (Douglas Cooper) called it, provoked him to write a letter to *The Listener* (8 September 1937) asking: 'Are we therefore to understand that Mr Moore dismisses the sculptors of the Renaissance? Does he only perceive Donatello as "overgrown with moss, weeds etc?"'

and to make us once more shape-conscious. To do this he has had to concentrate on very simple direct shapes, to keep his sculpture, as it were, one-cylindered, to refine and polish a single shape to a degree almost too precious. Brancusi's work, apart from its individual value, has been of great historical importance in the development of contemporary sculpture. But it may now be no longer necessary to close down and restrict sculpture to the single (static) form unit. We can now begin to open out. To relate and combine together several forms of varied sizes, sections and direction into one organic whole.

Shells and pebbles; – being conditioned to respond to shapes

Although it is the human figure which interests me most deeply, I have always paid great attention to natural forms, such as bones, shells and pebbles, etc. Sometimes for several years running I have been to the same part of the sea-shore – but each year a new shape of pebble has caught my eye, which the year before, though it was there in hundreds, I never saw. Out of the millions of pebbles passed in walking along the shore, I choose out to see with excitement only those which fit in with my existing form-interest at the time. A different thing happens if I sit down and examine a handful one by one. I may then extend my form-experience more by giving my mind time to become conditioned to a new shape.

There are universal shapes to which everybody is subconsciously conditioned and to which they can respond if their conscious control does not shut them off.

Holes in Sculpture

Pebbles show nature's way of working stone. Some of the pebbles I pick up have holes right through them.

When first working direct in a hard and brittle material like stone, the lack of experience and great respect for the material, the fear of ill-treating it, too often results in relief surface carving, with no sculptural power.

But with more experience the completed work in stone can be kept within the limitations of its material, that is, not be weakened beyond its natural constructive build, and yet be turned from an inert mass into a composition which has a full form existence, with masses of varied sizes and sections working together in spatial relationship.

A piece of stone can have a hole through it and not be weakened – if the hole is of a studied size, shape and direction. On the principle of the arch, it can remain just as strong.

The first hole made through a piece of stone is a revelation.

Lord goes on to ask what of Mino da Fiesole, Michelangelo and Bernini? And, I would add, Rodin. In one of several drafts of this sentence, Moore states that the blurring of form, and the extinction of shape were not quite so sudden, but had equally devastating results: 'Gradually since Gothic times sculpture in Europe had become more overgrown with moss & weeds & surface excrescences until no shape was discernible –'. He continues with Brancusi's role in restoring sculpture from this sorry, shapeless state of affairs: 'Brancusi in a way has been a martyr to the bad period before him, & has had to reduce sculpture back to the one shape unit, so that himself & others should realise that shape consciousness is fundamental in sculpture.' (HMF archive) See p.20.

The hole connects one side to the other, making it immediately more three-dimensional.

A hole can itself have as much shape-meaning as a solid mass.

Sculpture in air is possible, where the stone contains only the hole, which is the intended and considered form.

The mystery of the hole – the mysterious fascination of caves in hillsides and cliffs.

Size and Scale

There is a right physical size for every idea.

Pieces of good stone have stood about my studio for long periods, because though I've had ideas which would fit their proportions and materials perfectly, their size was wrong.

There is a side to scale not to do with its actual physical size, its measurement in feet and inches – but connected with vision.

A carving might be several times over life size and yet be petty and small in feeling – and a small carving only a few inches in height can give the feeling of huge size and monumental grandeur, because the vision behind it is big. Example, Michelangelo's drawings or a Masaccio madonna – and the Albert Memorial.

Yet actual physical size has an emotional meaning. We relate everything to our own size, and our emotional response to size is controlled by the fact that men on the average are between five and six feet high.

An exact model to $\frac{1}{10}$ scale of Stonehenge, where the stones would be less than us, would lose all its impressiveness.

Sculpture is more affected by actual size considerations than painting. A painting is isolated by a frame from its surroundings (unless it serves just a decorative purpose) and so retains more easily its own imaginary scale.

If practical considerations allowed me, cost of material, of transport, etc., I should like to work on large carvings more often than I do. The average in-between size does not disconnect an idea enough from prosaic everyday life. The very small or the very big take on an added size emotion.

Recently I have been working in the country, where, carving in the open air, I find sculpture more natural than in a London studio, but it needs bigger dimensions. A large piece of stone or wood placed almost anywhere at random in a field, orchard or garden, immediately looks right and inspiring.

Drawing and Sculpture

My drawings are done mainly as a help towards making sculpture – as a means of generating ideas for sculpture, tapping oneself for the initial idea: and as a way of sorting out ideas and developing them.

Also, sculpture compared with drawing is a slow means of expression, and I find drawing a useful outlet for ideas which there is not time enough to realise as sculpture. And I use drawing as a method of study and observation of natural forms (drawings from life, drawings of bones, shells, etc.).

And I sometimes draw just for its own enjoyment.

Experience though has taught me that the difference there is between drawing and sculpture should not be forgotten. A sculptural idea which may be satisfactory as a drawing always needs some alteration when translated into sculpture.

At one time whenever I made drawings for sculpture I tried to give them as much the illusion of real sculpture as I could – that is, I drew by the method of illusion, of light falling on a solid object. But I now find that carrying a drawing so far that it becomes a substitute for the sculpture either weakens the desire to do the sculpture, or is likely to make the sculpture only a dead realisation of the drawing.

I now leave a wider latitude in the interpretation of the drawings I make for sculpture, and draw often in line and flat tones without the light and shade illusion of three dimensions; but this does not mean that the vision behind the drawing is only two dimensional.

Abstraction and Surrealism

The violent quarrel between the abstractionists and the surrealists seems to me quite unnecessary. All good art has contained both abstract and surrealist elements, just as it has contained both classical and romantic elements – order and surprise, intellect and imagination, conscious and unconscious. Both sides of the artist's personality must play their part. And I think the first inception of a painting or a sculpture may begin from either end. As far as my own experience is concerned, I sometimes begin a drawing with no preconceived problem to solve, with only the desire to use pencil on paper, and make lines, tones and shapes with no conscious aim; but as my mind takes in what is so produced, a point arrives where some idea becomes conscious and crystallises, and then a control and ordering begin to take place.

Or sometimes I start with a set subject; or to solve, in a block of stone of known dimensions, a sculptural problem I've given myself, and then consciously attempt to build an ordered relationship of forms, which shall express my idea. But if the work is to be more than just a sculptural exercise, unexplainable jumps in the process of thought occur; and the imagination plays its part.

It might seem from what I have said of shape and form that I regard them as ends in themselves. Far from it. I am very much aware that associational psychological factors play a large part in sculpture. The meaning and significance of form itself probably depends on the countless associations of man's history. For example, rounded forms convey an idea of fruitfulness, maturity, probably because the earth, women's breasts, and most fruits are rounded, and these shapes are important because they have this background in our habits of perception. I think the humanist organic element will always be for me of fundamental importance in sculpture, giving sculpture its vitality. Each particular carving I make takes on in my mind a human, or occasionally animal, character and personality, and this personality controls its design and formal qualities, and makes me satisfied or dissatisfied with the work as it develops.

My own aim and direction seems to be consistent with these beliefs, though it does not depend upon them. My sculpture is becoming less representational, less an outward visual copy, and so what some people would call more abstract; but only because I believe that in this way I can present the human psychological content of my work with the greatest directness and intensity.

The Listener 18 August 1937, pp.338-40

The Nature of Sculpture

General Statements

Sculpture that is not symmetrical, perfect symmetry is death – nothing living is perfectly symmetrical –

Unpublished notes for 'A View of Sculpture' 1930, HMF archive

You see, I think a sculptor is a person who is interested in the shape of things. A poet is somebody who is interested in words; a musician is someone who is interested in or obsessed by sounds. But a sculptor is a person obsessed with the form and the shape of things, and it's not just the shape of any one thing, but the shape of anything and everything: the growth in a flower; the hard, tense strength, although delicate form of a bone; the strong, solid fleshiness of a beech tree trunk. All these things are just as much a lesson to a sculptor as a pretty girl – as a young girl's figure – and so on. They're all part of the experience of form and therefore, in my opinion, everything, every shape, every bit of natural form: animals, people, pebbles, shells, anything you like are all things that can help you to make sculpture. And for me, I collect odd bits of driftwood – anything I find that has a shape that interests me – and keep it around in that little studio so that if any day I go in there, or evening, within five or ten minutes of being in that little room there will be something that I can pick up or look at that would give me a start for a new idea. This is why I like leaving all these odds and ends around in a small studio – to start one off with an idea.

One of the things I would like to think my sculpture has is a force, is a strength, is a life, a vitality from inside it, so that you have a sense that the form is pressing from inside trying to burst or trying to give off the strength from inside itself, rather than having something which is just shaped from outside and stopped. It's as though you have something trying to make itself come to a shape from inside itself. This is, perhaps, what makes me interested in bones as much as in flesh because the bone is the inner structure of all living form. It's the bone that pushes out from inside; as you bend your leg the knee gets tautness over it, and it's there that the movement and the energy come from. If you clench a knuckle, you clench a fist, you get in that sense the bones, the knuckles pushing through, giving a force that if you open your hand and just have it relaxed you don't feel. And so the knee, the shoulder, the skull, the forehead, the part where from inside you get a sense of pressure of the bone outwards – these for me are the key points. You can then, as it were, between those key points have a slack part, as you might between the bridge of a drapery and the hollow of it, so that in this way you get a feeling that the form is all inside it, and this is what also makes me think that I prefer hard form to soft form. For me, sculpture should have a hardness, and because I think sculpture should have a hardness fundamentally I really like carving better than I like modeling. Although I do bronzes, I make the original which is turned into bronze in plaster, and although anyone can build a plaster up as soft mixture, that mixture hardens and I then file it and chop it and make it have its final shape as hard plaster, not as a soft material.

Forma 1964, pp.59, 63

Sculpture for me, must have life in it, vitality. It must have a feeling for organic form, a certain pathos and warmth. Purely abstract sculpture seems to me to be an activity that would be better fulfilled in another art, such as architecture. That is why I have never been tempted to remain a purely abstract sculptor. Abstract sculptures are too often but models for monuments that are never carried out, and the works of many abstract or 'constructivist' sculptors suffer from this frustration in that the artist never gets around to finding the real material solution to his problems. But sculpture is different from architecture. It creates organisms that must be complete in themselves. An architect has to deal with practical considerations, such as comfort, costs and so on, which remain alien to an artist, very real problems that are different from those which a sculptor has to face.

Roditi 1960, p.187

Sculpture should always at first sight have some obscurities, and further meanings. People should want to go on looking and thinking; it should never tell all about itself immediately. Initially both sculpture and painting must need effort to be fully appreciated, or else it is just an empty immediacy like a poster, which is designed to be read by the people on top of a bus in half a second. In fact all art should have some more mystery and meaning to it than is apparent to a quick observer.

Hedgecoe 1968, p.83

Sculpture is a very practical art. It's not like poetry which asks somebody to imagine what you wish to project. With sculpture you have to produce it. It's a real thing like building a house. So you have to relate it to the people who will live in it.

Hedgecoe 1986, p.86

To charge an 'abstract' shape with meaning – to impregnate form with vitality, – to give an organic life to non-realistic, non-representational sculpture –

To make a shape strangely significant, without knowing how, or why it is so.

Perhaps ability to do this comes about because of the sculptor's intense interest in all forms and shapes, – through empathy and human connections.

It is the antithesis to decorative 'niceness' or 'beauty' – it has about it something strange and perhaps disturbing, – rather than 'consoling' soothing and satisfactory.

Unpublished (?) notes, date unknown, HMF archive

I want to make sculpture as big in feeling & grandeur as the Sumerian, as vital as Negro as direct & stone like as Mexican as alive as Early Greek & Etruscan as spiritual as Gothic.

Unpublished notes for *Unit One* 1934, HMF archive

XVIII Dynasty Egyptian – Head of a Woman (princess?) in the Archaeological Museum, Florence

I would give everything, if I could get into my sculpture the same amount of humanity & seriousness; nobility & experience, acceptance of life, distinction, & aristocracy. With absolutely no tricks, no affectation, no self consciousness, looking straight ahead, no movement, but more alive than a real person.

Notes from Sketchbook 1955-57, Henry Moore Foundation

The great, (the continual, everlasting) problem (for me) is to combine Sculptural form (POWER) with human sensitivity & meaning, i.e. to try to keep Primitive Power with humanist content. Not to bother about stone sculpture versus modelling – Bronze versus plaster, construction – welding etc – but finding the common essentials in all kinds of sculpture.

Ibid.

65 *Bust of a Woman*, eighteenth dynasty Egyptian. Museo Archeologico, Florence

A last word about the possibilities of sculpture?

My belief is that no matter what advances we make in technology, and in the controlling of nature, and so on, the real basis of life is in human relationships. It's through them that we are happy or unhappy, and that we fulfil ourselves, or we don't. There is a great deal still to be done with three-dimensional form as a means of expressing what people feel about themselves, and nature, and the world around them. But I don't think that we shall, or should, ever get far away from the thing that all sculpture is based on, in the end: the human body.

Russell 24 December 1961

Truth to Material[11]

One thing you did recognise immediately is what you called its 'truth to material', a concept you later developed into a whole theory of sculpture. Could you explain exactly what you mean by 'truth to material'?

[11] For important early statements on truth to material, see *Unit One* 1934, p.191 and 'The Sculptor Speaks' 1937, p.195.

Well, this was in the air. Brancusi had already spoken about it. Gaudier-Brzeska, whom you mentioned earlier, had picked it up from Modigliani, and people like Epstein had already been carving direct before Gaudier-Brzeska. And this belief in direct carving came about by artists finding primitive art, by this interest in Negro sculpture and in primitive art, by using the materials in a natural way, instead of only making the material imitate flesh and blood, if that's what they were trying to make it, or hair, or fur, or whatever it may be. And this became a tenet among a lot of sculptors, and it was with me. It gave one a whole new direction in one's carving. I always have liked handling a hammer and chisel. I like pushing at the soft material of clay, but I'm happier when I use a hammer and chisel. The hardness of stone, and the resistance it gives you, can give you a kind of force and a power because you are fighting the material. And the material gives back some strength, like a kettle with a lid on will give you a feeling of power, whereas an open pan just left with no lid and boiling gives you no sense of power. Well, the same thing happens with the carving of stone. So I began to believe that you shouldn't lose this, you shouldn't do what Bernini did. I now admire Bernini tremendously, but at that time I looked upon him as the arch-sinner in carving, in that he was making stone behave like cloth, or like drapery, or like flesh and blood, and not keeping its stoniness. Even Michelangelo kept the stoniness.

Carroll 1973, pp.38-9

I began believing in direct stone carving, in being true to the material by not making stone look like flesh or making wood behave like metal. This is the tenet that I took over from sculptors like Brancusi and Modigliani. It made me hesitate to make the material do what I wanted until I began to realise this was a limitation in sculpture so that often the forms were all buried inside each other and heads were given no necks. As a result you will find that in some of my early work there is no neck simply because I was frightened to weaken the stone. Out of an exaggerated respect for the material, I was reducing the power of the form.

Then I became aware that in some examples of primitive art, the sculptor had been bold enough to make three-dimensional form out of a solid block, and it gave me courage to do it in my own sculpture. I found it very surprising that they had dared to make the necks as long as they had. Some of their carvings are so thin from the side that often you find them broken. Their vision had not been restricted by their material, and certainly some of the little figures of Cycladic times are remarkable examples of early sculptors being so concerned with realising their sculptural ideas that they had taken greater liberties with the material than I had thought were possible.

Hedgecoe 1968, p.45

Brancusi's dictum of truth to material, that is letting the material you are working in help to shape the sculpture, had a big influence on me. You didn't try to make in stone something that would have been infinitely easier to make in wire or metal. For instance, in stone you couldn't make a figure that was very heavy at the top and had thin ankles because it would simply break while you were carving it. Nor did you want to do what the later Greeks did – put a tree trunk up the back of one leg so that the other could be more realistic. Instead you wanted the material to have its say. So a thing in stone should look different from a thing in bronze; or that a thing in wood had qualities of its own, as thin as the branch of a tree, which stone can't be. This truth to material became a tenet.

Later, though, this became a restriction. After all, something can be so true to stone that it doesn't have any significant shape at all. It can be just a surface scratch or mark. So after a time, for me, this approach to sculpture became invalid because it is, of course, the vision behind a work that matters most, not the material.

I have done some sculptures in marble which have also been cast in bronze and I can see no reason why they shouldn't.

Hedgecoe 1986, pp.86-7

When I first began doing stone sculpture, about 1920, the most obvious thing about stone was its solidity. I began by trying to make sculpture which should be as stony as the stone itself, but afterwards I realised that unless you had some tussle, some collaboration and yet battle with your materials, you were being nobody. The artist must impose some of himself and his ideas on the material, in a way that uses the material sympathetically but not passively. Otherwise you are only behaving like the waves.

Hall 1960, p.104

When I began to make sculptures thirty years ago, it was very necessary to fight for the doctrine of truth to material (the need for direct carving, for respecting the particular character of each material, and so on). So at that time many of us tended to make a fetish of it. I still think it is important, but it should not be a criterion of the value of a work – otherwise a snowman made by a child would have to be praised at the expense of a Rodin or a Bernini. Rigid adherence to the doctrine results in domination of the sculptor by the material. The sculptor ought to be the master of his material. Only, not a cruel master.

Sylvester 1951, p.4

The Gothic church which forces the material as far as it will go is as true to its material as the Egyptian pyramid – or else if it weren't it would fall down – The Gothic artists in their churches understood their materials as well if not more than the builders of the Egyptian pyramid – who let the material completely dominate them.

There are two opposite attitudes to the material – typified by the Egyptian pyramids where the material completely dominates – & the late Gothic cathedral where the material is forced as far as it will go without being weak & falling down – my development has been from the egyptian domination of the material, to the Gothic opening out with arches & holes – But because I have had an admiration & liking for carving (over modelling) it has been a slow process, taking years to make each further step.

Unpublished notes c.1951, HMF archive

In your early days, you put 'truth to material', respect for the material he's working in, as the first necessity for a sculptor. Do you still feel the same?

No. There I've changed. I still think it tremendously important – but I used to exaggerate the importance. That's partly due to the state sculpture was in in this country thirty or forty years ago – it had become almost entirely representational and decorative. So it was necessary to get back to first principles and emphasise them afresh.

But what happens over a period of time is this. One starts out with certain ideas of one's own, and those ideas breed others – a whole fresh crop. It's impossible for a sculptor to keep lots of pieces of stone lying around his studio, or to go about constantly searching for the right piece to embody each idea that's working in his mind.

He may start by, so to speak, trying to liberate from a particular piece of stone the form he feels it contains. But in the end, though he still respects his material and doesn't ask it to do what it can't, he has to master it and not be at its mercy.

That's partly why I've turned more to bronze in the last ten years; it enables me to do things I couldn't do in stone. I was wanting to do upright figures. No stone figure, you know, can stand on its own ankles. You can stand on your ankles because of the marvellous arrangement of your bones and muscles, but if you were in stone you'd just break. That's why the Greeks supported their standing figures with tree-trunks, the Egyptians placed theirs against temples, and so on.

But bronze has tremendous tensile strength. You can make your figures long and thin, wider at the top than at the bottom, giving them uplift, a soaring feeling. And bronze lasts out-of-doors much better than stone.

'Henry Moore talks about My Work in a special interview with Tom Hopkinson',
Books and Art November 1957, p.29

Space and Form

SPACE AND FORM

Some definitions of sculpture.

My first sculpture teacher told me that 'sculpture is an infinite number of outlines.' This definition suggests looking only at the flat silhouette ① whereas sculpture should be looked at also from the middle outwards.

The next definition I came across was a better one, it was Rodin's 'Sculpture is the science of the hollow & the bump' ② a more three dimensional attitude – but still for me not including the spacial sense that sculpture should have. 'The hollow & the bump' describes surfaces only.

The next enlightening definition I found was the young sculptor Gaudier-Brzeska's 'Sculptural energy is the mountain'. This is still talking of surfaces, of relief, of projection rather than volume – for the mountain is a pimple on the earth's surface – it is the Earth itself which gives the full complete idea of form.

Complete three dimensional form – form in the round – is form in space, the far side of a form should be known when seeing the front of it, its volume should be comprehended, which is the space that the form displaces in the air – when fully comprehended form & space are one & the same.

① This concentrating on the outline, is one of the conventional (academic) methods of teaching life modelling. The student keeps turning the object & copying the outline until eventually he gets some more or less close approximation to the model – but this can be done, even cleverly done, without ever having felt the sculptural solidity of the model.
② This is somewhat similar to Ruskin saying that sculpture should have a 'pleasant bossiness' –
[...]¹²

Difference between modelling & carving in the approach to SPACE

Modelling begins with an armature, a thin form in space & gradually clothes that with the clay, wax, plaster or whatever modelling material is used – That is, you are given space & make forms in it.

Carving starts with a solid block which has surfaces but no space … The line of least resistance in directly carved sculpture is to make only relief form from different sides, to cut surface forms which have no complete existence, but are left embedded in the solid matrix. To make complete three-dimensional form in carving, it is necessary, besides thinking of the outer surfaces of forms, to think of the centres of forms, so that they exist from INSIDE OUTWARDS.

It is easy to get space (if only 'accidental' space) into sculpture produced by modelling, by building up onto an armature or by assembling separate pieces into one whole. But only if he has the most determined intention to have it will the sculptor make space an element in carved sculpture.

Unpublished notes c.1953-54, HMF archive

Some Notes on SPACE AND FORM in Sculpture

One distorts the forms in order to create space…

If space is a willed, a wished-for element in the sculpture, then some distortion of the form – to ally itself to the space – is necessary.

At one time the holes in my sculpture were made for their own sakes.

¹² At this point in the notebook there comes the passage headed 'Holes in Sculpture' quoted from 'The Sculptor Speaks', beginning with 'A piece of stone …' to 'hillsides and cliffs', see pp.195-6.

Because I was trying to become conscious of space in the sculpture – I made the hole have a shape in its own right, the solid body was encroached upon, eaten into, and sometimes the form was only the shell holding the hole. Recently I have attempted to make the forms & the spaces (not holes) inseparable, neither being more important than the other. In the last bronze Reclining Figure[13] I think I have in some measure succeeded in this aim. What I mean is perhaps most obvious if this figure is looked at lengthwise from the Head end through to the foot end & the arms, body, legs, elbows etc are seen as forms inhabiting a tunnel, in recession. Seen in plan the figure has 'pools' of space.

FORM FROM THE INSIDE OUTWARDS

Tension & inner force of forms.

Force, Power, is made by forms straining or pressing from inside. Knees, elbows, foreheads, knuckles, all seek to press outwards. Hardness, projection outwards, gives tension, force & vitality. Clenched fist symbol of power – of force.

Although carved sculpture is approached from the outside, if it ends by seeming to be sliced or scooped into its shape out of a larger mass, it will not have its maximum sense of bigness.

Undated notes early 1950s(?), HMF archive; reproduced in Man 1954 (n.p.)

Do you think it [wire sculpture] has contributed anything new to sculpture?

Yes. In the sense that there was and still is greater interest among young sculptors in space than in solid form, and an armature has a more obvious sense of space about it, more than a single solid form has. But one eventually gets to know that the understanding of space is merely the understanding of form, that space is only the shape that form would displace in air, or the distances between two things. If you hold your hand as I am doing now, the shape those fingers would enclose if I were holding an apple would be different from the shape if I were holding a pear. If you can tell what that is, then you know what space is. That is space and form. You can't understand space without being able to understand form, and to understand form you must be able to understand space. The idea that space is something new in sculpture is only held by people who don't know what space or form is.

How did you first arrive at your own early uses of space? I am thinking of your use of holes.

That was the attempt to understand three-dimensional form, and to try to grasp all kinds of form, whether hollow form, solid form, form projecting from a surface or form … well, every possible facet of three-dimensional reality. […]

When I look at you, I see the space that is made by your head resting on

[13] *Reclining Figure: Festival* 1951 LH 293; see p.275.

your hand and the space in between; your forearm is a single mass, your head is another, your head is being supported by that forearm at present, and that's resting on the knee that juts out. All this is giving space, all this is giving action and reality to form. It's not just drawing on the surface. To understand space, I have to begin to think of actual penetrations into the stone. The understanding of three-dimensional form is never-ending, and you can separate it into experiments. By making holes through a block, you can relate the front to the back, and so on. All these things are part of one's interest in understanding three-dimensional reality.

Hall 1960, p.104

I do not consciously use numerical proportions in my designs.[14]

Unpublished notes for *Unit One* 1934, HMF archive

I've always had a liking for squareness. The squareness of a right angle is a very vigorous action. This may be one reason why I appreciate Mexican and particularly Aztec sculpture.

Hedgecoe 1968, p.55

Eventually I found that form and space are one and the same thing. You can't understand space without understanding form.

For example, in order to understand form in its complete three-dimensional reality you must understand the space that it would displace if it were taken away. You can't measure a space without measuring from one point to another. The heavens have space that we can understand because there are points – the stars and the sun – that are different distances away from each other. In the same way we can only see space in a landscape by relating the foreground and middle distance to the far distance. To understand the distance from my thumb to my forefinger needs exactly the same understanding as distances in landscape.

Ibid., p.118

Holes[15]

The liking for holes came about from wanting to make space and three-dimensional form. For me the hole is not just a round hole. It is the penetration through from the front of the block to the back. This was for me a revelation, a great mental effort. It was having the idea to do it that was difficult, and not the physical effort. A very skilled gravestone memorial carver can carve a chain. I remember seeing a gravestone for a sailor, which had an anchor with a chain. The links were free, carved out of a solid piece of marble. It was very cleverly done but it had not required a sculptor to do it.

Ibid., p.67

66 *Figure* 1933-34 LH 137, travertine marble, height 40cm (15¾in)

[14] This is Moore's answer to question 13 in the questionnaire sent to members of Unit One: 'Do you consciously use numerical proportion in your designs?'.

[15] For an important early statement about holes in natural forms and in sculpture, see 'The Sculptor Speaks' 1937, p.195.

The hole as form – there is just as much shape in a hole as a lump.

Unpublished notes for 'The Sculptor Speaks' 1937, HMF archive

The holes are an expansion of three-dimensional form. They're one and the same. At a certain point I began to give my space a shape which could have turned into solid form if I'd thought of it the other way round.

Lake 1962, p.45

Holes & later work – one hopes is neither simply space in form, nor form in space, but both together.

Unpublished notes c.1951, HMF archive

There's no doubt a deep psychological explanation of the fascination of the hole.

Unpublished notes for 'The Sculptor Speaks' 1937, HMF archive

Size and Scale

You see, there is a difference between scale and size. A small sculpture only three or four inches big can have about it a monumental scale, so that if you photographed it against a blank wall in which you had nothing to refer it to but only itself – or you photographed it against the sky against infinite distance – a small thing only a few inches big might seem, if it has a monumental scale, to be any size. Now this is a quality that I personally think all really great sculpture has; it's a quality which, for me, all the great painters have – Rubens, Masaccio, Michelangelo – all the great painters, artists, and sculptors have this monumental sense. Perhaps it's because they don't allow detail to become important in itself, that is, they always keep the big things in their proper relationship and the detail is always subservient. I don't know what does it, but something … that is, an artist can have a monumental sense, and it's a very rare thing to have; what I'm saying is that it doesn't come from actual physical size. When the work has this monumentality about it, then you can enlarge it almost to any size you like, and it will be all right; it will be correct. But in doing it, if a thing becomes bigger than life-size, then as you stand and look at it, the angle that you might look at the head will be different from what you'd look at if it were small. Therefore it might need some alteration to give you the same feeling that you'd get from it if it were a different size. As you make a thing bigger or smaller, you alter to keep true to the mental vision you've had of it. But I don't know; I can't explain what it is that gives monumental scale to something. I think it's an innate vision, a mental thing rather than a physical thing. It's in the mind rather than in the material.

In trying to analyse what this big scale in a work comes from, perhaps, it is having an instinct so that the sculptor never forgets the big relevance of things, and no matter what amount of detail he puts into it, it is always subservient to the big general design of his form. For example, the Michelangelo Pietà in Saint Peter's in Rome is full of detail – the drapery, hands,

67 The diminutive lead *Reclining Figure* 1938 LH 192, 33cm (13in) in length, photographed by Moore against the skyline at Burcroft

faces. Everything in the sculpture is finished to the nth degree and yet the whole sculpture is monumental, mainly because I think that Michelangelo in doing the detail never forgot the whole big general design that he was making; so that to say, for example, that simplicity gives monumentality in itself isn't absolutely true. Simplicity alone, just leaving things out, will not produce monumentality; it may only produce emptiness. True simplicity is done not for simplicity's sake, but because you don't forget the essentials. It's done to keep the essentials and not because you like simplicity; it's only because there's something more important. Therefore it becomes simple because you're saying a big thing that has a big statement.

Forma 1964, pp.67, 73

First I asked him about size and scale. Moore said:

Every artist has a size to which he works. Michelangelo's was the sublime. You know his David – it's fourteen feet high. He carved that when he was twenty-one – an unbelievable feat for a young man, but he had already established his own monumental scale.

Watteau, to take an opposite, had a tiny scale. He could say everything he wanted, create his own special world, in a picture eighteen inches square. He didn't aim at grandeur; one can be on easy familiar terms with his creations. You could take a Watteau woman out to dinner; you couldn't take a Michelangelo woman out to dinner. You'd be terrified.

My own scale? It's just over life size. I think that's because I want my works to stand out-of-doors and be seen in a natural setting, and figures seen out-of-doors always look slightly smaller than they are.

The figure for Unesco [LH 416] I'm working on now is the biggest I've ever done. That's about twice life-size – and it's brought me an entirely new set of problems. One of them is to keep the distinction between strength and mass. It's easy in doing a work on a huge scale to imagine it's strong, full of vitality – which is what I want – when it's merely big and heavy.

Isn't it a relief to turn from working on a full-size figure to working on these little clay models?

Not a bit. Everything I do is intended to be big, and, while I'm working on the models, for me they are life-size. When I take one in my hand like this, I am seeing and feeling it *as* life-size. It's actually easier to visualise the small models in this way than, say, a half-size figure which would cover the top of a desk or table.

When I've got the model in my hand, I can be on all sides of it at once and see it from every point of view – as a sculptor has to do – instead of having to keep walking round. So in my mind there's never any change of scale at all.

'Henry Moore talks about My Work in a special interview with Tom Hopkinson',
Books and Art November 1957, pp.28-9

Anyhow, that thing of scale, of size, is a mixture of the two things, of physical size and mental scale … For example the little sketches of horses that Leonardo made in his sketch book were sometimes no bigger than a thumbnail, but you don't have that idea when you look at them. You think of a horse big enough to make a statue. And the same with Michelangelo sketches. There's a mental scale independent of the actual physical size.

I personally would like to think that the smallest sculpture that one makes has a bigness in it which would, if it had been necessary, have allowed the work to be enlarged without losing anything. In fact I would like to think that it would have gained, and in that sense I have an admiration, an ambition, a goal for something which looks big even in a photograph. I would like to think that one's works have about them a monumentality even if they're small. And I think that can happen.

There are some things like, for example, the Albert Memorial, that are really just enlarged small ideas. They're wrong in their scale, they haven't got their true physical size.

Interview with Donald Hall 1960; quoted in James 1966, pp.125, 127

The rightness of the size of a sculpture depends on where it is. My fourteen-foot *Archer* [LH 535] is somewhat too small for its location in front of the Toronto Town Hall, because I let the architect convince me to make it the size he thought it should be. But the second cast of the same piece which stands in front of Mies van der Rohe's museum in Berlin is right in size. The sculpture looks much bigger there, because it is not surrounded by tall buildings. You see it is not only set against a rather low building but against the verdant landscape of a park. Its size there is right, which demonstrates that the rightness of the size of a sculpture depends on where it is placed.

Seldis 1973, pp.195-6

And I like to see my sculpture on a large scale. Of course, you must have help to make such sculpture. I mean, an architect doesn't dig his own drains and lay his own bricks.

'Geoconversation: Henry Moore', *Geo*, Los Angeles September 1983, p.19

WOLFGANG FISCHER: How do you see the problem of scale and size in a historical perspective, say that some artists in some periods in history express themselves better on a small scale and others in a large scale. For example, Assyrian stone reliefs versus clay figures from Crete – Michelangelo and Bernini versus Renaissance medium-size bronzes – in short, that some artists in some periods of history express themselves better on small and others better on large scale.

HENRY MOORE: Undoubtedly, there are some artists whose ideas don't need large size. An example in modern art is Paul Klee. His imaginative, poetic small drawings would gain nothing whatever if they were ten times their size. In fact, their smallness allows you to enter into their rather fairy-like fantasy world better than if they were bigger works.

FISCHER: But I was thinking more of the three-dimensional.

MOORE: All right. Now I would think it would be a mistake to enlarge, say Staffordshire pottery figures. There are ideas even which are just not suitable for blowing up to over-life size. I have made some little sculptures, such as the 'Rocking Chair' groups – these were done to amuse my daughter when she was a child. They are just over 12 inches high. To have made them even half-life size – that is, three feet high – would have been wrong. They would have lost their toy-like quality.

Fischer 1971 (n.p.)

FISCHER: Yes, but in this case monumentality seems to be a stylistic quality.

MOORE: No, no, because you can teach style, but monumentality is a natural part of the vision of some artists, and it cannot be taught. Some artists have it and some don't. It doesn't mean doing colossal, large size works – someone like Morandi in his small still life paintings has such a sense – the bottles he paints can look like great towers in a landscape. This is just the way some artists alter things.

Ibid.

What are the things you most respond to, in art?

Well, if I were to go over the experiences that have stood out for me above all others, I think that nearly all of them would have what I'd call a quality of monumentality. It's not a question of size – a Cézanne can be only ten inches by eight and yet have absolute monumentality – it's a question of the mind behind the work.

Russell 24 December 1961

Tactile Experiences

HENRY MOORE: Tactile experience is very important as an aesthetic dimension in sculpture. Our knowledge of shape and form remains, in general, a mixture of visual and of tactile experiences. A child learns to judge distance by touching things, and our sense of sight is always closely associated with our sense of touch. That is why a blind man learns to rely more exclusively on the use of his hands. A child learns about roundness from handling a ball far more than from looking at it. Even if we touch things with less immediate curiosity, as we grow older, our sense of sight remains closely allied to our sense of touch.

EDOUARD RODITI: I used to know a German Orientalist, the late Professor Erwin Rumpf of Berlin, who was reputed to be one of the very rare Westerners to have an instinctively true appreciation of Japanese Art. He once explained to me that the aesthetics of the Japanese Netzuke figures – those little carved ivories that were used as buttons – required that the whole object be understood or read by feeling as explicitly as by seeing, and that Japanese art-lovers fondle them and comprehend the whole sculpture with the use of one hand.

MOORE: Blind persons have been known to model sculptures which are visually exciting. Still, there are limitations to the proportions of a blind artist's sculpture. Size would pose a great problem, and it would be almost impossible to conceive a very large figure, with a proper integration of the relationships of its masses as parts, without ever being able to have recourse to one's sight. Some people, misunderstanding the nature of tactile values, and perhaps wishing to be fashionable, will often say: 'I love touching sculptures.' That can be nonsense. One simply prefers to touch smooth forms rather than rough ones, whether these forms be natural or created by art. Nobody can seriously claim to enjoy touching a rough-cast sculpture, with its unpleasantly prickly surface that may be nonetheless good sculpture. No one likes touching cold and wet objects for example. A sculpture may thus be excellent according to quite a number of different criteria and still unpleasant to touch. But the tactile element remains of primary importance in the actual creation of most sculpture.

RODITI: [Bernard] Berenson has already discussed at great length the tactile qualities of a certain kind of painting, especially of the more sculptural art of Piero della Francesca or of Mantegna. But painting can suggest a whole range of tactile qualities, not only of sculptural awareness of roundness or relief that is suggested by Mantegna and Piero della Francesca, but also the awareness of texture that is suggested in a Courbet still-life, where the feathers of a pheasant and the fur of a hare can almost make your fingers tingle …

MOORE: But these last tactile qualities of painting can also degenerate into a kind of cheap illusion, like that of a performing magician. They exist, in a way, in sculpture too, for instance when a marble or bronze suggests the silky texture and the softness of human flesh. Actually, this is fairly easy to achieve, and many an outstanding sculptor is popularly admired for the finish that his assistants have given to his works.

RODITI: I have often been struck by the essentially tactile nature of certain distortions of the human form in your sculpture. It has seemed to me that these are sometimes inspired by tactile illusions of feeling, as opposed to the optical illusions that inspire most distortions in art.

MOORE: You are right. I believe that there can be distortions, tactile rather than visual in origin, which can make a sculpture much more exciting, though they may give an impression of awkwardness and disjointedness to an art-lover who is more accustomed to the distortions of painting. Sculpture with such tactile exaggerations can be so much more exciting than the smooth and merely pictorial ease that characterises most bad nineteenth-century sculpture.

RODITI: I have often felt that only Carpeaux, Rodin and Medardo Rosso, in the whole second half of the nineteenth century, really understood the purposes and the principles of sculpture.

MOORE: Rodin of course knew what sculpture is: he once said that sculpture is the science of the bump and the hollow.

Roditi 1960, pp.184-5

Whilst touching some sculptures can give pleasure, touch itself is certainly not a criterion of good sculpture. A particular pebble or a marble egg may be delightful to feel or hold because it is very simple in shape and very smooth, whereas if it were the same shape but with a prickly or cold surface, you would not like touching it. Of course you can tell the shape of something if you can put your hands all round it. But it is impossible for a blind person to tell you the shape of a building. The same applies to a large sculpture, in that, although the sense of touch is fundamentally important and implied, it is not physically necessary to touch a sculpture in order to understand its form.

Hedgecoe 1968, p.85

Subjects and Sources of Inspiration

I do not consciously use any form of symbolism in my sculpture (but I'm prepared to have it proved to me that unconsciously I do).[16]

Unpublished notes for *Unit One* 1934, HMF archive

Most artists have obsessions in their subject matter – some may be mainly landscape painters, some mainly figurative, others may do portraits or concentrate on animal painting, etc.

There are three recurring themes in my work: the 'Mother and child' idea, the 'Reclining figure' and the 'Interior–exterior forms'. Some sculptures may combine two or even all three of these themes.

Wildenstein 1979, p.28

Reclining Figure

From the very beginning the reclining figure has been my main theme. The first one I made was around 1924, and probably more than half of my sculptures since then have been reclining figures.

Hedgecoe 1968, p.151

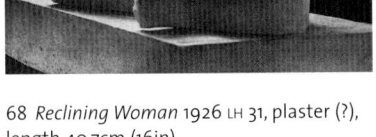

68 *Reclining Woman* 1926 LH 31, plaster (?), length 40.7cm (16in)

I want to be quite free of having to find a 'reason' for doing the Reclining Figures, and freer still of having to find a 'meaning' for them. The vital thing for an artist is to have a subject that allows [him] to try out all kinds of formal ideas – things that he doesn't yet know about for certain but wants to experiment with, as Cézanne did in his 'Bathers' series. In my case the reclining figure provides chances of that sort. The subject-matter is *given*. It's settled for you, and you know it and like it, so that within it, within the subject that you've done a dozen times before, you are free to invent a completely new form-idea.

Russell 1968, p.28

[16] This is Moore's answer to question 3 in the Unit One questionnaire, 'Do you consciously use any form of symbolism in your sculpture?'

Mother and Child

From very early on I have had an obsession with the Mother and Child theme. It has been a universal theme from the beginning of time and some of the earliest sculptures we've found from the Neolithic Age are of a Mother and Child. I discovered, when drawing, I could turn every little scribble, blot or smudge into a Mother and Child. (Later on, I did the same with the Reclining Figure theme!) So that I was conditioned, as it were, to see it in everything. I suppose it could be explained as a 'Mother' complex.

Hedgecoe 1968, p.61

The 'Mother and child' idea is one of my two or three obsessions, one of my inexhaustible subjects. This may have something to do with the fact that the 'Madonna and Child' was so important in the art of the past and that one loves the old masters and has learned so much from them.

But the subject itself is eternal and unending, with so many sculptural possibilities in it – a small form in relation to a big form, the big form protecting the small one, and so on. It is such a rich subject, both humanly and compositionally, that I will always go on using it.

Wildenstein 1979, p.29

I suppose the favourite form motives of any individual artist are an inescapable part of his make-up – (& could give a phychological explanation) (I might be able to give some sort of convincing reason for my liking of the mother & child theme from knowledge of my own history. I should find it more difficult to explain why so far I've found unending possibilities & variations on the reclining figure theme.

Unpublished notes for 'Art and Life' 1941, HMF archive

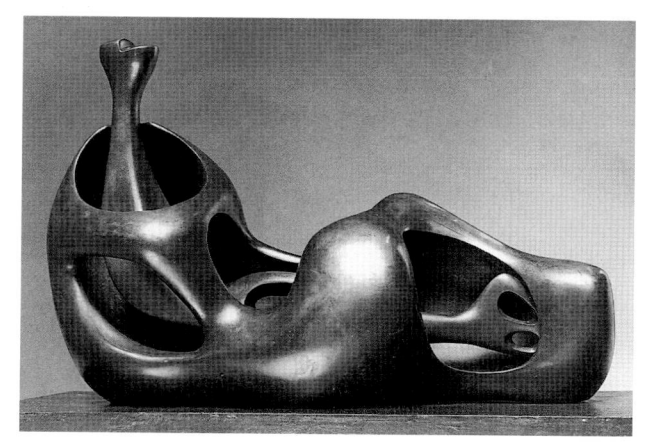

69 *Mother and Child* 1922 LH 3, Portland stone, height 27.9cm (11in)

Internal–External Forms

The idea of one form inside another form may owe some of its incipient beginnings to my interest at one stage when I discovered armour. I spent many hours in the Wallace Collection, in London, looking at armour.

70 *Working Model for Reclining Figure: Internal/External* 1951 LH 298, bronze, length 53.5cm (21in)

Now armour is an outside shell like the shell of a snail which is there to protect the more vulnerable forms inside, as it is in human armour which is hard and put on to protect the soft body. This has led sometimes to the idea of the Mother and Child where the outer form, the mother, is protecting the inner form, the child, like a mother does protect her child.

In conversation with David Mitchinson, 1980

What started you off on the Helmet idea?

I think it may be the interest I had early on in armour, in places like the Victoria and Albert Museum where one used to wander round as a student in the lunch hours.

And it may be that I remembered reading stories that impressed me and Wyndham Lewis talking about the shell of a lobster covering the soft flesh inside. This became an established idea with me – that of an outer protection to an inner form, and it may have something to do with the mother and child idea; that is where there is the relation of the big thing to the little thing, and the protection idea. The helmet is a kind of protection thing, too, and it became a recording of things inside other things. The mystery of semiobscurity where one can only half distinguish something. In the helmet you do not quite know what is inside.

Michael Chase, 'Moore on his Methods', *Christian Science Monitor*, Boston 24 March 1967

Titles

I don't give my sculptures high-falutin' or abstruse Greek titles. I prefer to call them 'Reclining Figure' or 'Mother and Child', simple descriptive names.

I decide the title of a sculpture after I have finished it. I didn't set out to do a sculpture called 'The Bird Basket' or 'The Bride' or even one called 'The King and Queen'. The naming of a piece of sculpture can start a line of thought for the person looking at it. I'm sure Paul Klee gave most of his paintings and drawings their titles after they were finished – or while working on them. There's one of Klee's pictures with lines going into water and forms underneath. He called it 'They're Biting' as though it showed a fisherman on the river bank dropping his line into the water and then getting excited that the fish were biting. A fuller appreciation eventually comes because it makes the observer look for the title's connection.

Hedgecoe 1968, p.109

New Ideas

When I first began doing sculpture about 1922 or so, I often worked direct in a piece of stone or wood, which might have been not a geometric shape but just an odd random block of stone that one had found cheaply in some stonemason's yard, or a log of wood which was a natural shape, and then I'd make a sculpture, trying to get as big a sculpture out of that bit of material as I could, and therefore one would wait until the material suggested an idea.

Nowadays I don't work so much in that way, as I have an idea, or an idea comes to me, and then I find the material to make it in, and to do that, the ideas that I may be concerned with, I'll produce several maquettes – sketches in plaster – not much bigger than one's hand, certainly small enough to hold in one's hand, so that you can turn them around as you shape them and work on them without having to get up and walk around them, and you have a complete grasp of their shape from all around the whole time. If the form, the idea, that you're doing is much bigger than that, then to see what it's like on the other side, you have to get up, walk around it, and this restricts your imagining and grasping what it's like as you can when it's small. But all the time that I am doing this small model, in my mind it isn't the small model that I'm doing, it's the big sculpture that I intend to do. It's as though one were drawing in a little sketchbook a tiny little sketch for a monument, or a tiny little drawing might be on the back of an envelope, but in your mind would be the equestrian statue that is over life-size. In the same way, these little plaster maquettes that I make, to me, are all big sculptures. Therefore, when I choose the one that I think has the best possibility and retains my interest, then it's only carrying out one's original idea in reality. For example, the maquette for this two-piece locking piece [fig.131] came about from two pebbles which I was playing with and which seemed to fit each other and lock together, and this gave me the idea of making a two-piece sculpture – not that the forms weren't separate, but that they knitted together. I did several little plaster maquettes, and eventually one nearest to what the shape of this big one is now pleased me the most and then I began making the big one. But in making the big one, the small one changes because you have to alter forms when they are bigger from what they are when they're small, because your relationship to them is a different one.

Forma 1964, pp.63, 67

Do you consciously try to get your mind working on a new piece? How do ideas come to you?

Well, in various ways. One doesn't know really how any ideas come. But I can induce them by starting with looking at a box of pebbles. I have collected bits of pebbles, bits of bone, found objects, and so on, all of which help to give one an atmosphere to start working. Sometimes I may scribble some doodles, as I said, in a notebook; within my mind they may be a reclining figure, or perhaps a particular subject. Then with those pebbles, or the sketches in the notebook, I sit down and something begins. Then perhaps at a certain stage the idea crystallises and then you know what to do, what to alter. You dislike what you've just made, and change it. At the end of a week you're sitting in that nice little easy chair with the bench in front, and there'll be probably some fifteen or so maquettes about five or six inches long, if it's a reclining figure, or that high if it's an upright. Then, either I know that a few of those are ideas I like or that I don't like any of them. If some are ones I like, then I'll do a variation on that idea, or I'll change it if I'm critical. Done in that way, the thing evolves. Always in my mind though, in making these little ideas, is the eventual sculpture which may be ten or twelve times the size of the maquette that I hold in my hand.

Hall 1960, pp.104, 113

DAVID SYLVESTER: Do a lot of the recent things begin from 'found objects'?

HENRY MOORE: Yes: finding driftwood and pebbles and bones – anything that starts one off as a reality for me now is a much better start than a drawing.

SYLVESTER: Do you add bits of clay or plaster to these objects?

MOORE: No. I look at them, handle them, see them from all round and I may press them into clay and pour plaster into that clay and get a start as a bit of plaster, which is a reproduction of the object. Then I add to it, change it. In that way something turns out in the end that you could never have thought of the day before. This to me now is the beauty of each day – if one is working – that by the end of it you might have had something happen that you couldn't possibly have foreseen.

SYLVESTER: Have any of the two-piece and three-piece reclining figures begun from 'found objects'?

Ideas from Old Bones

MOORE: Yes. On the extra piece of ground that we've got below our garden there must have lived a butcher who bred his cattle and he did the preparing of his carcasses and everything else, because whenever the garden is dug we find bits of old bones sawn across; and these always can start me off with

71 Found objects in Bourne Maquette Studio, Perry Green

an idea. But of course ideas must be in your mind to begin with. Although they may start from 'found objects' they finish as one's own invention. The value of certain kinds of modern sculpture may be that it opens people's eyes to nature, that they pick up things which they wouldn't look at otherwise; and they look at things with a new eye.

SYLVESTER: This is one of the ways in which the twentieth century has made nature imitate art. But you have collected these pebbles and bones for thirty years, haven't you? Did you previously use them as beginnings for sculptures?

MOORE: Not as much as I may do now. To begin with I was a stone-carver. For me stone was the essence of sculpture. The sort of effort that was needed to take a hard lump of stone and turn it into a willed work was what sculpture was.

SYLVESTER: When you did stone sculpture in the 'thirties a lot, did you ever imitate 'found objects'?

MOORE: No, in those days one had to buy odd pieces of stone from any stonemason that one found. And then you'd think: 'How can I make that into something in which I waste as little stone as possible?' Now, I wouldn't worry how much stone was wasted. Perhaps that's a bad thing, perhaps it's not. But this was very good discipline; it was like a young person having to make do on a budget instead of having a bank balance that he can draw on just as he likes.

SYLVESTER: Some of the things, then, have begun from pebbles and bones, and so on, but some haven't. Among the series of multiple-piece reclining figures, are there particular ones in which you did use such objects?

MOORE: In the first of the three-piece sculptures [LH 500], which is going to be shown soon, the middle piece, which was the pace-maker for it, was a vertebra of an animal that I found in the garden. And the connection of one piece through to the other is the kind of connection that a backbone will have with one section through to the next section. That's the only example I can immediately think of.

Sylvester 1963, p.306

Sometimes I make ten or twenty maquettes for every one that I use in a large scale – the others may get rejected. If a maquette keeps its interest enough for me to want to realise it as a full-size final work, then I might make a working model in an intermediate size, in which changes will be made before going to the real, full-sized sculpture. Changes get made at all these stages.

Levine 1978, p.57

In my sculpture, explanations often come afterwards. I do not make a sculpture to a programme or because I have a particular idea I am trying to express. While working, I change parts because I do not like them in such a way that I hope I am going to like them better. The kind of alteration I make is not thought out; I do not say to myself – this is too big, or too small.

I just look at it and, if I do not like it, I change it. I work from likes and dislikes, and not by literary logic. Not by words, but by being satisfied with form. Afterwards I can explain or find reasons for it, but that is rationalisation after the event. I can even look at old sculptures and find meanings in them and explanations which at the time were not in my mind at all – not consciously anyway.

Hedgecoe 1968, p.83

I believe that nothing should be taboo – no theory or prejudice should close one's mind to a discovery.

Unpublished notes *c.*1951, HMF archive

Theories – What I want is freedom – Not limitations within doctrinaire theories – Some people may get comfort & actual help from working within set limitations, from having taboos, – deciding that any particular degree of representation somewhere between all or none becomes academism, etc.

Ibid.

The Human Figure

In my opinion, long and intense study of the human figure is the necessary foundation for a sculptor. The human figure is most complex and subtle and difficult to grasp in form and construction, and so it makes the most exacting form for study and comprehension. A moderate ability to 'draw' will pass muster in a landscape or a tree, but even the untrained eye is more critical of the human figure – because it is ourselves.

Sylvester 1951, p.4

72 *Reclining Woman* 1928 HMF 564, pen and ink, chalk, wash, 333 x 420mm (13⅛ x 16½in). Private collection

There are three fundamental poses of the human figure. One is standing, the other is seated, and the third is lying down. Now, if you like to carve the human figure in stone, as I do, the standing pose is no good. Stone is not so strong as bone, and the figure will break off at the ankles and topple over. The early Greeks solved this problem by draping the figure and covering the ankles. Later on they supported it against a silly tree trunk.

But with either the seated or the reclining figure one doesn't have this worry. And between them are enough variations to occupy any sculptor for a lifetime. In fact if I were told that from now on I should have stone only for seated figures I should not mind it at all.

But of the three poses, the reclining figure gives the most freedom, compositionally and spatially. The seated figure has to have something to sit on. You can't free it from its pedestal. A reclining figure can recline on any surface. It is free and stable at the same time. It fits in with my belief that sculpture should be permanent, should last for eternity. Also, it has repose. And it suits me – if you know what I mean.

John D. Morse, 'Henry Moore Comes to America', *Magazine of Art*, New York March 1947, pp.100-1

The Head

Importance of the <u>HEAD</u> in figure sculpture. The head gives a scale to the rest of the figure – just because I feel the importance of the head, is why I do not make the head large & 'featured'.

Much primitive sculpture makes the head larger than life (& sometimes the rest of the figure is just a base for the head) because it wants to emphasise the expression of some obvious human – Michelangelo (& the later Greeks) made the head small because the sculptural rythmn & pose & the whole figure was what they were interested in – My heads are small just because I know how important the head is – what an important sculptural part the head plays in giving bigness & [a sense] of scale & size to the whole figure.

Unpublished notes c.1951, HMF archive

Some people have said why do I make the heads so unimportant. Actually, for me the head is the most important part of a piece of sculpture. It gives to the rest a scale, it gives to the rest a certain human poise, and meaning, and it's because I think that the head is so important that often I reduce it in size to make the rest more monumental. It's a thing that anyhow was done. The heads of Michelangelo's figures will sometimes go twelve times instead of the usual six and a half, which is the average. It is a recognised thing.

Freeman 1964, p.32

Nature may appear symmetrical sometimes, but it never is. Everybody's face, for instance, is asymmetrical. If you took the two halves of a person's face and reversed them, you'd get a different person.

Hedgecoe 1986, p.169

73 *Woman* 1957-58 LH 439, bronze, height 152.5cm (60in)

You don't need to represent the features of a face so as to suggest the human qualities special to a particular person. My own aim has not been to capture the range of expressions that can play over the features but to render the exact degree of relationship between, for example, the head and the shoulders; for the outline of the whole figure, the three-dimensional character of a body, can render the spirit of the subject treated.

When you observe a friend in the distance, you don't recognise him by the colour of his eyes (for these you are then unable to see) but by the effect made by his figure – the general disposition of his forms, the proportion and set of one mass to another.

Denys Sutton, 'Henry Moore: A Sculptor's Vision', The New York Times
22 March 1959

Hands

I have always loved hands, in common with most past sculptors. Rodin, for instance, made a very special study of hands. The first sculpture I did, or at least the sculpture that helped me to win a Royal Exhibition Scholarship to the R.C.A., was the modelling of a hand from life. Casts of this hand were later sent round to all the art schools as an example of how it should be done. I remember I enjoyed doing it quite enormously.

Hands, after the face, are the most obvious part of the human body for expressing emotion. That is why I concentrated on the hands in the 'King and Queen' in order to add to the sculpture an extra interest and meaning. This was missing in the little maquette, where the hands are rather rudimentarily and cursorily done.

Hedgecoe 1968, p.232

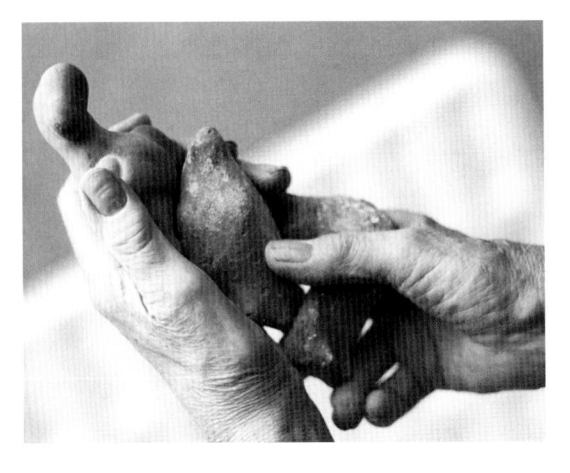

74 Moore holding flint stones

Hands can convey so much – they can beg or refuse, take or give, be open or clenched, show content or anxiety. They can be young or old, beautiful or deformed....

Throughout the history of sculpture and painting one can find that artists have shown through the hands the feelings they wished to represent. Rembrandt for example uses hands to express nearly as much as the head and its features.

Henry Moore, The Artist's Hands, Raymond Spencer Company
for the Henry Moore Foundation, Much Hadham 1980

The Human Figure as Inspiration

There have been two major influences on my work. The main one, perhaps, is drawing and modelling from the human figure – I have looked at the nude for half my life. Our own bodies, our own make up, have the greatest influence on art. If we were able to sleep on all fours or were the size of an elephant, for example, our architecture would be entirely different from what it is, so would our art. We know from our hands what things are much better than we would if we had hooves. From our bodies we understand nature; we can't get away from it and if the landscape were different so would our lives be. So the first influence on me came from studying, and trying to understand, the human figure.

Levine 1983, p.15

For me, everything in the world of form is understood through our own bodies. From our mother's breast, from our bones, from bumping into things, we learn what is rough and what is smooth. To observe, to understand, to experience the vast variety of space, shape and form in the world, twenty lifetimes would not be enough. There is no end to it.

Levine 1978, p.48

In the human figure one can express more completely one's feelings about the world than in any other way.

Wilkinson 1977, p.18

Natural Forms[17]

Besides the human form, I am tremendously excited by all natural forms, such as cloud formations, birds, trees and their roots, and mountains, which are to me the wrinkling of the earth's surface, like drapery. It is extraordinary how closely ripples in the sand on the seashore resemble the gouge marks in wood carving.

The upright exterior–interior form [LH 295] is like the petals which enclose the stamen of a flower. Besides acting as a protection, they provide an attraction.

Hedgecoe 1968, p.131

Nobody is sure how flintstones came about. I think some were formed by a natural casting process, since their strange shapes could not possibly be caused by wind erosion or constant wearing and fretting by the sea. The shapes of flintstones vary in character in different parts of the country. Having collected them for over fifty years on the beaches at Broadstairs [Kent] and in Norfolk and Dorset, I find a tremendous difference in the type of flintstone in the various localities.

Flintstones, pebbles, shells and driftwood have all helped me to start off ideas, but far more important to me has been the human figure and its inner skeleton structure. You can feel that a bone has had some sort of use in its life; it has experienced tensions, has supported weights and has actually performed an organic function, which a pebble has not done at all. In themselves pebbles are dead forms, their shape is accidental, and merely to copy them would not in itself create a sculptural form. It is what I see in them that gives them their significance.

Ibid., p.75

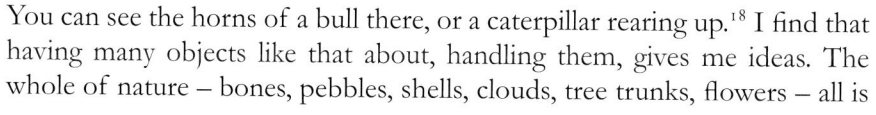

75 Bone with plasticine on which *Standing Figure: Knife Edge* 1961 LH 482 (see fig.130) was based

You can see the horns of a bull there, or a caterpillar rearing up.[18] I find that having many objects like that about, handling them, gives me ideas. The whole of nature – bones, pebbles, shells, clouds, tree trunks, flowers – all is

---

[17] For important early statements about natural forms, see *Unit One* 1934, p.192 and 'The Sculptor Speaks' 1937, p.195.
[18] Moore is showing Lake a curved, serrated shell.

grist to the mill of a sculptor. It all needs to be brought in at one time. People have thought – the later Greeks, in the Hellenistic period – that the human figure was the only subject, that it ended there; a question of copying. But I believe it's a question of metamorphosis. We must relate the human figure to animals, to clouds, to the landscape – bring them all together. There's no difference between them all. By using them like metaphors in poetry, you give new meaning to things.

Lake 1962, p.42

Materials

Stone

In those days, too, I loved stone, as I still do now. I actually love stone. A piece of stone, any piece of stone in a landscape, a big rock, anything in stone, I just love more even than I love wood.

Hall 1960, p.104

In stone sculpture you have to alter the malleable softness of flesh and blood into something that is harder and less bendable.

Ibid., p.492

I went to the stone quarries in Derbyshire and bought a lot of random blocks of Hopton Wood stone.[19] I had room and space enough at Burcroft to let the stones stand around in the landscape, and seeing them daily gave me fresh ideas for sculpture. Some of the stones were six or seven feet long and very odd shapes. […] This was very much a stone period in my life. In fact up to the war, nine out of ten sculptures I did were in stone. I still love stone.

Hedgecoe 1968, p.95

Granite is one of the hardest stones, it would last for thousands of years in any climate. Very few other stones will stay out of doors as well as bronze.

Ibid., p.143

I now use many varieties of marble, but in the early part of my career I made a point of using native materials because I thought that, being English, I should understand our stones. They were cheaper, and I could go round to a stonemason and buy random pieces. I tried to use English stones that hadn't been used before for sculpture. I discovered many English stones, including Hornton Stone, from visiting the Geological Museum in South Kensington, which was next door to my college.

Levine 1978, p.146

---

[19] This refers to the years 1936-37, see LH 163, 177, 178, 179. Moore also used Hopton wood stone in the mid-1920s, see LH 22 and 23.

White marble is a most pure and elegant material. In carving a sculpture, it is very important to match the right material with the particular subject in mind. In using white marble I give the forms a precision and refinement and a surface finish that I wouldn't try to obtain with a rough textured stone such as travertine.

Hedgecoe 1968, p.494

White marble emphasises elegance and refinement. That's why it's adored for all these memorials. It makes the dead people seem so distinguished.

Carll Tucker, 'Creators on Creating: Henry Moore', *Saturday Revue*,
New York March 1981, p.44

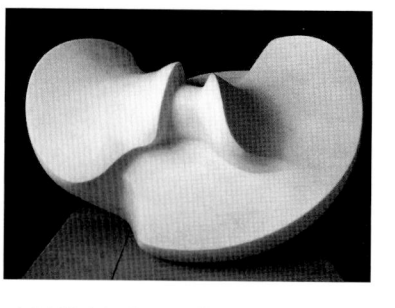

76 *Divided Oval: Butterfly* 1967 LH 571, white marble, length 91cm (36in). Private collection

Travertine has a quality – ruddy, powerful, strong. You feel you haven't got to handle it with kid gloves.

Ibid.

Roman travertine marble is a stone that I have loved ever since I first used it in 1932.[20] I like its colour and its rough, broken, pitted surface. Knowing these characteristics I did not give the plaster working model[21] a smooth surface.

Hedgecoe 1968, p.313

77 *Stone Memorial* 1961/69 LH 491b, travertine marble, length 180.5cm (71in). National Gallery of Art, Washington: Collection of Mr and Mrs Paul Mellon

Wood

As a youngster I didn't much like working in wood. I enjoyed working with stone – it had a strength and reality which easier mediums might not possess. And to begin with wood was a slow material to work in until I began to use an axe and a saw on big pieces – though you can only saw in a straight line. The finishing of wood is a slow process, too, because you have to cut across the grain or it splits. Also, a small wood carving takes longer and is more tedious to do than a small stone carving. I don't mean tedious in the sense that it is not enjoyable, I mean that one has to have more patience. For example, a small wood piece like the *Animal Head* [LH 1a] might take nearly as long as a life-size model in another medium. But wood is an easier material to work on than metal or stone. You cannot saw stone easily, for instance – it takes ten times as long as sawing a piece of wood. You cannot drill stone as easily either, whereas you can make holes in the wood that will help you to get into the material. Wood eventually became a freer medium for me and I could make things in it with arms and so on which would have broken in stone.

Wood carvers, and workers in wood, over the years have developed the tools that are most useful for dealing with wood. If you don't use the right

[20] The 1929 *Figure with Clasped Hands* LH 60 was Moore's first carving in travertine marble. He did not use it again until 1936, in *Carving* LH 164.
[21] *Working Model for Unesco Reclining Figure* 1957 LH 415.

tools things take longer, so you learn which tools suit. For example, you may find that a deeper gouge is more necessary in some woods than in others. For carving in stone the chisel is a flat one, but if you dig a tool inside the wood it can split it, so your tool has to be a curved gouge so that the two ends come out of the wood and don't bury themselves in it – only the middle of the gouge does the cutting. You have to work in a slightly different way, too, and you may have to take off smaller pieces at a time. The amount you can get rid of might be quite large, but it can't be detailed. In the finishing stages you have to nibble the wood, like a mouse making a hole.

When I was working on my *Reclining Figure*, 1939 [fig.99], I slowly came to the reason why, with time, big blocks of wood split more than small pieces. It is because the outside gets the warmth of the atmosphere and is drying and trying to shrink whilst, of course, the inside is still full of water and sap – the tree's blood – and can't shrink. So something on the shrunken outside – now a smaller area than it was – has to give way to cover the inside, and it splits.

When wood in a big block is being seasoned the air only drys out an inch a year, so if it is four feet in diameter it will take twenty-four years of slow seasoning for it to be seasoned right to the middle. Whereas, by piecing [piercing?] the block so that nowhere is more than six inches thick, it can be seasoned in three years.

Wood sculpture is no less permanent than any other sculpture if kept indoors under favourable conditions. Some wood sculptures not exposed to the weather conditions of hot and cold, dry and wet, can last almost indefinitely. But they can't be left out of doors because the rain, the wet, and the sun attack them. I remember an English painter friend buying a large wood sculpture made by a mutual friend, Zadkine, from Paris. It was in the garden down in Sussex and after about ten years the woodpeckers and the contrast of our English weather broke it to pieces and it fell apart.

All the different types of wood, so numerous and so varied, have their own individuality, each quite distinct from the others, just as an old piece of wood is so different from one that isn't seasoned. All woods vary enormously in hardness and softness, in the closeness of the grain, so there is a tremendous choice for the sculptor. The weightiness of some wood must also be taken into account in the work, because something that is very light must be treated in a different way from something that is very heavy. But it matters a great deal that the subject suits the material, or vice versa.

Boxwood

Boxwood has a close grain and takes a very high finish. That's why it was used a great deal in making woodcuts, because the lines could be built and then printed with ink. Box trees grow very slowly so they don't reach a large size and the slower the wood is in growing the harder it is. The soft woods – like poplar – grow very quickly. One or two sculptures I did came from blocks of wood I bought from a wood merchant in the East End of London who dealt in hard woods, a lot of which came from the tropics, but box-wood is English.

Beechwood

Beechwood is a silky kind of wood – you can give it a silky finish. It has a grain which is obvious, with a kind of undulating rhythm – upwards and downwards. It may have dark lines or lines that are hardly noticeable. The grain doesn't show as much in beechwood as it does, say, in elm, but it is a close-grain wood and, therefore, you can do small sculptures in it. The wood is suitable for carving and presents no special problems.

Elmwood

Elm on the whole has a grain that is very big and broad. It grows up to seven or eight feet in diameter. It wouldn't do to make a very small thing in elm because the grain would be like putting big stripes across a marble: across a face, for instance, they might come in the wrong place. You would never be able to control where the markings were going to come.

There was a timber merchant near me in Bishop's Stortford whom I got to know and to whom I went for wood. Whenever he got a very big elm tree he would let me know and I was able to use these for my reclining figures. I like working with elmwood because its big grain makes it suitable for large sculptures and because of the cool greyness of the wood.

Sycamore Wood

Sycamore is closer grained than elm, and more even. So though it is not a hard wood it will take a polish to give a high finish. Sycamore trees are common in England, and it is a very pleasant wood, suitable for carving.

Walnut and other Fruit Tree Woods

Walnut is harder than elm, as are the other fruit trees – apple, pear, plum and, on the whole, cherry. These are all good carving woods for smallish sculptures because the grain is tight and close and small in markings. But, again, one chooses the grain to suit the idea.

Ebony

Ebony is even closer grained – it hardly shows any grain at all. You can almost ignore the grain and treat it like a homogenous material – one that is the same all over. You don't need to see the linear pattern in it. It takes a very high finish: unfinished ebony would be rather a waste, like an unpolished diamond. Just as the rough diamond doesn't bring out the qualities of the stone, so ebony grains only when it is highly finished.

Lignum Vitae

Another of the tropical hard woods, lignum vitae has many of the same qualities as ebony. It is so dense and heavy that it actually sinks in water, and when carved it is harder than many stones. It is ideal for making a very thin upright figure – which can't easily be made in stone. I also found it an ideal body for my stringed figures.

78 *Mother and Child* 1938 LH 194, elmwood, height 91.4cm (36in). The Museum of Modern Art, New York: acquired through the Lillie P. Bliss bequest 1953

What wood can do that stone cannot is give you the sense of its having grown. Stone doesn't grow – it's a deposit.

Levine 1983, pp.20-3

An interesting point about working with wood is that it must come from a live tree. Dead wood, by which I mean wood from a tree that has died, has no qualities of self-preservation and rots away.

Hedgecoe 1968, p.335

Clay

Clay is wonderful stuff to punch and feel that the imprint of your fist is left in it.

Hall 1960, p.104

If you use clay it has to be kept in a malleable condition (if left untended for a week, it becomes hard and cracks), whereas you can leave plaster untouched indefinitely. To work on it again all you have to do is to soak it thoroughly in water, and then you can add further plaster to it as though you had only just left it for half an hour.

Hedgecoe 1968, p.300

Plaster

79 Moore working on the plaster for *Reclining Figure* 1963-65 LH 519 at Perry Green, 1964

Plaster is an important material for sculptors. Good quality plaster mixed with water sets to the hardness of a soft stone. I use plaster for my maquettes in preference to clay because I can both build it up and cut it down. It is easily worked, while clay hardens and dries, so that it cannot be added to.

Levine 1978, p.124

Any tools can be used for plasterwork, for example, kitchen tools such as cheese graters or nutmeg graters, spatulas, knives, or anything.

Ibid., p.114

I have a couple of young sculptor assistants, and between the three of us we will plan the armature. You need an armature because, with plaster sculpture, you have to build on something or you'd have a great big solid piece of plaster which is unhandleable and which takes ages to build up; so one makes an armature in wood with, perhaps, chicken wire roughly to the shape, but enlarged to scale. My assistants can do this after they've been with me for a few months or so and know the sort of methods I use. To have their help saves me a great amount of time. Once they have brought the work to within an inch or so of the measurements I intend it to be, I take it over, and it then becomes a thing that I'm working on as it would if I had brought it to that stage myself.

Hall 1960, p.113

This is how my plaster originals grow. At one time I used wire netting in making the armature, but this caused immense trouble when I made alterations which are always necessary in enlarging the maquette into a full size sculpture. Now for the armature I use only wood struts and scrim, a form of open-work sacking.

Hedgecoe 1968, p.345

The advantage of using plaster is that it can be both built up, as in modelling, or cut down, in the way you carve stone or wood.

Ibid., p.300

When working in plaster for bronze I need to visualise it as a bronze, because on white plaster the light and shade acts quite differently, throwing back a reflected light on itself and making the forms softer, less powerful … even weightless.

At first I used to have a tremendous shock going from the white plaster model to the finished bronze sculpture. But after forty years of working in plaster for bronze I can now visualise what is going to happen. The main difference is that bronze takes on a density and weight altogether unlike white plaster. Plaster has a ghost-like unreality in contrast to the solid strength of the bronze. If I am not absolutely sure of what is going to happen when the white plaster model is cast into bronze, I paint it to make it look like bronze. After a sculpture is cast it's too late, of course, to make any big alterations.

Hedgecoe 1986, p.159

Polystyrene

I first used polystyrene in the early 1960s, when I was asked to design the scenery for Mozart's opera *Don Giovanni*.[22] Certain parts of the scenery were made in polystyrene. From then on, I realised that it was going to save a lot of time, energy and effort. The previous method had involved working with a wooden or metal armature, wire netting, canvas and plaster – which is heavy material in itself. This meant that, for example, a single form of the 'vertebrae' [LH 580] would need three of us to move it round. I can move polystyrene alone, the material is so light. That is its advantage; its disadvantage is that it is easily damaged.

Levine 1978, p.133

How do you feel about working in polystyrene versus plaster?

I used to work in plaster for my big sculptures and make an internal armature. Then I'd stretch canvas and plaster over that and make refinements. That is all right, but it's nearly impossible afterwards to move it. You have to

---

[22] At the 1967 Festival of Two Worlds, Spoleto, the production of *Don Giovanni* opened the festival; it was conducted by Thomas Schippers, directed by Gian Carlo Menotti, with set designs by Moore.

saw it in pieces to send it to the foundry. Often, when you saw the shell, you find one part thick and another thin because you've been working on the outside and don't know what is inside. So it is a very uneven affair and can crack. Although it's still the way I like working, this new way of doing it in polystyrene is solid. You can make alterations easily and move the whole thing.

'Moore on Moore, Moore in Moore', *Intellectual Digest* August 1972, p.41

Concrete

These are about 1928, when I was experimenting with cement.[23] At the time reinforced concrete was the new material for architecture. As I have always been interested in materials, I thought I ought to learn about the use of concrete for sculpture in case I ever wanted to connect a piece of sculpture with a concrete building. The first method of using concrete I tried was building it up on an armature and then rubbing it down after it had set. This I had to do very quickly because the cement and the gritty aggregate mixed with it set so hard that all my tools used to wear out. Secondly, I tried casting in concrete.

Hedgecoe 1968, p.58

Bronze

Bronze is a reproductive material.

Unpublished notes late 1950s (?), HMF archive

I like using plaster as the preliminary material for my bronzes. When people talk about 'truth to material' it doesn't strictly apply to bronze, because a sculptor does not take a solid piece of bronze and cut it into shape as he does a piece of stone. For a bronze, he first has to make his original in something else. The special quality of bronze is that you can reproduce with it almost any form and any surface texture through expert casting. However, if you desire to achieve the real metallic quality of bronze, it is necessary to work on the surface of the sculpture after it has been cast.

Hedgecoe 1968, p.300

I'd like to go back now to your work in bronze. During the war you began to work in this metal more and more. In fact, between 1943 and 1947 I believe you cast over 140 bronzes. What was the appeal of bronze at this time?

Well, with the war there was the impossibility of doing large carvings, because one didn't know at a certain stage of the war whether, if you began a large carving, you'd have another week to finish it or not. So doing the shelter drawings loosened me up and freed me a little bit from being tied down by the material of stone and wood. And some of the things I thought

---

[23] *Mask* 1929 LH 64 and *Half-Figure* 1929 LH 67, both in cast concrete.

about were too open, too difficult, or at least would have been too slow to do in wood or stone. And so the bronze was a way of me working out a kind of humanist attitude that I think the shelter drawings and the coal mine drawings developed. And I'm glad it did. I'm glad that this happened. You see you can do a carving in bronze, in plaster for a bronze, in a quarter of the time. So I could get rid of four ideas and do four experiments – I mean not just formal experiments, but experiments in one's ideas too, in working out or expressing something, in getting rid of it. So I think this is the reason why I did so many bronzes.

Obviously casting in bronze involves very different techniques from, say, direct carving. But does it also involve a different approach, a different attitude towards the material to be sculpted?

Oh yes, because bronze can do anything. You can poise a life-size or over life-size equestrian statue on the two back legs, with the rest prancing and rearing in the air, with a figure on the back, and it's perfectly safe. This would be impossible in stone. But such things as that can be done in bronze. In fact bronze is not really a material on its own, as it were. It's a casting material. It's a reproductive material for any ideas you like to have. You never make the idea in bronze itself. You don't take a piece of solid bronze and bend it or model it. You cast it. You make it in something else and cast it into bronze. And a good bronze caster should be able to cast even feathers. So you can do anything, really, in bronze. This is its value. And you don't have to be bothered about the problems of how it will stand up, how it will weather, how it will do from a purely practical point of view. This is the beauty of bronze.

Carroll 1973, pp.46-7

Bronze is a wonderful material, it weathers and lasts in all climates. One only has to look at the ancient bronzes, for example, the Marcus Aurelius equestrian statue in Rome. I love to stand beneath this statue, because it is so big. Under the belly of the horse, the rain has left marks which emphasise the section where it has run down over the centuries. This statue is nearly two thousand years old, yet the bronze is in perfect condition. Bronze is really more impervious to the weather than most stone.

Levine 1978, p.148

Fibreglass

I haven't used fibreglass very much. Its only value to me is that as a material it is very strong yet light. For example, it was invaluable to me for the exhibition in Florence in 1972: I very much wanted to exhibit the large sculpture called *Locking Piece* [fig.131], but in bronze it weighed several tons. This made it impossible to transport it up to Fort Belvedere, where the exhibition took place. So I had a fibreglass cast made and used this. It was easy to put it together and to carry up to the fort, by hand even. Another large sculpture, *Large Two Forms* [LH 556], was also cast in fibreglass and shown in Florence. So the material served a useful purpose.

However, I wouldn't make and sell to anyone a sculpture in fibreglass to stand permanently outside because we don't know how long it lasts as a material or how well it weathers. Bronze we know lasts two, three, four thousand years.

For me, fibreglass is valuable only in casting a sculpture which already exists in a lighter, more portable form. No, I don't even make models in fibreglass. I make models in plaster because I am used to it, but also because I can change the model's shape easily, I can add to it, cut it down, soak it, leave it wet and rework it, even after a year. Fibreglass is awkward.

I have only ever cast one sculpture *only* in fibreglass, that is, not in bronze first or subsequently [LH 600]. This came about in 1969. I was given an elephant skull by my great friend Julian Huxley, the biologist. I have always been excited by bone forms, again, they are strong yet light. I did a lot of drawings of the skull and than made thirty to forty etchings of it over two years.[24] [...] Looking at the skull, drawing it and studying it gave me the idea of doing a sculpture of the skull. I didn't copy the etchings but evolved something new. What I had learned about its shape, form and colouring led me to make the sculpture in plaster and then cast it in fibreglass. The material brought out precisely the qualities of the bone: the colouring, the strength yet fragility. The materials – bone and fibreglass – shared a connection.

Viertes Internationales Plastik-Symposium, Art Studio Stiftung,
Lindau im Bodensee 1977

Working Methods
Carving and Modelling

At that time you were almost exclusively a carver, weren't you?

Yes, I like carving, as a physical occupation, better than modelling. I vividly remember the pleasure I felt when I first used a hammer and chisel. I was sixteen at the time, and I made a little war memorial, a roll of honour [fig.84], for the grammar school I was at.

When I was a student direct carving, as an occupation and as a sculptor's natural way of producing things, was simply unheard-of in academic circles, though Brancusi and Epstein and Modigliani had used it. I liked the different mental approach involved – the fact that you begin with the block and have to find the sculpture that's inside it. You have to overcome the resistance of the material by sheer determination and hard work. I liked that very much, and in fact I still prepare my plasters for bronzes with a mixture of modelling and carving.

But I don't want to put too much stress on the actual act of carving, or

[24] See p.296.

on the craftsmanship involved. Craftsmanship in sculpture is just common sense – anyone can learn it. It's certainly easier than in painting, I'd say. The mental grasp is difficult, and the three-dimensional conception, but the workmanship, which people like Eric Gill thought so important, can degenerate into a most awful mental laziness. like knitting or polishing the silver.

Russell 17 December 1961

I think it was perhaps my discovery of and excitement over primitive sculpture that made me more sympathetic to carving than modelling, for most primitive sculpture is carved.

Hall 1960, p.104

We all began to believe that carved sculpture was better than modelling, because there had been more human effort to make it, to shape it, you'd had to struggle, you'd had to work to do it. Now I realise that it doesn't matter how it is made but it mattered terribly then – the method you used, the tools, beginning with the point to split, to burst open the stone. It doesn't cut it, it bursts it. The claw tool, like teeth, like a series of pointings, but all tight together – one was very conscious of the method. Carving is a slower process and you have to visualise what you are trying to do, you have to know exactly what you are aiming for, whereas in modelling, you can alter it hundreds of times, you can add and take away. In carving you can only take away. It isn't that it's more difficult but it's more exacting.

When you are young you cotton on to an idea that helps you. I'm glad I did all of that carving – but I know now that there has been modelled sculpture which is just as good.

Hedgecoe 1986, p.69

In direct carving the resistance offered by stone gives a natural power to the work – as the kettle gives a sense of power emitting steam through the spout, in contrast with [an] open pan of water boiling – between modelling & sculpture I prefer carving to modelling. I prefer a hammer & chisel to a modelling tool. I enjoy the physical effort needed in carving & enjoy the resistance offered by the stone. Sculpture [is] a manly art which is perhaps why there are so many young ladies attracted to it just now.

Unpublished notes for 'A View of Sculpture' 1930, HMF archive

Difference between modelling & carving. Modelling begins with space – with nothing. Carving begins with solid block & makes space.

Unpublished notes c.1951, HMF archive

Carving can be a very, very soothing, jogging-along occupation, like digging a garden.

Hall 1960, p.113

231

Carving is a straightforward process of having a hard material and knocking, carving or bursting pieces off. The tools we have now for stone carving begin with what is called a pitcher, or a boaster, with which whole corners can be broken off. All stones tend to have a direction in which they break most easily because of their grain formation. Next comes the punch, or point, and we burst the stone all round with the point when we hit it. That allows us to get large amounts off at a time. After that comes a claw tool, which is really a series of punches and points all in one instrument. When used on the stone, it leaves a series of parallel grooves. This was a favourite tool of Michelangelo's. Next comes the chisel, which is flat.

Levine 1978, p.131

Woodcarving has to have a gouge, a curved tool, because wood has a fibrous grain. A flat tool could bury itself and split the wood instead of cutting it. So you have a gouge so that the two corners clear the wood and the cutting is done by the middle, curved part of the tool.

Ibid., p.115

Now that I am doing carving again,[25] it is natural that the carvings I did between 1920 and 1940, a period in which perhaps nine out of every ten sculptures I made were carvings, have influenced the work I am doing now. So in carving I am picking up, as it were, where I left off.

And yet in spite of the connection, my present stone carvings are less restricted. Whilst I still believe in keeping a stone quality, I am not as afraid of hurting the stone or damaging it as I used to be. Hence there is more freedom in my compositional ideas.

Hedgecoe 1968, p.450

Bronze and Lead Casting

To cast a large work into bronze is quite a major operation, but bronze casting on a small scale can, of course, be done by the sculptor himself. At one period of my career I thought I ought to know how bronze casting was done, and I did it myself at the bottom of the garden, along with my two assistants. We built a foundry in miniature of our own, and throughout one year I cast some eight or ten things into bronze. The experience was very valuable, but I now get all my casting done by long established bronze foundries with generations of experience in the work....

There are two main methods of bronze casting – the 'sand' process and the 'lost wax' process which I used. In this method, the founder (by the same moulding procedure that he would use to make a copy in plaster) makes a wax replica of the sculptor's original work. This wax replica is covered with a mixture of water, plaster and powder made from ground-up pottery – called grog – and this mixture sets hard, leaving the wax buried inside it. This mould is then baked in a kiln, when, through a hole left in the

[25] From the mid-1960s, Moore began carving once more during the summers he spent in Forte dei Marmi.

mould, the wax melts and runs out (is 'lost'), so you now have a space inside the mould exactly the shape of the original model, and into this hole you pour the molten bronze, and because of the baking in the kiln, the mould is conditioned to resist the enormous heat of the molten bronze.

Of course there are details you have to watch. For example, in an intricate model there must be 'leads' and 'runners' inside the mould so that the molten bronze runs into all parts and doesn't make any air locks, and you must know the exact temperature at which to pour in the molten metal, and have a furnace to bring it up to this great heat.

Except for the difficulty of melting bronze, I had done all this same metal casting in making my lead sculptures of 1938, '39 and '40, and I had then found that I could jump the early stage of casting by making my original sculpture directly in wax. Now, working direct in wax has many possibilities, since wax has a toughness about it that will allow you to do very thin forms – for example take that rocking chair sculpture of mine [LH 312] in which the back of the chair is in struts like a ladder, you couldn't make that construction in clay, nor in plaster, without awful trouble, whereas that was modelled directly in wax, easily and straightforwardly. Then all one had to do was to cover that with plaster and ground-up pottery and melt the wax out and cast it in bronze. By working direct in wax, one was able to make shapes and forms much thinner and more open than ever you could have done direct in plaster. Doing my own metal casting led me to doing those, and some other basket forms.... And one could do a sort of birdcage idea – one form inside another – which would be impossible to make in clay or plaster.

And this working direct in wax has become, with very many young sculptors, an understood and general method now. They model directly in wax and then just have that wax turned into bronze. It gives them a chance to do more spatial forms.

Have you made any more wax sculptures recently?

Not very many – at present. I make most of my sculptures direct in plaster – if they are going to be in bronze. That plaster original is sent to the foundry. The foundry then makes a mould and from that single mould it can make as many waxes as I intend the edition of bronzes to be.

How many do you have made?

Well, it varies according to the size of the sculpture and what demand there might be for it. One has to decide when a piece is done what edition you are going to make, just as a lithographer or an etcher will decide that he is not going to produce more than such and such a number. For example, of each of the Degas bronzes there are twenty casts.[26] In some cases of Rodin's there are thirty or forty casts of a work. I personally don't like having more than four or five casts made of a large sculpture, but of a very small piece one doesn't mind if the edition goes to ten.

[26] The posthumous editions of Degas's sculpture consist of one master set of bronzes; from this master set, two casts of each were made for his heirs and twenty for the art market.

What does it cost to cast a large, life-size sculpture?

It's a very expensive business. And this precludes young sculptors in the beginning of their careers from having their sculptures cast into bronze. A life-size sculpture, my *King and Queen* [fig.122] for example, costs over a thousand pounds to cast into bronze. When one is young, beginning, it tends to keep you from doing a large sculpture, certainly from having your large sculptures cast into bronze, unless a copy happens to be ordered.

You mentioned the process of patinating your bronzes when they come back from the foundry. What is this process and how do you do it?

I like working on all my bronzes after they come back from the foundry. A new cast to begin with is just like a new-minted penny, with a kind of slight tarnished effect on it. Sometimes this is all right and suitable for a sculpture, but not always. Bronze is very sensitive to chemicals, and bronze naturally in the open air (particularly near the sea) will turn with time and the action of the atmosphere to a beautiful green. But sometimes one can't wait for nature to have its go at the bronze, and you can speed it up by treating the bronze with different acids which will produce different effects. Some will turn the bronze black, others will turn it green, others will turn it red.

In doing your sculpture you have imagined a certain quality in the bronze. No sculptor works direct in bronze; you can't take a solid piece of bronze and cut it to the shape you want, so all sculptors who intend having their work in bronze are working with a mental idea of what it is going to look like, while they make it in some other material.

I usually have an idea, as I make a plaster, whether I intend it to be a dark or a light bronze, and what colour it is going to be. When it comes back from the foundry I do the patination and this sometimes comes off happily, though sometimes you can't repeat what you have done other times. The mixture of bronze may be different, the temperature to which you heat the bronze before you put the acid on to it may be different. It is a very exciting but tricky and uncertain thing, this patination of bronze.

It is entirely a matter of swabbing it with chemicals, is it?

And also afterwards you can then work on the bronze, work on the surface and let the bronze come through again, after you've made certain patinas. You rub it and wear it down as your hand might by a lot of handling. From this point of view bronze is a most responsive and unbelievably varied material, and it will go on being a favourite material for sculptors. You can, in bronze, reproduce any other material you care to.

Interview with Donald Hall 1960; quoted in James 1966, pp.137, 139-40

The next major thematic development in your work came at the end of the thirties with The Helmet *[fig.101] and the enclosure of an interior form within an exterior form. This is also interesting to me because it is cast in bronze, which is a material you hadn't been previously much inclined to use.*

They weren't cast in bronze to begin with. They were cast in lead. They have subsequently been cast into bronze from the lead. All those metal sculptures of 1938-40 were cast in lead in the Kent studio and in the open air. I had Bernard Meadows as a young Norwich student helping me. We constructed our own kiln, and they were all cast in lead. I didn't know about lead – I didn't know that you could put a little antimony with it and make it hard – so since then all the leads have been damaged. And they come back to me to be repaired, or to be salvaged – because in some cases if you drop a lead on the floor, on a hard floor, it will just collapse, whereas bronze is almost indestructible. So, to save the idea, I re-cast them into bronze, but they were all done originally in lead by me collecting bits of lead piping, bits of the construction of armatures which were made of a lead composition, and using my wife's pots and pans. You can melt lead on the kitchen stove, so it was quite possible for me to do my own casting, whereas with bronze the temperature is so high that you need a kiln, you need a furnace to do it. But with lead you can do it quite easily.

Carroll 1973, p.42

At one time I became very interested in doing my own bronze casting. I had an assistant then who was ambitious to be a bronze caster rather than a sculptor.[27] So I built a little foundry at the bottom of the garden. And I am very glad I did, because I learnt much about the characteristics of bronze which has been very helpful to me ever since. However, after a year of doing my own casting, I found the amount of time being taken up doing technical jobs was preventing me from doing as much sculpture as I wanted. Besides, professional bronze casters could do the job better than I. Now I send all my sculpture away to be cast and visit the foundry if necessary.

Hedgecoe 1986, p.159

I work out and apply all patinas myself. The chemical composition is largely determined by the climatic conditions in which the particular work is going to be set. I'm talking now of large-scale sculpture for siting in the open air. Different things will happen to the patina of bronze according to the kind of atmosphere in which it is gradually weathered. For instance, in itself bronze contains 90 per cent copper, a substance which is highly susceptible to atmospheric conditions. Near the sea a patina will change more rapidly to a green than it will in an atmosphere which is not fresh and clean. In an industrial atmosphere, laden with its many impurifications, the same patina will become black. I have to consider such facts as these and add to the make-up of the patinas, which are applied to the bronze castings, whatever chemicals will help adjust the eventual effects of atmosphere and weather-

[27] Bernard Meadows (see p.58, note 41) told me this was not true. He did in fact become a well-known sculptor, see *Bernard Meadows: Sculpture and Drawings*, edited by Alan Bowness, The Henry Moore Foundation in association with Lund Humphries, London 1995. Meadows told me that the little foundry at Hoglands was built in the late 1940s. 'It never really worked,' he said, 'because the furnace didn't get hot enough to melt the bronze!'

ing as near as possible to the ultimate appearance I have in mind. Although naturally this is to some extent an imponderable issue, since a patina will inevitably be subject to changes over which one can have no absolute control. Some sculptors leave the whole question of patinas to the bronze foundry. Not so myself. The addition of the patina is of great importance, and something which I must consider and evolve myself. My own patina is, of course, a preliminary to the one which nature will herself supply in time. Meanwhile the exercise of my own hand in this destiny is imperative.

Mervyn Levy, 'Henry Moore: Sculpture against the Sky', *Studio International* May 1964, p.179

Drawing[28]

Once I really became interested in drawing I tried to find out what drawing was, both as a science and as an art. Drawing is the expression and the explanation of the shape of a solid object on a flat surface, by the use of light and shade, and the understanding of the laws of perspective. I looked at the drawings of the Old Masters from the point of view of learning what drawing was. As a student in London I began to realise that good drawing was not copying the model, the tone values, the light and shade as in a photograph, not just the training of a copyist photographic eye. Nor was it even making the correct proportions or guessing the angles of outlines and such props to copying. It was an attempt to understand the full three-dimensionality of the human figure, to learn about the object one was drawing, and to represent it on the flat surface of the paper.

Wilkinson 1977, p.12

I spent two years at Leeds School of Art and four years at the Royal College of Art doing three or four days a week of modelling or drawing from life, trying to understand the figure. Afterwards I had seven years teaching life drawing and modelling at the Royal College and another seven years teaching it at Chelsea Art School. When I was looking at students' work I found I had to look perhaps even more intensely than at my own work. So altogether I had twenty years of continually concentrated observation and attempt at understanding the human figure.

The pure outline is a shorthand method of drawing. This is how Matisse drew at the end of his life and also Picasso. But they began their careers with this kind of highly finished three-dimensional drawing using light and shade, and then later in life simplified their styles. This is the real way to understand things.

Hedgecoe 1968, p.38

If I didn't like the look of them [the models], I tried to change them into human beings one liked better.

Wilkinson 1977, p.18

---

[28] For an important early statement about drawing, see 'The Sculptor Speaks' 1937, p.196.

Every few months I stop carving for two or three weeks and draw from life. At one time I used to mix the two, perhaps carving during the day and drawing from a model during the evening. But I found this unsatisfactory – the two activities interfered with each other, for the mental approach to each is different, one being objective and the other subjective. Stone is so different from flesh and blood that one cannot carve directly from life without almost the certainty of ill-treating the material. Drawing and carving are so different that a shape or size or conception which is satisfying as a drawing might be totally wrong realised in stone. Nevertheless, there is a connection between my drawings and my sculpture. Drawing from life keeps one visually fit – perhaps acts like water to a plant – and it lessens the danger of repeating oneself and getting into a formula. It enlarges one's form repertoire, one's form experience. But in my sculpture I do not use my memory or observations of a particular object, but rather whatever comes up from my general fund of knowledge of natural forms.[29]

Henry Moore, Sculptor: An Appreciation by Herbert Read,
A. Zwemmer, London 1934, pp.13-14

When my sculpture was mainly carving I would be having many more ideas than I was able to carry out and I would get rid of ideas, if that is the right phrase, by drawing to prevent them from blocking each other up. Often I would make pages of drawings of ideas. On one sheet of paper there could be as many as thirty projects, such as Stringed Figures, all produced in a few hours. One of them would hold my attention and I would think it was the best one. And then I would have to settle down to the longer job of making it into a sculpture.

Hedgecoe 1968, p.100

<u>SCULPTORS' DRAWINGS</u> There is a general idea that sculptors' drawings should be diagrammatic studies, without any sense of a background behind the object, or of any atmosphere around it. That is, the object is stuck on the flat surface of the paper with no attempt to set it in space – & often not even to connect it with the ground, with gravity. And yet the sculptor is as much concerned with space as the painter.

He must make the object he draws capable of having a far side to it, that is make it an object in space, not an object in relief, (only half an object stuck on the paper, and stopping at its edges) – It is necessary to give it the possibility of an existence beyond the surface of the paper.

Any wash, smudge, shading, anything breaking the tyranny of the flat plane of the paper, opens up a suggestion, a possibility of S P A C E.

Undated notes early 1950s(?), HMF archive; reproduced in Man 1954 (n.p.)

DAVID SYLVESTER: You were telling me a little while ago that you didn't work in the old way any more, beginning by drawing. Your way used to be

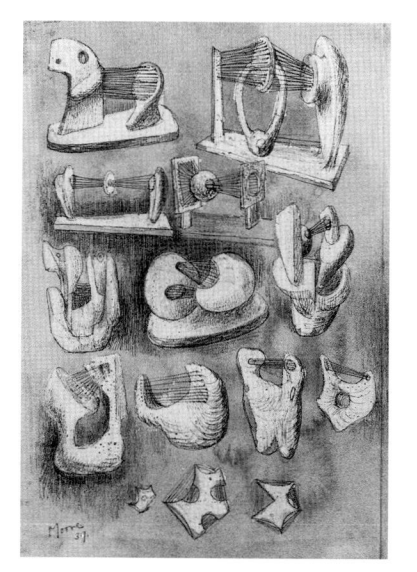

80 *Fourteen Ideas for Sculpture* 1939
HMF 1460, pencil, crayon, wax crayon, watercolour wash, pen and ink, 275 x 190mm (10¾ x 7½in). Lillian Heidenberg Gallery, New York

---

[29] A slightly different version of this statement was published in *Henry Moore: Sculpture and Drawings* 1944, pp.xxvii-xxviii.

to fill pages, sketchbook pages, with drawings, a variety of drawings. And you would go through these, selecting things that seemed interesting ideas. Then you would make a sketch model from a drawing and go on from there. This was your method for many years, wasn't it?

HENRY MOORE: Yes.

SYLVESTER: When did you start to do that?

MOORE: I think that was when one wasn't sure of ideas and directions. And it is also true that, being so young, one had lots of influences mixed up in one's mind, so that drawing was a means of generating ideas and also of sorting them out. Now I find that when what seems to me a good idea comes, I recognise it a bit quicker than perhaps I used to do.

SYLVESTER: May I get this idea straight about drawing as a means of generating ideas? How much automatism was there? Was it when the pencil was on the paper that things began to happen? Or were you actually carrying out things you visualised clearly in your head before you drew them?

MOORE: One used to use both methods. Sometimes you would sit down with no idea at all, and at some point you'd see something in the doodling, scribbling – whatever you call it; and from then on you could evolve the idea. That would be a way of doing it, say, late in the evening. Early in the morning I used to find one would start off with a definite idea, that, for instance, it was a seated figure I wanted to do. That in itself would lead to a lot of variations of the seated figure: you would give yourself a theme and then let the variations come, and choose from those which one seemed the best.

SYLVESTER: When you say you started with this, was it simply the idea that you wanted to do some sort of seated figure, or did you actually have a seated figure visualised in your head as something that you could see?

MOORE: One tries – at least one tried when younger – to fit in one's mental ambition for sculpture with the immediate ideas one had. I thought I knew what good sculpture was. But also, too, I was interested in particular subjects – especially reclining figure, and mother and child. But one has to amalgamate one's ideal of good sculpture; just as Michelangelo had an ideal of good sculpture when he said that a good piece of sculpture could be rolled down a hill without breaking. It proved that he had in his mind a vision of what was good sculpture.

SYLVESTER: This idea of a piece of sculpture that could roll down a hill without breaking was closely tied up with the thought of contrapposto, which implied making the figure compact.

MOORE: Sometimes you can begin from the two opposite ways. You can begin with the idea that you are searching for a good sculptural idea, or you begin with the human idea, the mother and child, and you try to make it become a good sculpture: that is, you amalgamate life and art, and how you do it, whether you start from the art side or the life side, in a way doesn't matter, as long as the amalgamation comes.

SYLVESTER: But when you have in mind, shall we say, a 'Moore Seated Figure', would you actually, before beginning to draw, visualise what you were going to put down?

MOORE: I tried to avoid visualising the finished product until a later stage.

SYLVESTER: So in the morning drawing as well as the evening drawing you really were using drawing as a means of generating ideas?

MOORE: Yes. I still like drawing just as much as ever, but there seems to be less time to do the sculpture one wants to do. Drawing has always been to me the lesser activity.

SYLVESTER: Your main work in the last few years has been a series of multiple-piece reclining figures. Has any of these started from a drawing?

MOORE: No.

SYLVESTER: And what was the last important work you did that did start from a drawing?

MOORE: I think probably the 'Family Group' ones. The family group ideas were all generated by drawings; and that was perhaps because the whole family group idea was so close to one as a person; we were just going to have our first child, Mary, and it was an obsession.

SYLVESTER: What about the Unesco figure [fig.126]?

MOORE: That didn't begin from a drawing; neither did the Lincoln Center figures [LH 518, 519].

SYLVESTER: But earlier than Unesco: the seated figure of a pregnant woman [LH 435]?

MOORE: That kind of idea can't begin from a drawing; in that particular case there is a sort of sense of touch of the back of that figure which is what my own mother had when I had to massage her when she suffered from rheumatism. This must come from actuality, from the handling of the material, of the 'thing'. 'The Warriors' [fig.124] began from a little pebble that led one on from a stump of a leg, to add to it the back and to add to it the arm and the shield. This you couldn't do by drawing.

Sylvester 1963, pp.305-6

Because now I am aiming at sculpture that is truly three-dimensional, I want it to vary from whatever angle I look at it. Although it is a unified idea, it is not symmetrical. To explain its shape by drawing I should require at least twenty or thirty drawings. At one time, when my ideas were more frontal, I would often start a sculpture from an idea I'd produced in a single drawing and work out what was to happen at the sides and at the back as I went along, but, with the kind of sculpture I do now, I need to know it from on top and from underneath as well as from all sides. And so I prefer to work out my ideas in the form of small maquettes which I can hold in my hand and look at from every point of view.

Hedgecoe 1968, p.269

In your early work, drawing direct from nature had some significance beside the sketches for your sculpture. How important is drawing to you today?

As I have said earlier, I love drawing. To me it is an activity that I enjoy. I used to draw the idea and then model it or carve it. Now I can draw because

I no longer use drawing for my sculptures so much and I make maquettes. I can now use drawing divorced from sculpture. I can draw for the pleasure of looking more intently and intensely at the object that I am drawing. I think that drawing is a – drawing, even for people who cannot draw, even for people not trying to produce a good drawing, it makes you look more intensely at whatever you are trying to draw, whatever you do if you just look. Just looking alone has no grit in it, has no sort of mental struggle or difficulty. That only happens while you are drawing. Therefore, I would suggest that if people like something they should try to draw it. If they are in love with a girl they should try to draw the girl. Looking at my grandson, drawing him and looking to draw, makes me know more what he is like than if I just look at him every day.[30] You wake up every morning in your bedroom, you look through the bedroom window, you have a certain view, can you draw it? Can you tell me, are there two trees, are there two lamp posts, are there what? 99 out of every 100 would not be able to tell you at all, although they have probably seen it for twenty years. But let them draw it two or three times and they will understand and look, and they will know. Drawing is a method, amongst other things, but one of its great values is observation and to learn about nature. Of course, I see reality with the eyes of a sculptor. Recently, in the winter, the trees for me were more interesting than in the summer, because they showed their sculptural aspect. Trunks of trees are very human. A branch that comes out from the main trunk is like an arm coming out from a body. I have been drawing trees quite a bit. To me they have a connection with human life. The trunk is like the body, and the branches getting a little thinner the further they get away from the trunk, are like the extremities. Drawing also teaches you to have eyes that are correct. By drawing you must guess, you must be able to judge – the length of a nose … if you are trying to draw a face you must be able to judge, and this is very important in your sculpture. This is why I think that drawing from nature, drawing from life (which I sometimes do, though not as much as I used to), is extremely important.

Erich Steingräber, 'Henry Moore's Maquettes: Observations on the Methodical Evolution in his Work', Pantheon, Munich July-September 1978, p.258

Etching and Lithography

Well, I really began to want to do graphic work, or prints, when I discovered that one could change a print without losing what you'd got already. It has its own, special possibilities. In a graphic work you can try out ideas and not lose the previous one, because you can retain the previous states – and you've got prints of it, anyhow. So it allows you to experiment. You get something, when you make a print, which you can't foresee exactly. There is a slight change, there's a difference. There's the kind of difference that you get, say – not quite the same – but a potter, when he makes the glaze on

---

[30] Moore made several studies of his first grandchild, Guston Danowski, who was born in 1977; see HMF 77(32)-(41), 78(63)-(65) and fig.148.

81 Moore in Hoglands Maquette Studio 1970, working on a copper plate for the Elephant Skull etchings

a pot and then puts the pot in the kiln to be fired, when it comes out the colour is always a surprise. So that you get this kind of surprise, too, in graphic work, which can seem to be an accident. You don't think out every step in a logical way, you have to have accidents, or what seem to be accidents, and you must take advantage of them.

Interview with Nigel Rees, *Kaleidoscope*, BBC 22 May 1975

Well, it was a departure in this sense,[31] that I've done some etchings and I like etching, and I think etching compared with, say, lithography is a more natural thing for a sculptor because etching is a very direct thing. Lithography if you are doing it in two or three colours you have to do one colour separate from the others and you have to wait until you see them superimposed and all this, and it's a kind of what …? In my opinion it's more suited to a painter. Whereas etching, you draw with the point and etching is more like sculpture, and I prefer etching to lithography as a graphic medium.

Interview with Alan Haydock, *The Arts this Week*, BBC 20 June 1971

In the past few years, I have done much more graphic work than I used to, and for etching and lithography I must have all the tools around me. I have adapted a small studio and had a printing press put into it, where I do my etching. Etching has to be separated from lithography or ordinary drawing because dangerous acid is used in the process.

Levine 1978, p.116

[31] Moore is referring to the Elephant Skull etchings, see p.296.

In the same way, there are drawings and prints that you can look at for long periods and return to again and again, always discovering new meanings. Rembrandt's etchings do this for me: it is wonderful how he makes shadows that have mysterious, unbelievable sonorities. Turner, whether on canvas or on paper, can create almost measurable distances of space and air – air that you can draw, in which you can almost work out what the section through it would be. The space he creates is not emptiness: it is filled with 'solid' atmosphere. In Hercules Seghers[32] there is a mystery in the depth and the modelling. By the slightest change in tone and technique he can push a surface back, giving it a sensitivity of form only just discernible in its subtlety.

Auden Poems, Moore Lithographs, British Museum, London 1974 (n.p.)

Sculpture and Architecture

On modern English buildings[33]

Peter Jones Store; Highpoint flats (Tecton); the Giraffe House at Whipsnade (Tecton); Arnos Grove Underground Station (SA Heaps and Adams, Holden and Pearson); house in Church Street, Chelsea (Gropius and Fry); the Village College, Impington, Cambridgeshire (Gropius and Fry); and Serge Chermayeff's house in Sussex

Architects' Journal 4 May 1939, p.719

The difference between Sculpture & Architecture

Architecture & sculpture both deal with the relationship of masses. In practice architecture has a functional or utilitarian purpose, which limits it as an art of pure expression. Aesthetically architecture is the abstract relationship of masses. If sculpture is limited to this, then in the field of scale & size Architecture has the advantage. But sculpture not being tied to a functional, utilitarian purpose can attempt much more freely the exploration of the world of pure form.[34]

That which architecture cannot attempt freely, but sculpture can, is the combination of abstract qualities of form composition (of abstraction) with the human element – it can be organic as against geometric. I look upon complete abstractions as valuable experiments for the sculptor in learning the principles of sculpture (of form composition & design) but I find I want the organic thing in my work – that a work which lacks it does not have, for me, as full a meaning.

And again, in architecture, the functional purpose, gives the architect a (critical) connection with reality in his design problems which is missing in purely abstract sculpture – This (critical) connection with reality in organic sculpture (biomorphic abstraction) is the human expression element.

---

[32] Seghers (1589-after 1633) was a Dutch landscape painter and experimental etcher to whose work Moore paid tribute in two etchings of 1971, *Hommage à Seghers* CGM 171, 172.

[33] Moore was one of four 'important people' who were asked to list modern buildings that they admired.

[34] This paragraph, in a slightly altered form, appeared in Moore's short contribution to *Circle* 1937, see p.193.

(Stone architecture is different from stone sculpture for it is hollow – the strains & stresses come on the shell not the centres.)

Perfect solution of its functional problem does not produce architecture in the full meaning – A machine which functions well whether its an aeroplane or a machine for living in – (a house) has a beauty not of art but of nature – The design of a bird for least wind resistance is not art – etc.

Unpublished notes for 'The Sculptor Speaks' 1937, HMF archive

SCULPTURE AND ARCHITECTURE[35]

During the 'functional period' of architecture, around twenty or thirty years ago, the modern architect had no use for sculpture in connection with his buildings. This was perhaps a good thing, both for the sculptor and the architect, for the architect was concentrating on his architecture and it freed the modern sculptor from being just a decorator for the architect and allowed him to concentrate on his own art in isolation.

However, it has now become clear that architecture is the poorer for the absence of sculpture, and the sculptor, by not collaborating with the architects, misses the opportunities of his work being used socially and being seen by a wider public.

I am sure the time has come for architects and sculptors to work together again.

Typed text 1952, HMF archive

When I am asked by an architect to find or make a sculpture to go with his building I am never very excited about it.

I know there will be problems. All architecture is geometric with dominating horizontal and vertical lines, and these are so insistent that if any asymmetrical sculpture is put with it you will find somewhere these distracting lines very evident in the background. In fact the building's geometry is so insistent that to find a position far enough away for the sculpture to have its own scale or presence may be impossible.

Spender 1978, p.9

I have never seen a person or a piece of sculpture against architecture that I would say can be seen perfectly from every point of view. I just don't know it. When dealing with an architectural situation, I attempt to consider certain things that can go wrong. There is a kind of right size for every such situation. I think that in the Lincoln Center piece [fig.82] its size in relation to the four buildings all around it and to the plaza is just about right. This is the thing I tried to think about. I don't work with architects except on these generalised problems like size. I don't like doing commissions in the sense that I go and look at a site and then think of something. Once I have been asked to consider a certain place where one of my sculptures might possibly be placed, I try to choose something suitable from what I've done or from what

[35] These appear to be notes for 'The Sculptor in Modern Society' 1952, see pp.139-40.

82 *Reclining Figure* 1963-65 LH 519 at the Lincoln Center for the Performing Arts, New York

I'm about to do. But I don't sit down and try to create something especially for it.

Seldis 1973, pp.176-7

If it's a figure [in front of a building] you'll find its head cut off, or that the body is split down the middle. It's no good putting an upright figure against a skyscraper. Sculpture is like a human being. Architecture is inhuman.

Spender 1978, p.32

The Elgin Marbles

When I first saw these marvellous sculptures as a young man, they were in galleries far more suitable in scale, and they were lighted to much better advantage. It was not so many years ago that the Elgin Marbles were moved to and dwarfed by these galleries built by and named for Lord Duveen.[36] Here is a prime example of the blindness of architects to the true meaning of sculpture. It's simply yet another instance of money thrown away to belittle great art while celebrating one donor. Anyone can see how inappropriate the column size of this room is to the scale of the sculptures and how the various pieces are installed too high up to be seen properly.

It's time that the myth of architectural primacy be debunked. Sculpture was central when the early temples were built about the statuary of the Gods, not architecture.

Seldis 1973, p.169

[36] The Duveen Gallery at the British Museum was completed in early 1939, but damaged by a bomb the following year. Restoration was not begun until 1960; the gallery opened in 1962.

Rievaulx Abbey, Yorkshire

I have always thought Rievaulx Abbey to be a most impressive monument. In its present state it is more sculpture than architecture. When architecture is unusable it inevitably becomes aesthetically the same as sculpture. This is perhaps why I like ruins. For example, the Parthenon. Now that the light passes through it, it is far more sculptural than if it were all filled in.

Hedgecoe 1968, p.27

Sculpture in Landscape[37]

Perhaps what influenced me most over wanting to do sculpture in the open air and to relate my sculpture to landscape comes from my youth in Yorkshire; seeing the Yorkshire moors, seeing, I remember, a huge natural outcrop of stone at a place near Leeds [Adel Rock] which as a young boy impressed me tremendously – it had a powerful stone, something like Stonehenge has – and also the slag heaps of the Yorkshire mining villages, the slag heaps which for me as a boy, as a young child, were like mountains. They had the scale of the pyramids; they had this triangular, bare, stark quality that was just as though one were in the Alps. Perhaps those impressions when you're young are what count.

Forma 1964, pp.53, 59

Sculpture is an art of the open air. Daylight, *sunlight* is necessary to it, and for me its best setting and complement is nature. I would rather have a piece of my sculpture put in a landscape, almost any landscape, than in, or on, the most beautiful building I know.

Sylvester 1951, p.4

Some time ago – in 1951 to be exact – I remarked that 'I would rather have a piece of my sculpture put in a landscape, than in or on the most beautiful building I know'. It has been quoted a good deal since then, and has acquired the slightly pontifical air of a 'statement', but for me it summarised many experiences.

I believe that sculpture is an art of the open air; daylight, – sunlight is necessary to it, and for me its best setting and complement is nature. A critic writing about some painting at the Venice Biennale wrote that sunlight was cruel to art, but he probably only meant, cruel to painting. Painting in its final state is an indoor art. You can't expose a Rembrandt, or a Cézanne to full sunlight and expect it to look its best. Painting is an illusionistic art, a substitute for reality. But good sculpture can be at home out of doors because it is a real thing, as a tree is real.

Since the very beginning of my sculpture career, I have made most of my sculptures working in the open air. I believe that natural light (rather than

[37] Sculptures in landscape settings are also discussed in a number of the entries on individual works by Moore; see for example pp.258, 269, 271, 275.

studio lighting) makes the sculptor produce forms which are complete and real like the nature around him. I want my sculpture to stand up to the changing light and weather (especially of England), so that near to, and far away it reads as three dimensional form.

Perhaps of all the outdoor placings of my sculpture, the three works of mine belong[ing] to Mr. W.J. [Tony] Keswick, and placed on his estate in Dumfriesshire, Scotland, satisfy me most.[38] His estate covers some three thousand acres, of farm, grouse moor, and sheep-grazing land, and the three pieces of sculpture are widely separated from each other. All three works are beautifully placed, but I think the position of the 'KING AND QUEEN' [fig.122] is the one I like the most. [...]

When Mr. Keswick invited me to stay with him, I went all over his land, and there are not only the wild hills and moors, but woods and lawns, and a lake with an island in the middle. I saw at least twenty or thirty sites for sculpture which are separated from one another by hillside or trees, so that one could never see more than one sculpture at a time. There was such a large variety that I feel that every large sculpture I have done could find a suitable setting there. He showed me a scar in one hillside – a kind of scooping out, that formed a natural dais. We thought that this would be the right spot for the 'KING AND QUEEN', and here eventually the two figures were placed. They look across forty miles of countryside into England.

Sculptors must be gratified by the growing number of open air exhibitions of sculpture which are being held everywhere. These exhibitions provide a test of their work, and give some of their most ambitious things a sort of roving commission to go out into the world to meet a larger public and make new friends. There is a danger nevertheless that the open air exhibition may swing things too far one day. There is a danger that people will confuse their love of flowers, and gardens, and visits to the park with an interest in sculpture.

And we shall have to fight against sculpture being reduced to ornament in landscape gardening just as we had to fight against its so called function as *architectural* ornament. And now too, we shall have to fight against the *new* role that some architects want us to play. They want to call us in when the building is completed yet still looks 'as if it needed something'. They *talk* of architecture and sculpture as 'one art', but in practice they want the sculptor to be a last minute humaniser.

The setting makes a difference to the mood in which one approaches a sculpture, and a good setting is one in which the right conditions are present for a thorough appreciation of its forms, but a setting cannot *alter* it. The sculpture remains what it is, wherever one sees it, and some of those revelations of sculptural form that alter a man's life have come to me in dark crowded corners of the British Museum.

'Sculpture in Landscape', *Selection*, Winchester autumn 1962, pp.12, 15

---

[38] *Standing Figure* 1950 (fig.112); *King and Queen* 1952-53 (fig.122); *Upright Motive No.1: Glenkiln Cross* 1955-56 (see fig.125).

From what I have seen of your recent work, you seem to be mainly interested in outdoor sculpture now. Why is this?

Well, I have always liked sculpture in the open air, and I like making sculpture which will stand outside in nature. I'm now able, for all sorts of practical reasons, to satisfy this desire, whereas in earlier days some of my sculpture had to be small in size. You can't make a small piece of sculpture stand outside in nature. It just gets lost. The open air reduces a thing in its scale. If you stood a real man on the pedestal of some of the public statues, one would find how much bigger than real life are even the things which look life-sized. They have to be.

Really, I have been concerned with outdoor sculpture nearly all my life. I had no studio, so I worked out-of-doors. It may also be that my liking for landscape and for nature has made me want to work out-of-doors, too, because I find a tremendous pleasure in actually working in the open air. To work shut inside a studio at times when the weather is good is like being in a prison for me.

You said that life-sized sculpture outdoors needs to be a little larger than life. Are there other formal requirements for such sculpture?

Yes. And here again I think that the habit of having open-air sculpture exhibitions may be a good thing for sculpture and sculptors. If you work in a specially lit studio, it is a temptation to push your sculpture into a position where things look better, where their less good views can be turned to the wall, and where the lighting suits them. Now in ordinary daylight – particularly English daylight, which can be very diffused and very even – only a sculpture which has a completely realised form will tell at all. Incised relief or surface scratchings won't show in dull English weather. Only your big architectural contrasts of masses – real sculptural power, real sculptural organisation – will tell at all on a dull day. Therefore, if one gets used to working out-of-doors, one will be challenged into making sculpture that has some reality to it – like the reality of the nature around it.

Hall 1960, p.103

WOLFGANG FISCHER: Do you think that nature itself is the most important master in scale or could a genius of the artist invent a scale coming from within, so to speak, from the laboratory of his mind?
HENRY MOORE: You mean by putting his work in nature.
FISCHER: Yes.
MOORE: Nature being real, if you put a piece of sculpture in relation to nature, the two must play against each other. Some areas of nature have a powerful domination, others are gentler and more accommodating, and in putting a sculpture in nature this 'mood' should be considered.

I have never been to the Grand Canyon. I know it only from films and photographs. To see it in actuality must be an overwhelming experience. It would be impossible for a piece of man-made sculpture to compete with it.

An example of a perfect setting of sculpture is Stonehenge (which I consider is sculpture, not architecture). As you approach Stonehenge, you see it on the bare brow of a rise of ground, outlined against the sky, powerful, monumental and grand.

If Stonehenge were in a hollow depression of ground and looked down upon from above, it would not have had the continuous attention and admiration it receives.

If you reduced Stonehenge by half, – if all the stones instead of being 20 feet were only ten feet high, to the smallest only four feet, then Stonehenge would not hold the dominating place in people's mind that it does. There is a photograph that Irina, my wife, took when we were looking at Stonehenge about 20 years ago, with me against one of the stones.

FISCHER: And have you still got it?

MOORE: Yes, and one will see that the human figure is a very tiny thing, that you could get about 20 life-size figures out of such a stone. So the size of Stonehenge does matter.

If you put Stonehenge in the Grand Canyon, it would be lost, it would be nothing.

Fischer 1971 (n.p.)

SCULPTURE in the Open Air looks smaller than when seen in the enclosed spaces of indoors. Landscapes, clouds, the sky, impinge on the sculpture & reduce its bulk – Thin linear forms tend to get lost.– It seems that in the open air a certain minimum bulk is needed, to contrast with the great spaces of the sky & large distances.

Undated notes, HMF archive; reproduced in Man 1954 (n.p.)

The sky is one of the things I like most about 'sculpture with nature'. There is no background to sculpture better than the sky, because you are contrasting solid form with its opposite space. The sculpture then has no competition, no distraction from other solid objects. If I wanted the most fool-proof background for a sculpture, I would always choose the sky.

Spender 1978, p.9

DAVID SYLVESTER: A great deal that has been written about your work has emphasised the landscape nature of the works themselves, especially the reclining figures. You have been living here in Hertfordshire for twenty years or more, but you were brought up in Yorkshire; are you aware of particular landscapes as shaping your work. Are they childhood landscapes or are they the landscapes of Hertfordshire, or what?

HENRY MOORE: No, they are of Yorkshire. To me the slag heaps round Castleford in my youth were huge mountains, they were like the Alps. When I go back and see them now, I see them in the same way; these heaps of slag have the same scale as the pyramids. Hertfordshire is only a setting for things because there are no roughnesses, there are no harsh impacts. I often long here for a bit of a hill that can put things against the sky. The ideal setting for my sculpture is where Tony Keswick has put those four things of mine in Scotland, near Dumfries,[39] in a landscape which is, I should say, exactly as it was 30,000,000 years ago. It's landscape as primitive man saw it. There are parts of Yorkshire that are like that.

Sylvester 1963, p.307

How important to me that Tony Keswick bought that 'Standing Figure' [fig.112] and placed it there without telling me until he invited me to see it. The setting is marvellous and so is that of the King and Queen [fig.122] and the Cross [LH 377]. All are placed perfectly. Seeing them has convinced me that sculpture – at any rate, my sculpture – is seen best in this way and not in a museum.

Spender 1978, p.26

---

[39] The three bronzes in note 38 above, and *Two Piece Reclining Figure No.1* 1959 LH 457.

83 *Reclining Figure* 1929 ʟʜ 59, brown Hornton stone, length 84.5cm (33in). Leeds City Art Gallery

CHAPTER FIVE

WORKS BY HENRY MOORE

Castleford Secondary School Roll of Honour c. 1916

The first serious wood carving I did was the Roll of Honour for the secondary school at Castleford. The art teacher was Miss Alice Gostick, a very sympathetic and helpful teacher. When the First World War began in 1914 I was just sixteen and still at school. By 1917 quite a number of old students of the secondary school had joined the armed forces, and some had already lost their lives or had been wounded. The headmaster decided that there should be a Roll of Honour on which their names would be inscribed.

Miss Gostick knew that I liked carving wood (although until then I had used only a penknife) and she gave me the responsibility of designing and carving such a Roll of Honour. She also provided me with proper woodcarving tools – various gouges and a mallet – and the large oak panel from which it was carved.

Levine 1983, p.54

84 *Roll of Honour* c.1916, height 174cm (68½in). Castleford High School, on loan to Leeds City Art Gallery

Head of a Girl 1922

One of my earliest wood sculptures was this *Head of a Girl*. It was carved from a piece of firewood which was about to be burnt. I rescued it, perhaps because it had a bend in it and was not straight like the other pieces. When I came to carve it, the bend became an important factor in the idea, and suggested to me a shy young girl looking downwards.

Ibid., p.61

Standing Woman 1923

The carving shows an influence from Negro sculpture, when I was learning all I could from sculpture in the British Museum. For example, the bent knees, which give a sense of physical action to the figure, are typical of much Negro sculpture. Incidentally, most Negro sculpture is in wood; it is the material most easily available in their environment.

Ibid., p.62

85 *Head of a Girl* 1922 LH 4, wood, height 23.2cm (9½in). City of Manchester Art Galleries: Rutherston Loan Collection

Mother and Child 1924-25

I remember I started it before going off on the travelling scholarship when I'd been put on the staff of the Royal College of Art and I began it and left

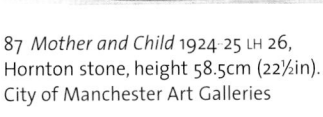

it unfinished and when I came back four months later I completed it. But this still has in it the four sided, pressed, compressed sense of a block, which although monumental in a sense, my criticism of this kind of work would be and was that the mother has no neck, that the child has no body because the head of the mother is taking the place of the body. That is at this stage I hadn't got enough command of direct carving to give the forms a full three-dimensional existence.

James 1975

West Wind 1928

In 1928, I agreed to carve a relief for the Underground Building at St James's, although I had never felt any desire to make relief sculpture. Even when I was a student I was totally preoccupied by sculpture in its full spatial richness, and if I spent a lot of time at the British Museum in those days, it was because so much of the primitive sculpture there was distinguished by complete cylindrical realisation. I was extremely reluctant to accept an architectural commission, and relief sculpture symbolised for me the humiliating subservience of the sculptor to the architect, for in ninety-nine cases out of a hundred, the architect only thought of sculpture as a surface decoration, and ordered a relief as a matter of course. But the architect of the Underground Building was persuasive, and I was young and when one is young one can be persuaded that an uncongenial task is a problem that one doesn't want to face up to. So I carved this personification of the North Wind,[1] cutting as deeply as the conditions would allow – to suggest sculpture in the round.

Sculpture in the Open Air 1955

86 *Standing Woman* 1923 LH 5, walnut wood, height 30.5cm (12in). City of Manchester Art Galleries: Rutherston Loan Collection

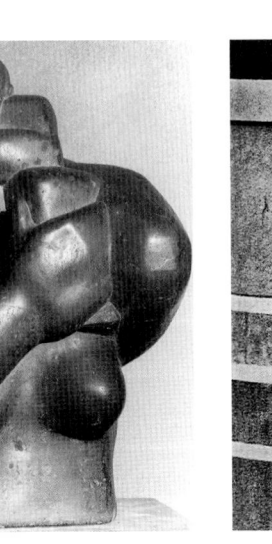

87 *Mother and Child* 1924-25 LH 26, Hornton stone, height 58.5cm (22½in). City of Manchester Art Galleries

88 *West Wind* 1928-29 LH 58, Portland stone, length 228.6cm (96in). London Underground Headquarters at St James's Park station, London

[1] Moore must have thought that his relief carving represented the North Wind. As Dennis Farr has pointed out, *West Wind* was incorrectly called *North Wind* in *Henry Moore, Sculpture and Drawings*, 1944 and 1957. See Dennis Farr, *English Art 1870-1940*, Oxford University Press 1978, p.250, n.2.

In 1928, Charles Holden, the architect, asked me to go to see him. His firm, Adams, Holden & Pearson, were then the chief architects for *London Transport*; Holden was the main designer in their team of architects.

He told me that they were building new headquarters for London Transport in St James's. Seven sculptors had been approached; Epstein was going to do two large Portland stone sculpture groups for the lower part of the building, one to be called *Day* and the other *Night*. They planned to have a tower to the building, an idea inspired by the 'Tower of the Winds' in Athens, Eric Gill would do two of the stone reliefs high up on the tower. Holden then asked me whether I would also do one of the reliefs, the one to be called the *West Wind*.

At that stage in my career I did not (and still do not) like sculpture that represents actual physical movement – sculpture that appears to be jumping off its pedestal. I was also prejudiced against relief sculpture itself as being too much akin to painting, and also because relief sculpture figured too prominently in art schools' teaching. I was trying to think and to produce sculpture fully in three dimensions.

So when Holden was talking about winds, I had these problems in my mind and I said that I did not think this would be a sympathetic subject for me. Holden said 'I'm not asking you to do a sculpture which is being blown away by the wind.' He talked to me like a father – he was very much older than I. After much playful argument, I said I would think about it. A little time later, it was still on my mind and I began making drawings on the subject altho' still fighting the idea. Slowly I realised that it might be wrong to give the title *West Wind* to a static figure and then I hit on the idea of a figure suggesting a floating movement, thinking of the character of the four chief winds – North being cold and hard – a male wind; South – a warm female wind; East – a hard, cutting wind and West, a rainier and softer wind – I made drawings, trying to express something of this character. You see the drawings are mainly of women.

The drawings in the sketchbook helped me to sort out my ideas. While none exactly prefigures the final sculpture, they show my searching, my groping towards it. At the end, when the sculpture on the building was finished, I was very pleased to have had the actual physical experience of doing it.

Sketchbook 1928: The West Wind Relief, Raymond Spencer Company,
Much Hadham 1982

Reclining Figure 1929

Well this was, what, 1929, and I think up to that time is the most successful of the reclining figures that I'd done [fig.83]. It has a definite influence from Mexican sculpture, from that particular figure, the *Chacmool* figure.[2] Now except for the turn in the head of the *Chacmool*, which I think is a wonderful sculpture, you get a side view of the body, and the legs are both doing the same thing, both sides are both doing the same thing, that is it's a

[2] For further comments on the Chacmool figure, see p.97.

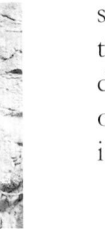

89 *Mask* 1929 LH 61, stone,
height 12.7cm (5in). Private collection

90 *Mother and Child* 1931 LH 106, sycamore
wood, height 76.2cm (30in)

91 *Girl* 1932 LH 112, boxwood, height 31.7cm
(12½in). Dallas Museum of Art, Foundation
for the Arts Collection: gift of Cecile and
I.A. Victor

symmetrical pose, and although I wasn't consciously trying to compete with this figure in the brown Hornton one, perhaps my desire to get more three dimensions into sculpture made me use a pose in which the top leg comes over and the body is twisted, the arm is up and the other arm is down, that is, I was using a much less symmetrical pose.

James 1975

This was the period when I had slight cubist tendencies, and in the square form of the Mother and Child[3] some of this influence shows. The whole rhythm of this reclining figure is a right-angled rhythm.

Hedgecoe 1968, p.53

I could make a list of some ten or twenty works which I know have been keyworks and which I know have solved some directions that I wanted to be satisfied with. Chronologically, it is first the figure I did in brown Hornton stone in 1929 influenced by the Mexican sculpture, particularly by the Chac-Mool figure. I realise now where the influence was, but it is very different. Except for the turn in the head, the figure is a symmetrical figure of which both sides are the same, the two legs are exactly in the same position, where in my Hornton stone figure there is a big difference, a big change and it also began to have something that my sculpture until then hadn't had, it began to have forms which really existed and worked against each other and with each other rather than one solid mass that was all crushed and stuck together. This had a freedom and yet kept a stormy strength and I knew when I finished it that it was the best sculpture I had done up to then.

Ionel Jianou, *Henry Moore*, translated by Geoffrey Skelding,
Arted, Paris 1968, pp.28-9

Mask 1929

In this mask I wanted to give the eyes tremendous penetration and to make them stare, because it is the eyes which most easily express human emotion. In other masks, I used the asymmetrical principle in which one eye is quite different from the other, and the mouth is at an angle bringing back the balance. I had noticed this in some of the Mexican masks, and I began to find it in reality in all faces.

Hedgecoe 1968, p.56

Mother and Child 1931

This was carved from a piece of sycamore tree trunk which was about thirty inches in height and approximately eighteen inches in diameter. It may be that the child seems somewhat compressed to the mother's chest because I was constricted by the roundness of the trunk. But this, perhaps, I welcomed as it increased the unity of the mother and child.

Levine 1983, p.66

[3] Moore is referring to *Mother and Child* 1929 LH 70.

Girl 1932

Boxwood suited a piece such as this because it is so hard and close in grain. I was able to get a detail which would have been very difficult had it been, say, a wide-grain elmwood.

Ibid., p.70

Two Forms 1934

Perhaps it can be thought of as a Mother and Child. I just called it 'Two Forms'. The bigger form has a kind of pelvic shape in it and the smaller form is like the big head of a child.

Hedgecoe 1968, p.76

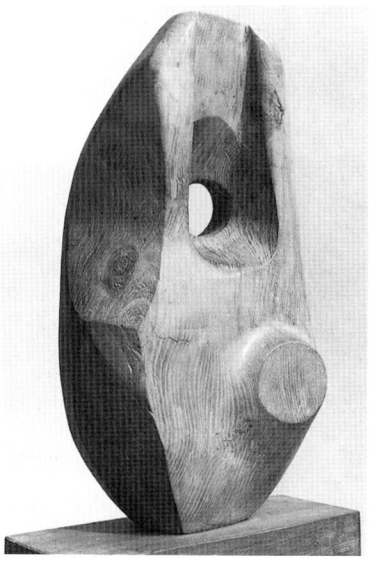

92 *Two Forms* 1934 LH 153, Pynkado wood, length 53.3cm (21in). The Museum of Modern Art, New York: purchase Sir Michael Sadler Fund 1937

Hole and Lump 1934

With this I was consciously concerned with simple relationships of form: here is the hole which is the opposite to the lump. I was putting an emphasis on this consciousness of form – of sculpture not being just an imitation of nature, but also an expression with three-dimensional form. I was also concerned less with the literary or representational side of works of art.

Levine 1983, p.87

Carving 1935

This is even more three-dimensional than my *Hole and Lump* made a year before. I was again consciously experimenting with form. I tried to place a small object inside another: this may have been the beginning of the interior/exterior idea. The ball was carved separately and placed inside at the finish of the piece.

Ibid., p.91

93 *Hole and Lump* 1934 LH 154a, elmwood, height 68.6cm (27in). The Henry Moore Foundation: gift of the artist 1977

Reclining Figure 1935-36

This is the first of the larger reclining figures I have carved in wood and it was already one of the recurring themes in my sculpture in wood, stone, and bronze. This carving is in elmwood, as are most of the large wood carvings. Until the prevalence of Dutch Elm disease in England, elmwood was the commonest and easiest wood to obtain in large pieces.

This sculpture was carved out of a rectangular block of elmwood which was about three feet long by two feet square. The grain, of course, was along its three-foot length. Elmwood has rather a large wide grain. For this reason it is not a happy choice for small sculptures, but in a large reclining figure the horizontal grain emphasises the horizontal pose. I found there were advantages in working on a large heavy block such as this. In the early roughing-out stages, instead of using only small gouges, it was possible to work with saws and an axe. This I enjoyed and it changed my attitude to wood-carving since in the smaller carvings I had sometimes felt the process of production was almost like a mouse nibbling to make a hole.

94 *Carving* 1935 LH 160, African wood, length 40.7cm (16in). Private collection

95 *Reclining Figure* 1935-36 LH 162, elmwood, length 88.9cm (35in). The Albright-Knox Art Gallery, Buffalo NY: Room of Contemporary Art Fund 1939

This first comparatively large wood carving led me, in later years, to produce wood reclining sculptures in even larger dimensions.

Ibid., p.94

Stringed Figures 1937-40

At one period, just before the war, in 1938 I think, I began the most abstract side of my work – the stringed figures. [...]

Well, I had gone one day to the Science Museum at South Kensington and had been greatly intrigued by some of the mathematical models; you know, those hyperbolic paraboloids and groins and so on, developed by Lagrange in Paris, that have geometric figures at the ends with coloured threads from one to the other to show what the form between would be. I saw the sculptural possibilities of them, and I did some. I could have done hundreds. They were fun, but too much in the nature of experiments to be really satisfying. That's a different thing from expressing some deep human experience one might have had. When the war came, I gave up this type of thing. Others, like Gabo and Barbara Hepworth, have gone on doing it. It becomes a matter of ingenuity rather than a fundamental human experience.

Lake 1962, p.42

Whilst a student at the R.C.A. I became involved in machine art, which in those days had its place in modern art. Although I was interested in the work of Léger, and the Futurists, who exploited mechanical forms, I was never directly influenced by machinery as such. Its interest for me lies in its capacity for movement, which, after all, is its function.

I was fascinated by the mathematical models I saw there [the Science Museum], which had been made to illustrate the difference of the form that is halfway between a square and a circle. One model had a square at one end with twenty holes along each side, making eighty holes in all. Through these holes strings were threaded and led to a circle with the same number of holes at the other end. A plane interposed through the middle shows the form that is halfway between a square and a circle. One end could also be twisted to produce forms that would be terribly difficult to draw on a flat surface. It wasn't the scientific study of these models but the ability to look through the strings as with a bird cage and to see one form within another which excited me.

Hedgecoe 1968, p.105

I began to use wood for these pieces when I had the idea of contrasting the thin lines of the strings with the transparency – like looking into a bird cage. It is much easier to drill holes in a wood body or framework than in stone, so wood was the ideal material for the stringed figures.

I remember someone like Gabo[4] seeing my experiments when he came to London and congratulating me on the whole idea. It fascinated him. He developed this string idea so that his structure always became space itself, whereas I like the contrast between the solid and the strings. The string and the 'open' idea was the side I was trying to relate and develop. This perhaps was the culmination of that process in which I was making an outside shape a sculpture in its own right (Interior/Exterior forms), yet one which was not completed until each part was connected to the other. When I connected one side to the other you could see through *and* inside.

Levine 1983, p.26

Stringed Relief 1937

This was the first of my 'stringed' figures. The two outside upright pieces are part of a beechwood shoe tree which I bought in the Caledonian Market. They are screwed on to the base which has a rounded mound; this is an integral part of the flat base. Together they provided the foundation for the strings which are the spatial element in the sculpture.

This first stringed figure experiment led to a series in which I explored spatial but transparent form. I found it exciting and full of possibilities. It led to a series of works.

Ibid., p.102

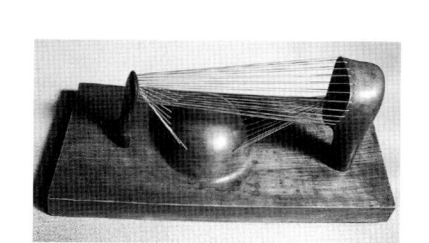

96 *Stringed Relief* 1937 LH 182, beechwood and string, length 49.5cm (19½in). Private collection

Bird Basket 1939

The *Bird Basket* to me is one of the special stringed figures that I made. It has got an organic form to it although the strings are abstract straight lines. It is called the *Bird Basket* because it has the handle of a basket over the top and strings that show the little inner piece as a bird inside a cage – at one end is the head and at the other end the tail. The title is a mixture of the two forms and the two words 'Bird' and 'Basket' are significant because they were arrived at in a practical way.

---

[4] Miriam Gabo recalled that in the late 1930s, after seeing one of Moore's stringed figure sculptures in his studio, Gabo declared: 'Strings, I'll show them what to do with strings.' Martin Hammer and Christina Lodder, *Constructing Modernity: The Art and Career of Naum Gabo*, Yale University Press, New Haven and London 2000, p.288.

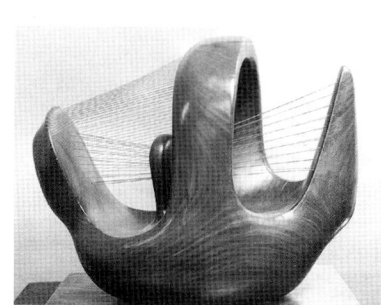

97 *Bird Basket* 1939 LH 205, lignum vitae and string, length 41.9cm (16½in). Private collection

What also makes me treat it as something special in my mind is that lignum vitae is one of the hardest woods in nature, and it can take a very beautiful surface and very thin edges like those at the left-hand side. Also it was more like carving a stone and at that time I still preferred stone to any other material.

This one is the most ambitious stringed piece I made. That also is perhaps why I value it, or would be more upset if it were destroyed than if some of the others were.

Ibid., p.106

Recumbent Figure 1938

The best architects of my own generation began to think seriously about sculpture in relation to their buildings in the late thirties. And when they came around to it, some were persuaded not to have sculpture *on* a building, but *outside* it, in a spatial relation to it. And the beauty of this idea of a spatial relationship is that the sculpture must have its own strong separate identity.

98 *Recumbent Figure* 1938 LH 191, green Hornton stone, length 139.7cm (55in). Tate, London

The architect Chermayeff[5] was thinking along these lines when he invited me, in 1936, to look at the site and lay-out of a house that he was building for himself in Sussex. He wanted me to say whether I could visualise one of my figures standing at the intersection of terrace and garden. It was a long, low-lying building and there was an open view of the long sinuous lines of the Downs. There seemed no point in opposing all these horizontals, and I thought a tall, vertical figure would have been more of a rebuff than a con-

---

[5] The architect and designer Serge Chermayeff (1900-96) was born in Russia and educated in England. Among his early design work were studios for Broadcasting House, London (1931). In 1940 he emigrated to the United States of America, where he taught design and architecture at Harvard and Yale universities.

trast, and might have introduced needless drama. So I carved a reclining figure for him, intending it to be a kind of focal point of all the horizontals, and it was then that I became aware of the necessity of giving outdoor sculpture a far-seeing gaze. My figure looked out across a great sweep of the Downs, and her gaze gathered in the horizon. The sculpture had no specific relationship to the architecture. It had its own identity and did not *need* to be on Chermayeff's terrace, but it so to speak *enjoyed* being there, and I think it introduced a humanising element; it became a mediator between modern house and ageless land.

When Chermayeff sold his house, and went to live in the United States, the Contemporary Art Society bought the Reclining Figure and presented it to the Tate Gallery, and now it is usually indoors, but has occasional airings.

I liked its position in the first open-air exhibition at Battersea Park, where it was in distant communication with my Three Standing Figures [fig.110]. But it had a pretty tough experience when it was a war-time refugee in New York. It had been lent to an international exhibition at the New York World Fair, and as it was still there when war broke out, The Museum of Modern Art kindly took it over and exhibited it, throughout the war, in its sculpture garden. When it came back it was in a very weather-worn condition owing to the extremes of heat and cold in New York, and its proximity to the sea. But at least I discovered that Hornton – a warm, friendly stone that I like using – is not suitable for exposure in intemperate climates.

Sculpture in the Open Air 1955

For me this was a bigger freedom in stone than I'd had up to then, not forcing the stone to weakness, keeping still its stony strength and yet losing the tyranny of the four sided block.

James 1975

London

One thing I forgot to ask you about last night, concerning the transport of the figure to & from New York – which is, that because the stone the figure is carved in (Hornton stone) can only be quarried in limited thickness, the figure had to be made of 3 horizontal layers of stone, which are dowelled & cemented together. Its perfectly sound to do that, because the stones are laid on their natural beds, as they should be in ordinary building – But it means that in moving it about, it should not be lifted except from the bottom, so that there's no risk of any separating … I meant to ask you who I ought to tell this to, so that whenever its moved, that is remembered.

From a letter to Kenneth Clark, 15 March 1939

Reclining Figure 1939

This was carved in Kent. The wood was obtained from a timber merchant in Canterbury. It was for me my most 'opened-out' wood carving – you can

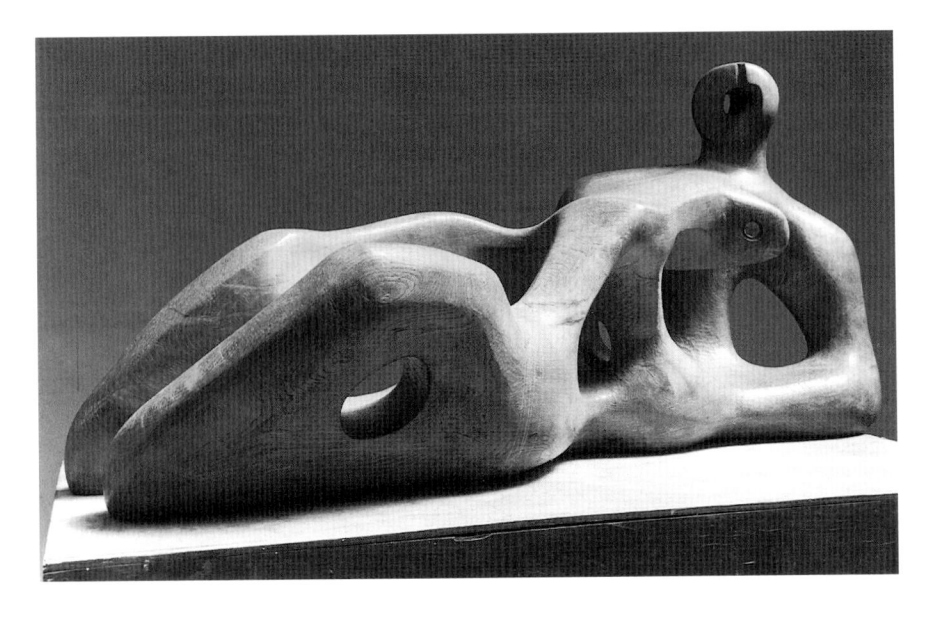

99 *Reclining Figure* 1939 LH 210, elmwood, length 205.8cm (81in). The Detroit Institute of Arts: Founders Society Purchase with funds from the Dexter M. Ferry Jr Trustee Corporation

look from one end to the other through the series of tunnels. It was also the most ambitious carving in wood I have ever done: I realised I could do a larger-than-life sculpture using saws and an axe in blocking out the first approach to it. Wood responds to atmosphere so in this composition I had to allow for that and the shrinkage.

This was a moment of great excitement in my work. This piece for me represented a special stage in my development; it was an advance in wood carving and a great struggle to do.

Levine 1983, p.113

This is […] an example of where with wood you can open out much more than you can with stone, and here the tunnelling, the opening and the spaces were meant to be as significant as the form itself.

James 1975

Three Points 1939-40

In 1940 I made a sculpture with three points, because this pointing has an emotional or physical action in it where things are just about to touch but don't. There is some anticipation of this action. Michelangelo used the same theme in his fresco on the ceiling of the Sistine Chapel, of God creating Adam, in which the forefinger of God's hand is just about to touch and give life to Adam. It is also like the points in the sparking plug of a car, where the spark has to jump across the gap between the points.

There is a very beautiful early French painting (*Gabrielle d'Estrées with her sister in the bath*),[6] where one sister is just about to touch the nipple of the

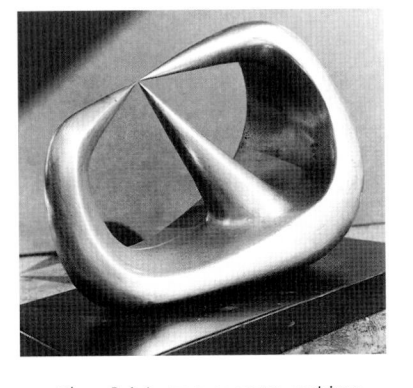

100 *Three Points* 1939-40 LH 211, cast iron, length 19cm (7½in)

[6] The Second School of Fontainebleau, *Gabrielle d'Estrées and One of Her Sisters c.*1595 (Louvre, Paris). In 1979 Moore did a drawing of this painting, HMF 79(89), based on a postcard reproduction.

other. I used this sense of anticipation first in the *Three Points* of 1940, but there are other, later works where one form is nearly making contact with the other. It is very important that the points do not actually touch. There has to be a gap.

Levine 1978, pp.28-9

The Helmet 1939-40

'I did the first of these in about 1940,' [Moore] said. 'I was working on the idea of a form within a form. This idea of protection, of shelter within armour, has been a theme with me for twenty years or more. It may have some psychological thing behind it, the mother-and-child idea, perhaps. You see, if this helmet weren't smooth, it wouldn't have that idea of "helmet". I meant it to have a kind of mechanical vitality.' He turned the helmet around so that the back was facing us. There was a large cutaway area. 'It wouldn't have this feeling of mystery, either, just as in a kind of armour. It's a caricature of the human figure, in a sense.'

Lake 1962, p.41

Shelter Drawings 1940-42

We owned a little Standard coupé and as a rule we used it when going into town. But one evening we arranged to meet some friends at a restaurant and for some reason or other went into town on the 24 bus instead of going by car. We returned home by Underground, taking the Northern Line train to Belsize Park station. It was a long time since I'd been down the tube. I'd noticed that long queues were forming outside Underground stations at about seven o'clock every evening but hadn't thought much about it, and now for the first time I saw people lying on the platforms at all the stations we passed; Leicester Square, Tottenham Court Road, Goodge Street, Euston, Camden Town, Chalk Farm. It happened to be the first night on which a big anti-aircraft barrage was put up all round London. I think it was done to help the morale of Londoners more than anything else: it made a terrific noise and gave the impression that we were hitting back at the raiders in a big way. When we got out at Belsize Park we were not allowed to leave the station because of the fierceness of the barrage. We stayed there for an hour and I was fascinated by the sight of people camping out deep under the ground. I had never seen so many rows of reclining figures and even the holes out of which the trains were coming seemed to me to be like the holes in my sculpture. And there were intimate little touches. Children fast asleep, with trains roaring past only a couple of yards away. People who were obviously strangers to one another forming tight little intimate groups. They were cut off from what was happening up above, but they were aware of it. There was tension in the air. They were a bit like the chorus in a Greek drama telling us about the violence we don't actually witness. [...]

I never made any sketches in the Underground. It just wasn't possible. It would have been like making sketches in the hold of a slave ship. One

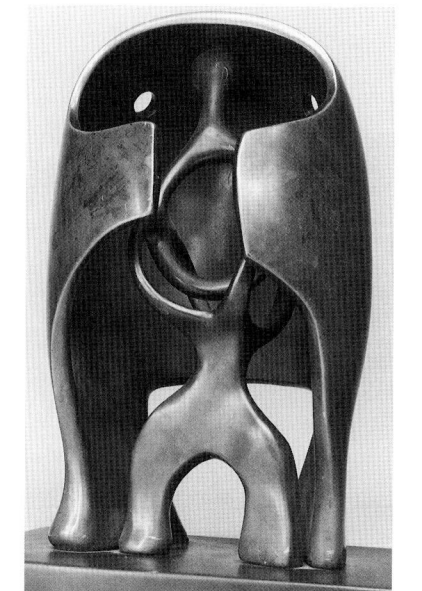

101 *The Helmet* 1939-40 LH 212, bronze, height 29.2cm (11½in)

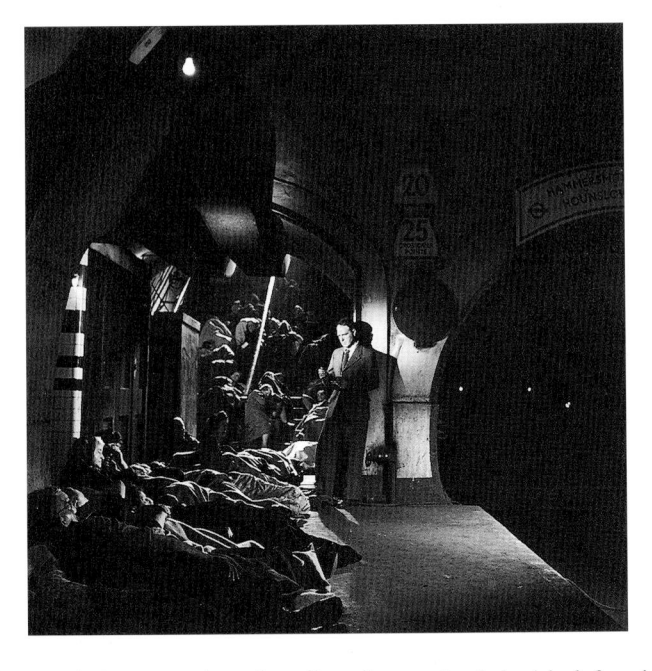

102 Moore on the platform of Holborn Underground station, September 1943, during the filming of *Out of Chaos*.
Photo © Copyright Lee Miller Archives

couldn't be as disinterested as that. Londoners had decided for themselves that the Underground was the safest place to be, and nothing was organised. There were no sanitary arrangements and no bunks. Some people brought their own mattresses, others simply lay on the concrete platform. Instead of drawing, I would wander casually past a group of people half a dozen times or so, pretending to be unaware of them. Sometimes I climbed the staircase so that I could write down a note on the back of an envelope without being seen. A note like 'two people sleeping under one blanket' would be enough of a reminder to enable me to make a sketch next day. Kenneth Clark saw some of these sketches and pointed out that I now had no excuse for refusing to be an official war artist.

I started a sketch-book, putting down ideas for drawings to be carried out later, sometimes adding the verbal notes made in the tube. The first sketch-book now belongs to Kenneth Clark. The one belonging to my wife was started immediately after the first was filled.[7] I started two others, but a lot of the pages were torn out and used for other purposes and they are no longer in existence. I think there's a school exercise-book with a few scribbles in it somewhere in the house, but that's all. The two sketch-books that survived are identical in format. They are cheap, tear-off pads with a cardboard back and originally contained a hundred sheets of thin paper quite suitable for jotting down ideas. They probably came from Bryce-Smith's artists' supply shop in Camden Town, where I bought most of my materials, and I seem to remember that they cost 1/6d each. They were bought before I had any intention of doing the shelter drawings. [...]

Being a war artist, I was entitled to a petrol allowance, and as Much

[7] The first Shelter Sketchbook is now in the British Museum; the second is in the collection of the Henry Moore Foundation.

Hadham is only thirty miles from the centre of London – at night we could see the red glow in the sky from the London fires – I was able to go to and fro in the Standard coupé. I went up to London for two days each week, spending the nights in the Underground, watching the people, and coming up at dawn. Then I would go back to Much Hadham and spend two days making sketches in the tear-off pad. The rest of the week I would be working on drawings to show to the War Artists Committee. I showed them eight or ten at a time and they would take about half of them. I was allowed to do what I liked with the others.

103 *Tube Shelter Perspective: The Liverpool Street Extension* 1941 HMF 1801, pencil, wax crayon, coloured crayon, chalk, watercolour wash, pen and ink, 477 x 432mm (18³/₄ x 17in). Tate, London: presented by the War Artists' Advisory Committee 1946

I had a permit which got me into any Underground I wanted to visit. I had my favourites. Sometimes I went out to the station at Cricklewood, and I was very interested in a huge shelter at Tilbury, which wasn't a tube station but the basement of a warehouse. But the shelter which interested me most of all was the Liverpool Street Underground Extension. A new tunnel had been bored and the reinforcement of the walls completed, but there were no rails, and at night it was occupied along its entire length by a double row of sleeping figures.

The sketches were done with pen-and-ink, wax crayons and water-colour. I used the wax-resist technique, which I had discovered by accident some time before, when trying to do a drawing for a three-year old niece of mine with the two or three stumps of wax crayon which she provided.[8] Her father is a schoolmaster and they lived at the house adjoining the school, so he suggested that I could get some watercolours from one of the class-

[8] Ann Garrould, daughter of Moore's sister Mary, is the editor of the six-volume catalogue raisonné of Henry Moore's drawings.

rooms, and it was a sort of magic to see the watercolour run off the parts of the drawing that had a surface of wax. I found it very useful when dashing down ideas in the sketch-book to be able to let the watercolour run over areas that had already been treated with crayon. I managed to get some of the white crayon that's used for marking glass, and applied it to areas that I wanted to remain white. When the coating of wax is too thin, the watercolour soaks through, and it will be seen that in a few of the sketches small patches of watercolour have invaded areas of another colour.

It was strangely exciting to come out on to the street in the early hours of the morning after a big raid, and I used to go down the back streets to see what damage had been done. It was on one of these journeys that I saw a whole family – three generations of them – sitting quietly together outside a blasted tenement building, waiting for something to be done for them. And another time I saw an injured girl being brought out of a mass of debris with her hair all fluffed out by dust and plaster.

Bunks were not provided in the shelters until several months after the bombing began; nor the canteens and decent sanitary arrangements. But from my point of view, everything was then becoming too organised and commonplace. Up to perhaps the first two months of 1941 there was the drama and the strangeness, and then for the people themselves and for me it was all becoming routine.

Henry Moore, *Shelter-Sketchbook*, Marlborough Fine Art, London 1967

In your own work, the shelter drawings would be the counterpart of 'Guernica', wouldn't they?

Certainly the shelter drawings did seem to get through to a much larger public than I'd ever reached before, and it did seem to me an extraordinary and fascinating and unique moment in history. It wasn't the outward things that touched me, as an artist – I mean, aeroplanes were still aeroplanes, and men in uniform are no different from men in civilian clothes. But to me at the time of the blitz it seemed that nothing like it had ever happened in the world before. There'd been air-raids in the other war, I know, but the only thing at all like those shelters that I could think of was the hold of a slave-ship on its way from Africa to America, full of hundreds and hundreds of people who were having things done to them that they were quite powerless to resist. And perhaps that did get through to the public and make a difference to our relationship: anyway, it's from that moment that I didn't need to teach for a living.

Russell 17 December 1961

Coalmine Drawings 1941-42

By the end of 1941 I had spent almost a year doing the Shelter drawings, and I was losing my initial enthusiasm and excitement. The shelters themselves had been tidied up and organised so that all their strangeness had gone. My great friend Herbert Read suggested that I should visit my native town of

Castleford in Yorkshire and go down the mines, which were of essential importance in winning the war.

And so for about two weeks I went every day down Wheldale Colliery at Castleford and sketched the miners at their various tasks, especially those working at the coal face.

104 Moore sketching Jack Hancock in Wheldale Colliery, Castleford, 1942

This pit is one of the deepest in the Castleford area. When the pit-cage reaches the bottom of the shaft there is still close on a mile to walk, and finally one has to crawl on hands and knees to reach the coal face where the roof is only 3 feet high. The thick choking dust, the noise of the coal-cutting machines and the men shovelling and pickaxing, the almost unbearable heat and the dense darkness hardly penetrated by the faint light from the miners lamps, the consciousness of being nearly a mile below ground, all made it seem at first like some terrible man-made inferno. But after the first few days I got used to it, and before the end I was taking it as naturally as the miners themselves.

To record in drawing what I felt and saw was a new and very difficult struggle. There was first the difficulty of seeing forms emerging out of deep darkness, then the problem of conveying the claustrophobic effect of countless wooden pit-props, 2 or 3 feet apart, receding into blackness, and of expressing the gritty, grubby smears of black coal-dust on the miners' bodies and faces at the same time as the anatomy underneath. I made the larger coalmine drawings back home in Hertfordshire, from sketches and diagrams and written notes done in the mine.

I now believe that the effort of making these drawings was of great value for my later 'black' drawings and graphics. In 1941 I was not particularly aware of Seurat's drawings. It was only later that I came to admire him, especially in the last ten years since I have owned two of his drawings myself.[9] I look at these almost every day, and I feel that my recent 'black' drawings also owe a lot to him.

Auden Poems, Moore Lithographs 1974 (n.p.)

[9] Moore came to own three Seurat drawings: *Two Carts* c.1883, *The Lamp* c.1883 and *Reading* c.1883-4 (fig.105).

105 Georges Seurat, *Reading* c.1883-84, conté crayon, 311 x 241mm (12¼ x 9½in). Private collection

Yet I did not find it as fruitful a subject as the shelters. The shelter drawings came about after first being moved by the experience of them, whereas the coal-mine drawings were more in the nature of a commission coldly approached. They represent two or three weeks of physical sweat seeing the subject and that number of months of mental sweat trying to be satisfied carrying them out.

It was difficult, but something I am glad to have done. I had never willingly drawn male figures before – only as a student in college. Everything I had willingly drawn was female. But here, through these coal-mine drawings, I discovered the male figure and the qualities of the figure in action. As a sculptor I had previously believed only in static forms, that is, forms in repose.

106 *Miners at Work on the Coalface* 1942
HMF 1992, pencil, wax crayon, coloured crayon, watercolour wash, pen and ink, 330 x 635mm (13 x 25in). Birmingham Museum and Art Gallery: presented by the War Artists' Advisory Committee 1947

And in both these subjects I think I could have found sculptural motifs only, if I'd tried to; but at the time I felt a need to accept and interpret a more 'outward' attitude. And here, curiously enough, is where, in looking back, my Italian trip and the Mediterranean tradition came once more to the surface. There was no discarding of those other interests in archaic art and the art of primitive peoples, but rather a clearer tension between this approach and the humanist emphasis. You will perhaps remember my writing you in 1943 that I didn't think that either my shelter or coal-mine drawings would have a very direct or obvious influence on my sculpture when I would get back to it – except, for instance, I might do sculpture using drapery, or perhaps do groups of two or three figures instead of one. As a matter of fact the *Madonna and Child* [fig.107] for Northampton and the later *Family Groups* actually have embodied these features. Still I sometimes wonder if both these and the wartime drawings were not perhaps a temporary resolution of that conflict which caused me those miserable first six months after I had left Masaccio behind in Florence and had once again come within the attraction of the archaic and primitive sculptures of the British Museum.

Sweeney 1947, pp.184-5

Without the war, which directed one's direction to life itself, I think I would have been a far less sensitive and responsible person – if I had ignored all that and went on working just as before. The war brought out and encouraged the humanist side in one's work.

Wilkinson 1977, p.36

Madonna and Child 1943-44

When I was first asked to carve a 'Madonna and Child' for S. Matthew's, although I was very interested I wasn't sure whether I could do it, or whether I even wanted to do it.[10] One knows that Religion has been the inspiration of most of Europe's greatest painting and sculpture, and that the Church in the past has encouraged and employed the greatest artists; but the great tradition of religious art seems to have got lost completely in the present day, and the general level of church art has fallen very low (as anyone can see from the affected and sentimental prettinesses sold for church decoration in church art shops). Therefore I felt it was not a commission straightway and light heartedly to agree to undertake, and I could only promise to make note-book drawings from which I would do small clay models, and only then should I be able to say whether I could produce something which would be satisfactory as sculpture and also satisfy my idea of the 'Madonna and Child' theme as well.

There are two particular motives or subjects which I have constantly used in my sculpture in the last twenty years; they are the 'Reclining Figure' idea and the 'Mother and Child' idea. (Perhaps of the two the 'Mother and Child' has been the more fundamental obsession.) I began thinking of the 'Madonna and Child' for S. Matthew's by considering in what ways a 'Madonna and Child' differs from a carving of just a 'Mother and Child' – that is, by considering how in my opinion religious art differs from secular art.

It's not easy to describe in words what this difference is, except by saying in general terms that the 'Madonna and Child' should have an austerity and a nobility, and some touch of grandeur (even hieratic aloofness) which is missing in the everyday 'Mother and Child' idea. Of the sketches and models I have done,[11] the one chosen has I think a quiet dignity and gentleness. I have tried to give a sense of complete easiness and repose, as though the Madonna could stay in that position for ever (as, being in stone, she will have to do). The Madonna is seated on a low bench, so that the angle formed between her nearly upright body and her legs is somewhat less than a right angle, and in this angle of her lap, safe and protected, sits the Infant.

The Madonna's head is turned to face the direction from which the statue is first seen, in walking down the aisle, whereas one gets the front view of the Infant's head when standing directly in front of the statue.

107 *Madonna and Child* 1943-44 LH 226, Hornton stone, height 149.9cm (59in). Church of St Matthew, Northampton

[10] In 1942 the Revd Walter Hussey commissioned the *Madonna and Child* to commemorate the fiftieth anniversary of St Matthew's Church, Northampton.
[11] Moore made numerous drawings, including HMF 2171-2186, and twelve maquettes LH 215-222, 222a-225 for the Northampton *Madonna and Child*.

In sculpture which is related to architecture, actual life-size is always confusing, and as S. Matthew's is a large church, spacious and big in scale too, the 'Madonna and Child' will be slightly over life-size. But I do not think it should be much over life-size as the sculptor's real and full meaning is to be got only by looking at it from a rather nearer view, and if from nearby it seemed too colossal it would conflict with the human feeling I wish to express.

Church of S. Matthew, Northampton, 1893-1943, St Matthew's Church, Northampton 1943

We've already mentioned the reclining figure as the major theme in your work. The other major one has been the mother and child, and I suppose your first masterpiece in this mode would be considered to be the famous Northampton Madonna. As this was a commissioned work, can you tell me how the commission came about, and what were some of the formal problems you had to solve in executing it?

Yes. I've perhaps done only two or three commissions. By commission I mean a commission in the sense that a Renaissance artist would be given the conditions and the subject matter and everything else. I fought shy of this, except I did do a thing on an underground station for the architect, who was very nice and very fatherly and persuaded me to do it.[12] Then the next persuader was the vicar of the Northampton church. I met him because the Chelsea School of Art, where I'd finished my teaching during the war, had been evacuated to Northampton, and I went to give a composition criticism. I was doing the shelter drawings at the time, and I met Canon Hussey, as he then was, and he said that his father, who had been the vicar of this church before him, had left some money for a sculpture for the church and would I think about doing a madonna and child for him. And I said, 'I don't think so. I'm busy anyhow with the shelter drawings.' And he said, 'I don't mean now, but may I come and see you?' And he used this kind of approach, of never pushing the moment, but of coming and seeing me. And eventually I said all right. Also, as I had not done any sculpture for nearly two years, through doing the shelter drawings and the coal mine drawings, I wanted to get back to sculpture, and yet I hadn't got the themes in my mind. So this was a way of beginning. But I still felt unsure of being able to do it, and I said to him, 'If you will give me two or three months, I'll do some little ideas, some little maquettes. And if my friends such as Herbert Read and Kenneth Clark think that what I produce is all right, then I'll consider it.' And I did this. And we had them all out on the mantelpiece at the Upper Terrace house of Kenneth Clark's. And I'd already decided which one I thought was best, because I could see it as stone and see it finished. And they agreed that this was it. But I still held to the idea that if I didn't like it at the end he wasn't to have it. And, anyhow, he was only going to give me about £300 for it, which is all he gave me, although it didn't matter to me because I had begun to sell a few shelter drawings and financially I was better off than I had been

[12] Charles Holden, see p.253.

before the war. Anyhow, this is how it came about. But I was definitely uncertain that I could produce what I would consider a religious work of art,
rather than a secular one, because none of my mother-and-childs, which I
had experimented with since 1922, was meant to be a madonna and child.
They were all meant to be just on the mother-and-child theme of the big
form protecting the small form, of the relationship of a small form with a
big form – of all the things that are implied in the mother-and-child idea
other than this religious one of the madonna and child. And I didn't know
that I could do it. Although I was baptised and confirmed and made to go
to church as a boy, I am not a practising Christian. But I still respect people's
beliefs enough to not want to put something in a church which people
would feel had nothing whatever to do with religion, or with religious feeling. […]

Eternal?

Yes, eternal. Now one of the things that satisfies me in a way about that
Madonna and Child is not my own feelings about it, but those of the wife of
a great friend of mine. I won't say the name, but she was a very sensitive and
very nice person, and her son was a brilliant boy. He was at either Oxford or
Cambridge, I forget which, and had a nervous breakdown because he was
working so hard. He didn't recover, and he remained a case and had to go
to the asylum in Northampton. And she told me that this was a terrible
affair for her and her husband, and she used to go and see him once a week,
although she never knew whether the next week, perhaps, he might not be
a little better. And she said that always on those occasions, after visiting him,
she would go and sit in the church in Northampton, in front of this *Madonna
and Child* of mine, and she said that it gave her tremendous comfort and
assurance and it helped her a lot. Now that is infinitely more satisfying to me
than to hear some art critic say that it's a good piece of sculpture.

Carroll 1973, pp.43-4, 46

I couldn't, for instance, have wished for a better foil to my Madonna and
Child in the Church of St Matthew at Northampton than Graham Sutherland's Crucifixion. Both the tranquillity of the carving, and the passionate
violence of the painting gain something by the contrast. The difference
would have been too sudden, too dislocating if these two works had been
side by side, but the fact that one cannot see them both together, but has to
turn away from the one to see the other produces a kind of equilibrium.

Sculpture in the Open Air 1955

Memorial Figure 1945-46

I think the figure I carved in 1945 and 1946 in memory of Christopher
Martin[13] has found a perfect setting in the grounds of Dartington Hall; there

---

[13] Christopher Martin (1902-44) founded the art school at Dartington Hall, Devon, and remained its head
for ten years until he died prematurely of tuberculosis.

108 *Memorial Figure* 1945-46 LH 262,
Hornton stone, length 142.2cm (56in).
Dartington Hall, Devon

are other parts of those lovely gardens that may well have been equally suitable, but it was this setting I had in mind when working on the maquettes.
The figure is a memorial to a friend who loved the quiet mellowness of this
Devonshire landscape. It is situated at the top of a rise, and when one stands
near it and takes in the shape of it in relation to the vista one becomes aware
that the raised knee repeats or echoes the gentle roll in the landscape. I
wanted it to convey a sense of permanent tranquillity, a sense of *being* from
which the stir and fret of human ways had been withdrawn, and all the time
I was working on it I was very much aware that I was making a memorial to
go into an English scene that is itself a memorial to many generations of
men who have engaged in a subtle collaboration with the land. Obviously, it
would be out of place in a wilder, more rugged setting.

Ibid.

I tried to make a figure which could rightly be called a memorial figure. I
wanted the figure to have a quiet stillness and a sense of permanence as
though it could stay there for ever; to have strength and seriousness in its
effect and yet be serene and happy and resolved, as though it had come to
terms with the world, and could get over the largest cares and losses.

The Gardens at Dartington Hall, text by Dorothy Elmhirst,
McNally, C. Eric, Dartington 1961

I intended the Dartington sculpture to be calm, gentle, and contemplative,
in keeping with the character and personality of Christopher Martin. In the
same year I was carving a large elmwood Reclining Figure [fig.109] (formerly
in Cranbrook Academy of Art) which is very different in feeling. Perhaps
the two sculptures express what some critics see as two opposing sides in

my work – the 'tough' and the 'tender'. I am happy to think I may have these two sides. To understand or feel anything deeply, you must know its opposite.

Finn 1976, p.266

Reclining Figure 1945-46

This, I think, was the best really big block of wood I obtained – it was over six feet long and I found it in a timber merchant's yard in our nearest big

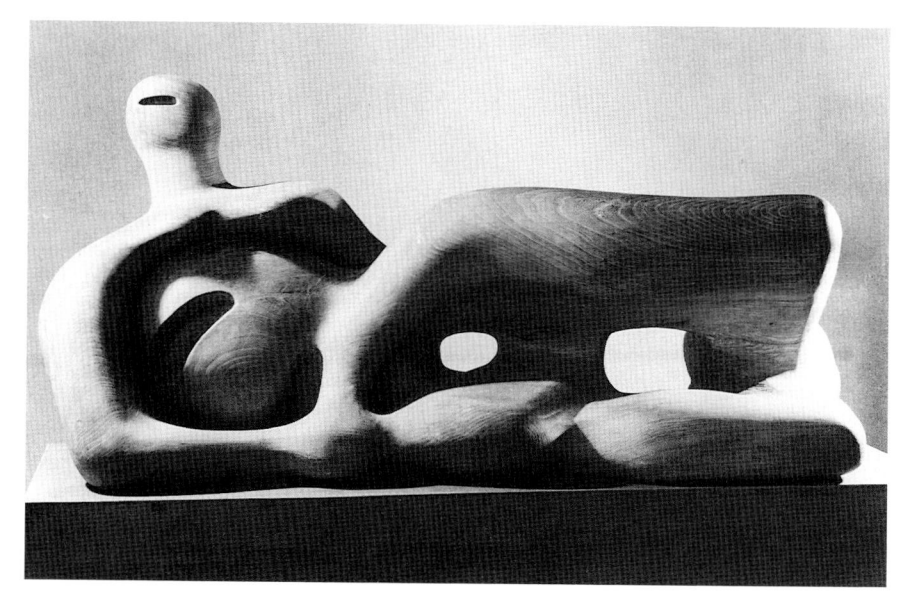

109 *Reclining Figure* 1945-46 LH 263, elmwood, length 190.5cm (75in). Private collection, on loan to the J.B. Speed Art Museum, Louisville

town. It was a fine and wonderful block and I started with great enthusiasm. I took many photographs of the progress and development of this sculpture – something I hadn't done before. I think I managed in this carving to get a richer, fuller three-dimensional sense than in large wood sculptures I had done so far. Perhaps the large bulk of this block enabled me to give it some sense of monumentality.

Levine 1983, p.116

Three Standing Figures 1947-48

This group, made in 1947-48, was not done especially for the position it now occupies in Battersea Park. The project was on the way before the Contemporary Art Society thought of commissioning it. The Museum of Modern Art in New York had said that they wanted from me a large work, and I had their request in mind when I decided to carve this group in Darleydale stone, which stone I chose because it would have weathered well and kept clean in the sea air of New York. In the smoke-laden atmosphere of London, especially being near Battersea Power Station, I think the stone will slowly go darker, it may perhaps look very well when nearly black. At present though, in its in-between stage, it is looking rather dirty. But it is no

110 *Three Standing Figures* 1947-48 LH 268, Darley Dale stone, height 210cm (84in). Borough of Wandsworth, London: gift of the Contemporary Art Society 1948, installed in Battersea Park

use being over-concerned about its surface appearance for the next few years.

When the Contemporary Art Society decided that they wanted to offer it to the London County Council Parks Committee, The Museum of Modern Art agreed to wait for a large work, and later they had a cast of the Stevenage Family Group [fig.111]. The three figures were well sited when they were shown in the first open air sculpture exhibition at Battersea Park, but they couldn't remain there because the tree to the right of one of them was rotten, and after it was felled the site lost a good deal of its attractiveness. But I was very happy about that original situation. The slight rise overlooking an open stretch of park and the background of trees emphasised their outward and upward stare into space. They are the expression in sculpture of the group feeling that I was concerned with in the shelter drawings, and although the problem of relating separate sculptural units was not new to me, my previous experience of the problem had involved more abstract forms; the bringing together of these three figures involved the creation of a unified human mood. The pervading theme of the shelter drawings was the group sense of communion in apprehension. But I only wanted a hint of that mood to remain in the three figures.

I wanted to overlay it with the sense of release, and create figures conscious of being in the open air; they have a lifted gaze, for scanning distances.

Sculpture in the Open Air 1955

Family Groups 1944-49

When Walter Gropius[14] was working in England before the war he was asked by Henry Morris,[15] Director for Education in Cambridgeshire to design a large school at Impington, near Cambridge. It was called a Village College and was meant to be different from other elementary schools because it was meant to put into practice lots of Henry Morris's ideas on education. Such as, that the children's parents should be catered for in the school, and that the school should be the centre of social life of the surrounding villages. The school had a lecture theatre, a hall where they could have plays and films – even sleeping accommodation for parents if they were held up there in winter evenings, etc. Gropius asked me to do a piece of sculpture for the school. We talked about it and I suggested that a family group would be the right subject. However, it never got further than that because there was no money. Henry Morris tried unsuccessfully to raise money by private subscription. Gropius left England for Harvard University. Later the war came and I heard no more about it until, about 1944, Henry Morris told me that he now thought he could get enough money together for the sculpture if I would still like to think of doing it. I said yes, because the idea right from the start had appealed to me and I began drawings in note book form of family groups. From these note book drawings I made a number of small maquettes, a dozen or more (some of which appear in the Lund Humphries book).[16] Some of the maquettes were ideas for bronze, but most of them were for stone because for the Impington school I felt stone would be the suitable material.

I must have worked for nine months or so on the *Family Group* themes and ideas, but again, Henry Morris found it difficult to raise money for the sculpture, and also my maquettes were not liked by the local Education authorities, and again nothing materialised. I carried out three or four of the six inch maquettes more fully in a slightly larger size for my own satisfaction, and then I went on with other work.

About two years later, 1947, John Newsom, the Director of Education in Hertfordshire, a friend of Henry Morris, and having similar progressive ideas on education, told me of a large school being built by Hertfordshire Education authorities. It was being designed by F.R.S. Yorke and Partners, very good architects. Newsom and Yorke knew of the projected Impington sculpture and now said as that had fallen through would I be prepared to do a piece of sculpture at their new school at Stevenage. I agreed, for here was the chance of carrying through one of the ideas on a large scale which I had

[14] The German-born architect and industrial designer Walter Gropius (1883-1969) was a pioneer of modern 'functional' architecture. From 1915 he directed the Weimar School of Art, which he reorganised in 1919 as the Bauhaus. Gropius lived in London from 1934 to 1937, where he worked on factory designs and housing estates for the home counties. He emigrated to the USA in 1937, where he became Professor of Architecture at Harvard University.

[15] For Moore's tribute to Morris see p.89.

[16] Moore is referring to the third edition of *Henry Moore: Sculpture and Drawings* 1949, plates 70g, 70h, 70i, LH 237, 230 and 229.

wanted to do. I went to see the school and chose from my previous ideas the one which I thought would be right for Stevenage and also one which I had wanted most to carry out on a life-size scale. This was a bronze idea [LH 259] (the one which the Museum[17] bought from my exhibition in 1945).

Again, though, money was a problem – eventually it was solved by me agreeing to do the sculpture at cost price (i.e. price of bronze casting, transport and materials etc.) if I could be allowed to make extra casts which I could dispose of myself.

So the explanation why you have a photograph with dates 1945-49 on the back is that the small version [LH 259] was made in 1945 and the large version [fig.111] in 1949. The main differences between the two are in the heads, especially in the head of the man. In the small version the split head of the man gives a vitality and interest necessary to the composition, particularly as all three heads have only slight indications for features. When it came to the life-size version, the figures each became more obviously human and related to each other and the split head of the man became impossible for it was so unlike the woman and the child. (There is different connection between things which are three feet from each other, as the large heads are, and things which one sees in the same field of vision only two or three inches apart.)

The large sculpture was finished in 1949 and cast for Stevenage at a small bronze foundry[18] here in England. The group was really too big for them to handle and they had lots of difficulties, in fact they took a whole year to do it, with a great deal of worry over it to me. That is why we are having the other casts made by Rudier in Paris.

Letter to Dorothy Miller,[19] 31 January 1951; quoted in James 1966, pp.224-5

111 *Family Group* 1948-49 LH 269, bronze, height 152cm (60in)

The first cast of this family group [fig.111] was made for the Barclay Secondary School at Stevenage, under the scheme brought in by the Hertfordshire County Council for spending a fraction of one per cent of the building estimates on pictures and sculptures for its new schools. (The scheme unfortunately has since been dropped.) The architect wanted a free-standing group out of doors, and had a position ready for it in his plans. I went out to Stevenage while the school was under construction and tried out a rough life-size silhouette made in cardboard of the Family Group just for its scale. It was to be in front of a curved baffle-wall about 20 ft. long by about 8 ft. high, on the left of the main entrance, but the space between the baffle-wall and the drive-way is limited, and the space between the sculpture and the baffle-wall is not great enough to tempt one to go round to the back of the sculpture. I realise that from the architect's point of view the position he had decided upon was the proper one. For the baffle-wall played a part in the architecture – it masked an awkward juncture of the building – and

[17] The Museum of Modern Art, New York.
[18] The bronze *Family Group* 1948-49 LH 269 for Barclay School, Stevenage, was cast at the Fiorini and Carney Foundry, Michael Road, Fulham, London.
[19] See p.67, note 55.

without sculpture in front of it, it might have seemed unjustifiable. The fact remains that it is a position that does not allow the Family Group to be, in the full sense of the term, free-standing. We stood it as far away from the wall as possible, but one can only see it from a limited number of views, one cannot get those sudden revelations that occur when one comes upon a sculpture from an unexpected angle. In such circumstances architects might consider the use of a turn-table, not to keep the statue slowing turning – that would be a horrible idea – but to present another view of it every month or so. And if a sculptor knows that his work is going to be seen all round, it is a further impetus to sculpt all round.

Sculpture in the Open Air 1955

Standing Figure 1950

I had in mind when making it that it should be placed out of doors in relation to nature. I think the caption should be 'Sculpture in Landscape – Standing Man'.

It is placed on a lonely moor in Scotland and the bleak nature of the landscape brings out the skeletonic, stark and solitary quality of the work, and in my opinion shows how sculpture and nature can augment each other and have a real poetic connection.

'Art Today', *World Student News*, Prague 1955, No.4, Vol.9, p.7

112 *Standing Figure* 1950 LH 290, bronze, height 221cm (87in). Glenkiln, Dumfriesshire

Sir William Keswick came to me after he had seen this piece in an exhibition (it may have been the second Battersea Park exhibition).[20] He told me about his sheep farm in Dumfriesshire, Scotland, and said its large acreage was unsuitable for agricultural farming because the ground was too rocky. I don't know whether he got the idea to put sculpture on his sheep farm after he saw the Battersea Park open-air exhibition, or whether he was inspired by his experience in China, where he had lived for many years, and where, he said, there are many examples of monumental sculptures in the open air. In any case, he bought this piece to put on his farm in Scotland.

He placed the sculpture himself on an existing outcrop of rock. Later I went up there and was thrilled with the beautiful landscape and at how well he had sited 'Yon Figure' (the sculpture's local name).

Finn 1976, p.296

These [the double heads] would be staring out into space. It's as though the back head is helping the front head to look in that direction. You double up as it were.

James 1975

Reclining Figure: Festival 1951

This Reclining Figure was commissioned by the Arts Council for the Festival of Britain in 1951. But I knew that the South Bank would only be its

---

[20] The exhibition was held in 1951.

113 *Reclining Figure: Festival* 1951 LH 293, bronze, length 228.5cm (90in)

temporary home, so I didn't worry about where it was to be placed. If I had studied a Festival site too carefully, the figure might never have been at home anywhere else. As it was, I made the figure, then found the best position I could. I was simply concerned with making a sculpture in the round. And it was out in the open most of the time I was working on it.

Sculpture in the Open Air 1955

This figure was perhaps my first conscious effort to make space and form absolutely inseparable. I became conscious of this aim halfway through the sculpture. In earlier works, particularly in my carvings, when I wanted to make space in stone sculpture it had been more difficult. Making a hole in stone is such a willed thing, such a conscious effort, and often the holes became things in themselves. But then the solid stone around them sometimes suffers in its shape because its main purpose is to enclose the hole. This isn't a really true three-dimensional amalgamation between forms and space.

I think this is the first sculpture in which I succeeded in making form and space sculpturally inseparable.

Finn 1976, p.287

This [the use of surface string] does come from the drawings. I don't know if there's anybody else who has used this kind of invention, but I invented at one stage a shorthand way of trying to show in a drawing the sectional line,[21] the form, the shape, without doing shading … At one stage I thought the sculpture was a little bit, what, well I was dissatisfied with the shape being shown as clearly as I wanted and so I used this drawing not trick, but

[21] For an explanation of the two-way sectional line method of drawing, see Wilkinson 1977, pp.16-17.

method idea on the sculpture and the strings had to be thin enough not to disrupt or confuse the surface. I mean you couldn't put a thick rope over. Cotton was a bit too thin, and so I used very thin string. And to some extent I think it does add an interest and form, it does give the shape more insistence than it would do on an absolutely plain surface.

In conversation with Alan Wilkinson, c.1980

Upright Internal–External Forms 1951-54

Much Hadham, Herts.

The first maquette [LH 294] for the wood 'Internal and External Forms' was produced in 1951. Later the same year I made the working model (24½" high), which was cast into bronze [LH 295]. The idea was always intended to be worked out over life-size, and to be in wood. But large and sound pieces of wood are not easily found, and it was after trying unsuccessfully for a year to find a suitable piece of wood that I decided I should have to make it in plaster for bronze, and this I did (6'7" high) [LH 296]. This was completed and about to be sent to the bronze foundry for casting when my local timber merchant informed me he had a large elm tree just come in which he thought would be exactly what I wanted. It was a magnificent tree, newly cut down, five feet in diameter at its base, and looked very sound. I bought it, and decided not to go on with the bronze version but to carry out the idea as originally intended as a wood sculpture.

I am very pleased this happened because I am sure that elm wood, in particular, with its large sized grain, varied, big and bold, makes it ideal in scale for large work. It was necessary for the Upright carving to be in wood, which is alive and warm and gives a sense of growth. (Wood is a natural and living material, unlike plaster or metal which are built up by man.)

These qualities were in harmony with the idea, which is a sort of embryo being protected by an outer form, a mother and child idea, or the stamen in a flower, that is, something young and growing being protected by an outer shell.

The large wood version [fig.114] was started in early 1953, only about a week after the tree had been cut down. Such a piece of wood, five feet in diameter, would have taken thirty years of special care and treatment to be seasoned, as on the average, wood seasons in a natural way one inch per year. Therefore, a sixty inch block takes thirty years to dry out to the middle. But by carving it slowly over a period of two years, and because its final form has no part more than five inches thick, it is now fully seasoned and the seasoning has been less precarious, and more thorough. (The hole at the base of the carving has been hollowed out from beneath.)

Without knowing your Gallery I can't say just how best to show it. I think it may need showing in the kind of light it has had in my studio where it has been made. That is, in a top light, which does not shine too directly into the interior, a light which lets the interior look like a cave, with some mystery in it.

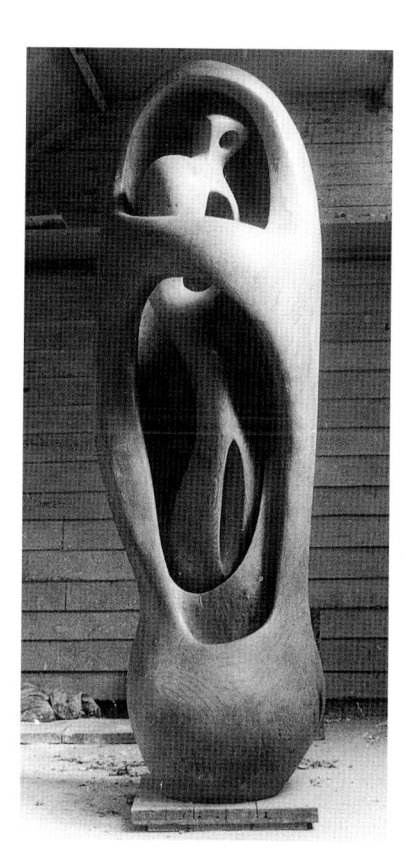

114 *Upright Internal/External Form* 1953-54
LH 297, elmwood, height 261.5cm (103in).
Albright-Knox Art Gallery, Buffalo NY

115 *Maquette for Mother and Child* 1952
LH 314, bronze, height 21.5cm (8½in)

I think its height need not be more than a few inches above the ground as already it looks large enough, and raising it would make it perhaps too cut off from the spectator. Its idea needs to be connected with the size of a human being and the spectator should be able to imagine himself standing in the place of the interior form.

Letter to Gordon Smith at the Albright-Knox Art Gallery, Buffalo 31 October 1955

Maquette for Mother and Child 1952

I've done many mother and child sculptures, and most of them have had this idea of the larger form in a protective relationship with the smaller form – the sense of gentleness and of tenderness. But this isn't always so with youth and age. It isn't always so with very young children or animals. They're ravenous. It's as though they want to devour their parent: their need for food, for growing, is such that they have no tender feelings towards the parent. Sometimes the parent has almost to protect itself – and this is the opposite side to what I usually did in my mother and child ideas. I wanted this to seem as though the child was trying to devour its parent – as though the parent, the mother, had to hold the child at arm's length.

The Listener 24 January 1974, p.105

Time–Life Screen 1952-53

I think architecture is the poorer for the absence of sculpture and I also think that the sculptor, by not collaborating with the architect, misses opportunities of his work being used socially and being seen by a wider public. And it was feeling that the time is coming for architects and sculptors to work together again, that brought me to do the double commission for the Time–Life building in Bond Street, of both the Bronze Draped Reclining Figure [fig.121] for the terrace and the carved stone screen [fig.120] at the Bond Street end of the terrace. I was first asked to do only the Reclining Figure, and was glad to, as that fitted in with my idea of free-standing sculpture in relation to architecture. It was at a later stage that the architect of the building approached me about the sculptured screen and I accepted the chance of working simultaneously upon two such entirely different sculptural problems.

It seemed to me that the screen must be made to look as though it was part of the architecture, for it is a continuation of the surface of the building – and is an obvious part of the building.

The fact that it is only a screen, a kind of balustrade to the Terrace with space behind it, led me to carve it with a back as well as a front, and to pierce it, which gives an interesting penetration of light, and also from Bond Street makes it obvious that it is a screen and not a solid part of the building.

With the perspective sketch of the building beside me I made four maquettes. My aim was to give a rhythm to the spacing and size of the sculptural motives which should be in harmony with the architecture. I rejected the idea of a portrayal of some pictorial scene, for that would only be like hanging up a stone picture, like using the position only as a hoarding for sticking on a stone poster.

This is the first of the four maquettes [fig.116]. I rejected it because I thought it too obvious and regular a repetition of the fenestration of the building.

This is the second maquette [fig.117]. I tried to vary this and make it less symmetrical but in doing so the rhythms became too vertical.

In this third maquette [fig.118] I tried to introduce a more horizontal rhythm but was dissatisfied with the monotony of the size of the forms.

This fourth maquette [fig.119] I thought was better and more varied and so this became the definitive maquette, although a further working model [LH 343] produced other changes.

Long before the carvings themselves were ready, I had to decide upon the shape and size of the openings of the screen, so that the architect could get it prepared and built into position before the carvings arrived on the site. The four big stones themselves were carved on a scaffolding erected in my garden – and, of course, without the stone frame screen round them. By the time I realised that they didn't really need a screen at all, the screen had been made and was in position on the building, and all I could do was arrange for the openings to be made larger, that is to say, as large as possible, without weakening the structure of the screen. I found too that my project really demanded a turn-table for each of the carvings, so that they could be turned say on the first of each month, each to a different view, and project from the building like some of those half animals that look as if they are escaping through the walls in Romanesque architecture. I wanted them to be like half-buried pebbles whose form one's eye instinctively completes. This idea of sculpture buried in a wall or jutting out from it is quite different from the idea behind Renaissance reliefs, where the solid is suggested by perspective. The Renaissance relief is a pictorial conception really and not a sculptural one. Trial and error is essential to the creative process, but unfortunately in the 20th century one cannot change one's mind on the job. I say 'in the 20th century' because I'm sure that the people who built Chartres Cathedral were able to have second thoughts. The carrying out of the fully developed idea of the Time–Life screen would have entailed elaborate reinforcement of the building and expense beyond the original estimates, but what has been done is the beginning of something, and the idea, particularly the turntable idea may yet bear fruit I hope in architectural sculpture of the future.

Sculpture in the Open Air 1955

116 *Time–Life Screen: Maquette No.1*
1952 LH 339, bronze, length 33cm (13in)

117 *Time–Life Screen: Maquette No.2*
1952 LH 340, bronze, length 33cm (13in)

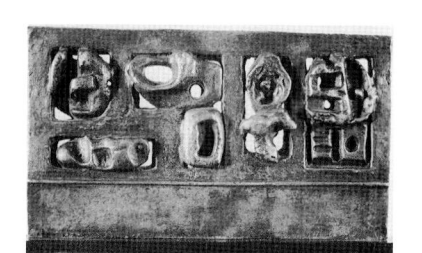

118 *Time–Life Screen: Maquette No.3*
1952 LH 341, bronze, length 33cm (13in)

119 *Time–Life Screen: Maquette No.4*
1952 LH 342, bronze, length 33cm (13in).
Art Gallery of Ontario, Toronto: gift of Dr Alan Wilkinson in memory of Betty Tinsley

120 *Time–Life Screen* 1952-53 LH 344,
Portland stone, length 808cm (26ft 6in).
Pearl Assurance, Time–Life Building, London

Draped Reclining Figure 1952-53

121 *Draped Reclining Figure* 1952-53 LH 336, bronze, length 157.5cm (62in)

I knew that the figure would be seen from the Reception Room and it seemed to me that in cold weather a nude – even an abstractish one – might look incongruous to people looking out at her from a warm room. So I became absorbed by the problems of the draped figure, and for a time I was back in the period of the shelter drawings, whose themes had demanded a concentration on drapery. But gradually I evolved a treatment that exploited the fluidity of plaster. The treatment of drapery in my stone carvings was a matter of large, simple creases and folds but the modelling technique enabled me to build up large forms with a host of small crinklings and rucklings of the fabric.

This figure was made for a small terrace, but because the terrace is in the open air I made it over life-size; if it stood up it would be a figure about 7 ft. high. A piece of sculpture that looks life-size in the studio always seems a bit under life-size when it's out in the open, and to look monumental it has to be a little larger than life.

Ibid.

I have tried in this figure to use drapery from what I think is a sculptural point of view.

Drapery played a very important part in the shelter drawings I made in 1940 and 1941 and what I began to learn then about its function as form gave me the intention, sometime or other, to use drapery in sculpture in a more realistic way than I had ever tried to use it in my carved sculpture. And my first visit to Greece in 1951 perhaps helped to strengthen this intention – so when I was commissioned to do a reclining figure to be placed on the terrace of the Time and Life building, New Bond Street, I took the opportunity of making this draped figure in plaster (for bronze).

Drapery can emphasise the tension in a figure, for where the form pushes outwards, such as on the shoulders, the thighs, the breasts, etc., it can be pulled tight across the form (almost like a bandage), and by contrast with the crumpled slackness of the drapery which lies between the salient points, the pressure from inside is intensified.

Drapery can also, by its direction over the form, make more obvious the section, that is, show shape. It need not be just a decorative addition, but can serve to stress the sculptural idea of the figure.

Also in my mind was to connect the contrast of the sizes of folds, here small, fine and delicate, in other places big and heavy, with the form of mountains, which are the crinkled skin of the earth. (This analogy, I think, comes out in close-up photographs taken of the drapery alone.)

Although static, this figure is not meant to be in slack repose but, as it were, alerted.

Sculpture in the Open Air, Holland Park, London 1954

King and Queen 1952-53

The 'King and Queen' is rather strange. Like many of my sculptures, I can't explain exactly how it evolved. Anything can start me off on a sculpture idea, and in this case it was playing with a small piece of modelling wax. It was at a time when I was thinking of starting my own bronze foundry. I had a young sculptor assistant who was keen on the technical side and wanted to know about casting bronze. I decided to cut out the first stage, which would have meant making a plaster cast, and to model directly in wax. Whilst manipulating a piece of this wax, it began to look like a horned, Pan-like, bearded head. Then it grew a crown and I recognised it immediately as the head of a king. I continued, and gave it a body. When wax hardens, it is almost as strong as metal. I used this special strength to repeat in the body the aristocratic refinement I found in the head. Then I added a second figure to it and it became a 'King and Queen'. I realise now that it was because I was reading stories to Mary, my six-year-old daughter, every night, and most of them were about kings and queens and princesses.

Eventually one of these sculptures went to Scotland, and is beautifully placed by its owner, Tony Keswick, in a moorland landscape. I think he rather likes the idea of the 'King and Queen' looking from Scotland across to England.

Hedgecoe 1968, p.221

122 *King and Queen* 1952-53 LH 350, bronze, height 164cm (64½in). Glenkiln, Dumfriesshire

Can you tell us something about the conception of the 'King and Queen'?

The idea for the 'King and Queen' was conceived by me with no particular setting in mind but with just my general feelings about sculpture in the open air.

The first cast of the sculpture was purchased by the city of Antwerp and placed in the outdoor sculpture museum at Middelheim Park. A year or so later Mr. Keswick decided to buy the final cast of it for his estate at Glenkiln.

Were the figures modelled in clay over armature?

No. The figures were built up directly in plaster.

Is the rock base natural, or was it partly or wholly built?

There is a natural outcrop of rock. The site is a natural bump on the high ground with outcrop of rock and grass, which is now mown short by sheep and rabbits grazing. The actual base is partly built of large stones from nearby, in order to make a level platform for the 'King and Queen'.

Who selected the site? You, Mr. Keswick, or the two of you together?

W. J. Keswick, inspired by Henry Moore, selected the site.

How long did it take to select the site once the idea of sculpture had come up?

The 'King and Queen' was tried in two other sites before coming to rest in the present one. This process took at least nine months. Mr. Keswick spends most of his time at Glenkiln, when not shooting, selecting sites for sculpture on the property.

Are there more sculptures on the estate than the two you sent?

Sculptures on the estate are:
>   'Standing Figure', by Henry Moore [fig.112]
>   'King and Queen', by Henry Moore
>   'The Visitation', by Epstein
>   'Madame Renoir', by Renoir

There are other smaller works, including a small Rodin.

Are there plans for more sculpture?

Nothing is planned. But, as and if Mr. Keswick has the means (which he is very doubtful) he hopes to go on with the idea of creating a large moorland 'gallery' for sculpture in 3,000 acres of ground.

Can the two pieces of sculpture done by you be seen from each other?

No, they are not visible one from the other.

How far apart are they?

They are far apart. Not in sight of each other. Half a mile apart – or more. They possess their environment. The whole point is that they should not appear as a jumbled collection.

Is the 'King and Queen' visible from some room of the owner's house?

The figures are not visible from any room of the owner's house. They are placed up on wild moorland and are quite alone. Possibly too much alone.

How much walking distance between first seeing the 'King and Queen' and reaching them?

From half a mile to one mile distance walking across the hill or along the hill roads – ten minutes or so, walking time.

Do they look in the direction of a specific object, house, hill, or lake?

They look out on the hills and over Glenkiln Loch. The 'King and Queen' have a magnificent view over the Loch looking out toward England over the border fifty miles away.

In making and placing 'King and Queen', did you consider the changing light and shadows cast by the sun?

Yes. They face south and slightly west.

What is the reason for what from the photographs seems a differentiation of treatment (in terms of naturalism) between the King's hand – particularly noticeable in the rear view – and his face?

Perhaps the 'clue' to the group is the King's head, which is a combination of a crown, beard, and face symbolising a mixture of primitive kingship and a kind of animal, Pan-like quality. The King is more relaxed and assured in pose than the Queen, who is more upright and consciously queenly. When I came to do the hands and feet of the figures they gave me the chance to express my ideas further by making them more realistic – to bring out the contrast between human grace and the concept of power in primitive kingship.

Art and Artists, University of California Press, Berkeley and Los Angeles 1956,
pp.104-7

It was a big subject, *The King and Queen*. When I was working on them, I was reminded of an Egyptian sculpture in the British Museum that I had seen many times of a seated figure of an official and his wife [fig.35]. But somehow the sculptor had raised them above this status and had given them greater dignity and self-assurance, almost a nobility of purpose to make them appear above normal life. I've tried to infect some of this feeling into my sculpture.

Hedgecoe 1986, p.156

Hand Relief No.1 1952

Much Hadham, Herts.

You are quite right in thinking it is the study for the hands on a larger work, actually of the KING AND QUEEN, 1952/53 [fig.122].

When I was making the large version of the KING AND QUEEN, and getting to working on the hands in detail, I got a little stuck with them, and contrary to any previous practice, I felt I needed to have a model of a real hand. And so I asked my wife to come into the studio and hold her hand in the position I required, – she posed for about a quarter of an hour and then said she couldn't stay any longer as the lunch she was cooking needed her attention. I then asked Mary, my daughter who was six years old, to come and hold her hand in the position I wanted, and in this way I was helped in completing the hands of the full-size sculpture.[22]

But the idea came to me of putting the two hands together in a relief composition, and this is how the plaque came about.

From a letter to Allan D. Emile, 21 October 1966

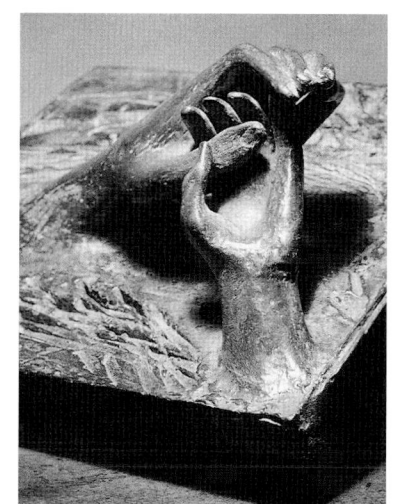

123 Detail of *Hand Relief No.1* 1952 LH 354, bronze (cast 1956), height 34.5cm (13½in)

Warrior with Shield 1953-54

The idea for *The Warrior* came to me at the end of 1952 or very early in 1953. It was evolved from a pebble I found on the seashore in the summer of 1952, and which reminded me of the stump of a leg, amputated at the hip.[23] Just as Leonardo says somewhere in his notebooks that a painter can find a battle scene in the lichen marks on a wall, so this gave me the start of *The Warrior* idea. First I added the body, leg and one arm and it became a

[22] Tam Miller, Moore's secretary from 1950 to 1956, also recalls standing in Moore's studio for two hours at a time with her hands on a little platform at elbow height.
[23] Moore sometimes gave conflicting sources for the evolution of sculptural ideas. See extract below, and the first two extracts on *Locking Piece*, p.291.

wounded warrior, but at first the figure was reclining. A day or two later I added a shield and altered its position and arrangement into a seated figure and so it changed from an inactive pose into a figure which, though wounded, is still defiant.

The head has a blunted and bull-like power but also a sort of dumb animal acceptance and forbearance of pain.

The figure may be emotionally connected (as one critic has suggested) with one's feelings and thoughts about England during the crucial and early part of the last war. The position of the shield and its angle gives protection from above. The distance of the shield from the body and the rectangular shape of the space enclosed between the inside surface of the shield and the concave front of the body is important.

Except for a short period when I did coal-mining drawings as a war artist, nearly all my figure sculpture and drawings, since being a student, has been of the female, except for the Family Groups, but there the man was part of the group.

This sculpture is the first single and separate male figure that I have done in sculpture and carrying it out in its final large scale was almost like the discovery of a new subject matter; the bony, edgy, tense forms were a great excitement to make.

Like the bronze *Draped Reclining Figure* of 1952-3 [fig.121] I think *The Warrior* has some Greek influence, not consciously wished for but perhaps the result of my visit to Athens and other parts of Greece in 1951.

Letter of 15 January 1955; quoted in James 1966, p.250

124 *Warrior with Shield* 1953-54 LH 360, bronze, height 152.5cm (60in)

The 'Warrior with Shield' began when I found a small stone in the garden which reminded me of the stump of an amputated leg. I added to the pelvis, then made the chest, and gradually it grew from the stump into the whole figure. I became very involved in it, as of course I do in everything. But this was different. My excitement was due to the fact that, apart from being concerned with the male figure in my coal-mining drawings, this was the first single male figure I had done in sculpture since my student days. In working on the 'Warrior with Shield', all the knowledge gained from the life drawing and modelling I had done years before came back to me with great pleasure.

Hedgecoe 1968, p.236

I would explain its [meaning] … being able to withstand aggression, being able to put up with the blows of fate … It still is a strong and masculine and powerful type. It's like the bull that is being attacked and yet will put up a spirited resistance and fight.

James 1975

Upright Motives 1955-56

In 1955 I was asked to consider making a sculpture for the courtyard of a new building [Olivetti] in Milan.

I visited the site and a lone lombardy poplar growing behind the building convinced me that a vertical work would act as the correct counterfoil to the horizontal rhythm of the building. This idea grew ultimately into the 'Upright Motives'.

Back home in England I began the series of maquettes. – I started by balancing different forms one above the other, – with results rather like the North-West American totem poles, – but as I continued the attempt gained more unity, also perhaps became more organic, – and then one in particular (later to be named 'Glenkiln Cross'), took on the shape of a crucifix, – a kind of worn-down body and a cross merged into one.

When I came to carry out some of these maquettes in their final full size, three of them grouped themselves together, and in my mind, assumed the aspect of a crucifixion scene as though framed against the sky above Golgotha. – (But I do not especially expect others to find this symbolism in the group.) In its great periods sculpture has been an outdoor art, an art of the open-air, and not an art only for drawing-rooms and museums. And I am very happy that this group is placed here at Otterlo to be seen in relation to landscape and silhouetted against the Dutch sky, – that sky whose vastness Rembrandt evoked even in his slightest landscape sketch.

Henry Moore: Drie Staande Motievan, Rijksmuseum Kröller-Müller, Otterlo 1965 (n.p.)

125 *Upright Motives Nos. 7, 1* and *2* 1955-56 LH 386, 377, 379, bronze. *Glenkiln Cross* in the centre, 335.5cm (11ft), is the tallest of the three. In situ at the Kröller-Müller Museum, Otterlo

One of the upright motifs, without my knowing why, turned into a cross-form and is now in Scotland. We call it 'The Glenkiln Cross', because the Glenkiln Farm Estate is where the first cast of it is placed. From a distance it looks rather like one of the old Celtic crosses.

Hedgecoe 1968, p.245

The top part definitely is in the form of a cross and it is like a figure but not complete arms but it is like a worn down cross. The body part is only half way down and the lower part is the column and on it are some little bits of drawing which don't matter sculpturally, which represent a ladder and a few other things connecting it with the crucifixion.

And I just let my fancy run in the lower part in making a little literary connection between this and the crucifix.[24]

James 1975

I often work in threes when relating things. Take the symbolic cross motif. I realised that, wherever it was placed with others, it had to be in the middle. When placed between two others, the three became a crucifixion group. The three of them are together as a group outside the Kröller-Müller Museum in Holland, and then there's another group of three in America, outside

[24] Moore didn't exactly let his fancy run free. The 'little bits of drawing' on the front of the column is indeed an apt description, for this was based on a sketch of an as yet unidentified oceanic object from New Ireland, which appears in the drawing *Ideas for Sculpture c.*1935 HMF 1236. The late William Fagg suggested to the author that the object which Moore copied may have been a *kepong* (head), or part of a panel from a Malanggan house.

the Amon Carter Museum in Fort Worth. However, in Scotland I think the single cross is probably better placed: seen from across the moor your attention is drawn towards it as if X marks the spot. From a distance a cross form stands out so much more than any other form.

Hedgecoe 1968, p.250

Unesco Reclining Figure 1957-58

126 *Unesco Reclining Figure* 1957-58 LH 416, Roman travertine marble, length 508cm (16ft 6½in). Unesco Building, Paris

EDOUARD RODITI: [...] But the London press has in recent weeks quoted or misquoted you very widely and stated that, before starting work on your Unesco assignment, you spent three or four months meditating the meaning of Unesco. [...]

HENRY MOORE: The press has very much exaggerated this aspect of my approach to the Unesco assignment. My friend Julian Huxley, the first Director General of Unesco, told me what he considered to be the purpose and meaning of Unesco, and this was, of course, a help to me in first formulating my thoughts on the subject.

RODITI: To me, it all sounds like a nineteenth-century assignment to design an allegorical group to be set above the main entrance of the building. I mean something like: 'The United Nations co-ordinating the efforts of Education, Science and Culture and guiding Mankind in its search for Peace.' I'm quite surprised that you didn't finally plump for a draped figure with a lantern held high, at arm's length, above its head.

MOORE: Eventually, after discarding many preliminary studies I decided on a reclining figure that seeks to tell no story at all. I wanted to avoid any kind of allegorical interpretation that is now trite. This particular reclining figure has perhaps turned out to be one of those that Sir Philip Hendy[25] has called 'wild ones'.

RODITI: How would you define your 'wild ones'?

MOORE: Well, they are sculptures which are inspired by general considerations of nature, but which are less dominated by representational considerations, and in which I use forms and their relationships quite freely.

RODITI: Your 'wild ones' are in a way what Goethe might have called your more 'dionysiac' sculptures.

Roditi 1960, p.181

[...] when I worked out the details, I realised the job was too big to do here, and so I went to Italy with the plaster model and worked there. The finished piece consists of four blocks of Roman travertine, excluding the pedestal base, of course. It is over sixteen feet long and weighs thirty-nine tons, but the original blocks weighed something like sixty tons before I went to work

---

[25] Hendy (1900-80) was director of the City Art Gallery and Temple Newsam, Leeds, 1934-45, and of the National Gallery, London, 1946-67. In 1941 he organised an exhibition of the work of Moore, Piper and Sutherland at Temple Newsam, the Tudor–Jacobean house presented to the Leeds City Art Gallery in 1922. The same year Hendy acquired for £220 the 1929 Hornton stone *Reclining Figure* LH 59 for Leeds. He and his wife Cicely became close friends of the Moores.

on them. That size and weight, of course, would have made it impossible to have done the carving here in my studio. Transport expenses alone would have been enormous, and I wouldn't have been able to handle such weights. I produced the full-size stone sculpture at Messrs Henraux's stone and marble works at Querceta, a small village at the foot of the Carrara Mountains, about a mile from Forte dei Marmi. The stone was quarried near Rome, but Messrs Henraux brought it from the quarries to their works at Querceta for me. There they have a large overhead crane, which simplified everything. But it took me nearly a year, with the help of two of Messrs Henraux's stone-carvers.

Unesco originally asked me for a bronze. I did some drawings with that in mind, but as I thought about it, I realised that since bronze goes dark out-doors, and the sculpture would have as its background a building that is mostly glass, which looks black, the fenestration would have been too much the same tone, and you would have lost the sculpture. So then I worked on the idea of siting the figure against a background of its own, but then, inside the building you wouldn't have had a view of the sculpture. Half the views would have been lost. So I finally decided the only solution was to use a light-coloured stone, and I settled on the same stone they've used for the top of the building: travertine. It's a beautiful stone. I'd always wanted to do a large piece in it. At the unveiling it looked too white – all newly carved stone has a white dust on it – but on my last trip to Paris, I went to Unesco, and I saw that it's weathering nicely. In ten or twenty years' time, with the washing of the Paris rain, it will be fine. Half of Rome is built of travertine.

Of course, it was a harder job than it would have been if I'd done it in bronze. When you carve, you're dealing with the absolute final piece. The practical problems are much greater than those you have with a large bronze. If I'd done it in bronze, the original would have been in plaster, and hollow. I'd have cut it up and shipped it off to the bronze founder, and the practical problems would have been his.

Lake 1962, pp.42-3

Two- and Three-Piece Reclining Figures 1959-63

'The *Two-Piece Reclining Figures* must have been working around in the back of my mind for years, really. As long ago as 1934 I had done a number of smaller pieces composed of separate forms, two- and three-piece carvings in ironstone, ebony, alabaster, and other materials. They were all more abstract than these. I don't think it was a conscious or intentional thing for me to break up the figures in this way, but I suppose those earlier works, from the thirties, had something to do with it. I didn't do any preliminary drawings for these. I wish now I had. One of them goes off to the Kröller-Müller Museum, and they've asked me if I have some preliminary drawings.

'I did the high one first [fig.127], then the more definitely reclining one [fig.129]. There's a third one [LH 478], even larger, that's just gone off to the foundry. I did the first one in two pieces almost without intending to. But after I'd done it, then the second one became a conscious idea. I realised what an advantage a separated two-piece composition could have in relating figures to landscape.' He walked over to *Reclining Figure No. II*, put his hands on the knees and the breasts. 'Knees and breasts are mountains,' he said. 'Once these two parts become separated, you don't expect it to be a naturalistic figure; therefore, you can more justifiably make it like a landscape or a rock. If it is a single figure, you can guess what it's going to be like. If it is in two pieces, there's a bigger surprise, you have more unexpected views; therefore, the special advantage of sculpture over painting – of having the possibility of many different views – is more fully exploited.'

127 *Two Piece Reclining Figure No.1* 1959
LH 457, bronze, length 193cm (76in).
Glenkiln, Dumfriesshire

Moore moved over to *Reclining Figure No. I*. He turned it slowly on its movable base. 'The front view doesn't enable one to foresee the back view. As you move around it, the two parts overlap or they open up and there's space between. Sculpture is like a journey. You have a different view as you return. The three-dimensional world is full of surprises in a way that a two-dimensional world never could be.'

Ibid., p.44

'The *Upright External/Internal Form* I did in 1952 and 1953 [LH 296] was a transitional stage from those early smaller pieces to these *Two-Piece Reclining Figures*, it seems to me in retrospect. I may do some that split into more than two parts. They are still one unit, not two or three separate figures. You'll note that *Number Two* is bolted in place on its pedestal. *Number One* isn't. But if somebody moved one of those parts one inch, straightaway I'd know.' Moore extended his arm into the open area between the two parts of the figure, then into its concavities. 'The space would be different, the angles through here, there. All the relationships would be changed.'

Ibid.

128 Georges Seurat, *Le Bec du Hoc,
Grandcamp* 1885, oil on canvas,
680 x 850mm (26 x 32½in). Tate, London

In doing these Reclining Figure sculptures (No.1 in 1959 and No.2 in 1960) it came naturally and without any conscious decision that I made them in two separate pieces, the head-and-body end, and the leg-end. In both sculptures I realised that I was simplifying the essential elements of my reclining figure theme. In many of my reclining figures the head-and-neck part of the sculpture, sometimes the torso part too, is upright, giving contrast to the horizontal direction of the whole sculpture. Also in my reclining figures I have often made a sort of looming leg – the top leg in the sculpture projecting over the lower leg, which gives a sense of thrust and power, as a large branch of a tree might move outwards from the main trunk, or as a seaside cliff might overhang from below, if you are on the beach. […]

129 *Two Piece Reclining Figure No.2* 1960
LH 458, bronze, length 259cm (8ft 6in)

In that sense I think these sculptures are more fully in the round than any previous work of mine. Being in two pieces the work separates itself from seeming to be *only* a representation of a reclining figure.

Both these sculptures are a mixture, an amalgamation of the human body with rock-forms and with landscape, and so like a metaphor in poetry giving to each element a new aspect, and perhaps a new meaning.

Mary Chamot, Dennis Farr and Martin Butlin, *Tate Gallery Catalogues: The Modern British Paintings, Drawings and Sculpture*, Volume II, Oldbourne Press, London 1964, p.459

While I was making it, my *Two Piece Reclining Figure* [fig.127] recalled for me Adel Rock and the *Rock at Etratat* by Seurat [fig.128].[26] This particular sculpture is a mixture of the human figure and landscape, a metaphor of the relationship of humanity with the earth, just as a poem can be.

Hedgecoe 1986, p.113

You know how sometimes in a museum they will reconstruct an animal, and they put a piece of knee, and then they will leave a blank with just a bit of armature, and then they put the foot. Now, the distance that they make the knee from the foot is terribly important. I mean if you took the foot and stuck it on to the knee, and didn't leave a space for the calf, you wouldn't have the proper relationship. Now the same thing applies in these two-piece and three-piece sculptures. The space between those pieces is just as important, and if somebody put them together in the wrong way it would be for me as wrong as if somebody put a knee and a foot too close together.

Carroll 1973, pp.49-50

DAVID SYLVESTER: Some of the things, then, have begun from pebbles and bones, and so on, but some haven't. Among the series of multiple-piece reclining figures, are there particular ones in which you did use such objects?
HENRY MOORE: In the first of the three-piece sculptures [LH 500], which is going to be shown soon, the middle piece, which was the pace-maker for

---

[26] Moore is referring to Seurat's *Le Bec du Hoc*, which he often saw when the painting was owned by Kenneth Clark.

it, was a vertebra of an animal that I found in the garden. And the connection of one piece through to the other is the kind of connection that a backbone will have with one section through to the next section. That's the only example I can immediately think of.

SYLVESTER: How did you come by the idea of the three-piece sculpture as distinct from the two-piece sculptures?

MOORE: The two-piece sculptures pose a problem of relationship: the kind of relationship between two people. It's very different once you divide a thing into three. In the two-piece you have just the head end and the body end, or the head end and the leg end, but once you get the three-piece you have the middle and the two ends; and this became something that I wanted to do. I tried several ideas before this one, and what led me to this solution was finding a little piece of bone that was the middle of a vertebra, and I realised then that perhaps the connection was through one piece to another – one could have gone on and made a four- or five-piece, like a snake carrying through with its vertebrae. In a way, the more pieces you make, the bigger the divisions are becoming, the easier it is: if you made a figure of ten pieces, then this dividing up would become a formula; it would become an accepted thing and if you had a head and shoulder, pelvis, two thighs, legs, two feet, you can place all those and you make it up into one figure.

Sylvester 1963, p.306

Standing Figure: Knife Edge 1961

This sculpture has been called *Standing Figure – Knife-Edge* also *Standing Figure – Bone* and again, *Winged Figure*. All three titles have some relevance to what it is, and how it came about.

Since my student days I have liked the shape of bones, and have drawn them, studied them in the Natural History Museum, found them on seashores and saved them out of the stewpot.

There are many structural, and sculptural principles to be learnt from bones, e.g. that in spite of their lightness they have great strength. Some bones, such as the breast bones of birds, have the lightweight fineness of a knife-blade. Finding such a bone led to me using this knife-edge thinness in 1961 in a sculpture *Seated Woman* (thin neck) [LH 472]. In this figure the thin neck and head, by contrast with the width and bulk of the body, give more monumentality to the work. Later in 1961 I used this knife-edged thinness throughout a whole figure, and produced this *Standing Figure*.

Sculpture has some disadvantages compared with painting, but it can have one great advantage over painting – that it can be looked at from all round; and if this attitude is used and fully exploited then it can give to sculpture a continual, changing, never-ending surprise and interest.

In walking round this sculpture the width and flatness from the front gradually change through the three-quarter views into the thin sharp edges of the side views, and then back again to the width seen from the back.

130 *Standing Figure: Knife Edge* 1961 LH 482, bronze, height 284.5cm (9ft 4in)

And the top half of the figure bends backwards, is angled towards the sky, opens itself to the light in a rising upward movement – and this may be why, at one time, I called it *Winged Figure*.

In a sculptor's work all sorts of past experiences and influences are fused and used – and somewhere in this work there is a connection with the so-called *Victory of Samothrace* in the Louvre – and I would like to think that others see something Greek in this *Standing Figure*.

Statement 1965; quoted in James 1966, p.278

Locking Piece 1963-64

The germ of the idea originated from a sawn fragment of bone with a socket and joint which was found in the garden. Given this theme, I made the complete sculpture.

Hedgecoe 1968, p.456

131 *Locking Piece* 1963-64 LH 515, bronze, height 293.5cm (9ft 7in). Tate, London

At one time I was playing with a couple of pebbles that I'd picked up, because behind my far field is a gravel pit and there are thousands of shapes and forms and one only has to go out there and I can find twenty new little ideas if I wish, immediately. Anyhow, I was playing with two pebbles which I found like that and somehow or other they got locked together and I couldn't get them undone and I wondered how they got into that position and it was like a clenched fist being tightly … Anyhow, eventually I did get it to [separate]; by turning and lifting, one piece came off the other. This gave one the idea of making two forms which would do that and later I called it 'Locking Piece' because they lock together.

In conversation with Alan Wilkinson, *c*.1980

When I made it, I was reminded of puzzles I played with as a child in which there were pieces that fitted together but were more difficult to take apart. To make two parts fit you had to put them together in a certain way and then turn them so they would lock.

Finn 1976, p.220

'Locking Piece' is certainly the largest and perhaps the most successful of my 'fitting-together' sculptures. In fact the two pieces interlock in such a way that they can only be separated if the top piece is lifted and turned at the same time.

Hedgecoe 1968, p.455

Knife Edge Two Piece 1962-65

'Sculpture (Knife-Edge Two Piece)' [LH 504] was finished in the summer of 1962. It has some connection with the figure I did the previous year, 1961, called 'Standing Figure (Knife Edge)' [fig.130] which was influenced by the study of bone forms. It has also some connection with the two-piece

132 *Knife Edge Two Piece* 1962-65 LH 516, bronze, length 366cm (12ft) outside the Houses of Parliament, London

sculptures I have been doing since 1959, where the problem of dividing the Reclining Figure into two, and later three pieces, occupied me.

Mary Chamot, Dennis Farr and Martin Butlin, *Tate Gallery Catalogues: The Modern British Paintings, Drawings and Sculpture*, Volume II, Oldbourne Press, London 1964, pp.459-60

When I was offered the site near the House of Lords for the 'Two-Piece Knife Edge' sculpture [fig.132], I liked the place so much that I didn't bother to go and see an alternative site in Hyde Park. I remembered as a young student, a sculpture called 'Rima' by Epstein,[27] a memorial to the poet W.H. Hudson. At the time this work caused a tremendous fuss. I demonstrated with a crowd of students against the general Philistine public, who hated it. It was tarred and feathered and goodness knows what. Six years ago I couldn't find it when I wanted to show it to a foreigner, which proves how easily one lonely sculpture can be lost in a large park. The House of Lords site is quite different. It is next to a path where people walk and it has a few seats where they can sit and contemplate it, unlike the placing of the very fine equestrian statue of Charles the First, in Trafalgar Square, which, in order to look at closely and appreciate in detail, you have to risk your life in crossing a maze of traffic.

Ibid., p.481

Nuclear Energy 1964-66

'Nuclear Energy', originally 'Atom Piece'. The title was changed because it was felt that some people might think that the word 'piece' meant peace.

Hedgecoe 1968, p.474

[27] *Memorial to W.H. Hudson (Rima)* 1923-25, Portland stone (Hyde Park, London).

It's a rather strange thing really, but I'd already done the idea for this sculpture before Professor McNeill[28] and his colleagues from the University of Chicago came to see me on Sunday morning to tell me about the whole proposition. They told me (which I'd only vaguely known) that [Enrico] Fermi, the Italian nuclear physicist, started, or really made the first successful controlled nuclear fission in a temporary building. I think it was a squash court – a wooden building – which from the outside looked entirely unlike where a thing of such an important nature might take place. But this experiment was carried on in secret and it meant that by being successful Man was able to control this huge force for peaceful purposes as well as destructive purposes. They came to me to tell me that they thought where such an important event in history took place ought to be marked and they wondered whether I would do a sculpture which would stand on the spot. Behind it later was going to be a building for the university, I think a library.

As they told me the story and the situation, I gradually remembered that only a fortnight previously, I'd been working in my little maquette studio (because I was trying to think as they told me what form or what shape such an idea brought to my mind) and the story reminded me of a sculpture I'd already done about six inches high which was just a maquette for an idea. I said to them that I thought I had done the idea as far as I would be able to and I showed them the maquette, and I said, 'I'm going to make this sculpture into a working model' because the maquette was only about six inches in height. I said to them, 'Would you wait until I've made this working model which will be about four or five feet in height and then when you see it, we could come to a decision whether it would really be suitable for your purpose?' When I had made this working model I showed it to them and they liked my idea because the top of it is like some large mushroom, or a kind of mushroom cloud. Also it has a kind of head shape like the top of the skull but down below is more an architectural cathedral. One might think of the lower part of it being a protective form and constructed for human beings and the top being more like the idea of the destructive side of the atom. So between the two it might express to people in a symbolic way the whole event.

Often my ideas grow from earlier ones and sometimes one of them refers to an initial idea and makes a variation on it. There is no doubt that this, the nuclear energy piece, has connections with previous sculptures that I've made which were based on skull forms or on dome-like forms with an interior to them. This piece became a combination of these two ideas. How successful or how much this can be conveyed to other people I don't know, it's just my interpretation.

David H. Katzive, 'Henry Moore's Nuclear Energy: The Genesis of a Monument',
Art Journal, New York spring 1973, p.286

133 *Nuclear Energy* 1964-66 LH 526, bronze, height 366cm (12ft)

---

[28] William McNeill was Professor and Chairman of the Department of History at the University of Chicago

The helmets in the medieval armour section of the Wallace Collection in London have always fascinated me. They have a purity of metal and a strength, outwardly; yet within, they convey an enclosedness, a quality of protection. These are the things I want to capture in my own variations on the theme.

Nuclear energy is not unlike this in its implications. It is a splendid force for good, and just as surely a force for evil. As I worked on this piece, I gradually saw the top part of it taking on the aspect of a skull – a death's head.

Summary of Information on the Site of the First Self-Sustaining Controlled Nuclear Chain Reaction,
Commission on Chicago Historical and Architectural Landmarks, Chicago 1971, p.2

Three Way Piece No.2: (The) Archer 1964-65

Over two years Revell[29] visited at least three or four times out here in Much Hadham. When I was doing the working model for the *Archer* [LH 534], he thought it would be absolutely the right configuration for the location on the square that he had in mind. As he was the architect of this building which was not yet completed, I let him tell me what size he thought it should be. Now I think he chose too small a size. I think that the building needed

134 *Three Way Piece No.2: (The) Archer*
1964-65 LH 535, bronze,
height 325cm (10ft 8in)

[29] The Finnish architect Viljo Revell (1910-64) won the international competition for the design of a new city hall and civic square in Toronto. He did not live to see *The Archer* unveiled in Nathan Phillips Square on 27 October 1966; see Wilkinson 1987, pp.3-9, and p.76 above.

something larger. As yet, in my own experience, I have never put a piece of sculpture with architecture where the sculpture has been too big. If there has been a fault, it's always been that the size has been too small. Nothing dwarfs sculpture more than architecture. The only one piece of mine that is absolutely right in relationship to the buildings around it is that at Lincoln Center in New York [see fig.82]. I wouldn't want it bigger, nor would I want it smaller.

Seldis 1973, p.227

But the second cast of the same piece which stands in front of Mies van der Rohe's museum in Berlin is right in size. The sculpture looks much bigger there, because it is not surrounded by tall buildings. You see it is not only set against a rather low building but against the verdant landscape of a park. Its size there is right, which demonstrates that the rightness of the size of a sculpture depends on where it is placed.

Ibid., pp.195-6

How I came to call it 'The Archer' is that the two forms in the middle of the sculpture, not at the top and not at the bottom, in the middle, to me have a kind of stretch in them, and one end is the shape of a bow and this to me at one stage just reminded me of pulling and stretching a bow, and that's why we call it 'The Archer'.

In conversation with Alan Wilkinson, c.1980

The Artist's Hands 1969-77

If one likes drawing hands, as I do, the nearest model is one's own two hands. These drawings were made to study hands generally. Hands, to me, are – after the head and face – the most expressive part of the human figure. Many other painters and sculptors have felt the same. Rembrandt, for example, uses hands to express nearly as much as the head and its features. Hands have always been of interest to me and, as a student, it was a hand I modelled, which helped to win me a scholarship to the Royal College of Art.

Wildenstein 1979, p.10

Hands can convey so much – they can beg or refuse, take or give, be open or clenched, show content or anxiety. They can be young or old, beautiful or deformed....

Throughout the history of sculpture and painting one can find that artists have shown through the hands the feelings they wished to represent. […]

The nearest model is one's own hands. […]

Over the years I have made numerous drawings of my hands in sketchbooks and from some of these studies I decided to make this series of etchings and lithographs.

Henry Moore, The Artist's Hands, Raymond Spencer Company
for the Henry Moore Foundation, 1980

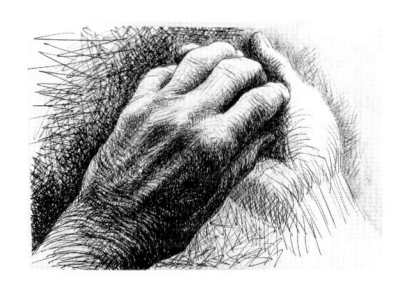

135 *The Artist's Hands,* page 65 verso from Notebook 1969-74 HMF 3215g, ballpoint pen, pencil, 176 x 254mm (6⅞ x 10in). Private collection

295

Elephant Skull Etchings 1969-70

The elephant skull was given to me in 1968 by my old friends Juliette Huxley and her husband, Julian Huxley, the well-known biologist. This skull had been in their garden in Hampstead for many years, but the London atmosphere was damaging it.

Juliette and Julian knew that I was very interested in the forms, shapes, and the structure which bones have in particular. Bones are the inside structure that nature uses for both lightness and strength. Take, for example, the skeleton of a bird – it is very light in weight, but it has to be strong to withstand all the energy and effort and the great strains and pressures of flying.

So in bones you can find the principles which can be very important in sculpture, and which can be used in making one's own sculpture. One does not copy the bones but uses the principles which nature has used to make strong forms out of this form. This is one of the reasons for my abiding interest in natural forms: the possibility of deriving important principles from them.

When Juliette Huxley said, 'Our elephant skull is beginning to deteriorate in London, would you like to have it?', I was delighted, and about a week later the skull arrived at my studio. The skull is three feet high and two feet wide and almost three feet from back to front. It is very monumental, a huge presence and very imposing.

As soon as I saw it I was very thrilled and knew I wanted to draw it. I find that you may think you are observing an object carefully when you stand and look at it, but you really look much more intensely if you try to draw it, because then you have to look very searchingly to understand its shape.

An elephant's skull is especially interesting to draw for it has tremendous varieties of forms, more than the human skull, more than in any other single bone-structure I know.

I did not draw the skull immediately I received it, but just looked at it each time I went into the studio, keeping in my mind the idea that sometime I would draw it to understand it better.

Then came the day when Gérald Cramer arrived; I had arranged to do a set of etchings for him. Cramer has a small gallery in Geneva where he specialises in exhibiting prints, engravings, and small sculptures; through him I had already made some etchings with the help of Jacques Frélaut, the main engraver and master printer of the long famous atelier Lacourière et Frélaut of Paris. This atelier has for years printed etchings and engravings for Picasso, Matisse, Miró and numberless other artists.

The arrangement with me was that instead of going to Paris to do my etchings, Frélaut should come and work with me in my studio here at Much Hadham. This first happened in 1968, when Frélaut came here for two weeks, bringing with him a number of copper plates of various sizes, and already prepared for use. On the first day's work I may make two or three drawings directly on the copper plates, Frélaut then bites these with the etching acid – but as I have not yet got my own printing press, the second day he has to take the plates to London, where he can use the press at the Royal College of Art (where I was once a student and then a teacher). On the second day while Frélaut is in London, I draw on two or three more plates, which will be printed by Frélaut in London on the third day. Collaborating in this way with Frélaut, at the end of a fortnight we may have produced prints of twenty or thirty etchings.

The night before Gérald Cramer came here, I had no clear pictorial ideas for etchings in my mind, for up to that time I had been concentrating on completing a large sculpture. It was my wife who reminded me that I had told her I wanted to make drawings of the elephant skull, and who suggested I should make etchings instead.

When Cramer and Frélaut arrived the next morning, this is what I began doing, drawing the skull directly with an etching needle on the copper plate just as I might have done with pen and pencil on paper.

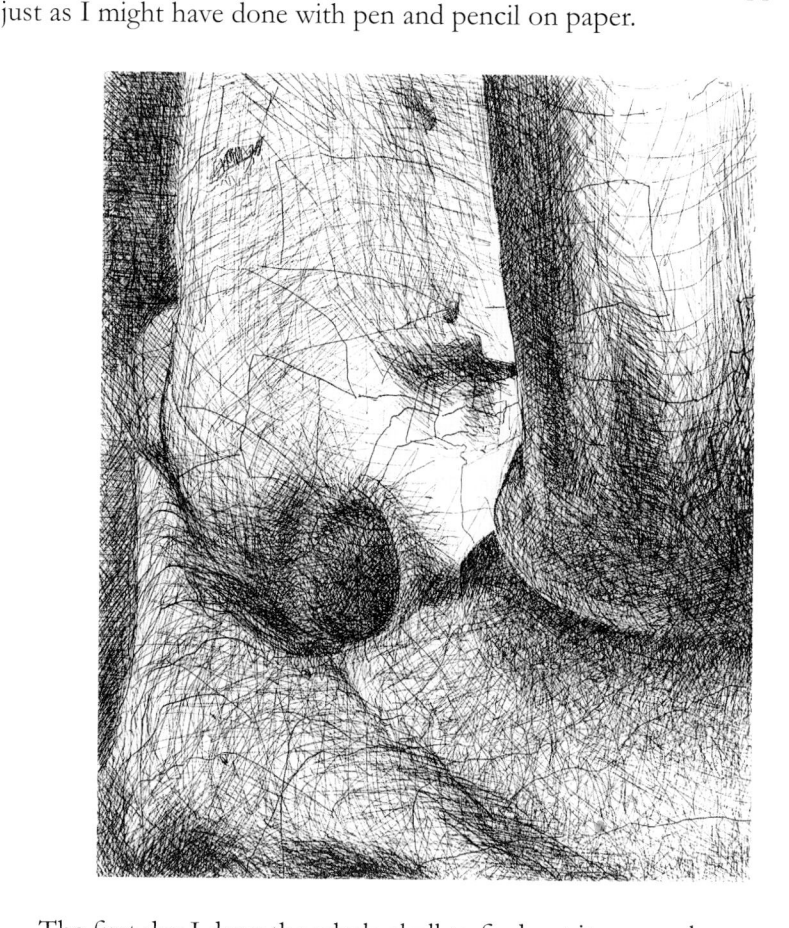

136 *Elephant Skull Plate XXII* 1969 CGM 133, etching, plate size 216 x 235mm (8½ x 9¼in); captioned by Moore 'Doric column and underground dungeons'

The first day I drew the whole skull to find out its general construction; gradually I became amazed at the complexity of it, and my interest and excitement grew greater each day I worked. By bringing the skull very close to me and drawing various details I found so many contrasts of form and shape that I could begin to see in it great deserts and rocky landscapes, big caves in the sides of hills, great pieces of architecture, columns and dungeons, and so this series of etchings is really a mixture of observation and imagination.

Typed statement 1970, HMF archive

Pen Exercises 1970

A Rembrandt pen drawing, looked at upside down, could easily be mistaken for a piece of completely abstract calligraphy. My 'Pen exercises' came out of my admiration for the drawings of Rembrandt – one of the greatest draughtsmen ever.[30] One can see in Rembrandt's drawings the pleasure he got out of just using pen and ink. He will give to a head and hand intense meaning and expression, but if you cover up the head and hand, then other parts of the drawing may appear as calligraphic flourishes.

So in the 'Pen exercises', I was finding expressive pleasure in the free use of pen and ink. The drawings began in that way, and some of them I later turned into figures or landscape, and one of them into a horse.

Wildenstein 1979, p.56

137 *Storm at Sea* 1970 HMF 3272, pen and ink, gouache, 175 x 254mm (6⅞ x 10in). The Henry Moore Foundation: gift of the artist 1977

Landscape Drawings 1970-79

From youth I have often drawn directly from landscape. But now I am often content just to look at and enjoy it.

Many of the landscape drawings I make now are not done through direct observation but are evidence of my general liking for landscape.

In fact, I can find a landscape in blots or random marks on paper, and my technique of drawing on blotting paper could be compared with the blot drawings of Alexander Cozens who made splashes of ink on paper and turned them into landscapes. The drawings of rock forms are connected with the great impression Stonehenge made on me, and even that first big outcrop of rock my father took me to see, as a boy, at Adel in Yorkshire.

All large forms, all rocks in landscape, have a primitive appeal. For example, people have always given names to isolated rocks, standing out at sea. In my drawings of landscape, a human scale is sometimes given by the presence of a temple, church steeple or similar object.

Ibid., p.22

138 *Arch Rock* 1979 HMF 79(46), charcoal, wax crayon and watercolour wash, 143 x 246mm (5⅝ x 9⅝in). The Henry Moore Foundation: acquired 1987

Stonehenge Lithographs 1972-73

The Stonehenge series of drawings and lithographs and the Auden illustrations were done only a few months apart. The Stonehenge drawings gave me a taste for using deep blacks and increased my feeling for the medium of lithography. [...]

The Elephant Skull series are etchings; the Stonehenge and the Auden series are lithographs. Of the two mediums I prefer etching. Technically and

---

[30] *Storm at Sea* (fig.137) is an adaptation of Rembrandt's pen drawing *Christ in the Storm on the Sea of Galilee* c.1654-55 (Kupferstichkabinett, Dresden).

physically I like using the fine point of an etching needle on metal rather more than soft chalk on stone. I began the Stonehenge series with etching in mind, but as I looked at, and drew, and thought about Stonehenge, I found that what interested me most was not its history, nor its original purpose – whether chronological or religious – or even its architectural arrangement, but its present-day appearance. I was above all excited by the monumental power and stoniness of the massive man-worked blocks and by the effect of time on them. Some 4000 years of weathering has produced an extraordinary variety of interesting textures; but to express these with an etching needle was very laborious, and after making two or three etchings I changed to lithography which I found more in sympathy with the subject – lithography, after all, is drawing on stone.

Auden Poems, Moore Lithographs 1974 (n.p.)

139 *Stonehenge IV* 1973 CGM 211, lithograph, 289 x 435mm (11⅜ x 17⅛in); captioned by Moore 'Inside the Circle'

In two or three lithographs I've tried to remember this moonlight effect. In those days, like many other things now spoiled by crowds, I don't remember anyone else being there, in the evening, or in the daytime.

Since that first visit to Stonehenge,[31] I must have been there again twenty or thirty times. Mary was for five years or more a boarder at Cranborne Chase School, and twice every term we drove to Crichel. On these occasions we stayed the night in Salisbury, and many times we went to look at Stonehenge. Quite often I took photographs, and now and then made little sketches.

Henry Moore: Stonehenge, introduction by Stephen Spender,
Ganymed Original Editions, London 1974 (n.p.)

140 Irina at Stonehenge, early 1960s

[31] See p.49.

Sheep Sketchbook 1972

My drawings of sheep began during the preparations in my studios for the big exhibition in Florence in 1972. The shippers and packers were all around, making such a disturbance that it was impossible to work, and I retired into a small studio which faces the field that I let to a local farmer for sheep grazing. I sat in this little studio making small plaster models or maquettes – I work differently now from the way I did as a young sculptor, and I now make maquettes in the round which I can imagine any size I like, but which I can hold in my hand and look at from any point of view.

I have always liked sheep, and there is one big sculpture of mine that I call *Sheep Piece* [LH 627] because I placed it in a field and the sheep enjoyed it and the lambs played around it. Sheep are just the right size for the kind of landscape setting that I like for my sculptures: a horse or a cow would reduce the sense of monumentality. Perhaps the sheep belong also to the landscape of my boyhood in Yorkshire. If the farmer didn't keep his sheep here, I would own some myself, just for the pleasure they give me.

These sheep often wandered up close to the window of the little studio I was working in. I began to be fascinated by them, and to draw them. At first I saw them as rather shapeless balls of wool with a head and four legs. Then I began to realise that underneath all that wool was a body, which moved in its own way, and that each sheep had its individual character. If I tapped on the window the sheep would stop and look, with that sheepish stare of curiosity. They would stand like that for up to five minutes, and I could get them to hold the same pose for longer by just tapping again on the window. It wouldn't last as long the second time, but altogether the sheep posed as well as a life model in an art school. Later I started to add settings, trying to make a pictorial arrangement. As I began to understand more about sheep, I could sometimes do further drawings in the evening from memory, or make a more finished drawing out of a rough sketch.[32]

The packing for Italy took about three weeks, so the first twenty or thirty pages were probably done then; but I went on drawing, because the lambing season had begun, and there in front of me was the mother-and-child theme. This is one of the favourite themes in my work: the large form related to the small form and protecting it, or the complete dependence of the small form on the large form. I tried to express the way the lambs suckled with real energy and violence. There is something biblical about sheep. You don't hear of horses and cows in the Bible in the same way; you hear of sheep and shepherds.

The technique is pen drawing, done with a ballpoint. There's no real difference between using a ballpoint and another kind of pen; the important thing is that you can make a blacker line by pressing harder. Later, in turning the pages of the sketchbook, I might want to emphasise certain points, and to do this I used a black felt pen. On some pages I used a grey watercolour wash to give a softer sense of distance. When I add colour – as I did

[32] Many of the sheep drawings were in fact based on photographs.

141 *Sheep: Back View* 1972 HMF 3343, ballpoint pen, wash, 210 x 251mm (8¼ x 9⅞in). Collection Fondation Veranneman, Kruishoutem

in several of these drawings – I may do it for some effect of drawing rather than for an explanation of the subject.

The large back view of a sheep on page 27 [fig.141] was meant to be the end of the sketchbook – like the end of a Charlie Chaplin film, where he turns his back and walks off. But I was still enjoying my sheep drawing, and so I went on with it. Later, when I came back from the Florence exhibition, and from carving in Italy through the summer, I found that the sheep had been shorn. They looked pathetically forlorn, naked, skinny, but shearing revealed the shape underneath the wool. I didn't like them as much when they were shorn. They must feel miserable; they certainly look it. So after a few more drawings of them in their shorn state, other interests took my attention, and the sketchbook ends.

Henry Moore's Sheep Sketchbook, comments by Henry Moore and Kenneth Clark, Thames and Hudson, London 1980 (n.p.)

Sheep Etchings 1972 and 1974

After the drawings came the etchings, where I found that I could get a finer and more sensitive line with the etching needle than had been possible with the pen I used in the drawing. Plate number I [CGM 226] is a general view looking at the sheep and the lambs in the landscape. Then there are the individual sheep suckling the lambs, numbers II, III, IV [CGM 196, 197, 199]. One can see the kind of thrust the lamb makes to extract the milk, there's a sort of violent little animal push. In number IV the head of the lamb is com-

142 *Sheep with Lamb I* 1972 CGM 196, etching and drypoint, 149 x 206mm (5⅞ x 8⅛in)

pletely hidden, there is a continuous enclosed form, almost the same as in some of my sculpture ideas, with the large form protecting the small, a kind of interior/exterior. In number V [CGM 227] there are the lambs at a different age, growing up and gradually getting fatter and fatter, because they just eat and eat. They're even a little further developed in number VI [CGM 201], the wool, the fleece, is getting softer and heavier, and I was also trying to show a little bit of change in the landscape, with the trees in the background. Number VII [CGM 228] is one of the sheep with the kind of look you get by tapping on the window – in a close-up you can see it just looking … sheepish. Then there comes a time when the wool is getting so luscious and so completely like a garment it's as though the sheep is wearing a fur coat: number VIII [CGM 229]. Later the wool becomes even thicker, almost like a ruff round the neck, it looks as if it could easily be taken off like a coat: number IX [CGM 230]. I was often fascinated by their back view and how in this particular sheep, number X [CGM 200], the foot gave a little twist as it was walking – this was the point I was trying to bring out. In number XI [CGM 231] they are with their coats off and looking more like goats. I wanted to connect the last etching with the early ones and so we have a lamb with fleece being suckled by its nude mother: number XII [CGM 232].

As well as these twelve etchings I made another two, one of which is a different version of a sheep and lamb [CGM 198] and the other a group of sheep I call 'Family' [CGM 233]. These we decided to use for the deluxe albums. Later, when we came to plan the deluxe edition it seemed to me a good idea to include the two etchings that I had drawn for the front and back of the cover [CGM 234, 235]. On the reverse were two sheep, without a background. For this I made another plate in etching and aquatint which came to be a snowscene with the two sheep walking across a field. On the front were a group of sheep in a landscape but also the lettering of the title. For this I made an aquatint background on a second plate. This was printed with the first plate after the lettering had been removed when the printing of the covers was finished. These two etchings together with the two smaller ones have now been printed on Japan paper and used only for the deluxe edition of this album [CGM 225].

Apart from liking the sheep I love drawing as an activity, trying to get and express sculptural ideas, but I love drawing from life which is a way of studying natural forms, just looking at something and trying to draw it, because I find that if you draw something you look much more intensely than if you just look without drawing. This is an absolute fact. You may look at a sight every morning, you may look out of your bedroom window every morning and see the sight of the village green or whatever you look out on to, but if you have not tried to draw it and you are asked what is there, I am sure you would not be able to say. But if you had been interested in drawing that scene, you would know it very much better.

People may think it's funny that someone like Henry Moore should draw sheep, as though it's unnatural to look, as though it's unnatural to want to draw from nature, as though one should become what you may call a sculptor of forms that are half invented, as though you shut your eyes to nature. It's a silly attitude; I see no difference, it's just two points of view in your attitude to form; one you draw directly from nature, the other you use your sum total of information and repertoire from nature. You are imagining or evolving a sculptural idea, but the two are not contrary activities; not to me.

Henry Moore, *Sheep*, Gérald Cramer, Geneva 1975

143 *Lullaby* 1973 CGM 271, lithograph, 289 x 305mm (11³⁄₈ x 12in)

Auden Poems, Moore Lithographs 1973

When Véra Lindsay[33] suggested that I should illustrate a selection of Auden poems I was at once interested in the idea, because I had known him ever since the 1930s and had always greatly admired him and his poetry; but it was some months before I felt I could really get going. I began with the most obvious poem – *Lullaby*, to me a very touching and beautiful one – in a straightforward way as if I were illustrating *Alice in Wonderland* or any other story. But after reading some of the other poems I realised that it would be impossible to treat them in the same way and I began to wonder what other ways there were of approaching the problem.

[33] In 1961 Véra Lindsay and her then husband John Russell, the art critic of *The Sunday Times*, had two interviews with Moore published in *The Sunday Times* on 17 and 24 December; a number of extracts from these interviews appear in this book. Lindsay had known the poet W.H. Auden since the 1930s, and in 1972 she brought him to Perry Green to discuss with Moore his illustrations for this project. Moore and Auden met again in Vienna in September 1973, only ten days before Auden died there of a heart attack.

The Shield of Achilles led me to do *Multitude*, and from then on the poems began to fit in with the mood and direction of my Stonehenge series. I decided not so much to illustrate as to complement, or even contrast. Two people who are very unlike each other can come together over something common to them both; the fact that Auden was a Yorkshireman, as I am, and that the Yorkshire landscape has always been a very exciting element in my life, made a strong link between us.

I found working on a book very different from doing a single drawing or print, or even a series of them without any text. One has always to think in terms of the book as a whole, and of the images not only in themselves but in relation to the text and as they will appear in their sequence, in relation to each other.

Auden Poems, Moore Lithographs 1974 (n.p.)

Drawings after Old Masters 1974-78

The drawings after Bellini came about through a very dear friend, the late Franco Russoli, who was the director of the Brera Gallery in Milan. He had the idea of asking some of his many artist friends to make interpretations of any picture in the Brera which particularly appealed to them. (The aim was to help the museum to raise funds.) I had no hesitation in choosing the 'Pietà' by Giovanni Bellini whom I would count among the ten greatest artists and humanists.

The two large drawings [HMF 75(13) and fig.144] show something I have already talked about – that human expression comes most strongly through heads but also through the hands. To intensify the emotional expression in my drawing – because I was only drawing a portion of the picture – I moved the hands closer to the two heads.

Dürer's 'Portrait of Conrad Verkell' [HMF 79(36)] is a tremendous drawing, and for some years I have had a reproduction of it on the wall in my studio.

Dürer has given the portrait such variety of form and has seen it in such a monumental way, that in explaining this to a friend, I said that I could easily make a landscape from the head. The lower part of the drawing is a demonstration of this.

The drawings after Donatello [HMF 78(11), 78(12)] were made during a television series on four Italian masters. I was asked to talk about Donatello, and I wanted to demonstrate in drawing how strongly his great dramatic power and humanity come out, even in reliefs.

Wildenstein 1979, p.69

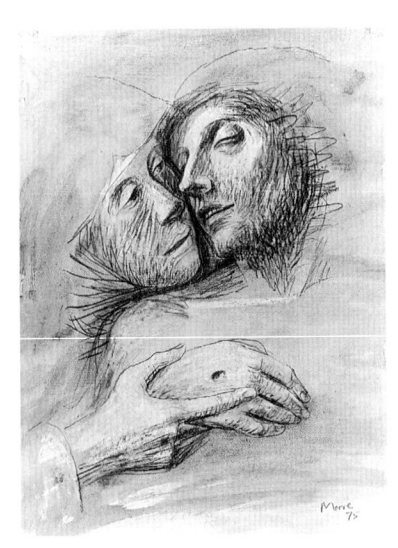

144 *Study after Giovanni Bellini's Pietà* 1975 HMF 75(14), pencil, charcoal, wax crayon, watercolour wash, gouache, 428 x 324mm (16⅞ x 12¾in). The Henry Moore Foundation: gift of the artist 1977

Trees 1975-78

I have always had a great liking for trees, and for tree trunks in particular. I like the bare trees in winter more perhaps than summer trees in full leaf.[34]

[34] Moore's etching *Trees V: Spreading Branches* 1979 CGM 551, based on the drawing illustrated, served as the model for the stained glass window 'The Tree of Life' for St Andrew's Church, Much Hadham. The window was made by Patrick Reyntiens and his son John, and dedicated on 30 July 1995.

The trunks of trees have, for me, a connection with the human body – their limbs branch out like arms and legs from the trunk of a figure. For me, too, trees have a definite affinity with sculpture. The immobility of a tree, rooted in the ground, has the kind of stability that I like in sculpture.

(A sculpture jumping off its pedestal is something I greatly dislike.)

Between two of our fields, where the sheep graze, there is an old hedge. Some parts of it must be nearly two-hundred years old. It has been chopped down again and again, it has been neglected, and severely massacred. So it has a long history, and its roots and branches suggested to me human figures – tortured, crucified and upside down.

Ibid., p.18

145 *Old Apple Tree in Winter* 1977 HMF 77(28), charcoal and watercolour, 241 x 290mm (9½ x 11³⁄₈in). The Henry Moore Foundation: acquired 1987

Reclining Figure: Holes 1976-78

I enjoy carving in wood, particularly if I can get a large log of wood from which I can rough-out the larger masses with saws and an axe. In England,

146 *Reclining Figure: Holes* 1976-78 LH 657, elmwood, length 222cm (87½in). The Henry Moore Foundation: gift of the artist 1977

until the arrival of elm disease, the wood most easily available in large pieces was elm. In my career I have carved five or six large over-life-size elmwood sculptures. Most of these sculptures (since I wanted to make full use of the bulk of the trunk) have one-directional growth, either vertical or horizontal.

Elm trees are usually straight-growing, but this last large block of elm which I acquired had a slight curve in it and was big enough to allow for a bend in the sculpture's pose. This is something which was not practical to do in my other large elmwood carvings. I always wanted to make in wood a figure that had a bend in its pose. Here I've been able to do it. For this reason I look upon this particular sculpture as having something special and different from the others. This piece will remain here in my personal collection. I remember working on it the night before it left for the retrospective exhibition at the Serpentine Gallery in 1978.

This was the largest elm log I have ever got hold of. The base of the trunk of the tree must have been a good seven feet in diameter. The late Harry Fischer, my friend who was the Director of Fischer Fine Art, heard that this very large tree was to be cut down and asked me if I was interested in acquiring it. I agreed very happily and when it arrived I was anxious to begin carving.

Being freshly cut down, the wood was not seasoned and was full of the tree's natural sap. To season wood, this sap has to be dried out and replaced by the ordinary atmosphere. This action takes place at the rate of about one inch a year. Therefore for the outside atmosphere to replace the sap in a log eighty-four inches in diameter it would take forty-two years for the atmosphere to replace the sap. This process has to take place very gradually, otherwise the outside shrinks too quickly and splitting occurs in the wood. However, I have found in my sculptural experience with wood that if, while it is still green, one reduces its bulk by blocking-out the main pose and opening up the sculpture so that no one part is more than six or seven inches in diameter – as this reclining figure is – then seasoning from the outside to the inside will take only three or four years. By keeping the sculpture myself and ensuring that it is kept in a controlled and even temperature, one ends up with seasoned wood in three or four years rather than in forty.

Levine 1983, p.139

Mirror Knife Edge 1977

I never mind making a bigger variation of a sculpture I have already done because I enjoy seeing a small maquette made larger. I would never reduce something from what it is to fit another place. That, I would think, was a diminishing of life.

The architect I.M. Pei[35] asked me to make a sculpture for his new extension to the National Gallery in Washington. When we had to decide, he came to my studio with photographs, plans and scale drawings of the building and suggestions of where he thought a sculpture could be placed. This was at the entrance to the new building. We both agreed that whatever sculpture it was, it would have to be on a very big scale, otherwise it would only look like somebody going in and out of the gallery. After some consideration we both thought that an existing sculpture, the *Knife Edge Two Piece* [fig.132] would be the right idea if made big enough, but we both agreed that if it were the other way round, that is, a mirror image of itself, it would suit better the entrance, because people could go through it into the gallery,

[35] Ieoh Meng Pei (b.1917) was born in China and emigrated to the United States in 1936. He studied architecture at MIT and Harvard. Among his best known buildings are the John Hancock Tower, Boston, the Bank of China, Hong Kong, and the glass pyramid at the Louvre in Paris. Pei was instrumental in acquiring Moore's six-metre high *The Arch* 1963/69 LH 503b for the library he designed in Columbus, Indiana, and the thirteen-metre long *Three Forms Vertebrae* 1978 LH 580a for the new city hall in Dallas, Texas.

whereas the other way they would be running into the wall. I thought it was a good experiment for me to have to do a sculpture as a mirror image. This was done and I think successfully.

In conversation with David Mitchinson, 1980

Child Studies 1977-78

I draw realistically, from life, for several reasons. One is that I want to look at the object and understand it more fully – and to draw for that purpose, you need ability in the purely technical, academic sense.

The many drawings I did years ago of Irina and Mary, my wife and baby daughter, were chiefly made to try to understand more about the mother and child relationship, which has always been one of my favourite themes.

These recent drawings, however, were not made solely to find out about children in general, they were done because of my great love for this particular child.[36]

Drawings done from love seem different in kind from purely observational drawings because one is emotionally involved.

Wildenstein 1979, p.8

Three Bathers – After Cézanne 1978

I now own a small Cézanne *Bathers* [fig.149] painting, and in talking about it to friends, I have often said, 'look what a romantic idea Cézanne had of women,' and, 'how fully he realised the three-dimensional world'. I felt that I could easily make sculptures of his figures.

148 *Child's Head: Three-Quarter View*, page from White Notebook 1977 HMF 77(34), pencil, 290 x 198mm (11³/₈ x 7³/₄in)

[36] Moore's grandson Guston Danowski, see p.240, note 30.

149 Paul Cézanne, *Three Bathers* c.1873-77, oil, 305 x 330mm (12 x 13in). Formerly in the collection of Henry Moore

150 *Three Bathers – After Cézanne* 1978 LH 741, bronze, length 30.5cm (12in)

Stephen Spender[37] in a letter to me said, 'your idea of showing that you could make sculptures of the Cézanne figures is fascinating. Why don't you do it?' Soon after his letter, I felt like proving it, and modelled each of the three figures in plasticine, taking about an hour in all. My idea was to show their existence completely in space, and perhaps to photograph them or make drawings, as it were, from behind the picture, showing them from all sides and demonstrating that they had been conceived by Cézanne in full three dimensions.

Levine 1978, p.129

I enjoyed the whole of this experiment. I had thought I knew our 'Bathers' picture completely, having lived with it for twenty years. But this exercise – modelling the figures and drawing them from different views – has taught me more than any amount of just looking at the picture.

This example shows that working from the object – modelling or drawing it – makes you look much more intensely than ever you do if you just look at something for pleasure.

Wildenstein 1979, p.74

Dorothy Hodgkin's Hands 1978[38]

The drawings of Dorothy Hodgkin's hands came about in this way. Sir Rex Richards,[39] the Vice-Chancellor of Oxford University and a Fellow of the Royal Society, knew of my liking for drawing hands. He told me that the Royal Society wanted a portrait of Dorothy Hodgkin who, besides being a Nobel Prizewinner, is also a Fellow of the Royal Society.

Rex Richards explained to me that from girlhood, Dorothy Hodgkin had suffered from an arthritic condition in her hands, yet she has carried out the most delicate and precise experiments for her work on X-ray crystallography. She is proud of having been able to do this in spite of what other people might think of as an insuperable handicap. She would be happy, he said, if I would like to draw her hands, and for the drawing to be used as a portrait of her.

I was delighted to be asked and at once agreed to do the drawing. In fact, an arthritic hand can be more moving than a perfect hand – the hand of a young girl, for example, though smooth and beautiful, can seem emptier of meaning.

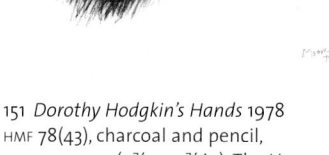

151 *Dorothy Hodgkin's Hands* 1978
HMF 78(43), charcoal and pencil,
252 x 327mm (9⅞ x 12⅞in). The Henry
Moore Foundation: acquired 1987

[37] Moore met the British poet Stephen Spender (1909-96) in 1934. When Spender was asked by the literary magazine *The London Mercury* to provide a portrait of himself, he said that he would only allow Moore to draw him. Four portrait drawings were executed in 1934 (HMF 1069-1072). The Moores became close friends of Spender and his Russian-born wife Natasha. Spender gave the memorial address at the thanksgiving service for Moore at Westminster Abbey on 18 November 1986.

[38] Dorothy Hodgkin (1910-94), the British chemist and crystallographer, used X-ray techniques to study the structure of steroids, penicillin, cholesterol, iodine and insulin. In 1964 she was awarded the Nobel Prize for Chemistry for her research into the structure of vitamin B12.

[39] Rex Richards, Professor of Chemistry at the University of Oxford, has been a trustee of the Henry Moore Foundation since 1989 and was Chairman from 1994 to 2001.

So Dorothy Hodgkin came and sat in my studio for two hours or so, for me to draw her hands. Later, I did some more work on these drawings and one of them [HMF 78(45)] now hangs in the Royal Society.

Ibid., p.13

Ideas for Sculpture: Collage 1978-79

152 *Reclining Figure: Sea Background* 1978 HMF 78(13), charcoal, chalk, gouache, collaged photograph and watercolour, 238 x 352mm (9³⁄₈ x 13⅞in). The Henry Moore Foundation: acquired 1987

The collage drawings are again ideas connected with sculpture, the backgrounds being used to give them density and reality, by suggesting an atmosphere around them.

Starting from collage helped very much. Using bits of photographs of flints, cutting them out, changing them and fitting them together, gave something to start off with, although the collage part might end up greatly changed in the final drawing.

As a young sculptor, I sometimes had to find an idea to fit an odd-shaped, random piece of stone. The collage drawings are a similar sort of process – making use of something which already exists, to suggest a new idea.

Ibid., p.44

Shut-Eye Drawings 1980-81 [40]

153 *Reclining Figures: Man and Woman* 1981 HMF 81(20), ballpoint pen, 252 x 355mm (9⅞ x 14in). The Henry Moore Foundation: acquired 1987

Over the last six months you have done about thirty 'shut-eye' drawings.

Yes, they are very quick to do. With a 'shut-eye' drawing you can't spend a lot of time because you don't know until you open your eyes what you are doing. [...]

Now the thing about closing your eyes, the subject that is mentioned has to be very obvious – almost a caricature of what the object is. It would not do for instance to try to draw a field of wheat. If someone said draw a donkey then immediately you have big ears and a biggish head. Or if they say a cow then you know there are the horns and an udder and so on [...]

Therefore when you try to do a 'shut-eye' drawing, the main characteristics are likely to come out stronger, but as you are not able to relate them to the others they come into odd relationships. But on the whole it produces the essence or the obvious point about an object.

In conversation with Ann Garrould, 4 June 1981

---

[40] For a further description of the making of the 'shut-eye' drawings, see *Henry Moore: Volume 5 Complete Drawings 1977-81* 1994, pp.x-xi.

Bibliographical sources

Henry Moore Bibliography, compiled by Alexander Davis, vols.1-5: The Henry Moore Foundation, Much Hadham 1992-1994

Catalogues raisonnés:

Henry Moore: Complete Sculpture, vol.1 1921-48 (*Sculpture and Drawings*), ed. Herbert Read 1944, 4th revised edition ed. David Sylvester 1957; vol.2 1949-54, ed. Sylvester 1955, 3rd revised edition ed. Alan Bowness 1986; vol.3 1955-64, ed. Bowness 1965; vol.4 1964-73, ed. Bowness 1977; vol.5 1974-80, ed. Bowness 1983, 2nd revised edition 1994; vol.6 1981-86, ed. Bowness 1988: Lund Humphries, London

Henry Moore: Complete Drawings, edited by Ann Garrould, vol.1 1916-29, 1996; vol.2 1930-39, 1998; vol.3 1940-49, 2001; vol.4 1950-76, in preparation; vol.5 1977-79, 1994; vol.6 1982-83, 1994: The Henry Moore Foundation in association with Lund Humphries, London

Henry Moore: Catalogue of Graphic Work [vol.I] 1931-72, ed. Gérald Cramer, Alistair Grant, David Mitchinson 1973; vol.II 1973-75, ed. G. Cramer, Grant, Mitchinson 1976; vol.III 1976-79, ed. Patrick Cramer, Grant, Mitchinson 1980; vol.IV 1980-84, ed. P. Cramer, Grant, Mitchinson 1988: Cramer, Geneva

The following publications are cited in abbreviated form throughout; other sources are given in full.

Auden Poems, Moore Lithographs 1974: *Auden Poems, Moore Lithographs*, exhibition catalogue, British Museum, London 1974

Berthoud 1987: Roger Berthoud, *The Life of Henry Moore*, Faber and Faber, London 1987

Carroll 1973: *The Donald Carroll Interviews*, Talmy, Franklin, London 1973

Finn 1976: *Henry Moore: Sculpture and Environment*, Abrams, New York 1976; Thames and Hudson, London 1977

Fischer 1971: *Henry Moore 1961-1971*, Interview with Wolfgang Fischer, Staatsgalerie Moderner Kunst, Munich 1971

Forma 1964: Warren Forma, *Five British Sculptors: Work and Talk*, Grossman, New York 1964

Freeman 1964: *Face to Face*, interviews with John Freeman, edited by Hugh Burnett, Cape, London 1964

Hall 1960: 'Henry Moore: An Interview by Donald Hall', *Horizon*, New York November 1960

Hall 1966: Donald Hall, *Henry Moore: The Life and Work of a Great Sculptor*, Harper and Row, New York; Gollancz, London 1966

Hedgecoe 1968: *Henry Spencer Moore*, photographed and edited by John Hedgecoe, words by Henry Moore, Nelson, London; Simon and Schuster, New York 1968

Hedgecoe 1986: *Henry Moore: My Ideas, Inspiration and Life as an Artist*, Henry Moore and John Hedgecoe, Ebury Press, London 1986

James 1966: Philip James (ed.), *Henry Moore on Sculpture: A Collection of the Sculptor's Writings and Spoken Words*, Macdonald, London 1966 (edition cited); Viking Press, New York 1967; revised edition, paperback, Da Capo Press, New York 1992

James 1975: *Henry Moore Looking at his Work with Philip James*, Visual Publications, London, New York, Toronto 1975: booklet, film strips and two audio cassettes

Lake 1962: Carlton Lake, 'Henry Moore's World', *Atlantic Monthly*, Boston January 1962

Levine 1978: *With Henry Moore: The Artist at Work*, photographed by Gemma Levine, Sidgwick and Jackson, London 1978

Levine 1983: *Henry Moore: Wood Sculpture*, commentary by Henry Moore, photographs by Gemma Levine, Sidgwick and Jackson, London 1983

Man 1954: *Eight European Artists*, photographed and edited by Felix H. Man, Heinemann, London, Melbourne, Toronto 1954

Roditi 1960: Edouard Roditi, *Dialogues on Art*, Secker and Warburg, London 1960

Russell 17 and 24 December 1961: John and Véra Russell, 'Conversations with Henry Moore', *Sunday Times* 17, 24 December 1961

Russell 1968: John Russell, *Henry Moore*, Allen Lane The Penguin Press, London 1968

Sculpture in the Open Air 1955: *Sculpture in the Open Air: A Talk by Henry Moore on his Sculpture and its Placing in Open-Air Sites*, edited by Robert Melville and recorded by the British Council 1955: typescript; copy in HMF library

Seldis 1973: Henry J. Seldis, *Henry Moore in America*, Phaidon, London; Praeger, New York 1973

Spender 1978: *Henry Moore: Sculptures in Landscape*, text by Stephen Spender, photographs by Geoffrey Shakerley, Studio Vista, London 1978

Sweeney 1947: James Johnson Sweeney, 'Henry Moore', *Partisan Review*, New York March-April 1947

Sylvester 1951: *Sculpture and Drawings by Henry Moore*, texts by A.D.B. Sylvester, Tate Gallery, London 1951

Sylvester 1963: 'Henry Moore Talking: A Conversation with David Sylvester', *The Listener* 29 August 1963 (from a BBC Third Programme broadcast)

Wildenstein 1979: *Henry Moore: Drawings 1969-79*, Wildenstein, New York 1979

Wilkinson 1977: Alan G. Wilkinson, *The Drawings of Henry Moore*, Tate Gallery, London/Art Gallery of Ontario, Toronto 1977

Wilkinson 1987: Alan G. Wilkinson, *Henry Moore Remembered: The Collection at the Art Gallery of Ontario in Toronto*, Art Gallery of Ontario, Toronto 1987

INDEX OF WORKS BY HENRY MOORE

Page numbers of illustrations are in italic type; passages dealing with a work in detail are indicated by page numbers in bold type.

Page numbers of illustrations are in italic type. Key passages dealing with a subject in some detail are indicated by page numbers in bold type.

Picture credits

All unacknowledged photographs, as well as many of those listed below, are in the Henry Moore Foundation archive.

Anita Feldman Bennet: p.65
Art Gallery of Ontario, Toronto: p.279 (lower right)
Ilario Bessi: pp.170, 223 (bottom)
Birmingham Museums and Art Gallery: p.266
Brancacci Chapel, Santa Maria del Carmine, Florence: p.156
The British Museum, London: pp.101, 105, 107, 108 (top), 109, 159
Castello Sforzesco, Milan: p.157
Chichester Cathedral: p.111
Crispin Eurich: pp.64, 226
David Finn: pp.103, 144
The Globe and Mail, Toronto: p.76
G.D. Hackett, New York: p.283
John Hedgecoe: pp.30, 33, 34, 36, 58 (top), 62, 63, 73, 221
Errol Jackson: pp.79, 241, 254 (bottom), 257 (top), 258, 276, 291, 292, 305 (bottom)
Felix H. Man: p.66
Lee Miller Archives: p.262
Lee Miller (Tate Gallery Archive): p.80
Michel Muller: pp.161, 301 (bottom), 309, 310 (top and bottom)
Museo Archeologico, Florence: p.200
Museo Nacional Centro de Arte Sofia, Madrid © Succession Picasso/DACS: p.167
Museo Nacional de Antropología, Mexico City: p.96
Museo Nazionale del Bargello, Florence, courtesy of the Ministry of Cultural Affairs: p.148
National Gallery, London: p.175
Philadelphia Museum of Art: p.146
Saidman: p.265 (top)
Tate, London: pp.145, 150, 151, 153, 155, 263, 274, 288 (bottom)
Angela Verren-Taunt/DACS: p.165
Budd Waintrob, New York: p.307 (top)
John Webb: p.304